# TOWN
### and
## COUNTRY

# TOWN

*and*

# COUNTRY

Race Relations in an
Urban-Rural Context,
Arkansas, 1865–1905

John
William
Graves

THE UNIVERSITY OF ARKANSAS PRESS
Fayetteville  1990  London

Copyright © 1990 by John William Graves
All rights reserved

ISBN: 978-1-55728-137-1 (cloth)
ISBN: 978-1-68226-138-5 (paper)
eISBN: 978-1-61075-431-6

Manufactured in the United States of America

24  23  22  21  20    5  4  3  2  1

Designer: *Ch. H. Russell*
Typeface: *Linotron 202 Caslon 540*
Typesetter: *G&S Typesetters, Inc.*

⊗ The paper used in this publication meets the minimum
requirements of the American National Standard for
Permanence of Paper for Printed Library Materials Z39.48-1984.

*Library of Congress Cataloging-in-Publication Data*

Graves, John William, 1942–
    Town and country: race relations in an urban-rural context, Arkansas,
1865–1905 / John William Graves.
        p.   cm.
    Includes bibliographical references.
    ISBN 978-1-55728-137-8 (alk. paper)
        1. Arkansas—Race relations. 2. Afro-Americans—Arkansas—
Segregation—History—19th century. 3. Reconstruction—Arkansas.
    4. Cities and towns—Arkansas—History—19th century. I. Title.
E185.93.A8G73   1990
978.7'00496073—dc20                              89–48316
                                                 CIP

*To My Parents*

*William A. Graves*
*and*
*Mabel Morehart Graves*

*In Remembrance*

# Acknowledgments

My initial interest in this subject began when I was still a child. As a young boy I listened with pride as the late Dr. Henry Calvin Lewis related stories concerning the political activities of my maternal great-grandfather, Henry R. Morehart. Mr. Morehart had been elected a Union Labor party state representative from Pulaski County, Arkansas, in 1888, and the following year Dr. Lewis had served as his page boy in the legislature, which then met in Little Rock at the State House on Markham Street. He recalled my great-grandfather's participation in the spirited sessions of the General Assembly and also his election campaigns. Dr. Lewis especially remembered that Mr. Morehart was a forceful speaker at local "schoolhouse debates," then a staple of political life in rural Pulaski County.

My academic involvement in nineteenth-century Arkansas history did not come until much later. While a graduate student at the University of Arkansas, I enrolled in Professor Gordon H. McNeil's class on historical methods and prepared for him a seminar paper on the enactment of the Arkansas Separate Coach Law of 1891. It was largely because of Professor McNeil's encouragement that I chose for the topic of my master's thesis the inauguration of segregation and disfranchisement legislation in Arkansas during the 1890s. My thesis advisor was Professor Walter L. Brown, former secretary-treasurer of the Arkansas Historical Association and former editor of the *Arkansas Historical Quarterly*. I am very indebted to him for having taken such a personal interest in my development as a scholar and for having shared with me in so many ways his extensive knowledge of Arkansas history.

Subsequently, as a doctoral candidate at the University of Virginia, I expanded the focus of my research, writing a dissertation on the history of race relations in Arkansas from 1865 to 1905. My dissertation advisor was the late Edward Younger, former chairman of the Corcoran Department of History and former dean of the Graduate School of Arts and Sciences at Virginia. The author remembers with great affection his wise counsel, his patience, and his unfailing help and concern.

Many individuals contributed to the preparation and research of the present manuscript. J. Morgan Kousser read my earlier dissertation and offered many extremely helpful suggestions for revision and improvement; I am particularly in his debt. Others who have read portions of my work at various times and have contributed valuable comments and insights include Ruth Churchill, Tom W. Dillard, August Meier, Michael O'Brien, Edwin S. Redkey, and Joel Williamson. Three former colleagues, Merry Kone Fitzpatrick, Eugene Jackman, and Betty Kissler have also been helpful in this regard. Of course, all of the above persons are absolved from any errors of fact or interpretation on my part.

The librarians and support staffs of several institutions have provided important assistance. Thanks is especially extended to the late Grace Upchurch and Helen Jo Adkisson and to Michael Dabrishus of the University of Arkansas Library; John L. Ferguson, Russell Baker, and Lynn Ewbank of the Arkansas History Commission; Lauren Stayton of the Alderman Library of the University of Virginia; Edwin G. Sanford of the Boston, Massachusetts, Boston Public Library; Kathy Sagebiel of the Southwest Texas State University Library; Philip Jones, David Walls, and Margaret Coakley of the Little Rock, Arkansas, Little Rock Public Library; and Marilyn Martin, Barbara Roberts, John Ragni, Valorie Newborn, Lee Ann Alexander, Harvey Peebles, and Robert Yehl of the Huie Library of Henderson State University.

A number of individuals helped me collect the photographs that accompany the manuscript, several of which were quite rare and difficult to find. I am very indebted to Tommy Devore, Tom W. Dillard, Lynn Ewbank, Andre Louis Guerrero, James W. Leslie, Linda Pine, and Bobby Roberts in this regard. The staff of the Arkansas Geological Commission also provided several maps.

In addition, special thanks is extended to Mrs. Cara Smith,

who invested much time and effort in typing the manuscript, and to Mrs. Marie Hughes, who assisted in typing also. My editor at the University of Arkansas Press, Ms. Debbie Bowen, provided much good advice and help in shepherding my manuscript to eventual publication. I am also appreciative of the financial assistance provided by Henderson State University, which awarded me a faculty research grant.

Four friends, Anthony C. Florek, Robert T. Hawkes, Jr., Douglas G. Holt, and James A. Means, provided me with a great deal of encouragement and moral support, as did my sister and brother-in-law, Martha Graves Siemers and William Siemers and my uncle and aunt, Irvin and Gaynelle Graves. Two deceased aunts, Mrs. E. A. (Ora Morehart) Thomas and Mrs. E. T. (Eleanor Morehart) Miller, cared for my mother during a period of extended illness, thereby enabling me to complete my graduate studies. A family friend, the late Mrs. Ruby Hawthorne Morton, similarly helped to care for my father in the months prior to his death.

I owe a unique debt to my parents, the late William A. and Mabel Morehart Graves. It was they who attempted to instill within me from an early age a moral consciousness and who urged me to cherish such values as integrity and honor and respect for truth. They also made many personal sacrifices in a great variety of ways that enabled me to pursue my education. Without their love and devotion, this book could never have been written.

Finally, I am especially grateful to Andre Louis Guerrero, former director of the Juarez-Lincoln Graduate Center of Antioch College and of the Ohio Commission on Spanish-Speaking Affairs and recent doctoral fellow and graduate of Harvard University. As noted above, he assisted me in obtaining several photographs that accompany the manuscript and also provided invaluable help in preparing the maps which are included. Moreover, through my years of association with him I have gained a perspective on the history of American race relations that I could never have acquired only by myself. More importantly, his whole life has been an example of personal courage and devotion to justice and the cause of humanity. To him, and to all of those who have made this study possible, I offer my sincere thanks.

# Contents

# List of Tables

# TOWN
### and
# COUNTRY

# Introduction

Since the first appearance of C. Vann Woodward's *The Strange Career of Jim Crow* in 1955,[1] Southern race relations in the latter half of the nineteenth century have received a remarkable degree of scholarly attention. Dozens of subsequent books and articles have investigated Woodward's central issue of the origins of Southern segregation as well as such related matters as the economic and psychological sources of white racial aggression, the racial attitudes and policies of Southern Redeemers and Populists, the political and social consequences of racially motivated disfranchisement laws, and the responses of Southern blacks to changing racial policies.[2]

If any one aspect of Southern race relations during this era has been neglected, it is urban race relations. This oversight is understandable in that the American South during this period was an overwhelmingly rural, agricultural region; according to the United States Census, even as late as 1900 only 17 percent of persons living in the South Atlantic states and 11.1 percent of persons living in the South Central states resided in urban areas of eight thousand persons or more.[3]

Census figures alone, however, can be distorting. As John W. Cell has observed, "In any modernizing society the early phases of industrialization and urbanization are much more important in forming persistent political and social patterns than would be readily apparent from purely quantitative measurements." As Cell notes, "Banks, lawyers, newspapers, fashionable seasons, and legislatures are all centered in cities. . . . It is to cities that histo-

1

rians normally look for those bursts of energy and sharp clashes of ideas that both produce and signify change. . . ." Quite simply, "cities set the pace and tone."[4]

This may have been particularly true as regards patterns of race relations that developed in the American South after the Civil War. There is growing evidence that the elaborate system of racial segregation that had emerged in Dixie by the first decade of the twentieth century initially appeared chiefly in urban areas.[5] After all, many of the traditional objects of segregation—streetcars, hotels, saloons, restaurants, theaters, and public parks, to name a few—were largely nonexistent in rural settings. Furthermore, in the countryside formal segregation was superfluous and unnecessary. If, as both Cell and C. Vann Woodward have pointed out, the intent of Jim Crow practices was to distinguish between superior and subordinate, in rural communities that was "made clear enough by slavery and then by its aftermath of paternalism and caste." If their intent was to maintain white supremacy and racial discipline, that was "handled in the country by direct, personal or 'vertical' control—whether by the 'boss man' or any white who chose to keep blacks in their place."[6]

Different circumstances existed in the cities and towns. Urban locales not only offered blacks greater anonymity and thus autonomy, but, as shall be shown, they also provided conditions that made possible economic and social mobility for some black town dwellers. As class lines began to cut across racial ones in the urban centers and the caste system showed signs of weakening, the "horizontal" system of segregation was instituted to separate the races and shore up white dominance.[7]

Although there is a developing consensus among scholars that Southern segregation had its genesis mainly (if not wholly) in urban areas, a great deal remains to be discovered concerning the emergence of urban segregation and the career of Jim Crow in the city. Heretofore, much attention has been devoted to the question "*When* did segregation first appear?" An even more important question, however, is "*How* and *why* did segregation appear?"[8] And at this juncture, one cannot help but discern a peculiar irony. The recent tendency of historians to treat urban and rural racial developments as discrete, separate phenomena, while logical and analytically useful, has contributed to a new form of segrega-

2.

tion. A major thesis of this study is that the urban centers of nineteenth-century Arkansas did not exist in social isolation. They were surrounded by an established agrarian culture with received racial traditions, and in developing their own racial practices, they would be influenced and shaped by the larger society of their time.

# I
# After the War

Away down yonder in the land of
cotton,
Old times there are not forgotten
—Stanza from *Dixie*

Only rarely and occasionally does a nation possess the sharp consciousness that it has reached the end of a historical era. For whites living in the American South, such a painful awareness was unavoidable in the spring of 1865. The victorious armies of the Union, backed by the superior population and industrial might of a triumphant North, had not merely crushed the attempt to establish an independent Southern Confederacy; in the wake of their advance, they had swept aside the South's peculiar institution of slavery, with the unique way of life it had flavored and sustained. A well-established social order "buttressed by every authority of learning, law, and constitution, supported by the church, the schools, and cherished devotedly by the people" had "perished quite completely."[1] All that was secure and familiar lay in the past; what the future held was unknown.

Of all the new adjustments confronting Southerners, assuredly one of the most pressing and perplexing was delineation of a new status for the freedmen, both in society and in law. In attempting to cope with this problem, inevitably white Southerners' responses were conditioned and limited by racial values inherited from prewar years. This was as true in Arkansas as in the rest of the South, although the *ancien régime* in the young frontier state had never been all that ancient. While slaveholding and the plan-

4

tation economy had developed rapidly in the last two decades of the antebellum period, as late as 1840, four years after admission to the Union, Arkansas could still report only 19,935 slaves among its population; in absolute terms, tiny Delaware alone possessed a smaller number of bondsmen.[2]

Nor, for that matter, had slavery been evenly distributed. Geographically and culturally there were really two Arkansases, divided by an imaginary line running diagonally from the northeast corner to the southwest corner of the state. East of this line was the lush, low-lying Delta of the Mississippi and Arkansas rivers and their tributaries; farther south lay the gently rolling timber lands of the Gulf Coastal Plain, traversed by the rich bottom districts of the Saline, Ouachita, Little Missouri, and Red rivers. Overflows and unhealthful swamps inhibited development of these alluvial areas, though by the eve of the Civil War they were witnessing the emergence of extensive plantations with large concentrations of slaves. By 1860, six southern and eastern counties contained over 50 percent slave populations;[3] reflecting this growth, the number of slaves in Arkansas had jumped to 111,115, approximately 25 percent of the state's inhabitants.[4]

North and west of the lowland regions, the Ozark and Ouachita mountains, separated by the Arkansas River, rose like enchanted isles above the endless prairies and plains of the American heartland. Within a few years after the Louisiana Purchase of 1803, a handful of pioneers had already begun to steer their ox wagons into these remote hills. The larger stream of immigrants poured around the mountains, but, as folklorist Jimmy Driftwood has described it, "there were some, families from the Tennessee Appalachians, most of them bearing plain Anglo-Saxon names like Lancaster, Copeland, Simmons, and Clark, who paused. They wound their way over steep wooded passes down into the winding virgin valleys to breathe a sigh of relief: 'Thank God, we're back home!'"[5]

A passionate attachment to the land characterized the people of the Ozarks, for they lived in a realm of surpassing beauty. Fresh air and intense morning sunlight, softened and diffused by mists and low-hanging clouds, produced at once a feeling of exhilaration and dreamy contentment. As the sun sank below the hills in the afternoon, a shifting play of light and shadow patterned the valleys and mountain walls. In winter the denuded forests and gray landscape sometimes produced a brooding air of melancholy, but springtime brought forth a new burst of life; flowering dogwood and redbud trees dotted the hillsides, interspersed between sprinklings of violets and fields of wild azaleas. Long, lazy summers gave time for hunting and for fishing and swimming in crystal-clear pools and mountain streams. With the coming of autumn the Ozarks were painted in somewhat somber hues: the deep blood-reds of blackjack oaks and the muted golden yellow tints of hickory and gum trees. In cool, deep ravines, scattered stands of sugar maples added an extra splash of color.

A few slaves arrived in the Ozarks along with the first white settlers, but their number was never great, and slavery was never able to take a firm hold in the mountains' hardscrabble soil. Most Ozark whites held no slaves at all, and those who did typically were small or middling farmers owning no more than a single family of bondsmen.[6] In 1860, 74 percent of Arkansas's slave population was located in the state's twenty-four lowland counties, while only 26 percent was found in the thirty-one counties of the north and west.[7]

These regional variations assumed heightened importance during the crisis of 1860–1861. Following Abraham Lincoln's election as President and the departure of seven Deep South states from the Union, a secession convention assembled in Little Rock to determine Arkansas's own course of action. Located near the exact geographical center of the state, at the very point on the Arkansas River where the mountains descend into the Delta plain, the capital city had in the past symbolized Arkansas's political unity. However, the convention which met in Little Rock in March 1861 accentuated intrastate divisiveness. Unionist delegates, chiefly from the upland districts, elected one of their own, David Walker of Fayetteville, convention chairman and by a narrow vote of thirty-five to thirty-nine turned back a secession resolution. Only after the firing on Fort Sumter did they reluctantly join representatives from the Delta in voting to carry Arkansas out of the federal republic.[8]

Even then, support for the rebel cause remained lukewarm in mountain areas, with many persons openly remaining Unionist in their sympathies.[9] As early as August 1862 Colonel M. LaRue

Harrison, for whom the town of Harrison, Arkansas, was later named, was able to organize a federal regiment of Arkansas troops. During the course of the war approximately fifteen thousand Arkansans, grouped in fourteen regiments, wore the Union blue; slightly less than two thirds of these troops were white volunteers, principally from mountain districts, with the remainder being black recruits from the eastern Delta.[10]

Moved by the prevalence of loyalist feeling in Arkansas and several other Southern states, President Lincoln, in December 1863, issued a proclamation offering pardons to former secessionists who would consent to take an oath of allegiance to the United States. Whenever 10 percent of the qualified voters of 1860 had taken the oath in any seceded state, this group could form a new Unionist state authority. Lincoln hoped that his "10 percent governments" would weaken the Confederate war effort, providing a basis for the subsiding of sectional passions and a speedy return of the Southern states to the nation's councils.

Already, on their own initiative, Arkansas Unionists had selected representatives to convene on January 4, 1864, in Little Rock (by then under federal military control) to establish a loyal government. When the delegates assembled, three to four dozen persons claiming to speak for twenty-two of Arkansas's fifty-four counties were present. The convention named John McCoy of Newton County in the Ozarks its chairman, drafted a new state constitution, and set up a provisional administration. At an election in March, over twelve thousand voters approved the constitution and elected Isaac Murphy as their new governor. Murphy, in his own person, represented the continuity of backing for the old republic among Unionist elements. A delegate from the Ozark county of Madison at the convention of 1861, he had been the only member to vote against secession after news of Fort Sumter.[11]

Support for the Union among whites did not automatically translate into affection for blacks, as the policies of the Murphy government soon demonstrated. Before the war, even the most isolated mountain areas had boasted at least a few slaves. And if slavery had been a relatively new institution within Arkansas, a large majority of settlers in the state had originally emigrated from the slave commonwealths of the older South. Particularly after 1830, defenses of slavery derived from the alleged inherent biological inferiority of Negroes had become commonplace throughout all of Dixie.[12] It is reasonable to assume that, for most whites, the idea that blacks could live in the community on terms of equality and full citizenship had simply become unthinkable. The widespread antipathy shown toward free Negroes in the antebellum period reflected not only a fear of slave insurrections but to a degree this prejudice. As early as 1843 Arkansas had prohibited the entrance of new free blacks into its borders and in 1860 had voted to expel its resident free blacks, despite the fact that they numbered less than a thousand.[13]

That native mountain Unionists in some measure shared a negative conception of black capacities is suggested by their constitution of 1864. The state's new organic law abolished slavery, repudiated secession, and disavowed the Confederate debt.[14] It also forbade passage of any law "prohibiting the education of any class" of the state's inhabitants.[15] Yet, no provisions were established for Negro suffrage, not even for blacks who were literate and held property or for black veterans of the Union army.[16] One section of the constitution was reminiscent of the antebellum statutes against free blacks; it specified that no Negro not already living in Arkansas could establish residence in the state, except by authority of the government of the United States or under proclamation of the President of the United States. Reflecting the delegates' strong feelings on the question, the new constitution mandated that the first session of the General Assembly meeting under its authority should adopt enabling legislation for the exclusionary provision.[17]

Blacks who desired the ballot for themselves could perhaps take some solace from the fact that they were not the only ones proscribed: initially, at least, a majority of former Confederates were disfranchised as well. Supplementing the basic loyalty oath required by Lincoln's proclamation, the first Unionist General Assembly demanded a second pledge from voters. The prospective elector not only had to affirm allegiance to the federal and state constitutions; he was also required to swear that he had not aided the Confederacy directly or indirectly since April 18, 1864, the date of Governor Murphy's inauguration.[18]

Protestations against the disfranchisement statute surfaced immediately. Former Confederate elements, objecting that the act barred from one half to two thirds of the prewar voting population,[19] initiated a test suit. In *Rison et al v. Farr*, the Murphy government's own supreme court struck down the state loyalty oath, finding it unconstitutional since the 1864 organic law contained no express authorization for restricting the adult white male electorate.[20]

The decision of the Unionist court may perhaps have been good law, but it made for disastrous politics. Overnight, the balance of power shifted in favor of the hitherto disfranchised ex-Confederates. In the August 1866 state elections these men, running as Conservative Democrats, swept all before them. Twenty-five Democrats were elected to the Senate, while only five of the seventy-nine representatives in the new House of Representatives were Unionist Republicans. Not a single member of the Unionist legislature of 1864 standing for reelection was returned.[21] Governor Murphy would still remain in office until the expiration of his original term in 1868, but he was no longer in control of events. Scarcely a year after the guns of war had silenced, the Unionists' old enemies on the battlefield were in control of the state government.

The actions of the "rebel" legislature of 1866–67 mirrored the attitudes of the white majority concerning what should be the new civil status of black people in Arkansas. The Des Arc *Citizen*, expressing the common view, enjoined the lawmakers "to throw around him [the Negro] certain restrictions," while giving him "certain rights and privileges, that he may be made most subservient to our purposes and interests." The editor believed that black suffrage was "more than we can swallow" and voiced reservations concerning schooling for blacks. "We cannot endorse too liberal an educational policy toward his children," he warned.[22]

Responding to these sentiments, the legislature passed a new statute conferring upon the freedmen such additional rights as were "demanded by humanity, as well as sound policy" but with "some exceptions, considered essential to the safety of society."[23] As specified by the act, the freedmen attained for the first time equality under the laws and the right of contract; furthermore, they were entitled to sue and be sued, to give evidence in court, to form legal marriages, and to hold property.[24] Blacks, however, were excluded from voting and were forbidden to intermarry with whites, serve on juries or in the militia, or attend school with whites.[25]

The legislature also indefinitely postponed action on bills designed to create a separate public school system for Negroes.[26] The lawmakers preserved some sense of equity by exempting blacks from payment of school taxes. The general impoverishment of the state after the war to a degree explains the reluctance to fund Negro schools, but there was also a widespread prejudice against the very idea of educating blacks, inherited from antebellum times.[27] Although the white Unionists had previously shown some disposition to make concessions to blacks on the matter of schooling, the attitude of the ex-Confederate elements reflected more obviously the strength of prewar traditions.

On a related matter, the legislature refused to ratify the proposed Fourteenth Amendment to the United States Constitution.[28] The amendment was designed in part to guarantee for blacks the rights of citizenship and assure for them the equal protection of the laws; while it did not require Negro suffrage, it encouraged it by threatening to reduce a state's representation in Congress and the Electoral College proportionate to the number of adult males disfranchised for any reason other than crime or participation in rebellion.

If Arkansas legislators seemed reluctant to accept completely the consequences of military defeat, their attitude was not appreciably different from that of the citizenry at large. Whites accustomed to the racial etiquette of slavery days naturally found it difficult to deal with blacks as free men. In the immediate aftermath of the war, Arkansas managed to escape the major race riots which afflicted some areas of the South; nevertheless, there were sporadic lynchings and outbreaks of violence.[29] There was also a pronounced reluctance to have close dealings with blacks in social situations; once the enforced contact and intimacy of slavery was gone, a tendency toward de facto segregation, though never hard or absolute, appeared.

Illustrative of this fact was an incident which occurred in 1866 at Wittsburg, a small eastern Arkansas town located on the St. Francis River in Cross County. A certain Mr. Thorn, a white plantation lessee who had recently arrived from the North, attempted to organize a school for local blacks. Thorn arranged for a Miss Celia Winchester, a black woman who had been graduated from

Oberlin College in Ohio, to come south and serve as the school's new teacher. He met her in person when her steamboat arrived at Wittsburg and escorted her to her lodgings at the local hotel. According to an eyewitness, "When the proprietor of the hotel learned that Miss Winchester was colored, he went out and bought a cowhide. He met Mr. Thorn on the street, held a pistol on him and cowhided him . . . Mr. Thorn stood and cried. He said that he was seventy years old and had never done any harm in his life. What he had done was not intended as a violation of custom."[30]

Actually, such examples of discrimination were not confined solely to the South. Free Negroes in the antebellum North had often encountered compulsory segregation, discrimination in employment, and restricted legal rights.[31] Only five of the sixteen Northern states in 1860 permitted Negroes within their borders to vote, and only one, Massachusetts, admitted them to jury service.[32] Southerners, however, failed to appreciate the extent to which the Civil War and the struggle for emancipation had begun to alter Northern attitudes. Nor did they understand that suspicious Yankees, fearful of some covert plan for a return to slavery, demanded a higher standard of egalitarian conduct from the South than they sometimes established for themselves. Violence, abuse of Negroes, repudiation of Unionists at the polls, election of many prominent former Confederates to office, refusal to ratify the Fourteenth Amendment or grant the suffrage to even the most qualified blacks—all these things convinced many Northerners that the rebel spirit was alive and well in the South and that white Southerners could not yet be trusted to administer political authority.

Determined not to be robbed of the fruits of victory, wary Northern voters gave top-heavy majorities to Republican candidates in the fall 1866 congressional elections. Over the veto of Lincoln's successor, President Andrew Johnson,[33] the Republican-controlled Congress passed three Reconstruction Acts in March and July, 1867. The acts abolished the existing governments in all of the former Confederate commonwealths save Tennessee, whose legislature had ratified the Fourteenth Amendment. Aside from that state, the former Confederate territory was divided into five military districts, with Mississippi and Arkansas constituting the fourth.[34]

Preparatory to the reestablishment of civilian authority, military commanders within each state were ordered to conduct a registration of voters, including both black and white males age twenty-one or older. Prospective electors were required to take a prescribed oath of loyalty to the United States Constitution. Persons, however, who had taken a prior oath to uphold the Constitution and then participated in rebellion against the United States were prohibited from subscribing to the new oath. Affecting many prewar state and federal officeholders, this stipulation was intended to exclude the old antebellum leadership class from the Reconstruction process. Even so, the majority of former Confederates were given the right to vote if they were willing to comply with registration procedures.

Upon completion of registration within a given state, voters were to select delegates to a constitutional convention, representation in the convention being based upon the number of registered electors within each county. The convention was to draft a new state constitution in conformity with the United States Constitution; it was also specified that the state's organic law would have to recognize black suffrage. Qualified electors were to ratify the new state constitution, and the state government created was to approve the Fourteenth Amendment. Once the Fourteenth Amendment was included in the federal Constitution, the state would then be eligible for full readmission and representation in Congress and the Electoral College.[35]

It was intended that the reconstructed state administrations thus established would be controlled by a coalition of blacks and native white Unionists who would thereafter possess the machinery for defending their rights. These governments would provide a powerful base for the Republican party in the South, hopefully assuring continued Republican hegemony in national affairs for decades to come.

Following passage of the first Reconstruction Act, Brevet Major General E. O. C. Ord assumed control of the Fourth Military District in the spring of 1867. Within Arkansas, Ord allowed Governor Murphy to remain in office until congressional Reconstruction was effectuated, although he refused to permit the General Assembly to reconvene. During the brief interlude of military rule, he proved to be a brisk, efficient, and reasonably impartial commander; with only a few exceptions, he permitted local and county officers elected in 1866 to remain for the time being at their stations.[36] None of these facts, however, could conceal the essential nature of his task. Belatedly, Arkansas's white majority had discovered what it was that pride went before.

The restoration of local "home rule" after the war had proven to be of limited duration, but the fleeting episode revealed the strength of inherited racial attitudes among native whites. Even former Unionists were unwilling to concede political or social equality to Arkansas's blacks, while among ex-Confederates there could still be found an unyielding spirit. Congressional Republicans responded with a determined resolution of their own, dismantling the existing state government, disfranchising many native leaders, and transferring political power into new hands.

# II

# Toward a New Order

We do not recognize that the
negro has any political rights
whatever. . . .
—Little Rock *Arkansas Gazette*,
   March 10, 1868

We are not here to ask
charity. . . .
—William H. Grey, black
   delegate to the Arkansas
   constitutional convention of
   1868

Pursuant with the requirements of the Reconstruction Acts, federal military authorities in Arkansas began appointing registration boards for the state between April and July of 1867. Republican nominees dominated most of the local boards, partly owing to the fact that former Confederates were barred from serving but also because of the apathy and demoralized condition of many Democrats.[1] Reflecting the dispirited mood of these latter persons, one Democratic editor gloomily admitted that the recent actions taken by his party during presidential Reconstruction had been a serious blunder; had the ex-Confederates acted with more restraint, he noted, Arkansas might have gained immediate readmission to the Union.[2]

As registration proceeded, however, Democratic leaders began to stir themselves to action. The *Arkansas Gazette*, the state's leading newspaper, implored every Democrat eligible to register to do so. Failure to enroll on the voting lists, the paper warned, would penalize one's home county, since the registration figures would serve as the basis for apportionment in the constitutional convention.[3] Another Democratic journal, the Pine Bluff *Dispatch*, tried to encourage the dispirited by suggesting that at least twenty-five thousand Democrats could legally register. Because this figure, it insisted, equaled the combined strength of the Negroes and white Unionists, the Democracy had a reasonable chance of continuing its control of the government. In addition, thousands of Union men and even some recent arrivals from the North would prefer working in concert with the Democrats to accepting black suffrage.[4]

While the Democrats foresaw capitalizing on such divisions, their own ranks were far from united.[5] By consenting to register, they would be recognizing the validity of the Reconstruction Acts and the legality of the new state government about to be created. For many, this was simply too much to concede.[6] Added to the former officeholders and others who were barred by law from taking the loyalty oath was a large body of "noncooperationists," men who in effect disfranchised themselves. While their attitude was principled, it further depleted potential Democratic ranks and enervated the Conservatives' strength.[7]

On September 26, 1867, General Ord issued an order declaring the registration complete; out of approximately 93,000 adult males in Arkansas, 66,805 had enrolled.[8] The election on a state constitutional convention was to begin on the first Tuesday in November and continue until finalized. Voters would cast their ballots for or against a convention and also select delegates in the event that a convention were held.[9]

The election proceeded as scheduled until culminated on December 5, the count being 27,576 FOR convention and 13,558 AGAINST, with approximately 24,950 registered persons not voting.[10] In spite of the extensive precautions taken by General Ord to ensure a fair contest, some Democrats lodged charges of fraud and partisanship against the election officers.[11] It seems likely, however, that the outcome was attributable principally to the great disarray and lack of a generally accepted policy within the Democratic camp—a view shared by most contemporary observers.[12]

From January 7 until February 14, 1868, the convention held its deliberations at the State House in Little Rock. All of the chief constituencies involved in the drama of radical Reconstruction had representatives present, though not in proportion to their numbers among the general population. Out of seventy delegates, seventeen were "Carpetbaggers" or outside whites who had entered the South since 1860, a majority of them while serving in the Union army or engaged in activities with the Freedmen's Bureau. Contrary to the popular stereotype, they were not penniless ne'er-do-wells who had arrived from their home states carrying all their worldly possessions in small cloth satchels. They were, in fact, the most prosperous and best-educated group in the convention. Several belonged to the more prestigious professions; occupationally, they comprised seven lawyers, three physicians, three farmers, a merchant, a manufacturer, an engineer, and a minister. Despite their relative youth and brief period of residency in Arkansas (median age thirty-four years, median residency five years), they had accumulated considerable wealth (median property holdings, four thousand dollars in real property and two thousand dollars in personal property), which encouraged them to settle permanently in the state.[13]

Nevertheless, their prior service with the Northern armies, plus their political activities in the Republican party and cooperation with Negroes, had estranged them from a majority of native whites; essentially, they remained aliens.[14] It is significant that they had been sent to the convention, not by white voters, but by blacks in heavily Negro districts bordering the Red, Arkansas, and Mississippi rivers.[15] Such isolation fostered among the Carpetbaggers a strong sense of group identification and cohesion; this, coupled with superior education, prior leadership experience, and youthful energy, gave them a tremendously disproportionate influence. One Carpetbagger, Thomas Bowen, was selected convention president, and he secured 78 of 184 committee assignments for his fellow newcomers.[16]

Local whites willing to cooperate with the congressional Reconstruction program, the legendary "Scalawags," provided twenty-three of the convention delegates. The typical member of this faction represented a predominately white district in western Arkansas and had lived in Arkansas for an average of eighteen of the forty-four years of his life. Nine of the native white "Radicals" were engaged in farming or related pursuits, but the group also included four physicians, three ministers, three lawyers, a merchant-farmer, a merchant, a brickmason, and one individual "at leisure." Five were former slaveholders, with one, Asa Hodges, having owned sixty-four slaves in 1860 and still possessing property valued at forty-five thousand dollars. Most Scalawags, though, were persons of modest means; the group's median property holdings were six hundred dollars in real property and four hundred dollars in personal property, indicating yeoman-class origins. Owing to their limited political backgrounds and a lack of consensus among themselves, especially on racial questions, they more often than not acquiesced in Carpetbagger dominance of the proceedings.[17]

Since the newly liberated freedmen tended at first to accede to the white radicals and look to them for leadership, only eight blacks were present as convention delegates. All represented eastern, central, and southwestern counties containing roughly two-thirds Negro-majority populations. None of the black delegates were illiterate, and their median total property holding was five hundred dollars. All but two appear to have formerly experienced enslavement; however, the Negroes' literacy and the fact that five were listed as mulattoes suggest a possible favored position in bondage.[18]

William H. Grey, a delegate from Phillips County, proved to be the most outstanding Negro spokesman in the convention. Born a free Negro in Washington, D.C., in 1830, in antebellum times he was employed as a servant to Virginia governor Henry A. Wise. Wise permitted him to attend sessions of the national Congress, and in this way Grey appears to have acquired considerable knowledge of parliamentary usage and debate.[19] The other antebellum free Negro, James T. White, a native of Indiana and likewise a Phillips County delegate, also took an active part in the deliberations.[20] So too did James W. Mason of Chicot County, an unusual former slave who had received a European education.[21] The remaining black delegates, while staying more in the background, still voted consistently in a rational way to protect and expand their race's interests.[22]

Seventeen Conservative Southern whites constituted the last faction in the convention (though there were five "nonaligned"

17

white Southerners not manifestly involved with any camp). Since the Reconstruction Acts prohibited many of the South's prewar leaders from voting or participating as delegates, the Conservatives were a younger group (median age thirty-nine years) than the white Scalawags. In spite of this, they were also wealthier, with median holdings of fifteen hundred dollars in real and one thousand dollars in personal property. In marked contrast to the Republican delegates, the districts they represented in southern, east-central, and northwestern Arkansas contained the smallest number of black voters (10.8 percent median). The Conservatives had not been unanimous in their original attitude toward secession; nevertheless, all but one had later accepted it as an accomplished fact and lent support to the Confederacy. At the start of the convention, they futilely pushed for readoption of the constitution of 1864 and later opposed ratification of the new 1868 constitution, in large measure because, as one of them put it, "it encourages the social equality of the white and black races."[23]

From the Conservatives' standpoint, the most objectionable feature of the 1868 constitution was its Negro-suffrage provision. As early as November 1865, James T. White, William H. Grey, and other black spokesmen had organized a mass meeting in Little Rock, reputedly the first Negro convention in the history of the state, where they had pressed for the enfranchisement of their race;[24] later, on the floor of the convention itself, Negro delegates united against proposals by Conservative member Jesse N. Cypert of White County which would have restricted the ballot to adult white males. William H. Grey capsuled the blacks' mood by stating:

> I am here as the representative of a portion of the citizens of Arkansas, whose rights are not secured by the Ordinance offered by the gentleman from White,—men . . . who have stood by the Government and the old flag in times of trouble. . . . From this and other considerations we are not here to ask charity at the hands of this honorable body, but to receive at the hands of the people of Arkansas, in Convention assembled, the apportionment of our rights, as assigned by the Reconstruction Acts of Congress.[25]

Grey went on to give an extensive review of past suffrage practices in the United States. Quoting from Justice Curtis's dissent in the Dred Scott case, he noted that free blacks had sometimes possessed the vote in antebellum days, even in some states of the South. To the charge that the freedmen were unprepared to exercise the franchise, Grey responded by pointing out that thousands of illiterate whites were already voting. "Why, sir," he observed, "every negro vote registered in this state I can duplicate with the vote of a white man that can neither read nor write; and still we are charged with ignorance. I do not deny it, but we are not isolated in that respect. If these men can vote, I see no injustice in permitting us to vote also." [26]

Grey denied that his people would use their new political power irresponsibly or in a spirit of vindictiveness; the charge of "Negro domination" was absurd on its face. Was it plausible, he asked, "that four millions of negroes scattered over this vast country" could control the vast majority of thirty million whites? "I have no antipathy against the white people of this country," he asserted, "and am not surprised at their strenuous opposition. History repeats itself: they have been as hard on men of their own race, when struggling for their own freedom. The noblesse of England,—the cavaliers—, had as little use for the clouted yeomanry and puritanic followers of Cromwell, as these gentlemen have for us. But time has a softening influence on all human prejudices." [27]

Throughout the proceedings black delegates reiterated these themes and continually emphasized the vital necessity of obtaining the ballot for themselves. Negro James T. White, echoing the democratic sentiments of many nineteenth-century Americans, averred that "the elective franchise is a god-given right, which comes to every man born into the world—be he black or white, green or gray, it is his right." White saw the Conservatives' argument that they were willing to grant Negroes equality before the law but not the ballot as hollow. By fighting in the Union army and cooperating with the Republican party, blacks had won the enmity of a majority of Southern whites and would "be crushed by the prejudice that we perceive exhibited [by Conservatives] in this hall." "How are we to live," he asked, "unless we have a power that will shove base men from the offices of the state? I thank God, to-day, that I may cast my vote with a Convention willing to accord equal rights to all." [28]

19

On two key tallies white Carpetbaggers and Scalawags combined to give decisive support to black suffrage demands. By a vote of fifty-three to ten, the convention rejected a Conservative proposal for readoption of the constitution of 1864 with its whites-only franchise provisions;[29] by a like margin, it turned down a Conservative minority report which would have incorporated similar voting features in the new 1868 document.[30] Insofar as the future of the new Republican coalition in Arkansas was concerned, however, it was ominous that the white Scalawags seemed to vote for Negro enfranchisement out of differing motives. Although some seemed inspired by genuinely democratic impulses, others supported enfranchisement with trepidation; while these latter recognized the step as a political necessity, they still worried that blacks might use their new power to demand greater advances in the social realm.[31]

Another issue which came before the convention suggested how easily the Republican bark might run aground on the shoals of the race question. On January 29, Conservative member John M. Bradley proposed incorporating within the state's new constitution a prohibition against legal marriages between blacks and whites. His measure drew instant fire from William H. Grey. The Phillips County Negro expressed his personal aversion toward interracial unions but objected to writing any form of racial distinction into the fundamental law of the state; moreover, he held that such marriage restrictions were simply unnecessary:

> In the constitutions of the Northern States, where such liberty is extended to men of all classes and colors, such outrages upon society are seldom committed. We hear nothing of them. Among the white people of the North, such provisions are never considered necessary. I cannot see why we should encumber our Constitution with such provisions. I scarcely think, that, with the intelligence and wealth of the white people of the country, they are going to make any overtures to us; and I am pretty sure our condition entirely prevents us from making any such overtures to them. It results, that the provision is superfluous. I know that such provisions have heretofore more or less obtained; but while the contract has been kept on our part, it has not been kept upon the part of our friends; and I propose, if such an enactment is to be inserted in the constitution, to insist, also, that if any white man shall be found cohabiting with a negro woman, the penalty shall be death. [Laughter and applause].[32]

John McClure, a Carpetbagger member who realized the potentially divisive nature of the miscegenation issue, moved to refer Bradley's proposition to the Committee on the Penitentiary. This effort failed, however, thirty-two to thirty-four, with a large number of white Scalawags joining the Conservatives in opposition.[33] An extensive debate then followed, with the Scalawags, especially, hopelessly split in their opinions and the tenuous Republican coalition on the verge of flying apart. Miles L. Langely, a white Reconstructionist representing Clark County, courageously asserted that any anti-miscegenation clause would be "in violation of the inalienable rights of man" as well as in contravention of the equal-protection clause of the proposed Fourteenth Amendment. "When you declare," he stated, "that in such a matter as marriage, I shall not choose for myself,—when you begin to limit me here, you may as well say I should not marry an English lady, a Dutch lady, a French lady. And indeed, people did think, a few years ago, it was very wrong to marry a foreign lady. They would have been just as much opposed to the social equality of the Dutch, or of the Yankees, as they now are to that of the negroes. This is simply a matter of prejudice. I contend it has no foundation." Langely vowed, "I shall record my vote against the proposition, if every other man in this convention votes otherwise. I am willing to record my vote, I can vindicate my course afterwards. It may make me unpopular now, just as it made me unpopular, in '62 and '64, to say that all mankind ought to be free."[34]

Carpetbagger Joseph Brooks lent strong endorsement to these convictions, holding that "When we shall have reached the period when legislative enactment shall be necessary, as to the arrangements of my parlor, or my bed-chamber, I hold that the convention, or the Legislature, will have passed beyond their legitimate domain."[35] Other delegates, though, took strong exception. Ira Wilson, a nonaligned Southern white, exclaimed, "I have promised the black people that I would give them suffrage, but never that I would give them my daughter. I told my constituency I would endorse nothing that looked to social equality of the races, their intermarriage, or anything of that kind; and it does chagrin me, and fill me with supreme contempt, for any man to talk of this being a matter of taste."[36]

The Republican leadership finally managed to have the Bradley proposition and other subsequent anti-miscegenation measures shunted into committee, but strains already produced by the convention discussions were apparent. Fearful that they were about to lose the crucial support of numbers of native Unionists, the Carpetbagger chieftains gave the whole subject sober reconsideration. On February 5, they brought forward a two-part resolution declaring, first, that the convention was "utterly opposed to all amalgamation between white and colored races, whether the same is legitimate or illegitimate" and, secondly, recommending that the next session of the General Assembly pass a new anti-miscegenation statute. The first section of the resolution carried unanimously, although Henry Rector, a mulatto delegate from Pulaski County, tried to abstain but was dissuaded by fellow representatives; the second section was endorsed by a vote of fifty-six to nine, despite the resistance of a number of Southern whites who demanded an organic prohibition. For the sake of party harmony, Negro delegates gave their backing to the resolution; they could at least find satisfaction in that they had kept any strictures out of the constitution.[37]

In its other work the convention introduced a number of major changes into the government of Arkansas. Remembering the hapless position of Isaac Murphy after the state elections of 1866, and perhaps anticipating extralegal intimidation against their followers in local districts, the Reconstructionists retained the four-year term for the office of governor and increased the chief executive's appointive powers.[38] Provisions for the legislature established a senate of twenty-six members and a house of representatives of eighty-two members, with representatives of both chosen from twenty-two electoral districts; apportionment of districts was to be based upon the number of persons who had previously registered for the convention election. This system was to remain until 1875. Then, and every ensuing ten years thereafter, new appointments would be made based on total population. In the meantime, however, legislative representation would be weighed in favor of heavily Negro Republican counties because of the fact that blacks had turned out in force for the convention registration while many whites had stayed at home. Within the electoral districts, moreover, lone white counties often were grouped with two or more predominately black counties, a method of gerrymandering designed further to enhance Republican strength.[39]

The franchise provisions of the constitution also promoted the interests of the Republican party. Among those barred from voting or holding public office were all persons disqualified by the proposed Fourteenth Amendment and the Reconstruction Acts, persons who had taken a prior oath of allegiance to the United States Constitution and then aided the Confederacy, those who "during the late rebellion violated the rules of civilized warfare," and those disqualified as voters or officeholders in the state or states from which they came. Individuals in the above categories, however, who "openly advocated or . . . voted for the reconstruction program proposed by Congress" and who accepted "the equality of all men before the law" were deemed qualified electors. The General Assembly, by a two-thirds vote of each house, was empowered to remove any constitutional disabilities from applicants who had "in good faith returned to . . . allegiance to the government of the United States"; in no case, though, could disabilities be lifted from anyone who, after adoption of the constitution, persisted "in opposing the acts of Congress and Reconstruction thereunder." [40]

Before registering or voting, all citizens were required to take a comprehensive loyalty oath, pledging fealty to federal and state constitutions and laws and acceptance of the civil and political equality of all men. Further, they had to agree not to "deprive any person or persons, on account of race, color, or previous condition, of any political or civil right . . . enjoyed by any other class of men" or to molest any individual because of his past adherences during the war or present political affiliations. [41]

Another feature of the proposed new constitution especially important for blacks was a provision empowering the General Assembly to erect a system of free public schools for the children of all races. The schools were to be financed by a one-dollar poll tax levied upon all adult male inhabitants; general state appropriations; county, township, and district property taxes; and by such revenues as might be procured from the sale of lands granted by the federal government. The question of separate, segregated school facilities was left discreetly unmentioned. Predictably, Conservatives opposed these educational provisions; they resented the new tax burdens which would fall on the shoulders of property owners, while fearing the possibility that the schools would promote "indiscriminate social intercourse" between the races. [42]

Additional noteworthy clauses in the constitution expressly disavowed the right of secession and outlawed slavery or involuntary servitude except as a punishment for crime. Also, the legislature was forbidden to make any compensation for emancipated slaves.[43]

On February 14 the convention completed its deliberations and formally adjourned, although subject to recall in the event that the constitution should be defeated. Voting on the document was to begin on March 13 and continue until terminated by military authorities. Simultaneously, elections for new state officers were to be held, conducted separately by judges appointed by a special commission of three Carpetbaggers established by the convention.[44]

The Republicans entered the contest with a well-oiled organization and smoothly functioning state committee inherited from the prior convention-delegate elections; complementing the work of these regular party vehicles, Union League and other Republican clubs labored to bring out a full vote and particularly helped to organize Negro supporters. The party platform endorsed the Reconstruction program and the proposed constitution, promised a system of free schools for blacks and whites alike, supported a program of internal improvements, and assured the people of the state that a Republican administration would promote honest and economical government. A full slate of candidates for state offices was fielded. Heading the ticket was General Powell Clayton, a former Kansas cavalry commander who had been in charge of the federal garrison at Pine Bluff during the war; after the cessation of hostilities, Clayton had remained in Arkansas, marrying a Helena woman and purchasing a plantation in Jefferson County.[45]

Though temporarily in the ascendancy, the Republicans were by no means confident of victory in the upcoming balloting. The Negro vote alone could not be expected to carry the day, and the difficulties of sustaining an alliance between blacks and a sizeable bloc of native whites were formidable. In western Arkansas there was the considerable faction of mountain Unionists to be courted; however, even in this region a majority of whites had ultimately backed the Confederacy, and most of these were now siding with the Democratic opposition. Still more troubling, some of the ex-wartime Loyalists were now beginning to cross over to the Democratic camp. This was partly because of distaste for the racial equalitarianism of radical Reconstruction, but not entirely:

24

political considerations were at work as well. Under the ante-bellum constitution of 1836, legislative apportionment had been based upon the number of adult white male inhabitants; with the enfranchisement of the blacks, the predominately white counties of the mountains would lose influence proportionately—especially so, since until 1875 legislative apportionment would be calculated upon the electors already registered within each county, with the number enrolled particularly heavy in some black districts.[46]

These factors encouraged the Democrats to throw off their spirit of lethargy and prepare for a genuine fight.[47] Preferring not to nominate candidates for state office but instead concentrate all their energies on defeat of the constitution, an enthusiastic party convention gathered in Little Rock on January 28 and proclaimed its support for a "white man's government in a white man's country." Emblems representing both the Democratic cock and the old Whig coon were prominently displayed, and conservative men of all political antecedents were urged to rally under the Democratic standard.[48]

Recognizing that the black-suffrage issue was their strongest card, Democratic leaders made repeated appeals for white racial solidarity throughout the canvass. While the party told Negroes that it would respect their basic equality before the law, this was as far as it would go. Lest there be any misunderstanding, the *Campaign Gazette*, a special edition of the Little Rock *Arkansas Gazette*, presented the Democratic philosophy with cogent frankness: "We do not recognize that the negro has any political rights whatever," the paper stated, "and his existence in the country is only tolerated by white men on the score of humanity."[49]

The election for ratifying the constitution, which began on March 13 and continued for over two weeks, marked the beginning of a sad tradition of fraud and violence which was to prove the worst feature of the heritage of Reconstruction in Arkansas. The Ku Klux Klan had already made its appearance and was busy terrorizing blacks in remote rural precincts.[50] Republican workers more than matched these efforts with their own dishonest tactics: Democrats alleged that individual Negro voters were marched and re-marched to the polls to cast their ballots again and again. Partisan registrars unscrupulously closed and then reopened the election precincts in ways designed to maximize Republican strength.

25

Returns themselves were doctored and tampered with to suit party purposes.[51]

Adding to the confusion, Congress passed on March 11, 1868, two days before the election began, a measure authorizing "any person duly registered in the State to vote in the election district where he offers to vote," provided he had resided in that district for ten days prior to the election and presented the proper credentials. On March 14 the War Department issued General Order No. 14 including these new directives, but it did not reach Arkansas until after the balloting was concluded. In Pulaski, Jefferson, and Washington counties, however, registrars had informally heard of the Congress's action and on their own initiative had admitted electors covered by the new provisions. Republicans contended that this explained a discrepancy in Pulaski County, where returns showed that the total votes cast exceeded by 1,195 the number of persons registered. If the tallies in the above three counties were accepted, the constitution would carry by the narrow margin of 27,913 to 26,597.[52]

Military authorities made no effort to resolve this dispute or conduct independent investigations of the various charges of fraud. Instead, they forwarded a copy of the returns and all allegations to Washington, D.C., for consideration. The army report did not deny that there had been irregularities but observed it unlikely that "any election for ratification of the constitution can be held in Arkansas where similar charges will not by some party be made, and probably with some foundation."[53]

The entire matter eventually passed to the Congress for adjudication. On May 8, 1868, Representative Thaddeus Stevens, speaking on behalf of the Committee on Reconstruction, brought forward an Arkansas statehood bill. Stevens declared that the voters of Arkansas had adopted a constitution in accordance with the stipulations of the Reconstruction Acts, established a government republican in form, and noted that their newly assembled legislature had just ratified the proposed Fourteenth Amendment. Stevens' bill passed both houses, was returned with President Johnson's veto, and then repassed in June 1868.[54]

On July 2, 1868, jubilant crowds of black and white Republicans filled the streets of Little Rock to witness Powell Clayton's inauguration as governor. Disconsolate Democrats kept a low profile, and the occasion passed without incident. Exercising a like restraint, Clayton delivered a moderate, temperate address in which he predicted a welcome end to sectional strife and the dawning of a bright era. Following the swearing-in ceremonies, a military salute of fifteen guns announced the admission of a reconstructed Arkansas into the American republic.[55]

# III

# The Legacy of Reconstruction

The rights we acquired in 1868
we expect to maintain.
—James T. White, black delegate
to the Arkansas constitutional
convention of 1874

For six years, from 1868 to 1874, Arkansas passed through the era of radical Reconstruction. The period was sometimes described by unsympathetic contemporaries and subsequent commentators as "black Reconstruction," an aberrant time when normal political conditions were suspended and replaced by "Negro domination" or "Negro rule."[1] Certainly as applied to Arkansas these terms are misnomers, or, at most, describe a half-truth. Blacks accounted for barely more than a fourth of the state's population, and under the initial convention registration of 1867, they comprised slightly under 35 percent of the enrolled voters. The test oath prescribed by the 1868 constitution disfranchised a sizeable bloc of white voters, yet even under that document Negroes could not control elections in their own right. In the 1872 governor's race, for example, 73,206 votes were cast, but there were only 22,921 adult black males residing in the state in 1870.[2] If every single eligible Negro had registered and voted in the above contest, the number of black ballots would not have exceeded 31 percent.

No Negro served as governor or lieutenant governor or sat on the supreme court bench, nor was any sent to Congress from

28

Arkansas under the Reconstruction administrations. Only two blacks held cabinet-level positions in the state government: one, the able William H. Grey, served as Commissioner of Immigration and State Lands from 1872 to 1874; the other, Joseph C. Corbin, a recently arrived immigrant from Ohio and an Oberlin graduate, held the post of Superintendent of Public Instruction from 1873 to 1874.[3] Moreover, in all sessions of the legislature during Reconstruction, and in the two decades afterward when Negroes still obtained the franchise, the number of black lawmakers was always less than it would have been had the blacks' representation been proportionate to their percentage of the state's population; in 1873, at the height of Reconstruction in Arkansas, there were only twenty black lawmakers in the General Assembly.[4]

Within the Republican party, despite intermittent racial flareups and patronage fights, blacks generally conceded primary leadership to white persons disposed to respect their rights and accord some recognition. Negroes sat in large numbers in the state conventions and on the state central committee; however, they never gained anything like complete control over these bodies. Sometimes the Clayton organization honored a trusted black lieutenant with temporary chairmanship of the state convention, but blacks were never able to win the powerful permanent chairman's slot. Among the twelve to sixteen Arkansas delegates who attended the national Republican conventions, there usually could be found two or three blacks, plus a few black alternates. A handful of recognized Negro leaders also received lucrative federal appointments as a reward for their loyalty and party activities.[5]

Nonetheless, if blacks did not control the Republican party, neither could they be ignored by it. Providing its largest constituency, they often managed to shape the direction of Republican policies and secure programs for advancement of their race. Nowhere is this more evident than in the field of civil rights. By using their political leverage within the Reconstruction administrations, Negroes were able to resist the incipient tendencies toward segregation which appeared in the aftermath of the war.

If these efforts were not completely successful, it was in part because blacks were not wholly consistent in their own attitudes concerning racial mixing. One of the most important developments in the evolution of the color line was the establishment of separate black churches; almost immediately upon emancipation, blacks deserted the predominately white congregations en masse and began founding their own religious institutions. Here, they could escape from painful encounters with white prejudice and condescension and could develop their own leadership capacities, social outlets, and forms of spiritual expression.[6]

A somewhat analogous pattern can be discerned in black responses to the inauguration of segregated schools. Over the bitter objection of Conservative delegates, Reconstructionists in the constitutional convention of 1868 had prevented provisions mandating segregated schools from being incorporated in the state's new organic law. The final document only stipulated that public schooling be made available to all children between the ages of five and twenty-one, regardless of race. Nevertheless, when the first Reconstruction legislature assembled in 1868, it adopted a new statute which provided for segregated public education. The measure passed unanimously in the Senate, and in the House of Representatives passed by a vote of thirty-seven to nineteen; the dissenting votes came from those who opposed the bill's segregation requirements. Still, despite this initial resistance, most Arkansas blacks appear to have soon acquiesced in segregated schooling without sustained protest. By the late 1870s, in fact, some blacks in Little Rock were requesting that only teachers from their own race be employed in the city's black schools.[7]

The black impulse toward separatism had its limits, however. Negroes could not isolate themselves from the operations of the economy and the larger society; any acceptance of color bars in the realms of commercial activities and public services could only impair their chances for progress. Reacting against nascent segregation restrictions and caste distinctions, Negroes in the 1868 General Assembly obtained passage of a new civil-rights law. The law forbade denial of first-class services to blacks in public accommodations or on public conveyances, with offenders subject to a two hundred- to five thousand-dollar fine and imprisonment in the county jail for up to twelve months, the latter to be imposed at the discretion of the trial judge.[8]

The effectiveness of the 1868 law is uncertain; clearly, in spite of its existence, some segregation continued.[9] The disappointing results prompted the Reconstruction legislature of 1873 to approve a second, more sweeping and strongly worded civil-rights act. The law covered public carriers, hotels, saloons, restaurants, and "places of public amusement" and required that owners or proprietors provide all persons "the same and equal" services at equal costs, regardless of race. Failure to comply could result in stiff fines and possible imprisonment. Another section of the act required that school districts furnish black children "like and equal" facilities to those given whites.

Whether this new law achieved greater results than the first is questionable. Rather surprisingly, it actually remained on the statute books until repealed in 1907, over thirty-four years after its adoption.[10] A survey of the reports of the Arkansas Supreme Court, however, shows that no appeals were ever carried under either the 1868 or 1873 statutes. Charles Nordhoff, a journalist for the New York *Herald* who visited Arkansas in March 1875, related that only one case had arisen under the 1873 act during its first two years of existence: a white saloonkeeper was fined $46.80, including court costs, for refusing service to black state senator R. A. Dawson and other black patrons. The New Yorker revealed his own feelings by stating: "The negroes have shown no disposition to make the law offensive."[11] Apparently, blacks liked to think they enjoyed the theoretical right of access to all public accommodations, but not many were anxious to undergo the emotional trauma of testing the statutes or risk the expense of unsuccessful litigation.

Even so, it is quite possible that the mere presence of the civil-rights measures had some influence. Although Nordhoff observed that some saloons in Little Rock "had two bars, one for each color," he "also saw in several cases black and white men drinking together."[12] Furthermore, testimony of contemporary black residents and a subsequent white visitor shows that, at least by the 1880s, Arkansas railroads had dropped earlier segregation arrangements. On the state's urban streetcar systems, segregation was not instituted until required by state enactment in 1903.[13]

In other areas persistence of the casual habits of the slavery period worked against appearance of color restrictions. For instance, the old practice of having servants live conveniently on one's property, usually in small quarters behind the main residence, inhibited the development of segregated housing patterns in cities

31

and towns. True, by the turn of the century older customs were beginning to be challenged by newer practices. When two out-of-state investors from Michigan, Henry F. Auten and Edgar E. Moss, began the new suburban development of Pulaski Heights at Little Rock's far western edge, they restricted land sales to white buyers. As one writer has noted, their policy of racial exclusion was "anything but subtle." In advertisement after advertisement, they stated that "Pulaski Heights is exclusively for white people" and insisted that "People who desire fine homes want an exclusively white neighborhood." [14]

Such an attitude undeniably represented the wave of the future, but even as late as 1900 it had not yet become omnipresent in the rest of the city. While there was a predominately black neighborhood in the central part of Little Rock, and a tendency for black families sometimes to cluster together elsewhere, still in numerous instances blacks and whites lived side by side [15] (see foldout map of Little Rock, 1900).

Similarly, both races shared common park facilities. Although the city directory of 1900 noted that privately owned Fulton's Park was "fitted up for the exclusive use of the colored people," other parks were at times utilized by both blacks and whites. For instance, an *Arkansas Gazette* article of August 10, 1897, entitled "Ex-Slaves Big Day," reported the celebrations of the Ex-Slaves' Association at Little Rock's West End Park, owned by the city's streetcar company. A little more than two months later, on October 14, the state Confederate reunion was held at the same place. [16] Occasionally, blacks and whites used the same park facilities at the same time. In 1892 the *Gazette* described a vocal-music concert at the city's Glenwood Park, owned by an earlier streetcar concern, as being "free for every man, woman, and child in Little Rock." Readers were assured, "There is room for all." No evidence was found that the concert was segregated in any way. [17]

Blacks as well as whites also had access to Little Rock's chief vaudeville house after 1885, the Capital Theater on Markham Street. Blacks do not appear to have been confined to the theater balcony but were likely being admitted to the main parquet section also, although it is not established whether on an integrated or segregated basis. [18] Incidental references to "Negro" saloons and restaurants can be found in almost any given year, but in some of these businesses, as late as the 1890s, the races mixed freely.[19] However, separate hotels and boarding houses were the general rule, in spite of state civil-rights laws.[20]

Concerning burial customs, as late as 1899 blacks were being interred in plots interspersed with those of whites in Mount Holly, Little Rock's original cemetery.[21] However, in 1888 a section of the city's new Oakland Cemetery was set aside solely for Negro use; black fraternal societies were given authority to administer the plots within it.[22] Even so, earlier traditions continued to linger on for years. In part, this was because of the persistence of the old practice of ex-slaves being buried next to their former masters. The Martin Cemetery, located near the Mabelvale community ten miles southwest of downtown Little Rock, the oldest cemetery in Pulaski County, provides a striking example: a former slave was interred in the Martin-family section of the cemetery as late as 1926.[23]

Throughout the state, ambiguity and confusion characterized the Reconstruction legacy in the sphere of civil rights. Widespread and pervasive racial discrimination continued; yet Arkansas blacks had managed to avoid a system of either total exclusion or total separation in public facilities. The absence of generally settled and agreed upon policies in race relations, coupled with the new reality of Reconstruction social initiatives and expenditures, meant that the opportunity for black mobility and advancement remained.

Perhaps the most important black gains under Reconstruction came in the area of public education. Before the Civil War, public schools had been almost nonexistent in Arkansas; a small state school fund had been created out of monies received from federal land grants, but, since no additional revenues were provided, as late as 1861 Arkansas could claim only twenty-five common schools exclusively supported by public financing.[24] While plans for a new system of free schools for whites had been laid under Isaac Murphy's administration, these had barely gotten under way before his government was dismantled.[25] The national Freedmen's Bureau struggled to maintain a few day schools, Sabbath schools, and night schools for Negro refugees, but its limited efforts barely began to touch black educational needs.[26]

Credit for the actual inauguration of mass education in Arkansas rightly belongs to the Powell Clayton administration. As authorized by the new constitution, the 1868 General Assembly empowered local districts to operate public schools for at least three months of every year. As noted previously, the same body also provided that separate schools for blacks and whites be maintained from the beginning, a factor which greatly mitigated white opposition.[27] A partisan vendetta from elements of the Democratic press did not prevent the schools from gaining in popularity, for by 1870 over 63 percent of white children and 50 percent of black children of school age were enrolled in classes.[28]

Important strides were also made in higher education. With the assistance of Morrill Act land-grant funds and a $130,000 contribution from the city of Fayetteville and Washington County, the radical government opened Arkansas's first state university in 1872.[29] The following year the legislature expanded the university program by commissioning a Branch Normal College for Negroes at Pine Bluff; operations at the latter campus were begun in 1875, just shortly after the close of Reconstruction.[30]

Initiatives in special education included the Arkansas Institute for the Blind. The Institute, started at Arkadelphia in 1859, had wrung a few appropriations out of the state during its early years but had at first largely been supported by private charity. In 1868 the General Assembly took over the school, moved it to Little Rock, and made it a public institution.[31] At the same time the Assembly incorporated an academy for deaf mutes, recently established in Little Rock, as a state school.[32] Unfortunately, Arkansas Negroes initially received scant benefits from these ventures: although the legislative acts creating them contained no racially exclusionary provisions, only a token number of blacks were placed in the deaf institute, and none in the blind school, until separate facilities were created in 1887.[33] Black patients were admitted from the beginning to the state's mental hospital[34] but were assigned to segregated wards, even though segregation was not required by law.[35] The asylum was formally created by the Republican legislature of 1873, but soon after the Reconstruction regime was toppled from power, and inadequate funding prevented its opening for a decade.

Blacks could take what little comfort they might from the fact that there were no segregation arrangements in the management of state prisoners; clearly, in all other aspects, care of inmates was lacking. In spite of his personal opposition,[36] financial exigency forced Governor Clayton to continue the leasing of state convicts to private contractors, a practice first begun in Arkansas in 1853.[37] Periodic exposés of brutal and inhumane treatment, with the death rate among convicts in some years in excess of 25 percent, did not stop economy-minded Democratic legislatures from continuing the lease system after Reconstruction; some reforms in care and supervision were introduced during the 1890s, but it was not until 1912, after decades of criticism and controversy, that the contract system was finally abandoned.[38]

The radical government also made little headway in shielding the rural poor from economic exploitation. The first Reconstruction legislature did pass, in July 1868, a new laborer's lien law. The law stipulated that claims for wages against an employer constituted a lien on his property; draconian penalties were imposed for any attempts to remove encumbered property from the borders of the state. While the lien act proposed to halt the cheating of Negro field hands by unscrupulous planters, most blacks did not have independent records of wages owed and in any case were usually too fearful, impoverished, and uninformed to avail themselves of the statute's protection.[39]

Whatever the limitations of its specific programs, the radical administration managed to introduce a broader concept of the state's social responsibilities to its citizens into the government of Arkansas. Since a majority of whites as well as blacks stood to benefit from its initiatives, particularly in education, these might under different circumstances have mollified white resistance and earned the Republicans greater support. However, in the absence of the extensive federal aid, the burden of underwriting Reconstruction policies fell upon state and local authorities—at the very time when Arkansas was reeling from the destruction wrought by the Civil War and could least afford increased expenditures for new services. This was especially true in southern and eastern counties, where plantation agriculture remained in great disarray.[40] The situation, bad to start with, was only worsened by the payment of extravagant salaries and fees well beyond what was necessary to open public offices to the less affluent.[41] Despite spiralling tax rates and property assessments,[42] the radical administration soon faced an empty treasury and a shortage of cash. As early as 1868 the Clayton government began the ruinous expediency of issuing state scrip for meeting expenses. Although the treasury warrants bore interest at 8 percent, and were receivable for various tax payments,[43] the state's shaky fiscal condition caused them rapidly to depreciate in value. By the fall of 1872 scrip had fallen to fifty-eight cents on the dollar, and by September 1874 it was selling for eighteen to twenty-five cents. The close of Reconstruction found Arkansas with an outstanding debt of $1,750,000 in scrip money.[44]

Issuance of the state scrip soon demonstrated the inexorable workings of Gresham's law. Smart taxpayers bought up the depreciated warrants to meet tax assessments, and the near worthless paper eventually made its circuitous way back into public coffers. State and local officers were compelled to pay accounts against the government, including teachers' salaries, in scrip; after 1870 this produced frequent teacher resignations, declining enrollments, reduced school terms, and in many instances the outright closing of schools, both black and white.[45]

In addition to the scrip obligations, Arkansas had accumulated a mountain of other debts to finance various public projects: total state indebtedness at the close of Reconstruction stood at $16,166,073.55, up from only $3,363,509.19 in 1868.[46] In some cases borrowed funds were used to good effect. For example, 413 miles of new railway trackage had been laid by 1874, and the Reconstructionists could claim that they had helped create a modern transportation system for Arkansas.[47] But for most of the remaining debt, few tangible results could be shown.[48] For years, the huge liabilities reinforced the mood of economy and retrenchment which marked subsequent Democratic administrations and dampened support for social initiatives and programs that might benefit the poor, including blacks. In 1884 a "readjustor" faction of the Democratic party succeeded in wiping out three-fourths of the debt through constitutional amendment, yet repudiation carried its own cost. Beginning in that year, and lasting until 1917, New York banks refused to handle any securities of Arkansas's state government.[49]

Factors other than economic chaos and financial mismanagement contributed to the undermining of the Reconstruction experiment. At least as significant was the inability of the Republican administrations to maintain public order. Because many native Democrats saw the radical government as a tyrannous usurpation, they had no qualms about attempting frankly revolutionary means to destroy it. Following the gubernatorial inauguration in the summer of 1868, nightriders of the Ku Klux Klan and other masked societies launched a bloody campaign of intimidation and reprisal.[50] In Crittenden County, a representative of the Freedmen's Bureau was murdered, and former Confederate general Thomas C. Hindman, who had shown some disposition to ally with the Republicans, was shot and killed at Helena. Congressman James Hinds was assassinated and party leader Joseph Brooks wounded while the two were on their way to a rally near Clarendon. At Searcy, in White County, the body of a Republican agent was thrown into a well. How many plantation Negroes and other obscure persons were killed is unknown, but Clayton numbered them in the hundreds.[51]

An effort to conduct a new registration of voters in time for the November 1868 presidential and congressional elections also elicited much violence; registrars were driven from their posts at gunpoint or otherwise chased away from their duties. When Clayton set aside the registration in eleven counties, Democrats charged him with acting from political motives; a modern study, however, has presented convincing evidence that the terror against registration officials was real and that the governor probably was justified in his action.[52]

Clayton waited until after the autumn balloting before unleashing his counterattack against the Klan. On November 4 he placed ten counties under martial law and later added several more to the list. A hastily recruited force of two thousand ill-disciplined militiamen, mostly black, moved through the state committing sundry killings, lootings, and rapines. Open warfare broke out at Center Point, in Sevier County, where a militia unit stormed and pillaged the town. In northeast Arkansas William Monks, a Missouri outlaw, teamed up with militia authorities to initiate a reign of brigandage. The state also employed a corps of private detectives who provided militia commanders with names of men to be arrested and, often, summarily executed.

After a campaign of four months, martial law was lifted and the militia companies retired; sporadic eruptions of violence persisted throughout the Reconstruction administrations, however, and occasionally militia units were sent back into action.[53]

Clayton argued that he had no choice, that his use of the militia was imperative under the circumstances. Perhaps so, but its employment invariably produced anger, alienation, and an erosion of public backing. Though not exclusively or perhaps even primarily responsible for the disorder of the Reconstruction era, as the party in power the Republicans suffered most from general dissatisfaction.

A final hindrance to the success of the Reconstruction program was internal strife and the resultant shattering of the state Republican organization. As early as the first Republican state convention, rival Carpetbagger and Scalawag groups vied for party control. The Carpetbaggers had managed to secure the gubernatorial nomination for Clayton; however, in an effort to restore harmony, Colonel James M. Johnson, an old citizen of Madison County in the Ozarks, was run for lieutenant governor. For the time being the breach was papered over, but after the election it reappeared, as the native Unionists found themselves slighted in patronage assignments and the letting of valuable state printing contracts.[54]

Further dissension appeared when Joseph Brooks, a former Iowa minister and leading Carpetbagger, broke away from the Clayton fold. As a delegate to the constitutional convention of 1868, Brooks had stood as an outspoken egalitarian and defender of Negro rights; a Methodist preacher of the old style, he had also taken the stump and done yeoman service in organizing black supporters for the Republicans. Brooks felt wronged, however, when the party denied him a seat in Congress. With a faction of Carpetbaggers and blacks behind him, he came forward on the floor of the legislature as an advocate of economy and began attacking Clayton's record of financial profligacy.[55]

Had the Democrats not been so disunited themselves, they might have benefited more immediately from Republican discord. After the ratification of the 1868 constitution and Clayton's inauguration, the Democratic state committee met in Little Rock on July 30 and issued an address to the people. The committee recommended an all-out effort in the forthcoming presidential and congressional campaigns. Although the radical state government was condemned as unconstitutional, all who could do so were urged to register, take the elector's oath with its pledge to uphold Negro suffrage, and work to send conservative men to the legislature.[56]

The policy of the state committee received the vigorous endorsement of the influential *Arkansas Gazette*. Two days following the committee's action the newspaper boldly declared:

> Now it has become necessary for self-preservation, a right enjoyed by the lowest of the animal kingdom, for such of our people as can do so to take this oath and vote in the coming election. We presume there are none among us who will not see the necessity of this course, and trust that none,—no, not one—will object to taking this oath. . . . In cases of this sort it has always been conceded that it is right to swear, and violate the pledge at the first temple of justice.[57]

On August 4, the newspaper reaffirmed this stand. "In regard to the propriety of urging our people to take the oath," it stated, "we will say frankly that we have not the time nor disposition just now to discuss the ethics of the subject. . . . In the present political struggle we believe that the end we seek will justify the use of ANY means."[58]

In private correspondence, William E. Woodruff, Jr., the *Gazette*'s publisher, elaborated upon this position and attempted to defend his newspaper's stance. Woodruff held that there was no "binding force in law or morals to an oath taken under duress" and cited the testimony of a number of former state supreme court justices and leading Arkansas attorneys who concurred with his view.[59] The present struggle was no ordinary political rivalry but really the continuation of a state of war. "I endanger my soul no more by taking this elector's oath," he insisted, "than I did . . . when I killed a man in battle. —False swearing (if you will) and the taking of human life are alike prohibited by religion and law. —As we are circumstanced the one act is no worse than the other."[60]

What appeared to Woodruff and the state committee as pragmatic and realistic, however, struck others as simply unscrupulous. "Noncooperationists" who had originally boycotted the constitutional convention-delegate elections were even more adamantly opposed to taking the new state voters' oath. Though sharing the

Democratic committee's abhorrence of the Clayton government, they held that the only honest way to combat the Reconstruction program was through a national alliance of conservative men in all parties and sections, as would later appear in the Liberal Republican movement.[61]

Representative of individuals of this persuasion was David Walker of Fayetteville, former antebellum Whig leader, ex-president of the secession convention of 1861, and briefly chief justice of the state supreme court during the latter period of the Murphy administration. Walker's Whig antecedents made him reluctant to cooperate with the Democratic organization, and his juridical mind balked at the idea of committing willful perjury. In a letter to Woodruff written September 24, he disclosed his opinion that the taking of the voters' oath was no minor issue of tactics; instead, it was a basic question of conscience:

> I have believed and yet believe that we should have adhered to that plank in the democratic platform which treats the Reconstruction Acts, and the State Governments made under them as void. But it seems that we are to abandon this plank, and step off squarely upon the negro equality plank of the Radical platform, and urge its adoption, to swear never to abandon it, and to invite the negroes to get upon it and vote with us. Are you in earnest in all this? Do you realy [sic] intend to fasten negro suffrage and negro equality upon the State? If such is realy [sic] your intention, then I can see how in good faith the voters oath may be taken. But if it is intended that the position shall be assumed, and the negro vote used to enable us to get in power that we may disfranchise him. Then, then—no, I will give no utterance to my feelings.
>
> I have thought it wrong to take any step which would commit us to this infamous state government, with its negro-equality provisions. But that step has been taken, and it is folly to oppose it now, for it has already gone forth, that in Arkansas at least, reconstruction is not a failure—that she has through her State Central Committee, consented to hold an election under the reconstructed state government, and has declared in favor of negro equality. . . . We stand in this degraded, humiliating condition before the world today, no effort which I or those who agree with me can make will change it."[62]

The persistence of such fundamental disagreements continued to debilitate the Democratic party and divide its ranks. However, the mere passage of time itself served to bestow a certain legitimacy upon the Reconstruction regime. Gradually, grudgingly, more and more persons of "noncooperationist" outlooks came to feel that it would at least be necessary to concede the radical state government's de facto existence and work temporarily within its political structure. Eventually, even Judge Walker acquiesced in this view.[63] Negro suffrage, moreover, once established, came increasingly to be accepted as a new fact of political life. Exposure to the more capable and honest type of black leader also began having a perceptible effect on the racial attitudes of some whites. As early as the constitutional convention of 1868, a Conservative delegate, referring to black spokesman William H. Grey, had declared, "You are an honorable man, sir, despite your color, and your kinky hair, and I have found you such."[64] Following a Little Rock school board election in February 1869 in which local blacks had demonstrated considerable independence and had elected a number of candidates over the official Republican nominees, the Arkansas Gazette commented, "We would much rather trust the resident blacks, who have been raised among us, to direct the interests of the community, than the unscrupulous strangers who try to use them as tools to their plans."[65] Whether wholly sincere or not, editorial statements like these inevitably had some influence on the formation of public opinion.

How swiftly new political currents were carrying the Democratic party toward previously unthinkable positions became evident in the state election of 1872. Long-simmering disagreements among the Arkansas Republicans at last boiled over, with various breakaway elements abandoning the regular Republican organization and fielding a separate ticket headed by gubernatorial candidate Joseph Brooks. Opponents labeled the rebels "Brindletails," derisively alleging that the strong-lunged Brooks bellowed at his audiences after the manner of a brindletail bull; in turn, Brooks' followers dubbed the regulars "Minstrels," from the fact that a prominent regular leader had once performed in a minstrel show.[66]

Convening in Little Rock on June 19, the Democratic state convention resolved to endorse the Brindletail nominees rather than place its own slate of candidates in the race.[67] A number of considerations lay behind the decision. For one, the Brindletails had allied themselves with the Liberal Republican movement

41

against the corruption of the Grant administration and were supporting the presidential bid of Horace Greeley. Many ex-Whigs and former "noncooperationists" within the Democratic camp, such as David Walker, still saw a national coalition of conservatives as the best way to undo the Reconstruction program; under the circumstances, they were willing to aid the candidacy of a man like Brooks, although ordinarily they would not have done so.[68] Brooks, moreover, had smoothed the way to cooperation by promising to work for removal of the test oath and disfranchisement provisions against ex-Confederates in the 1868 constitution. Politically, Brooks' favorable reputation within the Negro community could be expected to draw black votes away from the Republican regulars. And finally, Democratic assistance to the Brindletails would further encourage Republican division.[69]

The situation was not without its irony. Scarcely four years after proclaiming their support for "a white man's government in a white man's country," Arkansas Democrats were backing a leading Carpetbagger for governor who was best known for his racial equalitarianism and championship of black rights. In fact, running on the same ticket with Brooks were two Negroes, E. A. Fulton and Richard Samuels, candidates for secretary of state and superintendent of the penitentiary.[70]

A significant minority of the Democratic party found their state convention's policy hard to accept. Included in the group was a small cabal of important Little Rock lawyers and politicians, and William E. Woodruff, Jr., the *Arkansas Gazette* publisher. Less concerned with fostering a national union of conservatives than with destroying and replacing the 1868 constitution, they worried that endorsement of Brooks would prove inexpedient. By blurring party lines, it would hinder Democratic prospects for winning control of the legislature, a necessary first step in blocking radical programs and securing constitutional revision. Furthermore, they perceived the Brindletail leader as a man of will and determination, a charismatic figure who might reenergize the Republican organization and give it an extended lease on life.[71] Lending reinforcement to the above critics of the Brooks' endorsement were many rank-and-file Democrats throughout the state who disliked the Republican dissident's radicalism and racial beliefs.

These developments offered intriguing possibilities to the

Minstrel Republicans, who proved to be just as adept at the game of dividing the enemy as their opposition. In March 1871 Powell Clayton had resigned the office of governor to accept appointment by the Arkansas legislature to the United States Senate. At the same time, James M. Johnson was somehow persuaded to step down as lieutenant governor in exchange for the post of secretary of state, with the governor's chair then passing to state senate president Ozra A. Hadley, a faithful Clayton ally.[72]

It was generally assumed that Hadley would be chosen as the Minstrel standard-bearer in 1872; however, in a surprise move he voluntarily stepped aside, and the regular Republican state committee instead gave the gubernatorial nod to political unknown Elisha Baxter. A native Southern Unionist from north Arkansas,[73] Baxter had been named United States Senator by the Murphy government in 1864 but had never been permitted to take his seat by Congress.[74] Although he had served as a circuit judge during radical Reconstruction, he was not directly associated with the controversies surrounding the Clayton-Hadley administrations. Baxter entered the 1872 contest promising reform and a removal of voting strictures against ex-Confederates and skillfully attempted to co-opt for himself the Brindletail slogan of "universal suffrage, universal amnesty, and honest men for office."[75]

In attempting to broaden its base of support, each faction had nominated a candidate more representative of the ranks of its opposition than of itself. But, if confusing, the election also proved to be one of the most exciting in the state's history. The magnetic Brooks, especially, drew large crowds with his electrifying oratory. Years later a contemporary remembered that he "went through the State like a fiery cross, . . . denouncing Clayton . . . and all of them, telling the people that if they would elect him governor he would fill the jail so full of them that their legs would stick out the windows."[76]

While it is generally admitted that there were irregularities on all sides, the best evidence indicates that the Brooks' ticket probably won the contest. The Minstrels, however, controlled the registration machinery and election boards.[77] Totals from four counties were tossed out and other returns adjusted to show Baxter victorious over Brooks by the narrow margin of 38,584 to 34,622.[78]

The outcome left the followers of Brooks in a quandary, for the

1868 constitution invested in the General Assembly the authority to adjudge disputed elections and that body was still controlled by the Republican regulars. Heated talk of having reform legislators organize a second General Assembly, inaugurate Brooks as governor, and then throw the entire matter into the lap of Congress to decide was eventually discarded as imprudent. Brooks was left with little to do except to continue to protest, collect evidence of fraud, and wanly hope for some type of later federal intervention on his behalf.[79]

Although they had lost the recent election battle, the Democrats were unknowingly on the verge of winning the broader political struggle. Clayton and the Minstrel chieftains apparently had assumed that after having promoted Baxter they could readily control him, but the new governor soon demonstrated qualities of courage and independence. Baxter filled appointments on a nonpartisan basis, consulted with Democratic as well as Republican leaders, and scrupulously attempted to give both parties representation on registration and election boards.[80] He also made good on his campaign pledge to back the reenfranchisement of ex-Confederates.[81] With the full weight of the governor's office behind it, an amendment removing the voting disabilities imposed by the 1868 constitution cleared the General Assembly and was overwhelmingly approved in a special election held on March 3.[82]

These actions led to growing estrangement between Baxter and the regular Republican leaders, but a final rupture did not come until March 1874, when the governor refused to release additional state bonds to Arkansas railroads.[83] Baxter maintained that the original statute authorizing the railway aid bonds was technically flawed in several respects; by implication, all of the bonds issued under it were invalid.[84]

A number of the Republican chieftains had personal interests in the railroads and now faced the prospect of severe financial loss, but it would be simplistic to say that this was the only reason for their consternation.[85] Coming in the wake of the Panic of 1873, Baxter's action guaranteed a total collapse of the value of state railway bonds; the whole railroad-building program, one of the proudest achievements of the Republican administrations, was certain to be ruined.

The Arkansas Republicans stood on the banks of a political

44

Rubicon. Only a sense of desperation can explain their decision to disavow Elisha Baxter, the man they had recognized as chief executive for well over a year, and take up the dormant cause of Joseph Brooks (who was still being supported by some Democrats). Their new course was revealed on April 15, 1874, when the Pulaski County circuit court ruled that Brooks had been elected in 1872 and was the legal governor of Arkansas.[86] Brooks then immediately took the oath from Chief Justice John McClure; accompanied by a band of followers, he proceeded through a rainstorm to the State House and entered the Executive Office. As Elisha Baxter reported the incident: "Mr. Brooks, in person, with an armed force of a dozen or twenty, took possession of my room, and I was permitted the alternative of forcible and unseemly ejection, or of such arrest and punishment as he might see fit to inflict."[87] Before Baxter could take measures to reoccupy the State House, he found it filled with enemy soldiers.

Moving hurriedly to consolidate their position, Brooks' troops called in reinforcements and began fortifying the grounds around the Capitol.[88] With as much grace as he could muster, Baxter retreated to St. John's College in Little Rock, where the college's youthful cadet corps offered him protection.[89] Soon afterward, he declared martial law and established headquarters at the Anthony House, a hotel located four blocks east of the Capitol on Markham Street. In response to his appeals, over two thousand Baxter men converged on the city, while at least half that number rallied to the support of Brooks.[90] Each of the opposing armies was commanded by a former Confederate general, and many of the militiamen on both sides were black.[91]

The potential existed for a mass bloodletting; fortunately, however, the ensuing "Brooks-Baxter War" involved more melodrama than violence. Federal troops from the United States arsenal were stationed along Main Street to separate the combatants, with the intersection of Markham and Main forming the boundary between the two "camps." There were some threatening demonstrations and occasional skirmishes but no major engagements.[92] A brief encounter took place at Palarm Creek, sixteen miles upstream from Little Rock, where Brooks' troops firing from the banks of the Arkansas River captured the Baxter steamboat *Hallie*.[93] The only "battle" occurred at New Gascony in Jefferson

County on April 30: about one hundred Baxter men, mainly black field hands recruited from neighboring plantations by local resident King White, inflicted a loss of nine or so on a Brooks' force.[94] Throughout all the hostilities perhaps some two hundred were killed, but most of the deaths were caused by accidents.[95]

Arkansas escaped wholesale carnage primarily because it was understood by everyone that the final outcome of the dispute rested in Washington, D.C.[96] While the Grant administration was not eager to become enmeshed in the state's troubles, it was soon apparent that only federal intervention could avert massive disorder. Baxter urged the President to recognize that the General Assembly, which his followers controlled, had the authority to settle the dispute.[97] Brooks contended that, under the principle of judicial review, the courts should be the final arbiters and won a decision from the Arkansas Supreme Court sustaining his own claim.[98]

When the Baxter members of the legislature convened in special session in Little Rock, President Grant suggested that the Brooks' lawmakers be seated also and that both leaders disband their troops.[99] Baxter acceded to the proposal to admit the Brooks' members of the Assembly and promised to muster out his own forces in proportion to the number of Brooks' soldiers dismissed. However, he insisted that Brooks' militia be withdrawn from the State House and moved as far west of the building as his men were east; furthermore, he demanded that the federal authorities agree to acknowledge whichever contestant the legislature recognized as governor.[100]

While the Grant administration found these terms acceptable, Brooks rejected them, in part because they provided no guarantee of a full investigation of his allegations of election frauds in 1872. Angrily accusing the President of encouraging violence by his foot-dragging, he maintained that if Baxter or other persons alleging to be officeholders felt aggrieved, they should look to the Arkansas courts and not the federal government for redress.[101]

Brooks' truculence annoyed Republican officials in Washington and led to his undoing. Grant had always been embarrassed by Brooks' plea in any case; by upholding the Brindletail leader's claims, he would be calling into question his own supposed victory in Arkansas during the 1872 presidential election. In addition, the newspapers were beginning to hint that powerful railway interests were behind the movement to oust Baxter and install Brooks—and the last thing Grant needed was involvement in another possible scandal.[102]

On May 15, exactly one month after the imbroglio began, Grant acknowledged Baxter as governor and ordered the Brooks' forces to disperse.[103] Within a few days all the Brooks' militia were out of Little Rock, and Baxter and the General Assembly were again occupying the Capitol. The lawmakers refused to recanvass the results of the 1872 elections, and by the end of May all of Brooks' supporters had resigned or had been removed from their offices in the state government.[104] Proceeding to consolidate their hold, Baxter and his followers called a special election for June 30, at which voters were to be asked to approve a new constitutional convention; at the same time, they were to select delegates should the motion for a convention prevail.[105]

The election was conducted as planned, and the results showed the convention being overwhelmingly approved, 80,259 votes to 8,547.[106] Over seventy of the ninety-one delegates chosen were Democrats,[107] and only eight of the delegates were blacks.[108] There are indications that some black leaders, convinced that a convention was inevitable, decided upon a policy of accommodation; by working for a convention and cooperating with the white majority in the selection of its members, they evidently hoped to dissuade the Democrats from any attempt to take away their suffrage rights.[109] To a degree this may explain the lopsided nature of the returns, although in some instances they stretch credulity and lend plausibility to Republican charges of ballot-box tampering and other irregularities.[110] In Phillips County, for example, where blacks outnumbered whites by over two to one, the election tallies showed that 3,296 votes were cast for the convention and not one against it.[111]

The convention assembled in the House of Representatives chamber of the State House on July 14 and remained in session until September 7. The constitution which its members drafted embodied a strong distrust of centralized authority and a philosophy of limited government bred from the recent Reconstruction experience. Remembering the patronage machine created by Clayton and Hadley, the delegates stripped the governor of most of his appointive powers and reduced his term of office to two years.[112] Provisions were included for the popular election of both state and local officials,[113] with the right of suffrage not to depend on any previous registration.[114] The desire for economy led to a provision restricting the legislature from levying property taxes beyond 1 percent of assessed valuation[115] and to severe limitations upon its power to contract debts.[116] In addition, special restrictions were placed on local powers of taxation.[117]

Politically speaking, one of the most important sections of the constitution dealt with legislative apportionment. As observed earlier, apportionment under the radical constitution had been based upon the 1867 registration figures, a system which had given a measure of over-representation to the Delta region. Since a large majority of the state's black population was concentrated in the Delta, the effect had been to augment black political power. The new constitution established a house of representatives of not less than seventy-three nor more than one hundred members, with each existing county guaranteed one representative and the remaining representatives apportioned among the counties according to their adult male populations.[118] Election of state senators was based upon a district system, with each senator representing "as nearly as practicable" an equal number of adult male inhabitants.[119]

Although many features of the new constitution seemed to express a yearning to turn back the clock to pre-Reconstruction days, in some respects the document borrowed from radical ideas. For instance, provisions were kept for the maintenance of a system of free public schools for the children of both blacks and whites.[120] The constitution also acknowledged the political gains won by blacks during Reconstruction and contained no features abridging or curtailing their voting rights. Barely two weeks after the convention was into its deliberations, a motion was introduced making payment of a poll tax a prerequisite for the suffrage.[121] Black delegates, led by James T. White of Phillips County, offered strenuous opposition to the idea. It will be recalled that White, as a member of the constitutional convention of 1868, had been a forceful advocate of the initial enfranchisement of his race. Offering an amendment to strike the poll-tax amendment for voting, he now declared, "the rights we acquired in 1868 we expect to maintain. It is a premeditated plan by this convention to take as many of them as they can."[122]

Several Democratic members rose to deny the charge, and the black delegate's amendment to strike carried by a wide margin. However, some Democrats were motivated by a reluctance to disfranchise a portion of the white as well as black race, while others feared provoking federal intervention. Sebastian County delegate William M. Fishback, destined to become one of the state's future governors, pointedly noted that section of the 1868 Arkansas readmission bill which specified "the Constitution of Arkansas shall never be so amended or changed as to deprive any citizen or class of citizens of the United States of the right to vote who are entitled to vote by the Constitution herein recognized."[123] The message was not lost on the other members, a majority of whom were unwilling to risk a repetition of the sort of events which had doomed the Murphy government in 1866–68.

If the motives of the convention delegates were varied, the constitution they forged was nonetheless, in its strictly racial aspects, fundamentally broadminded and liberal. This was true not merely in regard to schooling and the suffrage;[124] in addition, the constitution's "Declaration of Rights" stated, "The equality of all persons before the law, is recognized, and shall ever remain inviolate; nor shall any citizen ever be deprived of any right, privilege or immunity; nor exempted from any burden or duty, on account of race, color, or previous condition."[125]

The convention designated October 13 as the date for an election upon ratification of the constitution and for selection of a governor and other state officials. In preparation for the contest, the state's Democrats met in Little Rock on September 18; out of a sense of gratitude and appreciation, the party tendered its gubernatorial nomination to its erstwhile opponent in 1872, Elisha Baxter. Baxter, though, was still anathema to a number of holdouts among the former "noncooperationists." For the sake of Conservative unity, he magnanimously declined the offer,[126] an action for which he was universally lauded.

When Baxter refused a second nomination, this time by acclamation, the Democrats chose Augustus H. Garland as their standard-bearer. A well-known member of the Little Rock bar, Garland had been a Whig in antebellum days and a Unionist delegate at the convention of 1861.[127] After Fort Sumter he became a reluctant secessionist, and during the war served as an Arkansas congressman, and later, senator, to the Confederate government in Richmond. In 1867 he was named United States Senator by the Murphy legislature, but, like most other representatives from the South, was not permitted to take his seat. Following this disappointment, Garland retired from active political involvements, devoting himself to his law practice and the replenishing of his fortune. In 1874, he reemerged to mastermind Baxter's successful behind-the-scenes legal strategy during the contest with Brooks.[128] Addicted to wearing old-fashioned rolling collars, a long broadcloth coat, and a wide panama hat, Garland combined a keen mind with a folksy, relaxed personality. Both flexible and principled, in the circumstances existing at the end of Reconstruction he was an ideal candidate.[129]

The Arkansas Republicans were seriously demoralized by President Grant's recognition of Baxter and subsequent events. Rather than field its own state ticket, the party simply chose to denounce as illegal Baxter's government and all measures taken since the decision of the Pulaski County circuit court. Nevertheless, several local Republican organizations did run nominees for office, and many of the rank and file turned out for the balloting.[130] In spite of the absence of any deleterious racial features in the constitution, blacks were apprehensive for the future, and most appear to have favored retaining the old 1868 document; although the constitution carried easily, 78,697 to 24,807, in all sections of the state the number of negative votes correlated very closely with the number of adult male black inhabitants.[131]

Garland and his fellow Democratic officeholders were quietly inaugurated on November 13, but the Arkansas Republicans made a last appeal to Washington, D.C. In the Congress, a special committee of the House of Representatives, chaired by Vermont Republican Luke Poland, investigated the Byzantine political situation in Arkansas: the committee carried out weeks of hearings and made two separate trips to the state to conduct an on-the-spot inquiry.

Attorneys for Joseph Brooks emphasized that the Arkansas courts had upheld his right to office, while stressing that the legislature had never afforded him an opportunity to present his evidence of election frauds committed in 1872. Garland warned that a failure to sustain his government would result in general strife. "There will be nothing but anarchy here," he alleged, "and

Mexico will be a paradise compared with it. This is as true as preaching." [132]

On February 4 the committee issued its long-awaited report, with all but one member recommending that it was not advisable to interfere with the existing state administration in Arkansas. Finally, on March 2, the House of Representatives voted, 150 to 81, to accept the report of the committee's majority. The House had recently upheld the radical regime in Louisiana by arguing that it could not go behind the certified election returns, and consistency demanded that the same position be adopted in the case of Arkansas. Powell Clayton bowed to the inevitable and wired the Little Rock *Daily Republican:* "The action of Congress on Arkansas affairs is conclusive. The validity of the new constitution and the government established thereunder ought no longer to be questioned. It is the duty of Republicans to accept the verdict, and render the same acquiescence which we would have demanded had the case been reversed." [133] Reconstruction in Arkansas had ended.

For Arkansas's blacks, the troubled Reconstruction period had left an ambivalent legacy. The Republican administrations, despite their considerable achievements, would be remembered by the majority of whites primarily for fiscal mismanagement, corruption, and political and social chaos. Because they were perceived to have played a prominent role in Republican affairs, blacks inevitably found that much of the negative feeling about Reconstruction would attach to themselves. Later, in the 1890s, memories of the disorder of the Reconstruction era would be invoked to justify forced removal of blacks from the democratic process.

Nevertheless, despite the antagonisms engendered, blacks benefited significantly from the Reconstruction experiment. Voting rights were secured and protected, and soon afterward, civil-rights statutes were enacted. These latter measures were infrequently enforced, but their presence still probably retarded somewhat the development of segregation practices. In addition, mass public education was made available for the first time to blacks.

Most important of all, Reconstruction developments had shattered the earlier white consensus on racial policy. More principled

51

conservatives had been inhibited by their own ethical and moral beliefs from employing every possible means to destroy the Republican opposition; more pragmatic individuals had readily resorted to fraud and violence to gain political mastery over the radicals, but, as expediency had demanded, some of them had proved just as willing to make overtures for black support. By the close of Reconstruction, Democrats as well as Republicans were actively courting the black electorate and were even recruiting and employing black troops in support of their cause. In the immediate aftermath of Reconstruction, Democratic leaders, defying criticism from white-supremacist elements in their own party, would continue to reach out to blacks and follow moderate racial policies.

# IV

# The "Redemption"

I shall strive hard to have Arks.
deserve the confidence bestowed
by our friends in Congress of both
parties. We are silently happy—
prudent and forgiving, and we
will try to let nothing mar the
victory.
—Governor Augustus H. Garland

Although some blacks had joined in the general celebrating following the Democrats' victories in 1874 and 1875, many of their leaders viewed the direction of events with trepidation.[1] However, there was no wave of recrimination, no massive proscription, not even a major diminution in the extent of Negro voting or officeholding. During his gubernatorial campaign, Augustus H. Garland had promised that, if elected, he would retain the Civil Rights Act of 1873 and protect black citizens' access to the ballot and to free public schools.[2] In his first proclamation as governor he struck a conciliatory note, declaring, "Should there be any indictments in the courts for past political offenses, I would suggest and advise their dismissal. Let the people of all parties, races, and colors, come together, be welcomed to our State, and encouraged to bring her up to a position of true greatness."[3]

Garland appears to have sincerely tried to carry through on these assurances. Shortly after he became governor, a delegation of whites from Lee County asked his cooperation in removing W. H. Furbush from office; Furbush, the black sheriff of Lee County, had been elected as an independent but had endorsed

Garland's gubernatorial bid. Garland asked if there was anything against the black's moral character or capacity. Receiving a negative reply, he responded: "I can't remove him; he was our staunch supporter during our whole trouble; he had, necessarily, to make some sacrifices and bear reproaches from his own people, and I shall sustain him."[4]

This incident was not an isolated one. In hopes of maintaining racial concord, Garland encouraged Democrats in the predominately black counties of the Delta to share offices with Negroes through an arrangement known as the "fusion principle." By this device, Republican and Democratic county committees met prior to the day of voting and allotted each other places on the ballot. A "compromise ticket" of blacks and whites would then be presented at the forthcoming election.[5] Typical of these understandings was the system launched in Jefferson County in 1878: Democrats usually named the county judge, county clerk, the assessor, and the state senator; while the Republicans chose the sheriff, the circuit clerk, and the three representatives in the lower house of the General Assembly; lesser county offices were similarly divided.[6] Beginning in the late 1870s and lasting through the early 1890s, fusion arrangements existed at one time or another in Chicot, Crittenden, Desha, Jefferson, Lee, Lincoln, Monroe, Phillips, and St. Francis counties, and perhaps others also. White officials benefited from fusion in that they were able to use the Negro vote to entrench themselves in power; blacks, for their part, were able to deflect charges of "Negro domination" and retain some voice in the affairs of government.[7]

The impact of the fusion system attracted notice from the moment of its inception. Charles Nordhoff, a reporter for the New York *Herald* who traveled through the cotton states in 1875, observed that white Democrats were cementing friendly political relations with black leaders in Arkansas.[8] Similar comments came from Dr. Jerome R. Riley, a Negro physician from Jefferson County. Riley, who had joined the Democratic party during Reconstruction, justified his action by noting that under the 1874 constitution and the Garland administration "more colored men were elected and are commissioned to offices of trust and pay" than had been true under the 1868 constitution and the Republicans;[9] Riley himself was at the time serving as enrolling clerk of the Arkansas House of Representatives through the patronage of Garland and Democratic leaders.[10]

Significantly, when Garland was named to the United States Senate by the Arkansas legislature in 1877, five black Republican representatives broke party ranks to cast their votes for him.[11] Their confidence was not misplaced, for Garland continued to recognize blacks with patronage rewards[12] and to espouse moderate racial views. In 1879, he expressly denied the contention of some Southern Democrats that the Thirteenth, Fourteenth, and Fifteenth Amendments to the federal Constitution could be declared invalid by congressional resolution; adopting an organic view of the Constitution, he maintained that although their ratification had been irregular, time and circumstances had made them "as firmly and fixedly a part of the Constitution as any of the other amendments." With obvious exaggeration, Garland insisted, "As Governor of Arkansas, I got the legislature to legislate directly and indirectly on these amendments. They are enforced in that State, and there is not a man in Arkansas . . . to whatever party he belongs, who would escape from them."[13]

When the United States Supreme Court nullified portions of the late Charles Sumner's civil-rights act in 1883, Garland even expressed sympathy for a proposed civil-rights amendment to the Constitution. Although he did not actually endorse the amendment, he declined to oppose it, stating, "Frankly and candidly, if white, black, or any other complexion of people in this country have not the equal protection of the laws I want to give it to them."[14]

Garland's position does not seem to have seriously damaged his standing at home, and it may conceivably have smoothed the way for his appointment as Attorney General of the United States during the first Cleveland administration. Two prominent Arkansas Negro leaders, Mifflin W. Gibbs, a Republican, and Jerome R. Riley, a Democrat, praised Garland for his sense of fairness in their respective memoirs;[15] when he died in 1899, an unusually large number of blacks in Little Rock are said to have attended his funeral services.[16]

Most of Arkansas's Democratic governors in the immediate post-Reconstruction era—the so-called "Redeemers"—continued to pursue conciliatory racial policies. Garland's successor, William R.

Miller, who served from 1877 to 1881, promised in his first inaugural address to use "the whole power of the state" to ensure blacks' legal and constitutional rights. Miller soon found an opportunity to honor his pledge, for in March 1877 several Negroes were killed by roving bands of marauders that had infested the area along the Arkansas-Louisiana state line. He sent two companies of militia, one white and one black, into Union County and offered a reward for the outlaws' arrest. Subsequently, a number of the ringleaders were captured in Texas and conveyed back to Arkansas for trial. When Miller received news that an armed body was preparing to attack the escorting officers and release the prisoners, he immediately directed that a detachment of the Hempstead County militia form a guard around the officers and protect them as they returned home.[17]

Such routine enforcement of the law may seem less than extraordinary; in fact, it required real political courage, for executive use of the militia was too reminiscent of Reconstruction experiences to be popular. Negro troops were especially disliked, as was highlighted by an incident which took place during the administration of Governor Thomas J. Churchill (1881–1883). In 1881, a local commander of the all-white militia of Pine Bluff proved so opposed to the employment of Negro recruits that he openly disobeyed instructions to enroll a newly organized black company. Governor Churchill, a former Confederate general, was not used to tolerating insubordination in the ranks; brushing aside adverse criticism, he personally ordered a court martial for the obstreperous commander and dispatched a Little Rock officer to muster in the blacks.[18]

By thus opposing the most extreme white supremacy elements within their party, the Redeemer leaders opened themselves to serious attack. Usually, however, they could expect support from important segments of the Democratic press, especially the influential Little Rock newspapers. The *Arkansas Gazette*, in particular, though not always consistent, often acted as a force for moderation in state politics. The newspaper, for example, gave strong endorsement to the compromise arrangements in black-majority population counties of eastern Arkansas whereby black Republicans and white Democrats divided local offices among themselves. In an 1889 editorial, it unreservedly condemned schemes for disfranchising black voters in these areas.[19] "The charge that good government cannot be secured [without disfranchisement] in counties where there is a large colored vote is not true," it declared. "Jefferson County, with an immense Negro majority, has as good a local government as there is in the south. So has Chicot, Phillips and other large Negro counties in this state. They have adopted the plan that justice and common sense suggests."[20]

On one occasion the *Gazette* even quoted an editorial from the New York *World* which boldly stated:

This is not a "white man's government," any more than it is a blue-eyed men's or a red-haired men's Government. It is a government by and for the people—all the people, without respect to race, religion, color, or previous condition of servitude. The Constitution makes it so, and back of and beneath the Constitution is the basic principle of the immortal Declaration that "all men are created equal and endowed by their Creator with certain unalienable rights." These are not glittering generalities. They are concrete truths, embodying the essence of Democracy . . . When the colored man becomes educated and by ability, interest and training is capable of joining intelligently in the business of government, he has just as much right to a part in it as the whitest citizen."[21]

The *Gazette* seemed implicitly to endorse these sentiments: it reprinted the remarks not in the usual space reserved for guest editorials but within its own editorial column and then itself immediately added: "The only discrimination possible under the constitution is that the fittest shall govern, and the test of fitness must be both disposition and ability to promote, by rules of common fairness, the country's best interests."[22]

As suggested by the above statement, concern for upgrading the caliber of the black electorate explains yet another facet of the Redemption era, continuing support by some whites for black schooling.[23] Governor Garland not only opened the Branch Normal College of the University of Arkansas at Pine Bluff for Negroes but named as the college's first principal Joseph Carter Corbin, former state Superintendent of Public Instruction under radical Reconstruction.[24] Because Democratic leaders gave priority to fiscal retrenchment, elementary and secondary schools, both white and black, were left separately and equally starved for funds.[25]

Nevertheless, the basic concept of public education was retained, and there was no obvious racial bias in the distribution of school resources. Under state law, areas having as few as thirty-five children of school age could incorporate as independent school districts;[26] by the mid-1880s, over three thousand districts had been established in Arkansas.[27] In an age when most schools usually aspired to only rudimentary instruction, this system could perhaps be justified; whatever its defects, as long as blacks had the vote it allowed for their maximum possible participation in school governance. As late as 1890, 20 percent of state school districts had a majority of Negro directors on their boards. Even "In the great majority of white districts," the Superintendent of Public Instruction reported, "the white boards give equal terms [to the Negro children] because they believe this to be right."[28] If official computations can be believed, for the whole state in 1890 the average per capita expenditure for enrolled white students was $5.87 and for black students $6.27, actually slightly higher for the blacks.[29]

Many of the racial policies and pronouncements of the Redeemer leadership would no doubt have seemed strange to later generations of white Southerners; for that matter, they irritated some whites of the time. The wish to avert possible federal intervention was partly responsible for the stances taken, but other factors were also involved. Perhaps chief among these was the widespread desire for social tranquility. For almost two decades, Arkansas had operated at a fever pitch of excitement. After the high drama of the secession crisis, the destruction of the Civil War, and the turmoil of its aftermath, Arkansans craved above all else quiet and order, stability and repose.[30] Writing during Reconstruction, Augustus H. Garland expressed a common feeling when he stated, "we have been . . . ground in between the upper and nether mill rocks—conservatism proper had been strangled, and bad men on both sides, desiring trouble and commotion have kept the country on fire, just as the late . . . war was inaugurated in 1860–61." Garland alleged, "I do not . . . mistake the facts, when I say that our people South—I mean those of social, pecuniary and moral responsibility—desire peace earnestly. . . ."[31]

The reference to "pecuniary responsibility" suggests a further consideration: social order was desired not merely for its own sake but was viewed as an integral part of the Redeemer economic program. Garland, a former Whig, shared the belief of many of his contemporaries that the South's future prosperity depended upon commercial and industrial development.[32] Although the treasury was virtually empty at the end of Reconstruction, his government appropriated fifteen thousand dollars for an Arkansas exhibit at the Centennial Exposition in Philadelphia, where the state's attractions were advertised to Yankee investors.[33] Under Garland and his successors, manufacturing and mining investments in excess of two thousand dollars per annum were exempted from all taxation until 1882.[34] Even after that date property of corporations and railroads was commonly assessed far below true value;[35] in addition, generous amounts of lands forfeited for back taxes were granted to existing and proposed railroads.[36] Supplementing these initiatives, the Redeemers encouraged immigration by offering vast quantities of public lands to actual settlers; homesteads not to exceed 160 acres could be obtained upon payment of a $5.50 fee.[37]

All of these incentives would be for naught without the maintenance of at least outward racial harmony. No industry would locate in a community wracked by violence, and election disorders and irregularities provided the worst sort of publicity for Arkansas.[38] The point was made repeatedly by Redeemer editors and politicians. Commenting on a theft of ballot boxes during the election of 1888, the Pine Bluff *Graphic* observed:

> You may talk about your natural resources, the fertility of your soil, the rich minerals sleeping in the bowels of the earth, the richness of your forests and the wealth hidden in the bosom of the mountains, and you may hold your immigration conventions, establish immigration bureaux, flood the country with circulars and pamphlets, but all will be of no avail until these election frauds, steals and robberies are blotted out.[39]

What was true for industry applied equally to agriculture. Throughout the post-Reconstruction era, Delta planters were eager to attract blacks to their fields and expand cotton production. Many were willing to tolerate Negro political participation, and even share offices with blacks, as a means of keeping their hands contented. It was no accident that Arkansas Democrats made some of their strongest overtures to blacks between 1878 and 1880, when thousands of Delta sharecroppers were threaten-

59

ing to migrate to Kansas in hopes of bettering their economic circumstances.[40] Negro leaders shrewdly capitalized on planter anxieties, warning that adoption of proscriptive measures against their race might lead to a mass exodus.[41]

Simple partisan considerations also help to explain the racial policies of the Redeemers. Hoping to deprive their Republican opponents of valuable ammunition, Northern Democrats constantly urged the Southern wing of their party to curb racial violence.[42] Local Democratic leaders, in turn, admonished their followers that persisting disorders could hurt the Democracy in presidential and national elections.[43] For that matter, Democratic chieftains could not rest easy with their ascendency in Arkansas. The end of Reconstruction had left the Arkansas Republicans crippled, but by no means was their organization completely moribund. In each of the presidential elections of 1876, 1880, and 1884, Republican presidential nominees won about 40 percent of the state's popular vote; Republican gubernatorial candidates could normally expect to garner around one-third of the ballots cast, and in several hotly contested congressional races, Republicans lost by only razor-thin margins.[44]

Although the Republicans obtained support from whites in some mountain districts and in the rising business community of Little Rock, from one-half to two-thirds of the party's strength came from black voters.[45] Since the Democrats presented themselves to the electorate as the party of white supremacy, their appeals to blacks were usually somewhat muffled. Nevertheless, they were eager to encourage as many Negro defections from Republican ranks as possible. Blacks were assured that under Democratic rule their right to acquire property would always be respected and that the ballot would "never be wrested" from them.[46] While the great majority of blacks stayed faithfully Republican, Democratic solicitations were not totally in vain: in state gubernatorial elections, Democrats often won from 20 to 25 percent of the black vote.[47]

It would be easy, if misleading, to exaggerate the benevolence of Redeemer racial policies. So long as their basic control and Democratic political domination were not in jeopardy, so long as their financial interests were not endangered, the Redeemers saw little harm in acknowledging the Negro's formal constitutional

60

rights. Public schooling was supported as a mechanism for inculcating the virtues of work and self-discipline among the lower orders and as a means of preventing attacks upon property from an ignorant electorate possessing the ballot. The Redeemers were chiefly concerned that they remain free to utilize the state's large pool of cheap labor without hindrance. At least as regarded the poorer classes, they opposed any sort of state interference in the impersonal workings of the competitive, capitalistic economy. In the words of one historian, their essentially bourgeois philosophy "was conservative, not in the sense that it denied the economic and social premises of a 'liberal' and atomistic society, but in its opposition to government action to relieve the misery of the unfortunate. . . ."[48]

With the exception of the homestead act, Democratic lawmakers of the 1870s and 1880s did almost nothing to ameliorate the lot of the impoverished rural masses, black or white. Indeed, many statutes were consciously designed to protect creditors, employers, and the wealthy and powerful. The legislature of 1875 adopted a measure reversing the relationship between a laborer's lien for wages and a landlord's lien for rents. Under the new statute, the landlord's lien took precedence over the laborer's in the absence of a written agreement to the contrary.[49] The same body regulated contracts between planters and agricultural workers. To protect an employer from unpaid debts for supplies, he was given a lien on all "produce raised" by his hands; the latter were also forbidden to leave the fields before the expiration of their terms of service. However, workers were shielded from arbitrary dismissal and were also given a lien on the crop to ensure payment of wages. Although the law was ostensibly protective of all parties, given the nature of Delta society it was usually the laborers who were prosecuted, fined, and jailed; fear of such punishment could virtually bind a hand to the plantation. The Little Rock *Daily Republican* referred to the measure as a "peonage act," which is essentially what it became.[50]

In another portentous step taken in 1875, the General Assembly validated the granting of mortgages on crops,[51] an action destined to hasten the spread of tenancy and the establishment of a one-crop system of agriculture within Arkansas; simultaneously, removal or disposal of mortgaged property without the consent of

61

the mortgagee was made a felony offense, punishable by imprisonment for one to two years.[52] This latter statute led to some extreme cases. In one instance, a white farmer was convicted for selling a small amount of mortgaged cotton in order to buy food for his ailing wife. It was admitted that the value of the remaining cotton crop was sufficient to cover his debts, yet the Arkansas Supreme Court upheld the sentence, stating that it had no choice but to enforce the law.[53] Public indignation led to a modification of the act in 1885. Although the claims of suppliers were strengthened by giving liens on crops for supplies precedence over any other mortgage or conveyance, the penalty for selling mortgaged property was reduced to a misdemeanor, punishable by a ten- to fifty-dollar fine and imprisonment for not more than ninety days in the county jail.[54]

Other types of crimes against property were covered by an extremely severe larceny law adopted in 1875.[55] Black slaves, denied the usual compensations of a free-labor system in antebellum days, often had few qualms about raiding their master's larder or otherwise engaging in minor thefts. The habit persisted after emancipation;[56] now, however, planters, although they continued to flog or otherwise punish their workers directly to some degree, increasingly looked to public authorities to reinforce plantation discipline. Under the larceny act, anyone stealing goods worth more than two dollars could be imprisoned by the state from one to five years. For items valued under that amount, the law stipulated incarceration in the county jail for up to a year and a maximum three-hundred-dollar fine.

Speaking against the larceny measure at the time of its enactment, Negro state senator John W. Williams of Phillips County pointed out that the end of the cotton season often left sharecroppers and hands cheated out of "all they have made, and they must live off somebody." Should the bill pass, he warned, "poor whites and blacks will be driven to the pen." Moreover, he insisted that when an individual was compelled to take food in order to survive, he was "not stealing," given the situation.[57]

Williams' fears as to the act's consequences were soon borne out. The *Arkansas Gazette* noted that of 552 convicts sentenced to the state penitentiary in 1877 and 1878, 414 were confined for taking "petty sums."[58] Blacks suffered most; although Negroes constituted barely more than a fourth of the state's population, black prisoners consistently outnumbered white, in some years by a ratio of more than two to one.[59] Many prisoners were also young, for age brought no special clemency. Because of the lack of a state reformatory school, youthful first offenders were confined alongside the most hardened criminals.[60] In 1892, it was reported that about one-fifth of the state's convicts were under the age of twenty-one. The youngest was age nine.[61]

The larceny act was also mainly responsible for a threefold jump in state prison population between 1874 and 1882, with the number of inmates rising from around two hundred to approximately six hundred.[62] Despite a $149,000 expansion of penitentiary facilities, there was still not sufficient room to house all inmates within prison walls, and the practice of leasing out convicts continued.[63] Dr. A. H. Scott, prison physician in 1879, publicly alleged that lessees were brutally mistreating convicts. His claim was substantiated by an official report for the following year, which showed an appalling 20 percent mortality rate among prisoners.[64] A legislative committee of 1881 deplored convict leasing as "cruel, inhumane, barbarous, and at variance with the civilization of the age," yet because of considerations of economy declined to recommend the system's abandonment.[65]

Acting upon the committee's report, the General Assembly extended leasing arrangements along the old lines, only stipulating that all new lease contracts should bring a profit to the state.[66] This modification caused a further deterioration in the care of prisoners, as was soon revealed in a series of blood-curdling exposés. The worst episode involved "The Horrors of Coal Hill." Early in 1888, a coroner's investigation revealed that convicts working in the mines of the Quita Coal Company at Coal Hill in Johnson County had suffered unbelievable abuse. Convicts had been worked barefoot even in winter, had been punished by having salt poured in their wounds, and in some cases had literally been beaten to death—one man received four hundred lashes before dying. A subsequent visit by the state prison board confirmed these findings. The board discovered that all the convicts were enduring cuffings, whippings, overwork, and a lack of adequate food and clothing. One hundred forty inmates, "black and white, well and sick," were housed in a bunkhouse ninety feet long,

63

eighteen feet wide, and twelve feet high. Prisoners were forced to sleep in their work clothes, with their beds consisting of piles of corn shucks and straw changed once in fifteen months—a "sickening stench" arose from these, and several were infested with vermin.[67]

When prisoners were asked why they had not requested treatment from the camp physician, they responded that they would be beaten by the guard through whom they were required to report. An unmarked graveyard near the compound contained the bodies of some sixty or seventy former convicts over which inquests had never been held as required by law. Prisoners testified that they had been given ample food for two weeks prior to the board's investigation but that before that time they had almost starved.[68]

Arkansas governor Simon P. Hughes and the other members of the state prison board had been alerted as to conditions at Coal Hill but had delayed their inspection for almost a year. They lamely excused their negligence by observing that under state statutes they were only required to supervise prisoners confined in the penitentiary, not in lessee camps. Hughes further noted that the legislature had not appropriated money for an inspection; however, at the time he had almost four thousand dollars remaining from his five-thousand-dollar contingency fund.[69]

County prisoners often fared even more poorly than state ones.[70] Hoping to alleviate pressures on the state penal system caused by the steadily increasing convict population, the legislature of 1881 raised the sum constituting larceny from two dollars to ten dollars.[71] However, persons stealing property valued under ten dollars could still be fined up to three hundred dollars and confined for up to a year in the county jail. The effect was merely to shift much of the convict burden onto local authorities. Anticipating such a result, the legislature authorized county courts to lease convicts to those parties offering "terms deemed most advantageous" to the county. Prisoners were given twenty-five cents credit on their fines for each day they worked but had to work two days for each day lost because of illness. They received no credit for Sunday or other times when their labor was not utilized, and attempts at escape could result in an extension of punishment. If a convict had been given a regular term as well as a fine, he worked out his fine first and then served his sentence. Consequently, actual length of imprisonment was often much longer than court judgments seemingly indicated. Although county sheriffs were charged with seeing that leased convicts be "treated with humanity," the law did not mandate specific times of inspection. When lessees were local planters or other persons of prominence, it was easy for sheriffs and county officials to overlook inadequacies in care. In such instances prisoners were left to the mercy of contractors, who had a vested interest in their exploitation.[72]

The Redeemers' dreary record of neglect cannot be ignored in any comprehensive evaluation of their social program. Nonetheless, it is true that, under Redeemer leadership, Arkansas blacks continued enjoying their newly won political gains for almost twenty years after the close of Reconstruction. At least in contrast with the racial policies later instituted, the Redeemers' earlier attitude appears restrained and conciliatory. In fact, it was the incomplete nature of the triumph of white supremacy in 1874 which left many whites disgruntled and dissatisfied. This particularly was the case in eastern Delta and other alluvial plantation districts. By 1890, fourteen Delta counties (out of seventy-five counties in the state) had over 50 percent black populations; in six of these, bordering the Mississippi and Arkansas rivers, blacks constituted approximately 75 percent or more of the inhabitants. Efforts to recruit new hands for the Delta cotton fields produced a continuing heavy influx of Negroes into the region—and rising fears among whites that they were being inundated by a black tide.[73] Paradoxically, even some of the white planters responsible for the black migration shared such anxieties.

One method of reducing tensions and preserving harmony was the fusion system, but fusion was a pragmatic political accommodation not really that popular with either race. Black spokesmen reluctantly accepted it only in hopes of forestalling violent attacks upon their followers. Ambitious younger whites resented having their own chances for preferment lessened by a political mechanism which divided offices with blacks and which gave the local white establishments tacitly allied with them a veritable stranglehold on power. And even many of the white politicians who directly benefited from the fusion arrangements probably disliked having to deal with black leaders on terms approaching equality.

Yet, the only alternatives to fusion were the use of fraud and extralegal intimidation to remove blacks from the democratic process or acceptance of complete black control.

Ironically, it was the Democrats' own constitution of 1874 which was responsible for this dilemma. By removing the governor's power to name county officials and transferring it back to county electorates, the document perpetuated Negro influence in areas with large black populations. In an 1888 letter to the *Arkansas Gazette*, an anonymous writer expressed the consternation of many Delta whites. Complaining that "The greatest blunder that Arkansas ever made was the abolition of the constitution of 1868," he noted, "We seemed to forget that an instrument . . . which was so potent in the hands of a handful of carpet-baggers could have been wielded with much more advantage by the white people of the state." The structure of the existing government, he grumbled, was "too exclusively local" and "too democratic":

> The present constitution would of course be good enough on this point for Northwest Arkansas if it were disconnected from the eastern and southern portion of the state. But while they have their heads buried in the Boston mountains [a chain of the Ozarks] in fancied security, they should not overlook the dangers to which their tails are exposed in the Mississippi valley. They ought to carefully read the fable of the belly and the members and this might be followed by the parable of the devil who refused to help his brother. The honest, intelligent men of Eastern Arkansas are as completely disfranchised and debarred from office by the present constitution as any white men ever were by the constitution of 1868, and this is not disproved by the fact that they occasionally accomplish something in spite of the constitution.[74]

Continuing, the writer admitted that Delta whites sometimes overcame local black opposition through the use of "fraud and force." "Desperate as these remedies are," he maintained, "and distasteful as they are to every honest man they are not to be indiscriminately condemned so long as self preservation continues to be the first law of nature." Who, he said, "would not hesitate to use either to baffle a burglar or to escape the violence of a lunatic. The justification in both instances is the same."[75]

Not all Democrats, by any means, were willing to countenance the use of illegal tactics to uphold white supremacy. The *Gazette* believed "the intelligent, tax-paying element must and does rule in every civilized country"[76] but insisted, "The plea that fraudulent elections are necessary to secure good government in certain localities is an attempt to cloak fraud with a respectability it can never wear. Crime is essential to nothing good on earth. Its touch blights every honorable thing with which it comes in contact."[77] The paper held the only solution to be "an equitable apportionment of the offices between the ignorant popular majority and the tax-paying minority, as is now done, with the best of results, in several counties in Arkansas."[78]

Actually, the practices followed in the Delta varied considerably from community to community, depending on such intangibles as the honesty and temper of local whites and the competence and attitudes of the blacks. Even the *Gazette* admitted that in at least five or six counties Democratic leaders routinely employed ballot tampering and other irregularities to sustain their hegemony.[79] Occasionally, they resorted to open violence; heavily black Phillips County affords an outstanding example. In 1876, the Republican gubernatorial nominee had carried Phillips by a vote of 2,672 to 1,010, and Hayes had defeated Tilden in the county presidential election of that year, 2,867 to 982.[80] However, in 1878 white Democrats, emulating the tactics of the "Redshirt" movement in neighboring Mississippi, organized several militia units. Republican meetings were broken up, threats issued, and voters were forcibly prevented from going to the polls. Two artillery pieces were brought down from Memphis and paraded over the country, "making the hills and valleys echo with their detonations." It is no great surprise that the county went Democratic in the September state and local election. Thereafter, the new Democratic county judge refused to place Republicans on returning boards, with predictable results in ensuring election contests. Republican leader Powell Clayton wryly commented, "Never since the days when Mahomet made his famous missionary tour with the Koran in one hand and the sword in the other was such an overwhelming and sudden conversion witnessed." Oddly enough, the new converts persisted in voting Republican at congressional and presidential elections where federal supervisors were present. Republicans remained frozen out of local government until 1886, when an altercation among the Democrats enabled them to ally with one of the white factions; via a fusion understanding, they regained a few offices and representation in the election machinery. Following this change, in the next gubernatorial election the Republican-backed candidate swept the county.[81]

A yet more obvious case of intimidation of blacks took place in Crittenden County. Blacks outnumbered whites in the county by over five to one, and Republicans usually won elections there by overwhelming margins. Because of a fusion agreement, however, white Democrats controlled a number of offices, including the important post of county sheriff. Trouble began brewing in Crittenden during the summer of 1888, when two Negro officials were charged with drunkenness. Shortly thereafter, a number of whites in Marion, the county seat, reported receiving threatening notes, and various other lawless and incendiary activities were alleged. On the day the two Negro officers' trial was to occur, a group of armed whites, including the sheriff, rounded up not only the accused but all other black officeholders and several black citizens, including a teacher, an editor, and a minister. The group of about twenty was then marched at gunpoint to the Marion railway station, placed on board a train for Memphis, and warned not to return.[82]

Fearful of passing back through the county, the group of black exiles fled to St. Louis and then reentered the state from the north over the Iron Mountain Railway; arriving at Little Rock, they requested intervention on their behalf from Governor Simon P. Hughes. The blacks denied the charges of drunkenness and wrongdoing and suggested that the anonymous letters had been secretly authored by whites to give a pretext for their expulsion. They noted that the circuit court had been in session at the time of the affair, presided over by a white Democrat; that legal redress had been readily available to the whites; and that, significantly, new local elections were only two months away.[83]

In light of the directly conflicting testimony, it is impossible to say what conditions had really been like in the county. What is clear is that the Negroes were removed from office without due process. After listening politely to their appeal, Governor Hughes stated that he could not act unless assistance was requested by the chief law enforcement officer of the county—the sheriff responsible for engineering the coup. Hughes insisted that the whole matter lay with the civil courts to resolve and observed, "if the exiles return and are murdered, the murderers are amenable to the law." Hardly reassured, the exiles decided against reclaiming their stations. In the ensuing fall election, an all-white slate won possession of the county government. Fourteen years after the end of statewide Reconstruction, Crittenden County was at last "redeemed."[84]

The Little Rock *Gazette* lamented the entire episode and suggested that the initial removal of the blacks had been illegal.[85] However, it did not condemn Governor Hughes for his passivity; nor did it vigorously press for the Negroes' reinstatement. The Crittenden troubles revealed the difficulty of adjusting traditional majoritarian democracy to the special circumstances of biracial communities, while exposing a central flaw in the position of the moderates. Without an implied threat of violence from whites, perhaps occasionally exercised, blacks in plantation counties would have no incentive for cooperating with the fusion understandings which moderates supported. The Redeemers' emphasis on harmony and cooperation merely obscured the hidden features of post-Reconstruction Delta politics: persisting race antagonism and fear.

# V

# Poverty and Paternalism: Black Life in the Country

> Honor and shame from no condition rise,
> Act well your part, there all the honor lies.
> —Alexander Pope, *Essay on Man*

A few days after the expulsion of Negro officials from Crittenden County, a white resident of Marion was interviewed by an *Arkansas Gazette* reporter and queried as to the new state of race relations in his town. The resident stressed the restored order, harmony, and tranquility in effect, warning that the black exiles need not try and return. In passing, however, he noted that the former black circuit clerk might eventually be allowed to come home since he was the only one of the deposed group who owned property in Marion.[1]

Although the rest of the Negro exiles could conceivably have owned property elsewhere, the comment nonetheless was a reminder of the anomalous situation of blacks in many parts of the Delta: through force of numbers they exercised majority political power, while economic power and control remained largely in the hands of the white minority. Lacking a secure financial base from which to defend themselves, Negroes found their legal rights and political gains precarious at best.

70

From the beginning of emancipation, blacks had appreciated the need for economic security, probably desiring title to their own farms and homesteads even more than the ballot. Their hopes in this respect were manifested as early as 1863 and 1864. Following the collapse of Vicksburg, a majority of planters along the Mississippi River abandoned their lands, leaving their cotton and corn standing in the fields and fleeing westward toward Confederate lines in Louisiana and Texas. Although these émigrés attempted to carry as many of their slaves with them as possible, thousands refused to go, instead escaping and making their way to Union encampments at Helena and other localities.[2]

The Negro runaways created a dilemma and headache for the Union-army commanders. Only a small proportion could be used effectively as laborers. Others could be enlisted in the military service, but Northern troops sometimes disliked fighting alongside black soldiers, an objection not completely overcome by the use of separate black regiments.[3]

Authorities eventually agreed that the best solution would be to place the refugees on vacated plantations leased to interested entrepreneurs and businessmen. Because of wartime scarcities, cotton prices had skyrocketed, and it was assumed that lessees could easily be found. The army, for its part, would be relieved of much of the trouble and expense of caring for the blacks. Putting the idle lands back into cultivation would help mitigate the national cotton shortage and even raise some funds for the federal treasury. Blacks, it could be argued, would benefit too, for they would be accorded an opportunity to earn money and accumulate savings; the leased plantations, furthermore, would act as schools for virtue, inculcating enterprise, self-reliance, and those qualities necessary for success in a free-labor economy.[4]

Bureaucratic scuffling between the War and Treasury Departments delayed immediate implementation of the leasing program, although some contracts were given in 1863. As finalized the next year, Major General Lorenzo Thomas assumed full command of the freed blacks and all leasing arrangements in the upper Mississippi valley, from Cairo, Illinois, south to the Department of the Gulf.[5] Colonel John Eaton, Jr., was named general superintendent of freedmen under Thomas, and he appointed Major W. G. Sargeant of the Sixty-third U.S. Colored Infantry superintendent for freedmen in Arkansas. Sargeant opened headquarters at Little

Rock and established offices at Helena, Pine Bluff, DuVall's Bluff, and Fort Smith.[6]

In order to assure just treatment of freedmen working for lessees, it was decided that provost marshals should be assigned to the various plantation districts. They would oversee contracts, settle all questions arising between employers and employees, keep a roll of workers on each plantation, and make sure that wandering bluecoats stayed away from the Negroes. Marshals were also to supervise creation of school districts for instruction of all children under twelve years of age.[7] Under the financial arrangements established, lessees paid no rent but were assessed a tax of two dollars per bale on cotton grown and five cents for every bushel of corn and potatoes raised.[8] For "respectful, honest, faithful labor" workers on plantations were guaranteed healthful rations, quarters, fuel, medical attention, education for their children, and clothing, with the cost of the latter to be deducted from remuneration. Flogging and cruel punishment were made indictable offenses, but drivers could whip younger boys with a hickory shrub out of the field if they thought it necessary. Minimum wages were set at ten dollars per month for men and seven dollars for women, children twelve–fourteen years old receiving half these minimums.[9] Variations in the above guidelines could be arranged with the mutual consent of the parties and approval of the provost marshals.[10]

Governed by these regulations, lessees in Arkansas during 1864 rented about one hundred abandoned plantations containing 50,270 acres and employing over 11,000 freedmen.[11] The experiment was not totally satisfactory. Raids by marauding Confederate bands disrupted operations, and early in September, when the crop was starting to mature, an infestation of army worms devastated the cotton; in consequence, only one-fourth of the usual production was realized.[12] Additional problems included a failure to appoint provost marshals or establish schools in many districts, and the inadequacies of the lessees, a majority of whom were retired federal officers with no prior experience in the cotton business or in dealing with plantation workers.[13]

Negro field hands disliked leasing arrangements because they so resembled slavery conditions. The hands worked in gangs, were constantly under the watchful eyes of white supervisors, could not leave the plantations without permission, and had at least half of their wages withheld until the cotton was picked and sold. While army regulations authorized deductions in rations and pay for feigned illness or poor performance, in practice distinctions were often overlooked; first-class hands and perennial shirkers drew identical pay, and some of the worst consumed the most food. When lessees attempted to make merit adjustments, much wrangling and bitter altercations ensued. There was little incentive for achievement or personal initiative and accomplishment. As had their Southern planter predecessors, Northern lessees complained about Negro thievery, shiftlessness, and general laziness.[14]

At first, lessees were inclined to ascribe such feelings to the ingrained habits of slavery. It is suggestive, however, that the experiment with free black labor was most promising when Negroes were given charge of their own affairs. In some districts the government permitted blacks to rent small farms or portions of plantations directly, lending them work stock and equipment and advancing money for expenses while they made the crop.[15] In the Helena district thirty or more took leases, and some sold their crop standing in the field before the omnivorous army worm appeared. The black lessees aggregate income was reportedly some forty thousand dollars, ten lessees realizing an aggregate profit of thirty-one thousand dollars. Two planted forty acres of cotton; their expenses were about twelve hundred dollars, but they sold their crop for eight thousand dollars. Another man leased twenty-four acres, accumulated expenses of less than two thousand dollars, and sold his cotton for six thousand dollars. Still another made a net profit of thirty-four hundred dollars on thirteen and a half acres. A fifth individual sold his crop on twenty-five acres for four thousand dollars, while a sixth, working seventeen acres, earned enough by the season's end to purchase a good house and leave a cash balance of three hundred dollars. A majority of the remaining black lessees sold their cotton in the seed at twenty-eight to thirty-three cents per pound, making on the average about five hundred dollars net profit on every ten acres cultivated.[16] The general superintendent of freedmen for Arkansas reported: "I cannot see that, in any particular, these colored men have been less successful than the white planters along side them.

73

When they employed hands, there is little if any complaint against them, either in the matter of rations, wages, or usage. Having undertaken small and manageable tracts of land, working them in good part themselves, and employing but a small number of hands, their crops have been more fully worked, and so have produced more bountifully."[17]

At the end of the Civil War, the national government did not pursue these encouraging results. By early 1865 it was apparent that the South could not continue long in the field. After peace was made, federal troops would presumably be disbanded, and all protection and discipline over the freedmen withdrawn. To fill the void, Congress passed the Freedmen's Bureau Act on March 3, 1865. The Bureau's powers were later expanded through renewal legislation, and, as finally established, it had authority to dispense rations to destitute blacks and whites, operate schools for freedmen, supervise labor contracts on plantations, and dispose of confiscated and abandoned lands. The original purpose of the act in reference to the latter was to sell in small tracts to freedmen and refugees properties not restored to old owners through amnesty and special pardon. President Andrew Johnson proved so liberal in the granting of pardons that much land was never available for sale, however.[18] Those properties not restored were bid for at public auctions. Since the Congress failed to provide a credit system or financing for the ex-slaves, confiscated plantations generally passed back into the hands of whites, either original or new titleholders.[19]

The Congress did approve on June 21, 1866, an act setting aside all federally owned public lands in Arkansas and other Southern states for use as homesteads for freedmen and for those whites who could take an oath that they had not borne arms against the United States. Public lands were to be reserved for homesteads until January 1, 1867, with Freedmen's Bureau agents to locate and estimate their value and aid settlers in securing them. Again, no credit provisions were created for blacks or others. Because most freedmen owned little more than the clothes on their back, not many could buy teams, seed, supplies, or maintain themselves during the first nonproductive year of clearing the ground. The poorest of credit risks, having no collateral, they found private loans unavailable in the capital-dearth, ruined South.[20] Though

Congressman Thaddeus Stevens of Pennsylvania and others persisted in calling for land confiscation and redistribution, their appeal, with its implied threat to the sanctity of private property, was ignored by the majority of Northerners.

The vision of "forty acres and a mule" died hard among black folk. At the constitutional convention of 1868, Phillips County Negro delegate William H. Grey tried in vain to stimulate interest in land for freedmen, but neither white conservatives nor radicals were responsive.[21] In 1870 two white radicals, Asa Hodges and Joseph Brooks, proposed carving 160-acre homesteads for freedmen out of swamp and overflow lands granted to Arkansas by the federal government. The idea got nowhere, in part because of federal restrictions that the transferred lands were to be used exclusively to raise funds for levee construction and in part because of the unsuitable character of much of the land itself.[22]

Nevertheless, a limited number of blacks did manage to acquire farms. During the Reconstruction period state property assessments and taxes soared. During the period 1864–1866, assessed valuation of property in Arkansas was $35,723,449; by 1873, the figure had climbed to $104,560,292. The annual tax paid into the treasury during the six years of radical administration, 1868–1874, averaged $1,112,419; by comparison, state property taxes had netted only $146,521 annually in 1864–1866.[23]

Although their number is not certain,[24] almost surely some planters who lost everything in the course of the war saw their holdings gaveled away at tax sales. Under a state law of 1868, lands not redeemed three years from assessment were to be auctioned off by the state auditor for the amount of back-due assessments. One such sale was advertised for the second Monday of February 1871 in the Little Rock *Weekly Republican*. The list of lands for sale occupied sixteen pages twenty-four by fourteen inches in fine print (nonpareil). From this list the editor of the *Arkansas Gazette* calculated that 15,416 tracts containing 3,622,405 acres of land were forfeited for taxes during 1869 alone.[25]

Democratic newspapers alleged that radical tax policies were deliberately confiscatory, a charge not completely denied by the Republican press.[26] Support for this view is offered by an 1868 law which specified that lands auctioned at tax sales were to be disposed of in twenty- to forty-acre tracts,[27] thereby allowing freedmen with small savings to enter the bidding. There are no available statistics indicating the exact number of blacks who acquired land in this way. Charles Nordhoff, who spent some time in Arkansas in the spring of 1875, estimated that one in twenty blacks owned farms;[28] no doubt many of these were acquired through tax proceedings.

Of course Negroes, after they acquired farms, also faced the problem of raising funds to meet taxes. Even so, a sizeable minority somehow were able to buy and hold land during and after Reconstruction. By 1900, the U.S. Census showed that of 46,983 black farmers in the state, 11,766 or 25 percent were owners or part owners of their land (among whites the figure was 63.3 percent).[29] Most of these black yeomen were marginal operators eking out a bare subsistence; 73.3 percent owned homesteads of fifty acres or under, and only 11.2 percent owned farms of more than one hundred acres.[30] The average annual gross value of product per Negro-owned farm was $382, and the average value of property, including livestock, buildings, tools, and equipment was $728.[31]

The extent of rural poverty and the minimal degree of economic progress most rural blacks had achieved is further documented by the official reports of the state auditor. In 1895, the General Assembly enacted a new law requiring that the amount of taxes paid by each race be listed separately for each county in Arkansas.[32] The auditor's report for the following year revealed that in the state's most heavily Negro counties, those with approximately 75 percent or more black populations and all located in the Delta, blacks paid only a minuscule amount of total taxes collected (see table 1). Ten years later, in 1906, the state auditor's report indicated a slight improvement, either in the economic circumstances of blacks or in the efficiency of tax collection, but still demonstrated the general impoverishment of blacks in plantation counties (see table 2).

A few black agriculturalists enjoyed a comfortable sustenance, even wealth. Of the Negro owners, 2.2 percent had farms of over 175 acres, and 0.1 percent owned over 1,000 acres.[33] One of the most remarkable figures in this latter class was Pickens W. Black. Born a slave in Alabama in 1861, Black, according to an account by his son, "got into a fight with one of his mother's boyfriends

## TABLE 1
### *TOTAL TAXES COLLECTED FROM BLACKS, EXCLUDING POLL TAXES, IN ARKANSAS COUNTIES WITH APPROXIMATELY THREE-QUARTERS OR MORE BLACK POPULATIONS, 1896.*

| County | Percentage Black Population (1890) | Percentage Taxes Paid by Blacks | Total Taxes Paid, Blacks | Total Taxes Paid, Whites |
|---|---|---|---|---|
| Chicot | 87.8 | 4.5 | $1,321.10 | $29,401.42 |
| Crittenden | 85.3 | No report | No report | No report |
| Desha | 79.5 | 3.6 | $1,006.13 | $27,773.58 |
| Jefferson | 73.2 | 4.2 | $4,982.51 | $119,269.16 |
| Lee | 75.2 | 11.7 | $4,060.54 | $34,837.02 |
| Phillips | 78.6 | 9.3 | $7,186.54 | $77,361.02 |

SOURCES: *Arkansas Biennial Report of the Auditor of State, 1897–1898* (Little Rock, 1898), 225–26; U.S. Census Office, *Twelfth Census, 1900,* I, *Population*, Pt. 1, 530. Totals include both real and personal-property taxes collected.

## TABLE 2
### *TOTAL TAXES COLLECTED FROM BLACKS, EXCLUDING POLL TAXES, IN ARKANSAS COUNTIES WITH APPROXIMATELY THREE-QUARTERS OR MORE BLACK POPULATIONS, 1906.*

| County | Percentage Black Population (1900) | Percentage Taxes Paid by Blacks | Total Taxes Paid, Blacks | Total Taxes Paid, Whites |
|---|---|---|---|---|
| Chicot | 87.1 | 8.8 | $6,794.97 | $77,447.75 |
| Crittenden | 84.6 | 8.4 | $6,868.95 | $81,673.15 |
| Desha | 81.7 | 8.4 | $6,349.28 | $75,698.02 |
| Jefferson | 72.8 | 11.6 | $26,989.71 | $232,148.40 |
| Lee | 77.8 | 25.4 | $14,543.57 | $57,194.24 |
| Phillips | 78.6 | 11.2 | $13,993.48 | $124,980.37 |

SOURCES: *Arkansas Biennial Report of the Auditor of State, 1907–1908* (Little Rock, 1909), 419–20; U.S. Census Office, *Twelfth Census, 1900,* I, *Population*, Pt. 1, 530. Totals include both real and personal-property taxes collected.

TABLE 3

*AVERAGE TAX PAID PER CAPITA BY BLACKS AND WHITES,*
*EXCLUDING POLL TAXES, IN ARKANSAS COUNTIES WITH*
*APPROXIMATELY THREE-QUARTERS OR MORE BLACK*
*POPULATIONS, 1896 AND 1906*

| County | 1896 | | 1906 | |
|--------|------|------|------|------|
|  | Blacks | Whites | Blacks | Whites |
| Chicot | $0.13 | $21.12 | $0.54 | $41.28 |
| Crittenden | No report | No report | $0.56 | $36.48 |
| Desha | $0.12 | $13.11 | $0.68 | $35.98 |
| Jefferson | $0.17 | $10.89 | $0.90 | $20.83 |
| Lee | $0.29 | $ 7.43 | $0.96 | $13.29 |
| Phillips | $0.37 | $13.58 | $0.67 | $22.02 |

SOURCES: Derived from *Arkansas Biennial Report of the Auditor of State,*
*1897–1898* (Little Rock, 1898), 225–26; ibid., *1907–1908* (Little Rock,
1909) 419–20; U.S. Census Office, *Twelfth Census, 1900,* I, *Population,*
Pt. 1, 530.

one night when he was 14 and ran off to Arkansas when he thought
the man was dead." He arrived in the state "flat broke and mighty
hungry," doing "any odd job he could lay his hands on, including
a five-week stint with the railroad, laying ties." Black "saved out
just enough to eat a little each day and put the rest away." He
accumulated enough to purchase a forty-acre farm and continued
saving and buying. Eventually he built a vast empire of over eight
thousand acres in Northeast Arkansas, working 360 families, Negro
and white, on his holdings. The little hamlet of Blackville, fifteen
miles south of Newport in Jackson County, preserves his name.[34]

Another successful Delta Negro was Scott Bond, who lived at
Madison in St. Francis County. Bond was the son of a nephew of a
former master who had leased the Bond family for a time during
slavery. A native of Mississippi, he was carried to Arkansas when
five years old. After emancipation he worked for a while with his
black stepfather on a farm, but his real chance came in 1877. In
that year a Mrs. Allen, a kinswoman of his old owner, rented and
later sold to him an estate of twenty-two hundred acres. By the

end of his life, Bond possessed nineteen farms aggregating five thousand acres, had three cotton gins, a store in Madison, a sawmill, and a gravel pit which supplied the Rock Island Railroad in Arkansas. In 1917 he turned down an offer of two million dollars for his combined properties.[35]

After achieving his fortune Bond returned on one occasion to Mississippi to visit his former master, a man named Goodlow, who was the uncle of Bond's white father. The family sent a carriage to meet him at the train station. As Bond approached the Goodlow home, he was surprised to find it "a great mansion with beautiful lawns." Bond was received by the family and entertained in their residence, which was adorned with fine furniture, gleaming mirrors, and imported carpets. After an hour's conversation about the young land of Arkansas, he finally summoned up enough courage to reveal his relationship to the family. He stated that he knew many Southern whites had fallen into hard times after the war and that if his father were in any distress he wished to aid him. The Goodlows acknowledged the blood tie amidst weeping and rejoicing, and Bond was invited to stay the night in the mansion. He discovered that his father, Wes Rutledge, had died in Texas ten years before. However, the Goodlows had him driven to Canton, Mississippi, where three of Rutledge's children by his white wife were doing business. Bond met and chatted with them, although he did not disclose that he was their half brother.[36]

Such an event was unusual in the South, for individuals like Scott Bond and Pickens Black were as rare and out of place in their society as the occasional Negro planter and slaveholder of antebellum days. Their true significance was captured by Pickens W. Black, Jr., in a 1971 interview published in the *Arkansas Gazette*. "My father," he observed, "was a fine, hard-working man and he did something unheard of for a black man, and most white men, of that time or even nowadays. He actually created something from nothing with no education or help from nobody. He was one in a million."[37]

♦    ♦    ♦

For most blacks, devoid of property or possessions, life was a matter of sheer endurance. Immediately after the war Negroes had shown an extreme reluctance to remain working as field hands on someone else's land. A number, it is true, continued serving as faithful retainers for their old masters' families, and occasionally a Southern widow or orphan escaped starvation because of their loyalty. They were lovingly pointed to in later years, out of genuine affection, and as proof of the allegedly benign character of the old slave system. If slavery were so cruel, the argument went, how could it have produced such devotion?

The fact was, however, that a majority of ex-slaves had left the plantation at the first opportunity.[38] Travelers in the South during 1865 and 1866 reported seeing great throngs of dusty, disheveled blacks wandering back and forth over the roads and highways. Some were simply enjoying the exhilarating sense of freedom, others getting away from harsh former owners; many were looking for long-lost relations separated by slave sales, others marking time until they received their forty acres from the government or until some opportunity turned up. Whites viewed this vagrancy as evidence of the Negro's innate childlike nature, his inability to work without white discipline and supervision. In a curious way, whether blacks remained on the plantation or not, slavery was seen as justified.

Although it was not recognized as such at the time, vagrancy, at least in some measure, represented the freedmen's version of a labor strike, a refusal to go back to work until they received their own homesteads. After a few months, however, desperation forced them to seek employment. Mrs. Alfred Holt Carrigan, wife of a planter of Washington, Arkansas, wrote on January 1, 1866, "It is the saddest time I ever knew. Our servants are faithful to us, nevertheless, the streets of Washington are crowded with Negroes hunting homes . . . Dr. Jett died; the family in deep distress. A great many are dying from trouble."[39] Death hovered over white and black alike in that dreadful period. According to one estimation, over five thousand freedmen's graves were made in North Little Rock in 1865.[40]

When blacks did return to work the land, there were painful adjustments for all concerned. Whites found it difficult to discard the peremptory attitudes and habits of the slave master; Negroes displayed a good deal of surliness and truculence. Nursing old and new grudges and wrongs, real and imagined, they enjoyed the delicious pleasure of talking back to whites with less threat of flogging. The diary of James M. Hanks, a Phillips County planter, records almost daily battles with hands.[41] The wife of another planter became so frustrated that she wrote, "I wish I might go to some large town and live the remainder of my life, so utterly weary am I of plantations past, present, and to come."[42]

The resumption of agricultural production necessitated new economic as well as social arrangements, for some way had to be found of paying the now free ex-slaves. Experiments with cash wages were tried but had many drawbacks, not the least of which was the scarcity of money. In an attempt to recoup their losses and pay hands, planters contracted heavy debts. Mrs. Carrigan tried to confine the sense of depression this created to her diary. On Christmas day 1865 she noted, "The children enjoyed themselves very much. They knew little how much their parents were suffering. Washington [Arkansas] was never in more distress. . . . Father gave Mr. C. his note due him for Negroes. The note was $5000 dollars, enough to make us poor for life. Debt is the cause of so much sorrow in the South now."[43]

High cotton prices after the war encouraged Arkansas growers in believing that they could see through the crisis and repay their heavy obligations. Newspapers encouraged everyone to roll up his shirt sleeves and go to work. Planters were told they must look to the future in "their present dilapidated state if they would be happy" and "must smile as if prosperous."[44] "Every man must be a producer," warned the editor of the Van Buren *Press*, "times are hard but with money scarce no man can slack."[45] Another writer encouraged whites to see that their children did all necessary work and chores about the house and farm and that they be given a trade. "The silly notion so prevalent heretofore that physical labor is inconsistent with good breeding must give way to a more practicable, a more sensible, and a more healthful sentiment."[46]

Arkansas planters endeavored to take the above advice to heart but seemed almost cursed with bad fortune. Owing to labor problems and a shortage of capital with which to buy supplies, a large portion of the land was not planted in 1866. Perhaps this was just as well, for in May disastrous overflows of the Mississippi and its tributaries, said to be the worst in twenty years, destroyed the crop. Generally, the year was a horrible calamity: "The spring was wet and cold, cutworms were destructive in the bottoms, and a drought in July and August injured late cotton."[47] The Van Buren *Press* declared it a heavy "blow to the energy of soul of the farmer and planter. . . . Men who had come home . . . had staked all on this crop. Almost all were compelled to go into debt for supplies. They have been forced to live almost from hand to mouth, saving every penny and using the strictest economy to get along this far."[48]

Arkansas cotton production in 1866 was only 190,000 bales, compared to 367,393 bales sold in 1859.[49] Conditions improved little in 1867, for once again ruinous spring overflows and summer droughts decimated the cotton. Cotton prices, while high, were not so good as expected. The average price per pound fell from 43.20 cents in 1865 to 31.59 cents in 1866 and continued dropping.[50] The federal cotton tax also ate into profits. First imposed as a feature of the Revenue Act of 1862, the tax, originally set at a half cent a pound, was raised to two cents, then to five cents, lowered to three cents in July 1866, and finally abolished in February 1868—after exacting approximately one million dollars from Arkansas growers.[51] After that date, state and local property taxes under radical Reconstruction more than made up for its removal.

Continuing turmoil concerning the labor supply, magnified by a southwide tendency for some black women to withdraw from labor in the fields and for black men to work shorter hours, only added to the planters' troubles.[52] Reflecting the general distress, the amount of land in farms decreased 20.6 percent between 1860–1870.[53]

Omnipresent poverty brought a gradual cessation of experiments in cash wages for hands. Wages in Arkansas averaged from fifteen to twenty dollars a month, including weekly rations, which were about the same as under slavery: one peck of cornmeal or flour, three to five pounds of bacon, one pint of molasses, and a quantity of great northern beans. If a hand signed for a whole year's service, he often secured rations for his family as well, plus use of a cabin, a patch of ground for a garden, privilege of common pasture for a cow or pig, and other advantages.[54] Total remuneration was actually higher in Arkansas than in the South Atlantic region and some other areas, probably because of the greater scarcity of labor in the state's still semi-frontier economy (see table 4).

# TABLE 4
## MONEY WAGES PLUS VALUE OF RATIONS, AGRICULTURAL LABOR, BY STATE, 1867 AND 1868, IN DOLLARS

| State | 1867 | | | 1868 | | |
|---|---|---|---|---|---|---|
| | Men | Women | Youth | Men | Women | Youth |
| Virginia | 102 | 43 | 46 | 102 | 41 | 45 |
| North Carolina | 104 | 45 | 47 | 89 | 41 | 39 |
| South Carolina | 100 | 55 | 43 | 93 | 52 | 42 |
| Georgia | 125 | 65 | 46 | 83 | 55 | 47 |
| Florida | 139 | 85 | 52 | 97 | 50 | 44 |
| Alabama | 117 | 71 | 52 | 87 | 50 | 40 |
| Mississippi | 149 | 93 | 61 | 90 | 66 | 40 |
| Louisiana | 150 | 104 | 65 | 104 | 75 | 60 |
| Texas | 139 | 84 | 67 | 130 | 72 | 63 |
| Arkansas | 158 | 94 | 78 | 115 | 75 | 67 |
| Tennessee | 136 | 67 | 65 | 109 | 51 | 45 |

SOURCE: U.S. Department of Agriculture, *Report of the Commissioner of Agriculture for the Year 1867* (Washington, D.C., 1868), 416.

In the aftermath of the war, many planters found the outlay for wages and supplies onerous to bear. Often use of the wage system had not proven very satisfactory anyway. From the planter's perspective, its most serious drawback was the instability of the labor supply, for it woefully failed to develop dependability, efficiency, and a sense of personal responsibility among workers. Even withholding a portion of wages due until the end of the season was no guarantee that the former slaves would remain to gather the crop; the problem of harvesting caused thousands of acres to lie fallow. One newspaper claimed that in 1869 a third of the Southern cotton crop was lost by failure of labor in gathering.[55] Planters who saw their hands slip away in August and September, faced with the emergency of picking cotton already made, offered wages of $1.00 to $1.50 per one hundred pounds. This began a self-perpetuating cycle; hands could break contracts, go to better fields, and earn five or six dollars in two or three days.[56]

Blacks, however, had their own reasons for disliking the wage system. As had earlier been the case with Northern lessees, they often worked in gangs under close white supervision; moreover, the best hands resented being paid wages identical to those received by the worst. Use of the system was most effective on large estates where owners could afford employing overseers and "riding bosses"; planters, their sons, and Northerners usually failed in these capacities. One of the few areas where it was retained was on plantations around Scott, Arkansas, owned by the Steele, Dortch, Alexander, and other families. Reminiscent of slavery times, hands and their drivers were called together each morning by the ringing of the plantation bell and were assigned tasks for the day or week.[57]

On the majority of plantations payment of wages in money eventually gave way to the use of the tenant system. Repeated crop failures exhausted the planters' slim resources, and as their debts mounted, they found satisfactory credit for hiring and furnishing more difficult to obtain. Compelled by empty pockets to abandon cash outlays for labor, they began substituting tenancy arrangements instead.

Principal variations of the tenant system were known as sharecropping, share renting, and fixed or cash renting. Sharecropping was frequently called farming "on halves" since half the proceeds from sale of the sharecropper's cotton went to the landlord. The "croppers" were assigned a section of land on the plantation, ranging from fifteen to forty acres or more, depending on the size of their family and their reputation as workers. The landlord provided mules, plows, hoes, seed, firewood, and cabins, with the sharecropper providing only his labor. Landlords also saw that their hands received medical care and rations, although costs for these items were deducted. They either operated their own plantation stores directly or arranged credit for their tenants through local furnishing merchants.[58] Owners dictated the amount and type of crop to be raised and reserved the right to employ extra hands if a tenant fell behind in his crop, charging him the extra expense for wages.

Favored tenants and old hands who had been lucky enough to win their landlord's good will were occasionally promoted to the status of share renters. To enter this class a tenant must have saved enough money to buy his own teams, seed, and farm implements. Then he needed only to ask the landlord for living quarters and land. Rentals varied but were customarily a third of the corn grown and a fourth of the cotton, hence the name "third and fourth" renter. Fixed renting, in which the tenant paid a smaller proportion of the crop and enjoyed greater freedom of management, was less common in the Delta, as was cash renting.[59]

Though begun at first out of necessity, the tenancy system soon won general favor. As economist Joseph D. Reid has noted, one reason for its widespread use may have been the ability of sharecropping to facilitate aggregate risk reduction.[60] Presumably, it was in the mutual interest of planters and sharecroppers to make necessary changes during the growing season in crop mix, fertilizer used, and so forth, since both parties would gain from needed alterations. Planters specifically benefited since the system, while it gave them less product, nevertheless relieved them of heavy wage payments, with the danger of contracting large debts being minimized. Labor costs were automatically adjusted downward in bad years, and there was a greater degree of permanence in the work force.

Even the tenant enjoyed some advantages. In theory, his rent was automatically reduced in bad years, and he became at least a semi-independent operator working his own parcel of land. To a degree family stability was enhanced, since husband, wife, and older children formed an economic unit, laboring together.[61] Moreover, so long as the tenant family remained on the plantation, the threat of starvation was gone. One economic historian, Stephen J. DeCanio, insists that sharecropping produced maximum efficiency and that, overall, returns to the laborer exceeded his marginal productivity.[62]

Other authorities, however, have presented a less sanguine view of the economic and social effects of the sharecropping system. Roger L. Ransom and Richard Sutch, in particular, argue that while admittedly sharecropping produced short-run advantages for landlords and tenants alike, it ultimately had deleterious long-run effects. Since both landlord and tenant shared output equally, neither would find it advantageous to pay for an improvement unless it increased output to the extent of more than twice the cost of the improvement. They also observe that sharecropping perpetuated the crop-lien system; under it, merchants and landlords demanded that tenants concentrate on producing cotton, which assured them payment in a readily saleable commodity and gave them a lucrative market for food supplies. Ransom and Sutch believe that this concentration on cotton, occurring during a time of falling world cotton prices, impeded Southern economic development[63]—a position disputed by DeCanio.

The argument among the economic historians is an important one, but it should not obscure one critical point on which they agree: that poverty and inequality were widespread in the rural South and that, in any absolute sense, opportunities for economic and social mobility for plantation workers were greatly restricted and limited. Even DeCanio concedes this, although he attributes the persistence of poverty to unequal ownership of the nonhuman factors of production.[64]

Unquestionably, evidence from Arkansas supports this consensus view that plantation workers as a group remained oppressed and impoverished. Under sharecropping arrangements, tenants customarily had to pay the planter for ginning and marketing their cotton and reimburse him for food and medical care. The mark-ups and interest charges for rations and supplies could be unbelievably exacting; profits ranged from 25 to as much as 300 percent on credit sales and from 20 to as high as 50 percent on cash sales.[65]

Conceivably, a sharecropper could labor for an entire year and not make a dime. Most planters refused to give written contracts or receipts for financial transactions. At the harvest's end they weighed their tenant's cotton and balanced his profit from the crop against his accumulated charges for supplies. Any remaining debts were then carried over to the next season. Year after year the hapless tenant found himself bound tightly in an inextricable straitjacket of peonage. To keep hands from becoming too dissatisfied, the wiser planters usually gave them a little money when settling annual accounts, often silently entering the sum in their books as a cash advance. For a tenant to leave was risky, as his creditor was protected by law and other planters would be hesitant to take him. In some instances he might find another landowner, hard up for hands, who would assume his obligations. Investigations by Gavin Wright have shown that there was considerable turnover in the Southern plantation labor force. As often as not, however, migrating brought little improvement. True, a measure of progress was possible for some tenants, but, frequently, debts only began accruing anew under each successive master.[66]

One aged ex-slave and former sharecropper, Henry Blake, bitterly recounted his own experiences in a 1930's interview with the Federal Writer's Project. He remembered:

> After freedom, we worked on shares a while. Then we rented. When we worked on shares we couldn't make nothing—just overalls and something to eat. Half went to the other man and you would destroy your half if you weren't careful. A man that didn't know how to count would always lose. He might lose anyhow. They didn't give no itemized statement. No, you just had to take their word. They never give you no details. They just say you owe so much. No matter how good account you kept, you had to go by their account and now, Brother, I'm telling you the truth about this. It's been that way for a long time. You had to take the white man's work on notes and everything. Anything you wanted, you could git if you were a good hand. You could git anything you wanted as long as you worked. But you better not leave him—you better not try to leave and git caught. They'd keep you in debt. They were sharp. Christmas come, you could take up twenty dollars in somethin' to eat and as much as you wanted in whiskey. Anything that kept you a slave. . . .[67]

One might well ask how a Delta planter, as often as not a pillar of his community and church, subscribing to a chivalric code of personal integrity and honor, could justify such exploitative conduct toward dependents.

The answer in part lies in the basic nature of Delta society. Life in the plantation South moved slowly in ordered patterns, governed by the ever-repeated cycle of the crop and the rhythms of the seasons. Changes came gradually, and to the occasional visitor time itself sometimes seemed suspended in the hot, torpid air. Each plantation county had its recognized first families; its quiet, sturdy yeomen; its quota of poor whites, some of them sharecroppers; and its black field hands. Each of these classes had its recognized and acknowledged place in the social order, and all were entwined together and connected in a web of reciprocal duties and obligations.

This is not to say that the plantation world was "feudal" in the European meaning of the word. Lingering and persistent frontier conditions lent a democratic flavor to everyday existence. For all his pretensions, the typical Southern planter was no haughty, aloof patrician. Even the wealthiest usually had "poor relations," and not uncommonly sons of planters and yeomen joined in hunting, fishing, and other diversions. Landowners took a close interest in their hands, getting them out of scrapes with the law, extending money and help in times of emergency, and otherwise lending assistance. In fact, it was exactly the centrality of personal relationships which sustained social harmony and the feeling of community.[68]

However, whenever an individual evinced too much dissatisfaction with his accustomed station, whenever he displayed too much personal ambition or restlessness, he was rightly perceived as a threat to the unity and stability of plantation society. While social mobility among whites was not unknown, especially in the turbulent postwar years, it was not really encouraged. Almost every sleepy Delta village had its eccentric individuals, but the social milieu generally did not approve of unbridled individualism. The town "character" was as often as not a person of unusual sensitivity whose talents, dreams, and inchoate yearnings had remained undeveloped and unfulfilled. The Yoknapatawapha novels of William Faulkner, set in the neighboring state of Mississippi, capture vividly the sense of gestalt wholeness and social conservatism in Southern rural culture. Especially is this so in Faulkner's negative portrayal of the fictitious Snopes family, presented as a tribe of amoral *arrivistes*, devoid of principle and possessing less intelligence than animal-like cunning.

If upward mobility was not exactly smiled upon in whites, it was positively forbidden to blacks. Those few blacks who broke through the barriers of racial caste and challenged their society's racial traditions could meet with intense animosity. Scott Bond, although a millionaire planter, was careful to have whites address him as "Uncle Scott" rather than as "Mr. Bond," telling them "I have my doubts as to whether you mean the word Mr. or not, and if you do you cannot afford it here in the south."[69] In spite of his caution, hostile white neighbors unsuccessfully tried to have his cotton seed boycotted by various cotton-oil companies.[70] On another occasion, they attempted, again without success, to prevent him through a court injunction from erecting a sawmill. Bond noted that the movement against his project "consisted of three-fourths of all the white men in the town in which I lived [the Delta village of Madison]. I felt that I was right and went about

the matter in a business way. I tried to explain to those people
. . . that I was harming no one by putting in this mill; that it
would give employment to a number of people and cause hundreds of dollars to be spent in the town, that would otherwise not
be spent. They said I should put in no saw mill here. 'This is a
white man's country, and white men are going to rule.'"[71]

Pickens W. Black likewise discovered that success could produce bitter enmity. On two separate occurrences his store at Blackville was destroyed by arsonists.[72]

As demonstrations of energy, initiative, and ability brought not
the esteem and praise of their fellows but rather heightened prejudice and, in some cases, real threats of violence, it is no wonder
that Delta Negroes commonly forsook ambition and aspiration.
Edward King, a correspondent for *Scribner's Monthly*, toured Arkansas and the lower Mississippi valley in 1874 and was struck by
the listlessness, slovenliness, and apathy of Negro tenants and
sharecroppers; quoting a local planter, King reported, "whenever
they could secure a little money the ground in front of their cabins
would be strewed with sardine boxes and whiskey bottles."[73] The
description fit many croppers accurately enough, who drew what
limited pleasures in life they could from immediate, hedonistic
gratifications. It seems plausible that denial of opportunities was
to a great degree responsible for their indolent behavior, yet planters used such conduct to rationalize further denials. Why pay
blacks higher wages, they argued, if the extra cash would only be
squandered on liquor, women, and other sundry dissipations?

Ultimately, of course, such social attitudes had their wellspring
in underlying economic realities. As Jay R. Mandle has observed
in his perceptive study *The Roots of Black Poverty*, the classic plantation economy is a "market-oriented but archaic social organization" distinguished by its own special class structure, culture, and
ideology. Mandle believes it appears when "the state of technol-
ogy allows profit-maximizing large-scale farmers to produce a
staple for a market" but only if they can obtain a supply of workers at a cost below what the market for labor would normally require. To get the needed workers, "some combination of coercion
and domination is required" and "that use of coercion defines the
class relations of the society." These class relationships in turn
give rise to and reinforce a culture "best characterized as paternalistic in which deferential attitudes are exhibited by the group

89

which is dominated and qausi aristocratic norms are accepted by the elite." Whereas slavery had provided the coercion to provide such a work force before the Civil War, the crop-lien system, peonage laws, violence, intimidation, racial discrimination, and the absence of alternative work opportunities achieved the same result after the war.[74]

The persistence of a plantation economy in Arkansas and of the social system and values it engendered, however, did not inhibit a continuing influx of blacks into the Delta. At the close of the Civil War much of the region, while dotted with plantations and scattered settlements, still contained acres and acres of uncleared wilderness. In the bottom lands along the White, Cache, and St. Francis rivers canebrakes were so thick that travelers sometimes could not journey in carriages or wagons but only on foot or on horseback. Haunting cypress swamps and marshes, breeders of mosquitoes and malaria, covered the "sunk lands" of Northeast Arkansas, a legacy of the New Madrid earthquake of 1811–1812. Bears, cougars, deer, and other wildlife made their homes in silent virgin forests, while beavers and otters scurried along the banks of innumerable creeks and streams, themselves teeming with bass, crappie, catfish, and gar. Above, the Delta sky was clouded each fall by great flocks of wild ducks, making their way southward along the Mississippi flyway.[75]

Gazing across at this scene from the high bluffs of Memphis or looking out from the decks of steamboats, observers sometimes concluded that the entire land of Arkansas was an isolated backwoods. In early pioneer days it gained an unsavory reputation as a haven for outlaws and desperadoes of every color and description. A common joke asked, "What was your name before you went to Arkansas?" In any vaudeville performance, the mere mention of the state was guaranteed to produce a guffaw.[76]

Even in the first days of the century this image was not entirely accurate, and it became less so with each passing decade. After 1840, particularly, Arkansas's eastern regions began attracting a large immigration from the older cotton states of the South. Established families, bringing capital and slaves, purchased the initial claims of frontiersmen. Small clearings were expanded and transformed, with a pattern of large plantations emerging.[77]

The Civil War and disorders of Reconstruction suspended this

90

process, but it began anew after 1870, promoted by a flurry of railroad building and levee construction.[78] Between 1860 and 1870, the total white population of Arkansas increased only 37,972, or 11.7 percent, and the total black population only 10,910, or 9.8 percent.[79] By 1880, however, renewal of immigration had boosted the white population 82.5 percent over the figure for 1860, while the black population rose 89.3 percent during the same period.[80] As might be expected, much of the increase in black population was concentrated in the alluvial counties of the Delta and other lowland areas. In the eight most important plantation counties in these regions, the number of blacks, already high to begin with, jumped almost 69.7 percent between 1860–1880. By comparison, the white population there increased only .07 percent,[81] actually declining in five of the eight counties—probably reflecting greater concentrations in property ownership (see table 5).

In the fertile, untapped soil of the Delta there were fortunes to be made, at least for those who had enough funds to buy and exploit the land and who could find sufficient hands to cultivate it.

TABLE 5

*BLACK POPULATION OF THE STATE OF ARKANSAS, 1860 TO 1900*

| Year | Total Population | Black Population | Percentage Black |
|------|------------------|------------------|------------------|
| 1860 | 435,450 | 111,259 | 25.6% |
| 1870 | 484,471 | 122,169 | 25.2% |
| 1880 | 802,525 | 210,666 | 26.3% |
| 1890 | 1,128,211 | 309,117 | 27.4% |
| 1900 | 1,311,564 | 366,856 | 28.0% |

SOURCE: *Population of the United States . . . 1860 . . . Eighth Census* (Washington, D.C., 1864), 134; *Ninth Census . . . The Statistics of the Population of the United States . . . 1870* (Washington, D.C., 1872), 4–8; *Statistics of the Population of the United States at the Tenth Census . . . 1880 . . .* (Washington, D.C., 1883), 3; *Eleventh Census of the United States . . . Population, Part I . . .* (Washington, D.C., 1895), 403; *Abstract of the Twelfth Census of the United States . . . 1900* (Washington, D.C., 1904), 40–41.

*Total population includes a very few Chinese and American Indians.

Securing an adequate labor force proved the most obdurate obstacle to success. As early as 1866 a call went out for a planters' convention, to convene in Memphis in the spring of 1867, for the purpose of considering ways of enticing blacks from the older plantation states.[82] There was also a good deal of talk about luring European and even Chinese laborers to the Delta fields. These latter groups, however, generally found the poor wages, limited prospects for mobility, and unhealthful climate of the region uninviting.[83] Resignedly, and in spite of continual grumbling about the blacks' slothfulness, planters decided that they would have to be the men for the work.

Immigration efforts began in an informal way, with a planter, sent by a few of his neighbors, going east to select hands he thought were reliable, sign them to contracts, and conduct them into the state.[84] Later the system evolved into private labor bureaus that opened offices, sent agents, advertised their activities to planters, and tried to establish a reputation for good service. In addition, railroad companies sometimes entered the business directly. R. A. Williams, an immigration officer for the Little Rock and Memphis Railroad, claimed to have brought twenty thousand blacks into the Arkansas and Mississippi Delta during 1891–1892 alone.[85]

Agents scoured the South Atlantic states,[86] using every persuasion to entice unsuspecting blacks into moving westward. The situation was not dissimilar from seventeenth-century Virginia, when sea captains and representatives of planters gave exaggerated accounts of that commonwealth's bountifulness while wooing white indentured servants to the New World. Delta immigration officials likewise portrayed Arkansas as a veritable New Eden, where the black newcomer could anticipate enjoying a life of luxury and ease. William Pickens, a Negro whose family migrated from South Carolina to Arkansas in 1888, recounted ruefully the blandishments employed:

> The agent said that Arkansas was a tropical country of soft and balmy air, where cocoanuts, oranges, lemons and bananas grew. Ordinary things like corn and cotton, with little cultivation, grew an enormous yield.
> On the 15th of January, 1888, the agent made all the arrangements, purchased tickets, and we boarded the train in Seneca, S.C., bound

## PERCENTAGE BLACK POPULATION OF ARKANSAS BY COUNTY, 1890

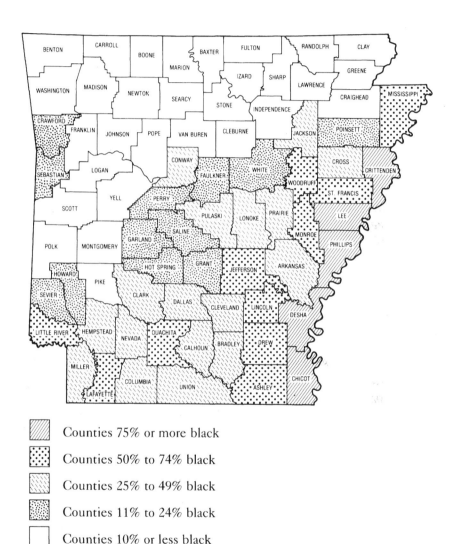

Counties 75% or more black

Counties 50% to 74% black

Counties 25% to 49% black

Counties 11% to 24% black

Counties 10% or less black

SOURCE: *Twelfth Census of the United States . . . 1900 . . . Population, Part I* (Washington, D.C., 1901), 530.

toward Atlanta, Ga. Our route lay through Birmingham and Memphis, and at each change of trains there seemed to be some representative of the scheme to see us properly forwarded, like so much freight billed for we knew not where. It was midwinter, but with all the unquestioning faith and good cheer of our race we expected to land at the other end of our journey in bright sunshine and spring weather.

And a comical-looking lot we must have been. We had no traveling cases, but each one bore some curious burden—sacks of clothes, quilts, bags, bundles, and baskets. When we left our home the weather was comparatively mild, but as fate would have it, the nearer we got to Arkansas, the colder it became. In Memphis the snow was deep and the wind biting. The faith and enthusiasm of the party grew less; perhaps the older heads were waking up to a suspicion. The further we got from our South Carolina home, the dearer it seemed, as is true of most things in their first abandonment.[87]

Reaching a small station in Arkansas, Pickens' family was met by two double-team wagons of the unknown planter to whom they were consigned. They were "hauled many miles through cyprus 'brakes' and snow and ice sufficiently thick to support the teams." "The older people," Pickens supposed, "had by this time comprehended the situation, but we children were constantly peering out from under our quilts and coverings, trying to discover a cocoanut or an orange blossom, while the drivers swore at the mules for slipping on the solid ice."[88]

At last arriving at their destination, the family was "stored away, bags, bundles, boxes and all . . . in a one-room hut to await the breaking of winter and the beginning of field work."[89] They were already deeply in debt, for they owed for their transportation, though just what that amount was no one knew. Moreover, during the first weeks of enforced idleness they had to draw on the planter for supplies of salt meat, cornmeal, and molasses. With the beginning of the cotton season these rations were augmented with a little better food, including sugar, coffee, and flour.

For the first year the children were kept home from school in hope of working off the sums owed the landlord. The smallest of the children helped hoe and pick cotton, and Pickens recollected having seen his older sisters drive a plow. The family's combined efforts, however, produced no remuneration, only bitter disappointment:

When the first year's settlement came around, and a half hundred bales of cotton had been produced by the family and sold by the planter, Father came home with sad, far-away eyes, having been told that we were deeper in debt than on the day of our arrival. And who could deny it? The white man did all the reckoning. The Negro did all the work. The Negro can be robbed of everything but his humor, and in the bottom lands of Arkansas he has made a rhyme. He says that on settlement day the landowner sits down, takes up his pen and reckons thus:

A nought's a nought, and a figger's a figger—
All fer de white man—none fer de nigger.[90]

During the second year Pickens and his brothers and sisters were allowed to attend the short midsummer and midwinter sessions of the plantation school. The school "was dominated by the interests of the planter; when the children were needed in the fields he simply commanded the school to close."[91] In spite of its deficiencies and the rudimentary instruction offered, the school was the one place in the plantation world where Pickens was able to develop pride in his own talents. He especially enjoyed the old-fashioned spelling classes. The assembled students stood in line and advanced toward the "head" or "foot" of the line according to their ability to spell. When a student missed a word, he was "turned down," and the first scholar to give the word correctly took his place in front of all those who had misspelled it in succession. If a student was absent from class, he automatically had to "go foot," regardless of his previous position in the line. Pickens had a bright sister who usually stood head, while he stood second. They impishly enjoyed staying home a day "for the exquisite pleasure of going foot and turning the whole class down."[92]

Pickens also looked forward to the visits of "An aged Negro, a characteristic Uncle Remus, [who] would come some nights and relate . . . quaint animal stories. The antics and cleverness of 'Bre'r Rabbit, Bre'r Bar, Bre'r Fox, Sis' Cow and Bre'r Tommy Mud Turtle," he recalled, "did much to enliven the dullness of the hours."[93]

Such pleasant experiences, however, were overshadowed by the family's persisting troubles. To minimize expenses during the second winter, Pickens' mother cooked and washed, while his father felled trees in the icy "brakes" to make rails and boards. No provisions were drawn from the planter, although "The old debt remained . . . and perhaps took advantage of this quiet period to grow usuriously."[94] Moreover, in the spring some of the family members came down with malarial chills and fevers. The medicine and physician "had to be secured on the feudal plan, the planter paying the bills."[95] Pickens remembered that under this system the physician had every temptation to neglect his patients. His pay was assured, and there was no competition. The family's suffering was acute: they had come "from an elevated, healthy country," and their constitutions "fell easy prey to the germs of the lowlands."[96]

With the gradual return of good health and the coming of the new cotton season

> the whole family plunged into work, and made a bigger and better crop. But at reckoning time history repeated itself; there was still enough debt to continue the slavery. If the debt could not be paid in fat years, there was the constant danger that lean years would come and make it bigger. But there was the contract—and the law; and the law would not hunt the equity, but would enforce the letter of the contract. It was understood that the Negro was unreliable, and the courts must help the poor planters.[97]

It was finally decided that "There was but one recourse—the way of escape." Pickens' father managed to have himself excused on some pretext for a brief trip to Little Rock. On the outskirts of the city, he found a landowner willing to advance money for railroad fares and rent a small farm. This might have seemed no improvement, but as Pickens noted, "a rented farm with a definite loan" was "a different proposition from a state of debt-slavery, where the creditor sells all the produce and does all the counting."[98]

One night shortly after his father's return, Pickens' family fled the plantation under cover of dark, like runaway bondsmen in antebellum times. The children and some goods were piled in a wagon, with the adults walking afoot. They traveled some twelve to fifteen miles through the night, reaching the nearby town of Augusta. There, early the next morning, the family caught the first train to Little Rock, and freedom.

# VI

# The Promise
of the City

Crossing the Arkansas River in a ferry-
boat, in May, 1871, I arrived in Little
Rock a stranger to every inhabitant. It
was on a Sunday morning. The air refreshing, the sun not yet fervent, a
cloudless sky canopied the city; the
carol of the canary and mocking bird
from treetop and cage was all that entered a peaceful, restful quiet that
bespoke a well-governed city. The
chiming church bells that soon after
summoned worshipers seemed to bid
me welcome.
—Mifflin W. Gibbs, *Shadow
and Light*

[Little Rock] has the settled, temperate, orderly society of an Eastern town,
but [is] democratic in its habits, and
with a cordial hospitality which is more
provincial than fashionable. . . . The
street cars and railways make no discrimination as to color of passenger.
Everywhere I went I noticed that the
intercourse between the two races was
friendly.
—Charles Dudley Warner, *Harper's
New Monthly Magazine*, September
1888

That William Pickens' father elected to remove his family to the
vicinity of Little Rock was probably no accident. Throughout the

latter half of the nineteenth century, the American South remained a depressed agricultural land, crushed first by the ruin of the Confederacy, and then later, in the 1880s and 1890s, by tumbling prices for cotton and other farm commodities. For most people, living was synonymous with poverty and grim endurance, with "getting by"; at least in economic terms, few men could reasonably expect to prevail but could only hope to survive.

Within this bleak world of thwarted aspirations and gloomy prospects, the newly developing cities and towns seemed to lighten a path toward individual advancement and possible success. Often, modern historians of the New South have minimized the importance of Southern commercial and industrial progress during the immediate post–Civil War decades and have sometimes denigrated or ignored entirely the concomitant phenomenon of Southern urbanization during the era. For example, writing in the *Origins of the New South*, C. Vann Woodward noted that the South's relative position in the national economy vis-à-vis manufacturing remained virtually static between 1860 and 1904; in 1860, he observed, the South had 17.2 percent of the manufacturing establishments of the country and 11.5 percent of the capital. By 1904 these figures were 15.3 percent and 11 percent respectively.[1] Moreover, such development as did occur was frequently in extractive industries or in primary manufacturing, areas of activity characterized by low wages and use of unskilled labor. (Concerning urbanization, Woodward, despite some references in the body of his text, did not regard the subject as important enough to warrant treatment in a separate chapter; indeed, the words "urbanization," "cities," and "towns" are not listed in the index of his book,[2] a striking omission when one reflects upon its title.)

Somewhat later, Paul M. Gaston of the University of Virginia treated the early effort at achieving Southern industrialization more sympathetically, stressing how the dream of an industrialized, urbanized "New South" helped sustain Southern morale after the South's defeat in the Civil War. Yet Gaston too, like Woodward before him, ultimately underscored the gap which remained between promise and performance, rhetoric and reality.[3]

While this emphasis has its obvious validity, it has an equally obvious danger: in stressing what was not achieved, it is easy to overlook what was. Undoubtedly, in their eagerness to attract outside investment the New South boosters and Redeemer politicians surrendered far too much. Their sins were legion: a cavalier attitude toward protection of the South's treasured resources, an insensitivity about numerous social neglects, acceptance of low-wage policies which ultimately retarded Southern economic growth, and acquiescence in neo-colonialist policies of both the federal government and some Northern corporations which, arguably, may possibly have inhibited the South's development. To a degree, however, this nearsightedness may only have been a measure of the Southern leaders', and the South's, desperation. What minuscule industrial base the South possessed in 1860 was practically demolished during the Civil War. Moreover, the enormous capital investment in slaveholding was utterly wiped out, and Confederate money and bonds had lost all value. Lacking any extensive foreign aid for rebuilding, the South had to look to herself and to private investment sources from outside the region to secure the badly needed funds for economic reconstruction. These facts make the compliant attitude toward business at least understandable.

It might be added that, even if there had been the disposition, there was at least in the beginning no precedent from nineteenth-century American experience to justify extensive government surveillance of business operations. Jacksonian democracy was the South's outstanding liberal tradition, and it had been largely laissez faire in its economic ideology. Furthermore, while exacerbated by outside exploitation, the worst features of the Southern industrialization effort—the low wages, the long hours and miserable working conditions, the callous disregard for the agricultural classes—have typified many modernizing societies going through the initial painful stages of capital accumulation. Far from being singular, the New South recapitulated a pattern traced by Great Britain and New England and in some respects still being repeated by developing countries today.

The point here is not to give a sweeping apologia but to try and place developments in a broader historical perspective. Despite severe limitations and deficiencies, the promoters of Southern business and industry did accomplish something. By the turn of the century the South, occupying a fixed geographic position, had regained the relative place in national manufacturing that she had possessed on the eve of the Civil War; this occurred during an era which witnessed completion of the "conquering of the Continent," the rapid growth of the Far West, and, in absolute terms, a total nine-fold increase in the product of American factories. In view of the peculiar handicaps the South possessed, this was, as Woodward himself observed, "no inconsiderable achievement."[4]

The most visible sign of the South's economic advance was her steady urban growth. It is true that the South remained the most predominately rural section of the country; by 1900, according to the United States Census, the proportion of the population residing in urban areas numbered only 11.1 percent in the South Central states and only 17 percent in the South Atlantic states.[5] Furthermore, many of the South's urban locales, despite the development of manufacturing, were still primarily regional distribution centers for Northern-based industries and corporations.

Nonetheless, as Gavin Wright's study *Old South, New South: Revolutions in the Southern Economy since the Civil War* has documented, important strides were continually being made.[6] Stimulated especially by a new burst of railway construction, thousands of villages and hamlets had become towns, and some of these latter were already becoming cities. A small but already potent urban bourgeoisie was appearing, and in many places pioneer Southern entrepreneurs had already founded some of their region's leading commercial houses. Profits and savings acquired from a variety of new business enterprises, deposited in local banks or plowed back into local investments, fueled the vital process of capital formation and urban development. Slowly, the rudimentary foundations for the transformation of Southern society and the Southern way of life were being laid. In any long-range view, this was perhaps the most significant historical phenomenon of the period.

Within Arkansas, the city of Little Rock provides the best example of the seminal changes which were occurring. Despite the fact that it was the seat of state government and Arkansas's largest urban grouping, Little Rock in 1860 was scarcely more than a sleepy country village, with a grand total of 3,727 inhabitants. By 1900, the capital's population had jumped tenfold, to 38,307 (by contrast, the state population roughly tripled during these years, from 435,450 to 1,311,564).[7] Although still only a good-sized town, Little Rock had already achieved a ranking as the nation's fourth largest inland cotton market and was handling 124,556 bales of the white staple through its brokers.[8] While the picturesque steamboat was beginning to disappear from the Arkansas River, six new railroad lines fed into Little Rock; during the seasonal year 1899–1900, 43,253 freight cars arrived at the city train depots, and outshipments amounted to 23,977 car loadings.[9] At the same time, 171 industrial establishments regularly employed 2,751 workers and processed or manufactured goods annually valued at a respectable $4,723,188.[10]

Flourishing retail businesses included 29 blacksmith shops, 38 dry-goods firms, 27 hotels, 2 ice houses, 43 restaurants, 170 groceries, and even one health-food store, the Egyptian Anti-Dyspeptic Meal Company. Two institutes offered cures for alcohol and opium addiction and must have enjoyed a brisk trade since Little Rock also supported its own brewery and 62 thriving saloons. There were nineteen music teachers, two cigar rollers, twenty-two dressmakers, and thirty-nine persons who kept boarders in their homes.[11]

Little Rock was expanding rapidly, but not rapidly enough for the ambitious men who had invested in it. The leading merchants of the day—among them Philip Pfeifer, Gus Blass, W. B. Worthen, Henry Rector, Charles Stifft, and M. M. Cohn—had organized a Board of Trade, a forerunner of the present-day Chamber of Commerce.[12] Hoping to attract capital from the Northeast, the board exuberantly advertised the virtues of Little Rock throughout the postwar decades. One of its promotional brochures, issued in 1891, exclaimed:

> How surprised must be the people of the Eastern states when they contemplate the great changes that have taken place within the last 40 years. At that time, Little Rock was a straggling village in the midst of a wilderness peopled by savages, but mark the change. A comfortable residence takes the place of a cabin, hotel supplants the tavern, better stores are built and the surveyor's stakes mark the outline of a city. . . . Now there reaches the ear the sharp clang of a thousand hammers, the thunder of long trains of passenger and freight cars, the scream of the locomotive and all the confused noises of the busy industries of a great city, until today, she stands a magnificent city of 30,000 souls.[13]

Thirty thousand was perhaps not really that magnificent, and any honest appraisal would have admitted that Arkansas's capital retained a pronounced countrified air. It was not unusual to see poultry and livestock in parts of the town, and many families kept their own fruit trees and vegetable gardens. Little Rock in 1891 was only settled to Battery Street on the west, Twentieth Street on the south, and Byrd Street on the east, so numbers of residents were within walking distance of the intersection of Markham and Main streets, the heart of downtown. In 1888 these two thorough-fares had been paved with granite blocks quarried at nearby Fourche Mountain, but most other streets were unimproved dirt—which turned into a thick gumbo after prolonged rains. One exasperated state legislator introduced a bill designating the city's principal roadways "navigable streams."[14] After a week of heavy spring downpours, the *Arkansas Democrat* admonished that muddy streets provided "no excuse for equestrians using the sidewalks."[15]

These primitive conditions dampened the enthusiasm of few Little Rock citizens, for progress was evident and the future appeared encouraging. The city's telephone system continually fascinated visitors from remote backwoods districts. Although several riding stables offered a wide range of horses for rent, public transportation was available in the form of streetcars. The car lines stretched to the very edge of town, and streetcars were so popular that trailers had to be hitched on during rush hours. The street railway company changed from mule-drawn cars to electric trolleys in 1891, just three years after the downtown business district saw its first electric street lamps installed.[16] The street lamps created such a stir that in faraway western Arkansas a large party of sightseers rode to the top of Mount Magazine, in a vain attempt to at least gaze from a distance at the lights of the city.

◆　　◆　　◆

Growing Little Rock seemed to offer a beacon of opportunity and hope for Arkansans of all backgrounds, but especially was this so for many of the state's Negroes. The town's attractiveness for blacks is suggested by the changing census statistics (see table 6). Out of the population of 3,727 in 1860, 853 persons were Negroes, almost all of them slaves; at the next census, however, in 1870, blacks accounted for 5,274 of a total 12,380 residents, an increase of from 23 to 43 percent;[17] while the percentage of black inhabitants varied somewhat after this time, blacks never constituted

## TABLE 6
### BLACK POPULATION OF LITTLE ROCK, ARKANSAS, 1860 TO 1900

| Year | Total Population* | Black Population | Percentage Black |
|------|-------------------|------------------|------------------|
| 1860 | 3,727 | 853 | 22.9% |
| 1870 | 12,380 | 5,274 | 42.6% |
| 1880 | 13,138 | 4,507 | 34.3% |
| 1890 | 25,874 | 9,739 | 37.6% |
| 1900 | 38,307 | 14,694 | 38.4% |

SOURCE: *Population of the United States . . . 1860 . . . Eighth Census* (Washington, D.C., 1864), 19; *Statistics of the Population of the United States of the Tenth Census . . . 1880 . . .* (Washington, D.C., 1883), 416; *Report on Population of the United States at the Eleventh Census: 1890, Part I* (Washington, D.C., 1895), 451; *Twelfth Census of the United States . . . 1900 . . . Population, Part I* (Washington, D.C., 1901), 609.

*Total population includes a very few Chinese and American Indians.

less than a third of the city's population during the remainder of the nineteenth century.

Visiting Little Rock in 1874, journalist Edward King was impressed by the strides its black population had made. "There the negro," wrote King, "has done much to increase one's faith in his capacity for industry and progress." He observed that "a large proportion of the colored people at Little Rock own their homes" and that "two aldermen,—black men and slaves up to the war, but now worth from $5,000 to $10,000 each—are sent up to the Council." Although Democratic Redemption was just around the corner, Negroes still held several important posts in the state government; among the black state officeholders, King found "many gentlemen of education and refinement" who "are graduates of Harvard University, of Oberlin, and of many of the best Western schools." But while Little Rock's black community contained "many noteworthy instances of progress among the negroes," this was "not so common in the back country," where most blacks were impoverished tenants or sharecroppers.[18]

King's observations concerning the discrepancy in conditions between blacks living in town and their fellows in plantation districts merits further examination. Negroes living in Little Rock probably did have a better chance for advancement, and one advantage they enjoyed was the people of the town itself. While certainly no Constantinople, the little Arkansas capital had a surprisingly heterogeneous population after the Civil War. Foreign immigrants streaming into America generally avoided the unprosperous states of the old Confederacy, but a small trickle of newcomers nevertheless made their way southward, frequently locating in the rising urban centers. In Little Rock the United States Census of 1880 showed that 1,446 of 8,611 whites in the town were foreign-born, almost one sixth of the white population.[19] Although the proportion of foreign-born began dwindling after that date, they remained a salient element in the community for years.

Among the many immigrant groups lending color and variety to life in the Arkansas capital were the Irish, who actually arrived before the war; a small colony established itself in Little Rock between 1848 and 1850, and scattered families continued to drift in from the emerald isle after that time.[20] By the latter part of the century, the Irish had pretty well melted into the larger native culture, but they still dominated the hierarchy and priesthood of Arkansas's small Catholic church and were active in their own social club, the Sons of Erin. Perhaps one mark of the degree of their assimilation was the action of the Most Reverend Edward Fitzgerald, bishop of Little Rock, when he attended the First Vatican Council in Rome in 1870; Fitzgerald was one of only two bishops in the world who voted against the Council's promulgation of the dogma of papal infallibility, an action which won him much loud acclaim from Arkansas Protestants. By and large Catholics encountered only minor hostility in Arkansas, in part no doubt because of their limited numbers; many of Little Rock's leading Protestant families enrolled their daughters in Saint Mary's Academy, a girls' finishing school operated by the Sisters of Mercy.

During the years in which the Irish first came, Little Rock also greeted its initial influx of German settlers.[21] These people, some of them refugees from the revolutions of 1848, were reinforced by a larger immigration from the fatherland in the 1870s and 1880s. By 1890 there were 1,465 persons of German, Swiss, or Austrian birth residing in Pulaski County,[22] making the Teutons far and away the largest immigrant group. Although they got along well enough with their neighbors, they tended to stick together, settling in Little Rock's east side near the old Arsenal grounds (later to become MacArthur Park). German Catholics established their own parish, St. Edward's, at 610 East Ninth Street in the area, while German Lutherans erected a church at the corner of Eighth and Rock streets. The Germans supported their own weekly newspaper, the *Arkansas Staats Zeitung;* a *turnverein;* and a veteran's society, the *Deutscher Krieger und Landwehr Verein.* There were also two chapters of the Saint Joseph's Society, a German Catholic service organization, and bands which played both classical music and popular songs and ballads. One Germanic novelty that older residents took to with gusto was the beer garden, several of which soon dotted the city.[23]

Despite their tendency toward clannishness, the Germans lost little time asserting themselves politically, regularly electing numbers of their group to the city council and the school board. Such families as the Reichardts, Geyers, Kraemers, and Reiglers, among others, established themselves as leaders of civic affairs.

Contemporaneous with the coming of the Germans, a small Jewish community made its appearance. A synagogue, Congregation B'Nai Israel, was established in 1870, and a Hebrew Relief Society and Hebrew Ladies Benevolent Association were formed.[24] A number of early Jewish settlers soon became prominent in local business life. Philip Pfeifer, Gus Blass, and M. M. Cohn all founded mercantile concerns which would grow into major department stores in the twentieth century. Another Jewish citizen, Herman Kahn, was instrumental in starting the Bank of Commerce, destined to evolve into one of the city's major financial institutions, the Union National Bank.

Several other groups found their way to the Arkansas capital. Two hundred Polish Catholic families settled in the Marche community, just outside of Little Rock, during 1878–1880. A sprinkling of Bohemians, Slavonians, Italians, Greeks, and Syrians arrived around 1900, and the city even had a tiny handful of American Indians and Chinese among its inhabitants.[25]

Joining the foreign-born was a large advent of newcomers from the Northern states. Most of these Yankees were not "Carpetbaggers" but simply adventurous persons looking for new fields of work and opportunity. A good number of them were Union-army veterans who had served in Arkansas during the Civil War, had grown to like the state and its people, and later decided to return. In 1888 the *Arkansas Gazette* pointed out that over half of Little Rock's population had been born in Northern states.[26] Immigration from above the Mason-Dixon line represented a continuing tradition since even in antebellum days the town had had an important Northern element; in fact, Chester Ashley, one of the principal founders of Little Rock in the 1820s, was a native of Massachusetts, a graduate of Williams College and the Litchfield Law School.[27]

Yankees, blacks, foreigners, and native whites all rubbed elbows in Little Rock, and while everyone's life was probably thus enriched, Negroes particularly benefited from this budding cosmopolitanism. Of course, not all of the arrivals were free from racial prejudice, and, for that matter, the Northerner or foreigner who turned against blacks in hopes of winning quick acceptance from local whites was not unknown.[28] But in some cases the intensity of prejudice and racial feeling may have been less. During his trip through the Southern states, Edward King noted, "the shrewd Hebrew . . . has entered into the commerce of the South in such a manner as almost to exclude Gentile competition." King ascribed the Jewish merchant's success to the fact that "[he] understands the freedman very well, and manages him in trade. The negro likes to be treated with consideration when he visits the 'store,' and he finds something refreshing and friendly in the profuse European manner and enthusiastic lingo of Messrs. Moses and Abraham."[29]

Despite the tinge of anti-Semitism in his remarks, King's observations about a willingness to have dealings with blacks may have been astute; the same lack of inhibition could have applied to other immigrant groups as well. For instance, Little Rock's Republican mayor between 1869 and 1871 was a corpulent 250-pound German, A. K. Hartman. Nicknamed "Count Bismarck" by the Democratic press, he had few compunctions about attempting a voting alliance between the city's Germans and its blacks.[30]

Personal ties were at least as important as partisan ones. Isaac T. Gillam, Jr., a Negro teacher and principal in the Little Rock schools in the late nineteenth and early twentieth centuries, lived for a time next to a German immigrant family. As an alumnus of Howard University who had done postgraduate work at Yale, Gillam was fluent in German and often conversed in that language with his neighbors. The families became good friends, visiting and exchanging books from each others' private libraries.[31]

Such instances of camaraderie were possibly rare. However, even if it is conceded that foreign immigrants and Northerners differed little from other whites in their racial attitudes, the mere presence and commingling of peoples of diverse origins and background must have fostered a modicum of "urbanity" and tolerance for difference. Negroes could not help but benefit from such a broadened perspective.

If blacks gained from Little Rock's less homogeneous population, their interests were likewise promoted by its distinctive political complexion. Arkansas was the most solidly Democratic state in the solid South; even in antebellum days it had proved unwaveringly loyal to the party of Jefferson and Jackson. From 1836, when Arkansas was admitted to the Union, through 1860, Democratic candidates had swept the state in every presidential election; every prewar governor was a Democrat, as were all members of the state congressional delegation, save for one Whig congressman in 1847.[32] The reasons for the state's Democratic affinities are not hard to discern. Once they had obtained their land, what many of the yeoman farmers of Arkansas desired most of their government was to be left alone. The Whig party of Henry Clay, with its nationalistic program of federal aid for internal improvements, high tariffs, and high taxes, won few disciples. Some planters in lowland districts, having economic and social ties with urban commercial elites and desirous of obtaining federal assistance in levee construction, were attracted to the Whig banner; nevertheless, many of the large slaveholders were as leery as the yeomen of intrusive federal power.

Little Rock's merchants, however, appraised their interests differently. Eager to open up new markets and bridge connections to Eastern states, they responded enthusiastically to the Whig promises of federal money for improved roads and railways. In almost every antebellum election, Little Rock stood valiantly as an island of Whiggery in a Democratic sea.[33] The turmoil of Reconstruction drove the majority of ex-Whig businessmen into the arms of the Democracy, but for many it was an unhappy marriage; the painted temptress, Republicanism, exuded a seductive charm.[34] As Little Rock historian Ira Don Richards put it, "These ex-Whigs, the dominant political faction in antebellum Little Rock, felt right at home in the party of Lincoln, Grant, and Hayes, a party that had endorsed and enacted into law Clay's old American system in a way the Kentucky statesman had never been able to do";[35] furthermore, they were "unimpressed by the white supremacy theme of the southern Democracy, especially should it conflict with economic interests."[36] Combining with other Republican elements, some of the former Whigs helped see Little Rock go for Hayes over Tilden in the presidential election of 1876, and for Garfield instead of Hancock four years later.[37] Until state-passed disfranchisement laws took effect in 1892, Republicans always had the margin of victory in every one of Little Rock's subsequent national elections.[38]

A number of Whig converts were only "presidential" Republicans, for Democrats gained control of the city administration in 1875. Once in power, they immediately increased the ward districts from four to six, squeezing as many blacks as possible into one ward in hopes of reducing their representation on the town council.[39] Party lines were fluid, however, and the Democrats' hegemony was tenuous; individual Republicans and third-party men could usually be found serving as aldermen. In 1887 an ostensibly "nonpartisan" ticket, with businessman William G. Whipple as its candidate for mayor, won control of city hall; Arkansas Republicans later ran Whipple as their gubernatorial standard-bearer in 1892.[40]

Unlike much of Arkansas, Little Rock maintained something approaching a viable two-party system, and the measure of party competition worked to the advantage of blacks. Republican business leaders naturally defended the suffrage rights of their black allies, hotly denouncing ballot-box outrages.[41] Periodic election irregularities did not prevent Negroes from remaining a force in local politics; from 1869 through the seventies and eighties, they always had at least one or two of their race on the city council.

Longest to serve was Green W. Thompson, who had a grocery store at 523 Center Street. First elected in 1877, Thompson held his position sixteen years, until his defeat as the city's last nineteenth-century black councilman in 1893.[42]

Negro voting power produced not only a representative voice in city decision making but also patronage rewards. Even Democratic administrations, anxious to siphon off Negro support, kept blacks on the police force and appointed them to minor positions in the city government.[43]

Political participation likewise worked to assure educational advantages for Little Rock's blacks. Just as on the city council, Negroes could regularly be found on the school board until disfranchisement took effect in 1893;[44] in addition, a black usually was appointed to the "Board of Visitors," which made an annual inspection of the capital's pedagogical institutions.[45]

To a degree, such input helped deflect the considerable opposition to Negro schooling which existed. Whites in Little Rock had originally refused to appropriate any monies for black education, and it had been introduced only after the advent of radical Reconstruction.[46] Despite growing evidence to the contrary, some persons stubbornly insisted that blacks were inherently ineducable.[47] For that matter, the whole concept of public education was suspiciously viewed by many as an alien Yankee importation, and only slowly did it gain in general respectability and acceptance; some of the well-to-do, particularly, saw the public schools as "charitable" enterprises and continued to enroll their own progeny in private academies—though this attitude waned as the years went by.[48]

Public apathy, racial prejudice, and limited tax sources were all evidenced in the statistics compiled for the *Annual Reports* of the school board. Total expenditures per enrolled pupil for 1879–80 were $11.32, with teachers and supervisors receiving an average annual salary of $587. School authorities failed to give comparative figures on expenditures per white and per black student or for white and black teachers' salaries; however, there were eighty students per teacher in white classrooms and eighty-two per teacher in black classrooms.[49] Teachers' salaries appear to have been based on competitive examinations, with all holders of "first-grade" licenses, and so forth, receiving the same fixed salary.[50] By 1892–93 the overall situation had improved, but only slightly, and chiefly for whites. Expenditures per enrolled pupil had increased to $14.80 and average annual teachers' salaries to $615.[51] The pupil-teacher ratio had dropped to sixty-seven per classroom in white schools but risen to eighty-seven per classroom in black ones.[52]

Overcrowded conditions and lack of a state compulsory attendance law (not adopted until 1909) encouraged a phenomenal drop-out rate for both races. As late as 1895–96, only 52 percent of white children and 45 percent of black children of school age were enrolled in classes at all; of those attending, 56 percent of the white and 70 percent of the black students were in the primary department, consisting of the first four grades. By contrast, the high-school departments, comprising grades ten through twelve, accounted for 5 percent of white and 4 percent of black enrollment.[53]

Lamentable as the situation was, conditions in Little Rock schools looked good when measured against the rest of the state. City voters regularly approved the maximum five-mill district tax levy allowed by Arkansas's 1874 constitution.[54] From early Reconstruction days onward, capital-city schools offered a full nine-month term, while as late as the 1890s most rural schools operated for less than three months.[55] The average state expenditure per enrolled pupil in 1891–92 was $4.80, two-thirds less than the figure for Little Rock.[56] Few one-room country schoolhouses aspired to teach more than the basic "three R's," but Little Rock opened a high-school department for whites in 1870 and for blacks in 1873.[57] Each offered courses in English, Latin, French, German, drawing, vocal music, bookkeeping, the natural sciences, and higher mathematics.

As a member of the Board of Visitors, William G. Whipple observed Union High School for Negroes in 1880 and came away impressed. He gave the black physics scholars a two-hour impromptu examination over electricity and magnetism, reporting "[they] acquitted themselves well and creditably. . . . Scarcely a question was missed . . . Most of the class seems to have a clear understanding of the reasons and principles of the subject which to the majority of minds is quite abstruse and difficult of comprehension." He concluded, "No class, colored or white, could have done much, if any better."[58]

Unusually ambitious students who completed the high-school

program could enroll in one of the capital's three private Negro colleges. The Freedmen's Aid Society of the Methodist Episcopal Church [North] began one of these in 1877. Originally known as Walden Seminary, the school was renamed Philander Smith College in 1883, after a native of Oak Park, Illinois, whose widow gave $10,500 for construction of the first building. The John F. Slater fund also contributed to the school, as did local whites, who provided needy students with room and board in their homes, and sometimes tuition, in exchange for light house and office work. By 1910, over seven thousand Negroes had received instruction at Philander Smith.[59]

Black religious denominations founded the other two colleges. Negro Baptists organized Arkansas Baptist College in Little Rock, beginning in 1884; however, the school did not really get on its feet until 1887, when a persevering young black educator, Joseph A. Booker, became president. Booker presided over the institution until the mid-1920s and was largely responsible for its survival and growth. White Baptists and local and Northern philanthropists gave some assistance, but the college was "built almost entirely by the colored people . . . with the small pittance which they saved from the wash tub, cotton field and cook kitchen."[60] Black Methodists of the African Methodist Episcopal Church likewise financed their own school; originally begun in 1886 as Bethel University, the school was renamed Shorter University in 1892, in honor of A.M.E. bishop James A. Shorter. The school removed briefly to Arkadelphia in 1891 but relocated in North Little Rock in 1897.[61]

All of the Negro colleges offered the standard liberal-arts curriculum and a number of vocational and home-economics courses. As did many contemporary institutions, they also conducted a "Preparatory Department," really a high-school program; this latter was especially directed toward the needs of those students from rural areas who had been denied the benefits of secondary-level instruction.

Aside from the possibility of a good education, Little Rock's schools and colleges gave blacks another decided advantage—employment. Philander Smith College received its first black president, the Reverend James M. Cox, in 1897, and Arkansas Baptist College and Shorter University had always had black administrators; all three colleges included black faculty. In the public schools use of black principals and teachers steadily increased. The superintendent's report of 1877 noted, "There is a growing desire on the part of the colored people to have their schools supplied with teachers from their own race. With this desire we are in hearty accord, and we hope the day is not far distant when a sufficient number of well-educated efficient colored teachers can be found."[62] During the 1880s and early 1890s, white teachers in Negro schools were transferred to white institutions, and new openings in the former were filled with Negro applicants. This policy had the effect of further separating the races, but it undeniably gave educated blacks desperately needed professional employment; moreover, since Negroes were not permitted to teach in white schools, the policy could be justified in terms of equity.

Some of the pioneer black teachers were at first poorly prepared for their work, but almost all were dedicated and hard-working and gained competence with experience.[63] Little Rock's first Negro teacher, Mrs. John Herbert (Charlotte) Stephens, served in the city schools for seventy years, from 1869 to 1939; a former slave of the Chester Ashley family and an Oberlin graduate, Mrs. Stephens improved the minds of generations of black children and won the affection and respect of black and white alike. She lived long enough to witness the dedication of the city's Stephens School, named in her honor, on October 8, 1950.[64]

Negro education was also promoted by the concern manifested by white administrators. J. R. Rightsell, the city school superintendent during most of the late nineteenth century, was remembered by Negroes for his sincere interest in black teachers and pupils.[65] Rightsell and Board of Education president Frederick Kraemer constantly appealed for increased appropriations to reduce classroom loads in their *Annual Reports*.[66] For the highly motivated black student, Little Rock schools offered at least the chance of personal betterment and success. John K. Rector, one of four members in the Negro high school's 1879 graduating class, went to Lincoln University in Pennsylvania, Harvard, and Yale, and returned to become a principal of Little Rock's Bush Elementary School.[67] Another graduate of the same class, Miss Susan Patillo, married an A.M.E. clergyman and faculty member of Wilberforce University.[68] Possibly the most distinguished graduate in subsequent years was William Grant Still, a graduate of M. W. Gibbs High School in 1911; Still became a nationally known composer and a conductor of the Los Angeles Symphony Orchestra.[69] William Pickens, a member of the high-school class of 1899, attended Yale, where he received a Phi Beta Kappa key and won the Ten Eyck Prize for Oratory. Pickens afterward became a college professor and a staff officer of the NAACP.[70]

These persons would have been exceptional in any race, and naturally not all Negroes were so academically inclined. For the less bookish, Little Rock offered ample social diversions. A simple age, conversation provided a chief source of entertainment, and there was much home visiting back and forth. Quilting parties, a legacy from frontier days, were occasionally enjoyed by the women. When a prized quilt was almost ready to be taken from the frame, friends were invited in to help finish it and to celebrate the completion with a party. Husbands of the women would arrive at supper time "and everyone would sit down to a tremendous meal: a large baked chicken at one end of the table, a little pig at the other; half a ham in the center, with biscuits, three kinds of cornbread, all sorts of vegetables, cakes and pies."[71]

Community activities included church socials and "cakewalks," chautauqua functions, bands, baseball clubs, drill teams, cycling societies, Ex-Slaves Association meetings, and Emancipation Day celebrations.[72] One of the most popular was the *Maifest*.[73] Introduced during Reconstruction by a German schoolmaster, the festivity was taken over by a Union Board of Negro religious groups. An annual "Queen of the May" was chosen and crowned with a wreath beneath an arch of roses. Older black residents remembered it as "a lovely joyous day of games and laughter, food and relaxation."[74]

Fraternal societies were as well liked by blacks as by whites. The city directory of 1900–01 listed forty-three separate black lodges in town, and this total appears to have been an under-enumeration.[75] One worldwide fraternal order had its origins in Little Rock. In 1882 a young black, John E. Bush, was standing on a city street corner conversing with a prominent white. An aged Negro woman approached and asked that they give her something to assist in burying her dead husband. Both men contributed, but the white remarked, "I cannot see or understand your race. When they work they throw their earnings away and whenever a Negro dies or needs help the public must be worried to death by Negro beggars—it is a shame!" Stung by the comment, Bush and a fellow employee in the United States Postal Service, Chester W. Keatts, proceeded to found the Mosaic Templars of America. By 1913 the order operated a burial and insurance program, a building and loan association, a hospital at Hot Springs, and owned a two-hundred-thousand-dollar headquarters building at Ninth and Broadway streets in Little Rock; there were eighty thousand dues-paying members in twenty-six states, Central and South America, the Canal Zone, and the West Indies.[76]

As the history of the Mosaic Templars suggests, fraternal societies did more than provide social outlets; in the absence of workmen's compensation, Social Security, unemployment benefits, or other amenities of the welfare state, they aided blacks in surmounting perennial exigencies and troubles.

For the less straitlaced, the Arkansas capital offered entertainments other than church gatherings and lodge meetings. The city race track on the far east side of town attracted throngs of black and white devotees. Bawdy houses, called *maisons de joie* by the more worldly, could be found near the riverfront east of Main Street.[77] A number of white patrons preferred the services of light-skinned mulatto women, locally known as "Creoles." In some years prostitutes were required to wear their hair short, as in ancient Greece, and were only permitted to shop in the downtown business district one afternoon a week—a day when married women remained grimly shuttered in their parlors.[78] At night, however, the street walkers roamed the city at will; Mount Holly cemetery was a favorite assignation spot.[79]

Little Rock also had a drug problem since cocaine use had entered the country through the Gulf ports and made its way up the rivers to Arkansas.[80] Saloons, gambling houses, and dives of every sort and description luxuriated in rank profusion. The *Arkansas Gazette* complained in 1888 that "notorious gambling-lottery concerns are kept openly in several parts of the city where the young, the unsophisticated and the unwary are entrapped and fleeced. Poor and ignorant negroes squander daily the hard earning that should go to the support of their families."[81] Some of these resorts, such as the Congo House on East Markham Street, were exclusively for Negroes; in others, however, the color line dissolved amidst carefree abandon. In 1891, a newspaper reporter gave readers a tantalizing view of one of these latter, located just across the Arkansas River in North Little Rock (then called Argenta). "It consists," he wrote, "of a store building composed of a bar and lunch counter in the front room, a billiard hall and a dance hall in the rear, in which at one end is a raised platform or stage, where the most obscene and revolting orgies are enacted. In the same lot are several cabins occupied by the lowest type of women who have given up their lives to prostitution. Here white and black mingle together, and it is here that toughs and criminals of all classes make their rendezvous."[82]

Barroom brawls and Saturday-night knife fights were the least savory aspect of black life in Little Rock. However destructive and self-defeating, these activities served as a poor-man's therapy, a chance to "let off steam," release tensions, and forget hardships. And for many blacks, living was hard enough. A majority of the town's Negroes, refugees from the plantations, had limited educations and few advanced skills. Toiling as day laborers, porters, and domestic servants, they earned bare subsistence incomes. The tax returns for Pulaski County in 1896, although they also included country precincts, still clearly establish that most Little Rock blacks, like their rural counterparts, lived in poverty. Ten years later, the tax returns for 1906 revealed only limited improvement (see table 7).

However, even the poorest urban black received cash wages instead of working for shares, with the planter keeping all books and financial records. If an employer proved too irascible or difficult, the black man could quit and go searching for another job without threat of fine or peonage. Not many blacks could realistically expect any dramatic improvement of their lot, but there was always hope for the children. William Pickens recounted that his family's "move cityward was not prompted, as is usually charged in such cases, by any desire to get away from work, but by the high motives of education and the future."[83] Pickens' mother "died of overwork and consequent broken health. She had been determined to keep her children in school and had worked from early morning till late at night to that end." He "seldom waked early enough to catch a glimpse of her" and before her return at night

## TABLE 7
### *TOTAL TAXES COLLECTED FROM BLACKS, EXCLUDING POLL TAXES, IN PULASKI COUNTY, ARKANSAS, 1896 AND 1906*

| Year 1896 | Percentage Black Population (1890) | Percentage Taxes Paid by Blacks | Total Taxes Paid, Blacks | Total Taxes Paid, Whites |
|---|---|---|---|---|
| | 46.4 | 2.4 | $6,609.99 | $275,309.40 |

| Year 1906 | Percentage Black Population (1900) | Percentage Taxes Paid by Blacks | Total Taxes Paid, Blacks | Total Taxes Paid, Whites |
|---|---|---|---|---|
| | 46.1 | 3.3 | $19,218.51 | $576,050.85 |

SOURCES: *Arkansas Biennial Report of the Auditor of State, 1897–1898* (Little Rock, 1898), 226; ibid., *1907–1908* (Little Rock, 1909), 420. U.S. Census Office, *Twelfth Census*, 1900, I, *Population*, 530. Totals include both real- and personal-property taxes collected.


## TABLE 8
### *AVERAGE TAX PAID PER CAPITA BY BLACKS AND WHITES, EXCLUDING POLL TAXES, IN PULASKI COUNTY, ARKANSAS, 1896 AND 1906*

| Year | Blacks | Whites |
|---|---|---|
| 1896 | $0.30 | $10.87 |
| 1906 | $0.66 | $16.92 |

SOURCES: Derived from *Arkansas Biennial Report of the Auditor of State, 1897–1898* (Little Rock, 1898), 226; ibid., *1907–1908* (Little Rock, 1909), 420; U.S. Census Office, *Twelfth Census, 1900*, I, *Population*, Pt. 1, 530.

"sleep had weighed down" his eyelids.[84] Pickens himself earned money for his books and school supplies at an assortment of odd jobs: building fires and running errands at a local hotel, working at a sawmill and stave factory, and, later, laboring on a construction gang for the Choctaw railroad. Progress wiped out his favorite job, that of oarsman for a skiff ferry operating across the Arkansas River; in 1897 the public-spirited citizens of Little Rock constructed a free bridge across the river, and "the famous old ferry that had existed from the foundation of the city was then to die. The passing of the old ferry," he remembered, "seemed the passing of a friend. I had usually carried a book on my oarsman's seat so that I could read or study while waiting for passengers; and as I rowed to and fro I had conjugated Latin verbs to the stroke of the oars."[85]

Many Negroes spent their entire lives doing the type of work which engaged Pickens during his boyhood.[86] A minority, however, managed to attain a measure of financial security and success; by the latter part of the century, a nascent class of skilled artisans, craftsmen, and small businessmen had emerged. A survey of Little Rock's black community made in 1898 listed eight Negro-owned wood and coal yards, ten blacksmith firms, twenty-nine barber shops, a cigar and tobacco stand, two hotels, nine restaurants, two jewelry stores, three tailor shops, four newspapers, a drug store, and a mortuary; there were fifteen cobblers, fifteen dressmakers, two upholsterers, and two confectioners. Some Negroes had won entrance into the professions; the same survey named fifty-five teachers and educators, thirty-eight ministers, six lawyers, five physicians, and one dentist.[87]

A few Little Rock Negroes had acquired considerable wealth. Asa L. Richmond, a Negro contractor, was mentioned in 1889 as owning thirty-three houses in the capital which brought him two hundred dollars per month rent.[88] Calvin Sanders, a city alderman from 1868 to 1870, owned a farm on the outskirts of town and a city block on which he erected ten houses.[89] William LaPorte, another prosperous black, was a former runaway slave who had lived in Canada, traveled throughout Europe, and served in the famous Fifty-fourth Massachusetts Regiment during the Civil War. In 1865 he settled in Little Rock and entered the plasterer's trade; "by hard work and close economy" he amassed twenty thousand dollars wealth, owning nine houses.[90]

Isaac T. Gillam, Sr., was a veteran of the Second Arkansas Regiment. Family tradition relates that he got his start in life after the war by purchasing a wounded cavalry horse which recovered and won several races. Gillam served as a Little Rock city councilman during the 1870s and was elected a state representative on the Greenback party ticket in 1879; in 1882 Democrats nominated and elected him Pulaski County coroner. A successful blacksmith and property owner, he was able to see his son, mentioned earlier, enter Howard University and Yale. His oldest daughter, Cora Alice, was one of the earliest graduates of Shorter College and later became a faculty member of that institution. Later, in the twentieth century, Little Rock's Gillam Park would be named in his honor, and Little Rock's Gillam School would be named in honor of his son Isaac T. Gillam, Jr., who became principal of the city's M. W. Gibbs High School for blacks.[91]

James E. Rector served on the Little Rock school board and was for fourteen years United States Superintendent of Mints; his son, John K. Rector, also mentioned previously, attended Lincoln University.[92] Among other well-to-do blacks were Soloman Winfrey, a contractor, brick mason, and property owner;[93] Albert Desha, a justice of the peace and landowner;[94] and George E. Jones, a grocer, realtor, and undertaker. Jones possessed enough capital to build a three-story brick office building, occupying half a block, at the corner of Ninth and Gaines streets; in addition, he owned sixty rental houses in Little Rock. Active in the Knights of Pythias and a pillar of Allison Presbyterian Church, his estate was estimated as "being worth easily $50,000" at the time of his death in 1902.[95]

Among distinguished Negro professional men was Dr. J. H. Smith, a dentist who left Illinois and came to Little Rock after the great Chicago fire of 1871; a biographical account published in 1898 noted, "This popular dentist whose office is at 701 Main St., is one of the most successful practicians in the city, and is the only colored man of that profession in the capital. Notwithstanding the sharp competition by reason of the many proficient white dentists, he has a large and lucrative practice among the wealthy white class." Smith's success, the writer believed, "destroys the old and foolish saying that if a man is a Negro he is not respected by the wealthier class of citizens. In him is clearly demonstrated that if you have what the wealthy or any other class of citizens want and do what they want done you will be respected by them and have their patronage." Dr. Smith, the writer concluded, was "a true example of manhood and a most satisfying exponent of racial possibilities."[96]

Little Rock's veteran Negro lawyer was Thomas P. Johnson, who first hung up his shingle in 1870.[97] The leading attorney in latter years was Scipio A. Jones, who was admitted to the bar in 1889 and licensed to practice before the Supreme Court of the United States in 1905. Jones served as counsel for the Mosaic Templars and other fraternal orders and led a successful suit to improve conditions for prisoners at the Pulaski County penal farm.[98] Of the many educators, one of the most respected was J. Talbot Bailey, a graduate of Atlanta and Howard universities. Bailey taught as a professor at Philander Smith College during the 1880s and also was president of Shorter University for the year 1886–87. Something of a Renaissance man, he also found time to edit two newspapers, the *Arkansas Herald-Mansion* and the Little Rock *Sun*, as well as read law and enter practice before the United States Supreme Court.[99]

While all of the above men left their mark on the world, by far the most prominent black leader in the Arkansas capital was a remarkable Victorian soldier of fortune named Mifflin Wistar Gibbs. Born a free Negro in Philadelphia in 1828, Gibbs as a youth had volunteered for action in the antislavery cause and the underground railroad, making the acquaintance of Frederick Douglass and Charles Lenox Remond and helping usher to freedom such celebrated escapees from bondage as William Box Brown. In 1850, young Gibbs left the East to join the frantic California gold rush; realizing that there was more than one way to gather wealth, he began importing fine shoes and boots—then commanding gilt-edged prices—into San Francisco. He was soon a rich man and able to assist in founding *The Mirror of the Times*, California's first black newspaper. In 1858 gold strikes on the Frazier River in British Columbia lured Gibbs northward, where he again repeated his mercantile triumphs. He won a coveted contract for building a railroad into the anthracite coal fields on Queen Charlotte Island, which, despite trouble from hostile Indians, he completed within the specified period. Settling on Vancouver Island, Gibbs constructed "one of the most beautiful villas in Victoria," later sold to the attorney general of the colony for use as his private residence. He was elected to the Victoria council from "the most aristocratic ward" in the city. Financially secure enough to withdraw from active business operations, Gibbs was able to live comfortably off the income from his investments.[100]

At this point many persons might have rested on their laurels, but Gibbs was excited by the new possibilities for blacks in the United States after the Civil War. Returning to America, he entered law school at Oberlin, Ohio, being graduated in 1870. At a convention of colored men in Charleston, South Carolina, he made the acquaintance of William H. Grey and other Arkansas blacks, who persuaded him that their state was fertile ground for a man of his talents. In 1871 Gibbs moved to Little Rock, where he gained instant recognition. He was appointed county attorney of Pulaski County and elected municipal judge of Little Rock in 1873. His fair and impartial conduct of the latter office won him confessed admiration from white Democratic antagonists and the life-long appellation of "Judge Gibbs."[101]

His political star in the ascendant, Gibbs became the chief black lieutenant of state Republican leader Powell Clayton. He was chosen a Republican candidate for presidential elector in 1876 and the following year was appointed federal land registrar in Little Rock. He held the post until 1889, when he was promoted to United States Receiver of Public Monies; in addition, Gibbs filled the important post of secretary of the Republican state central committee from 1887 to 1897 and was an Arkansas delegate to the Republican national conventions in 1880, 1884, 1892, and 1896. He achieved the capstone of his career in 1897 when the efforts of Powell Clayton and the Arkansas organization secured him the United States consulship to Tamatave, Madagascar. Old age was beginning to take its toll, however, for Gibbs decided to step down from his diplomatic duties in 1901. He returned to Little Rock, publishing the next year his memoirs, *Shadow and Light*, a sprightly and interesting account of his life and times.[102]

After Gibbs left for Africa in 1897, his position as Arkansas's preeminent black Republican was taken by another Little Rock resident, Mosaic Templar leader John E. Bush. Born in Tennessee in 1856, Bush and his mother had been carried to Arkansas during the Civil War as their master's family fled before advancing Union armies. Left an orphan at the age of seven, he "became a drifter, eating and sleeping wherever he could" and gaining a reputation as a troublemaker.[103] When forced to enroll in school, though, he became a conscientious student, even taking a job as a brick moulder to earn money for his education. An honor graduate of the Little Rock high-school class of 1876, after commencement he worked for three years as a school principal in Little Rock and Hot Springs and then entered the railway mail service. Bush's marriage to Cora Winfrey, daughter of wealthy contractor Soloman Winfrey, and his leadership in the Mosaic Templars opened the way for political advancement. He represented Little Rock's sixth ward at the Republican state convention in 1883, and the next year he was selected as secretary of the Republican state conclave. Pulaski County Republicans elected him temporary chairman of their convention in 1892; also in that year he and two other blacks, Mifflin W. Gibbs and William LaPorte, were Arkansas delegates to the Republican national convention. In 1894 Bush was listed as secretary of the Pulaski County Republican organization.

Bush in part was politically successful because of his close association with white Republican chieftain Powell Clayton, who remained after Reconstruction the dominant figure in Arkansas Republican affairs. Bush, along with Mifflin W. Gibbs, helped thwart an incipient black revolt against Clayton in the 1880s. When asked by the grateful and much-relieved white leader what he wanted, Bush responded, "Your influence as long as you have any and as long as I deserve it." Clayton replied, "You have it." True to his promise, Clayton (despite occasional equivocations) joined Bush and other Negroes in keeping at bay "lily-white" movements within state Republican ranks.[104] Under their tacit understanding, blacks supported Clayton's primacy and in turn were assured a subordinate yet important voice in the Arkansas Republican party.[105] Bush himself, with Clayton's backing, was appointed United States Receiver of Public Lands in 1898, a post he retained until Democrats elected Woodrow Wilson as President in 1912.[106] For fourteen consecutive years he filled his position "without a scandal or a charge of corruption."[107]

Examples of Negro social mobility and progress were most pronounced in Little Rock but could be found to some extent in

## TABLE 9
### BLACK POPULATION OF ARKANSAS'S SIX LARGEST TOWNS, 1900

| Town | Total Population* | Black Population | Percentage Black |
|---|---|---|---|
| Fort Smith | 11,587 | 2,407 | 20.8% |
| Helena | 5,550 | 3,400 | 61.3% |
| Hot Springs | 9,973 | 3,102 | 31.1% |
| Little Rock | 38,307 | 14,694 | 38.4% |
| Pine Bluff | 11,496 | 5,771 | 50.2% |
| Texarkana | 4,914 | 2,078 | 42.3% |

SOURCE: *Twelfth Census of the United States . . . 1900 . . . Population, Part I* (Washington, D.C., 1901), 609.

*Total Population includes a very few Chinese and American Indians.

Arkansas's smaller towns. Fort Smith and Hot Springs, in western Arkansas, had lesser black populations (see table 9) and offered more limited political prospects; however, they supported a minuscule petite bourgeoisie class of artisans and merchants.[108] Texarkana, in the far southwest, was the boyhood home of ragtime composer Scott Joplin, who placed the setting of his opera *Treemonisha* in Arkansas.[109] On the other side of the state, the Mississippi River town of Helena was the residence of black Reconstruction leaders William H. Grey and James T. White.[110] J. N. Donohoo, a Phillips County state legislator and prominent Republican leader, lived nearby.[111] Another leading Helena resident was the Reverend E. C. Morris, who in 1894 founded the National Baptist Convention; by 1906, with 2,261,607 members, it had grown to become the largest black religious denomination in America.[112] Just outside Helena was Southland College, a missionary institute operated by the Quakers, or Society of Friends, from 1864 to 1925.[113]

The town of Pine Bluff, located down the Arkansas River forty miles southeast of Little Rock, occupied an especially significant place in Arkansas Negro life.[114] In addition to being the county seat of heavily black Jefferson County, it was the home of the

Branch Normal College for Negroes of the University of Arkansas.[115] Two smaller schools also were established there: the Presbyterian Board of Missions for Freedmen opened the Richard Allen Institute in 1885,[116] while Arkansas Catholics began the Colored Industrial Institute in 1889. The secretary of the Board of Trustees of the latter school was a second-generation Irish priest and Confederate veteran, Monsignor J. M. Lucey. Lucey was not only a friend of black education but proved to be an outspoken foe of lynching. He is also remembered for having publicly opposed, in 1891, a proposed new law calling for segregation of railway passengers.[117]

Politically speaking, Pine Bluff's blacks were second only to those of Little Rock for the weight they carried within Arkansas's Republican party. Negro resident A. M. Middlebrooks was a Republican candidate for presidential elector in 1888 and afterwards federal deputy revenue commissioner for the Eastern District of Arkansas.[118] The city's most outstanding black politician was Ferdinand Havis, a former Desha County slave who had come to Pine Bluff after emancipation and had learned the trade of barber. In 1871 he was elected a Pine Bluff city councilman for a two-year term and in 1873 was sent to the state legislature by Jefferson Countians. He was appointed a colonel in the Baxter forces during the "Brooks-Baxter War" in 1874; in that year he also was returned to the city council, where he served continuously until disfranchisement got underway in the early nineties. He held the position of Jefferson County assessor from 1873 to 1877 and that of county circuit clerk from 1882 until 1892; from 1890 to 1892, he additionally filled the office of county clerk.[119]

Havis, Mifflin W. Gibbs, and John E. Bush formed something of a black triumvirate within the Arkansas Republican organization. Regularly serving on the state central committee with the other two men, Havis was also a delegate to the Republican national conventions of 1880, 1884, 1888, and 1900. He received the caucus vote of the Republican members of the legislature of 1887 for United States Senator from Arkansas and was for several years chairman of the Jefferson County Republican Committee. Havis was also much involved in civic affairs, belonging to the Freemasons, Odd Fellows, and United Brothers of Friendship; for a time, he served as National Grand Master of the latter organization. He also constructed a two-story brick building on the northeast corner of Second and Main streets in downtown Pine Bluff, which housed both a saloon and meeting hall. In addition, an 1889 biography noted that "he owns about 2,000 acres of land and is quite wealthy."[120]

Pine Bluff could also boast having among its numbers Arkansas's most successful urban black businessman, Wiley Jones. An ex-slave, Jones in the first years of freedom had worked for a time as a porter and teamster and had finally become a barber and saloonkeeper. In spite of his humble origins, he quite obviously possessed the Midas touch. By the 1880s he owned property scattered throughout Pine Bluff as well as the city race track (with a stable of trotting horses worth fifty thousand dollars) and the Colored State Fair Grounds. Jones was a key figure in organizing the state fair. Beginning in 1886, the event attracted twenty thousand visitors annually to Pine Bluff, much to the satisfaction of white and black merchants alike. In addition, Jones also owned a major Pine Bluff streetcar system until 1894, when he sold his interests to another streetcar syndicate. Asked by an enquirer in 1893 to estimate the value of his total assets, the black entrepreneur joked, "They tax us pretty lively here, so you may just put me down at $200,000." Other reports stated that $300,000 was a more accurate figure.[121]

The achievements of the more successful blacks often proved inspiring to others of their race. The statements of one young black, John Gray Lucas, typify the pride which many felt. A native of Marshall, Texas, Lucas grew up in Pine Bluff, attending the public schools there and the Branch Normal College of the University of Arkansas. Continuing his education in the North, he was graduated from the Boston University School of Law in 1887, the only black in a class of fifty-two and one of seven who were graduated with honors.[122] While a law student, Lucas was interviewed by the Boston *Daily Globe* and was asked specifically about racial conditions in his home town. In the reporter's transcription, Lucas almost appeared to bubble over with enthusiasm. He pointed out that in Pine Bluff three of the eight city councilmen were black and that Negroes filled the offices of county coroner and circuit court clerk; furthermore, Negroes composed half the police force and half of the local justices of the peace and often served on juries. A black man, he noted, owned the city streetcar system. On public carriers throughout the state "there was neither distinction nor separation [by race]." Contrasting the lot of Massachusetts blacks with conditions in Arkansas, Lucas was unimpressed by the former. In fact, he wondered aloud why "more colored young men from the North did not make Arkansas their home. It is an inviting field for them, and a grand opportunity to make something of themselves."[123]

◆     ◆     ◆

Evidence suggests that some talented Northern blacks were taking Lucas's brand of advice to heart. During Reconstruction and after, until the 1890s, superior economic conditions and political opportunities in Dixie, especially in the cities, were drawing numbers of them southward. Joseph C. Corbin, Mifflin W. Gibbs, William LaPorte, and Dr. J. H. Smith are examples of the type in Arkansas. Native blacks who went north for their education, like Charlotte Stephens, John K. Rector, and Lucas himself, often returned upon completion of their schooling.

Part of this migration had to do with changing attitudes among some of the South's white population. As previous studies by David R. Goldfield, Paul M. Gaston, and others have demonstrated,[124] urbanization had facilitated the appearance of an authentic bourgeois class within Southern cities, bringing forth a new social milieu and new social values. Whereas the climate in plantation districts almost discouraged individual mobility and advancement, that of the cities fostered these attributes. Old ties and family connections remained important, but the town merchant and urban booster praised enterprise, initiative, bustle, and ability, particularly the ability to raise capital and make money. Blacks who demonstrated these qualities sometimes won a degree of genuine respect, a respect which went well beyond the condescending paternalism of the *ancien régime*.

Travelers in Arkansas were often struck by how much this was so. Even as late as 1899 Charles Stewart, a Chicago Negro reporter, observed, "While in Little Rock I have visited the offices of . . . successful negro lawyers and have seen white men go in to consult them. Negro doctors have white patients. Negro merchants have white customers and the like." He asked, "Could these evidences be considered taking away the manhood of a race? When I say that the negro has a better time in the south than in the north I am accused of catering to southern sentiment and prejudice, but the man who deals in facts and who visits this country must agree with me." [125] In a similar vein African Methodist Episcopal bishop W. B. Derrick, when first assigned to head his church's conference in Arkansas, stated, "The relations existing between the races, I must honestly confess . . . to be far better than I had any conception they were. I am surprised at business relations between employers and the willingness on the part of the business element to accord recognition to colored men." [126]

Local black leaders occasionally offered collaborating testimony. In his 1902 autobiography Mifflin W. Gibbs sharply attacked disfranchisement and other late regressive tendencies in Arkansas. Nevertheless, he wrote, "It can truly be said of Little Rock that the press and leading citizens have been more just and liberal to her colored citizens than any other Southern city. I well remember when her institutions relating to commerce, literature, professions, Board of Trade, Real Estate Exchange, bar and lyceum were open to us, whilst two-thirds of their members were our political opponents." [127] Gibbs was not merely referring to the Reconstruction period, for newspaper accounts show him attending meetings of the bar association and real-estate exchange at least as late as 1888. [128]

Gibbs not only belonged to professional associations but conducted intimate business dealings with whites. An 1889 sketch listed him as a partner in the Little Rock Electric Light Company and a shareholder in other enterprises. [129] At a statewide immigration convention held in Little Rock in 1888, Gibbs was a member of the predominately white delegation from Pulaski County, whereas A. M. Middlebrooks, Wiley Jones, and the Reverend E. C. Morris were among similar groups from Jefferson County and Phillips County. The meeting was a conference of Arkansas's most influential business and civic leaders, called to discuss ways of attracting capital and labor into the state. [130]

Other blacks acquired equal prominence. When a Little Rock streetcar company underwent financial reorganization in 1895, Chester W. Keatts, the cofounder of the Mosaic Templars, was named court-appointed receiver of the bankrupt firm. Keatts

126

posted personal bond of forty thousand dollars and spent over a year disposing of the corporation's properties; he earned special commendation from the bench and the general satisfaction of all concerned.[131]

Wiley Jones of Pine Bluff likewise developed important connections with his white business counterparts in that city. In June 1889 he formed a partnership with Edward B. Houston, a well-known white real-estate developer and contractor, for the purpose of creating Pine Bluff's first modern suburb, the town of White Sulphur Springs. Located seven miles west of Pine Bluff, the town became a fashionable summer resort and remained so well into the early twentieth century. Land was plotted and lots sold to noted Pine Bluff citizens, and a large hotel and nearby park were constructed. Subsequently, ownership of the enterprise was expanded through the incorporation of the White Sulphur Springs Land and Improvement Company in 1892; Jones was a major shareholder in this latter concern, along with Houston and several other leading white businessmen.[132]

Commercial intimacies worked to dissolve opposition to black political participation and officeholding. When Mifflin W. Gibbs was nominated by the Republican state committee for the appointment as United States Consul to Tamatave, Madagascar, in 1897, the Democratic *Arkansas Gazette* actively backed his efforts to obtain the post. "Judge Gibbs," the paper editorialized, "is one of the best educated colored men in the south and a man of advanced and progressive ideas. He is a leader among his race . . . and commands the respect of all who know him. He has lived in Arkansas many years and has acquired much of the world's goods through business tact and honest effort. He is worthy of the position not only on account of the influence he commands in the ranks of his party, but by reason of his fitness for the place."[133]

One might suppose that white responses would be different in the case of a local federal appointment. However, such was not always the case. In 1901, John E. Bush faced opposition in his bid for reappointment as receiver of the United States land office in Little Rock. Politics never made stranger bedfellows than in the coalition formed against Bush: it consisted of "lily-white" elements within the Arkansas Republican party and Boston, Massachusetts, Negroes who distrusted his choice friendship with

Booker T. Washington. In his successful fight to retain his office, Bush secured endorsements from Washington and Powell Clayton and from Little Rock's white business establishment. The mayor, board of trade, bar association, every bank in the city, and "business houses without exception" all forwarded letters of recommendation to President Theodore Roosevelt. Horace G. Dale, chairman of the Pulaski County Democratic Committee, telegraphed the White House, "It affords me pleasure to indorse the application of John E. Bush for reappointment as receiver of the U.S. land office. I have known him for twenty-five years (we were boys together) . . . and he has the confidence of both white and colored people here. He is to my personal knowledge a credit to his race and to the community. I think his reappointment will give general satisfaction."[134] F. J. Ginnochio, secretary of the Democratic county committee, affirmed these remarks, wiring, "I have known Mr. Bush for thirty years, and during that time I have never heard one word against his character. . . . He is a colored man of whom we are all justly proud; he stands well in this community and is a credit to his race. He is one of the foremost colored men in the State, and his appointment would be satisfactory to the public generally, without regard to politics."[135]

With backing from Little Rock whites, Bush won his fight for reappointment and held his position until 1912; he was one of the few Southern black officeholders to escape the "black broom" movement of President William Howard Taft to reduce Negro influence in Republican affairs.

Bush's confirmation in 1901 has gone almost unnoticed by historians. Yet, it is noteworthy that it occurred just two years prior to the much-publicized Indianola, Mississippi, affair; in the latter incident, President Roosevelt closed a rural post office because of white demonstrations against a new black postmistress.[136]

Of course, business associations and political dealings did not usually translate into social relationships. Occasionally, however, even here caste lines were breached. During his first month in office, President Theodore Roosevelt incurred the ire of many Southern whites by inviting Booker T. Washington to dine with him at the White House. The furor aroused caused Opie Read, the nationally known humorist, to recall another dinner given twenty years previously in Little Rock.

128

The dinner in question had occurred in 1880, during Ulysses S. Grant's extensive tour of the South. Grant's Southern visit had been transformed into a lavish ritual of sectional reconciliation, a means by which Southern whites could demonstrate their renewed loyalty to the American government. In Little Rock a "grand parade" attended by fifteen to twenty thousand persons had been staged for the former Union-army commander, and in the evening a "grand banquet" was given in his honor at the city's stylish new Capital Hotel. A reporter for the New York *Graphic* described the banquet as "the largest and most sumptuous entertainment . . . that the local Delmonico had ever attempted, and . . . in every respect a magnificent success. Plates were laid for 250 guests. Everyone came in festive array and the solid men of Little Rock felt themselves proud to be numbered in the chosen band."[137] Among those present were such dignitaries as Little Rock mayor John Gould Fletcher, Arkansas governor William R. Miller, and outstanding leaders of both parties and of Little Rock society.

Also "numbered in the chosen band" was a black Arkansan, Mifflin W. Gibbs. Read recounted that at the time he was an editor of the *Arkansas Gazette* and had been seated next to Gibbs at the dinner. The person who had originally been asked to respond to the fourteenth toast, "American Citizenship—Its Duties and Responsibilities," had been unable to attend, and Read had arranged for Gibbs to talk in his stead. When Gibbs spoke, "Every guest was spellbound, and General Grant was astonished." Read made note of Gibbs' "earnest speech" in the next day's issue of the *Arkansas Gazette,* and he subsequently stated that the black man had "scored the greatest oratorical triumph of the affair."[138]

Gibbs' attendance at the Grant banquet was an aberration from the prevailing etiquette, and it is probable that he was invited only because of the special nature of the occasion. Other indications, however, point to a weakening of traditional racial mores in Little Rock. In 1889 Frederick Douglass paid a visit to the city, staying at the home of black dentist J. H. Smith. A white reporter for the *Arkansas Gazette* was sent to interview Douglass but seemed almost more impressed by the elegant appointments in Dr. Smith's home than by the distinguished visitor. Of Dr. Smith, the journalist described him as "a colored man, but with so complete a polish in manners, dress, language and appearance that he may

129

truly be called a negro in name only."[139] The comment, while unintentionally rude, was revealing; personal wealth and individual refinement seemed to have had a marked effect on at least one Caucasian's perception of blacks.[140]

The most persuasive testimony concerning racial progress in Little Rock came from Frederick Douglass. When queried by the *Gazette* reporter about his reception in the Arkansas capital, Douglass proved as outspoken as ever, complaining bitterly about having been refused service in a local restaurant. By and large, however, he seemed favorably impressed. When asked about the attitudes of local blacks, he responded: "It gives me a great deal of pleasure to find that the race, as a whole, enjoys a large degree of contentment at the relations existing between it and your own race. I find that the colored man is a citizen in feelings as well as in law, and he talks Little Rock and Arkansas with a great deal of enthusiasm, and expresses a profound faith in the future greatness of your city and state." Perhaps Douglass had his doubts, however, for he added, "It is a condition of affairs that I trust may continue and strengthen."[141]

Still, Douglass basically reaffirmed these observations in a later interview with the Indianapolis (Indiana) *World*, a black newspaper which occasionally printed reports about blacks in Arkansas and elsewhere in the South. In response to a question about his recent Arkansas trip, Douglass commented:

> I was told by some friends that the time was unpropitious for me to visit Arkansas, but I have the pleasure to state that not a single incivility was shown me while there. On the contrary, to all appearance, the people were as civil as any people south of Mason and Dixon's line. On Thursday I visited both branches of the State Legislature, and had not been in my seat as a spectator five minutes before a member moved that the courtesy of the body be extended me. I am not sure but the action in some measure was a desire to assure me of the liberal feeling of the State. There was no objection in either house to the motion.[142]

Douglass also noted, "I was surprised to find some colored men so well fixed in Arkansas. For instance, there's Wiley Jones, of Pine Bluff, who owns the street railroad, and another colored man owns fine horses, one of which is valued at $10,000."[143]

During his visit to Little Rock, Douglass had given a public lecture at the Capital Theater on Markham Street. Blacks and whites had crowded to hear the famous speaker; seated behind the podium were Judge Mifflin W. Gibbs, Councilman Green W. Thompson, Professor J. Talbot Bailey, and Dr. J. H. Smith, as well as such prominent whites as Pulaski County judge W. F. Hill and former Little Rock mayor John Gould Fletcher. The audience, however, had been racially separated, whites being grouped on one side of the hall and blacks on the other.[144] Moreover, just two years after the ceremony honoring the former abolitionist and veteran civil-rights leader, Arkansas legislators, meeting in Little Rock, would enact a new state "Jim Crow" law, a statute requiring racial separation of passengers on railroads.

The Douglass lecture illustrated perfectly both the promise of the city and the very real barriers which remained against black advancement. Among whites, older inherited prejudices clashed head-on with newer urban perspectives, and few individuals displayed much logical consistency in their racial views. Furthermore, the very process that worked to erode caste feelings, that of rapid black social mobility, also created new fears, envies, and status anxieties among white people.

The latter phenomenon has been described by sociologist Pierre L. van den Berghe in his comparative history of race relations in several Western countries.[145] Van den Berghe notes that when older, paternalistic styles of race relations based on a master-servant model begin to be challenged by the upward mobility of a previously subordinate group, the dominant race sometimes responds by instituting new forms of physical separation. In this way it attempts to mark out and maintain its superior place in the social hierarchy. "To the extent that social distance diminishes, physical segregation is introduced as a second line of defense for the preservation of the dominant group's position."[146]

In the new competitive type of race relations, "contact declines, miscegenation decreases, racial ghettos appear." Members of the lower caste are no longer perceived as lovingly childlike and irresponsible but instead as "uppity," aggressive, and insolent. The benevolent condescension and sense of *noblesse oblige* of former times is replaced by race hatred and virulent bigotry, often expressed in sudden upwellings of violence, such as lynchings and race riots. "The earlier master-servant model that established social distance with etiquette" now "gives way to sharp competi-

131

tion between the subordinate race and the working class of the dominant race. The latter joins the upper class to form a 'herrenvolk' democracy to put the excluded race down."[147]

Signs of the possible development of such a racial pattern were beginning to appear in Arkansas's urban centers by the late 1880s and early 1890s. For example, in 1892 Little Rock witnessed the grisly lynching of a young black accused of assaulting a five-year-old white girl. An inflamed mob of five hundred persons battered down the gates of the state penitentiary, smashed open the door to the cell block where the Negro was confined, and carried him to the corner of Fifth and Main streets, where he was strung from a telegraph pole. "Before the body had risen above the heads of the mob, a shot was fired . . . followed by a regular fusilade . . . blood from the body of the victim forming a pool underneath."[148] When Arkansas governor James P. Eagle, just returning to the city, attempted to intervene, the mob turned and assaulted him, and he perhaps barely escaped the rope himself. The following morning the *Arkansas Gazette*, in a display of yellow journalism rivaling Hearst and Pulitzer, headlined, "His Excellency Attacked by a Mob! . . . In the Capital Itself!"[149]

There were other, less violent, manifestations of racial feeling. Working class and lower middle-class whites were most threatened by the Negro's rise since they competed with blacks for jobs and depended to a great degree on their skin color for a sense of self-esteem and self-worth. One indication of this was the competition and rivalry of white and black barbers in the city.[150] Hostility was not confined exclusively to these classes, however; in 1889 a body of white Episcopalians objected to the seating of delegates from St. Phillip's parish, a new black congregation in Little Rock, in their church's diocesan convention. Equally noteworthy, though, is the fact that Episcopal bishop Henry Niles Pierce adamantly rejected their exclusionary demands.[151]

Clearly, the larger record discloses that the progress of blacks in Little Rock and Arkansas's other urban centers could generate both positive and hostile tendencies in urban race relations. Why then, one wonders, was it the latter which, beginning in the 1890s, increasingly prevailed? Van den Berghe's typology itself perhaps provides part of the answer, but to a considerable degree the explanation can also be found in the attitudes and reactions of rural Arkansans. None of the forces which served to weaken caste attitudes and traditional social arrangements within the town existed to any appreciable extent in country districts, where inherited outlooks still held sway. Rural visitors to the cities were disturbed and frightened by the erosion of caste lines they encountered and by the recognition received by middle-class blacks.

Indicative of rural hostility was a book authored by Charles E. Nash, a doctor and former planter and plantation owner from eastern Arkansas. The mouth-filling title of his work, published at Little Rock in 1900, was *The Status of the Negro, from a Negro's Standpoint in His Own Dialect—A Country Negro Visits the City and Takes in the Surroundings—His Conversation after His Return*. The book's plot concerns a rural black named Jim who journeys to Little Rock and is corrupted by the town's environs. Jim meets several urban middle-class black types, a minister, a teacher, and a politician, all of whom are presented as pretentious, empty-headed buffoons. Under their pernicious influence Jim is driven to steal a red-bandanna handkerchief from a store, is arrested, and forced to work off his fine on the city road gang. He has profited from his experience, however, for when a black attorney offers to plead his case for five dollars, he replies, "I got no five dollars, neider can you get me outen dis scrape, kase the white man put me in, an' he got mo' sense dan you." Properly chastened, Jim, a wiser man, returns to his cabin on the plantation.

At one point in the dialogue the author, speaking through Jim, compares the town Negro to an ornery mule who leads all the farm livestock into the corn patch every night, eats his fill, and then eludes capture the next day by hiding in the woods. What should be done with him? The mule can't be killed, it is admitted, "kase he good to work, an' make plenty for hisself an' de whole family." Rather, "keep dat mule in de lot. Make de fence ten rails high, an' stake-an'-rider it so he can't get out; den he be useful an' can't steal. Den let de white folks keep de nigger at home, an' don't turn 'em out to come to town and steal people's stuff. Keep him in his place; dat's what I say." [152]

The upshot of the tale, given in Dr. Nash's own voice, is that "Jim goes home satisfied that freedom does not free him from either punishment or labor, and settles down to make a living by honest work, and learns the lesson to keep away from the city." [153]

# VII

# Agrarian Revolt: 1888 and 1890

Ill fares the land, to hastening
ills a prey,
Where wealth accumulates, and
men decay.
—Oliver Goldsmith, "The
Deserted Village"

At the same time that the fortunes of some urban blacks were rising, those of many rural whites were declining. The post–Civil War years witnessed growing distress in Southern agriculture, the causes which were complex. Between 1860 and 1910, United States cotton production jumped from 3,841,000 to 11,609,000 bales, while the nation's population soared from 31,443,321 to 91,972,266; contemporaneously, beginning in the 1870s, the federal government reverted to gold standard, withdrawing wartime greenback dollars from the economy and demonetizing silver coinage. The result was a sharp currency contraction and severe deflation, the amount of money in circulation falling from approximately fifty dollars per capita in 1865 to around fourteen or fifteen dollars per capita by the 1890s.[1]

Eastern financial circles generally applauded the government's "sound money" program. Bondholders who had purchased federal securities with depreciated greenbacks were paid in gold, and the currency scarcity allowed bankers and creditors to assess high interest charges on loans. For numerous other Americans, however, the effects were calamitous. Tighter money meant higher unemployment for industrial workers and plummeting crop prices and incomes for farmers—for Southern cotton growers, cotton prices dropped 47.7 percent between 1874–77 and 1894–97. Individuals with mortgage payments to meet or other fixed indebtedness were especially hard hit.[2]

If federal monetary policies were a chief source of the farmer's troubles, other factors nonetheless exacerbated his plight. There were of course the agriculturalist's timeless enemies of drought and flood, but added to these there were myriad man-made difficulties. High protective tariffs enacted by Republican-controlled Congresses excluded foreign manufactured goods from the United States, forcing farmers to purchase their equipment and supplies from domestic producers at an artificially bloated cost. Railroads, owned increasingly after 1880 by Northern investors and financiers, favored large shippers and exacted high freight payments, especially at small rural communities served by only one line. Pools, trusts, and holding companies worked to destroy business competition and raise expenses. In addition, the federal government's National Banking Act of 1862 neglected the South, failing to provide adequate credit outlets and facilities.[3]

Denied access to ordinary commercial loans, Southern farmers increasingly had to depend on the pernicious crop-lien system for assistance: persons too hard pressed to pay cash on the barrel bought their fertilizers, seed, coffee, flour, and other goods on credit obtained from neighboring furnishing merchants—often at exorbitant rates of interest; the markup on commodities purchased in this way could be from 30 to 70 percent above the usual cash price. To ensure payment, the storekeeper demanded a lien or mortgage on the coming year's crop; proceeds from the sale of the crop were applied to the farmer's account, with any remaining debt carried over to the next season. Since the merchant retained a first lien on all future crops until the initial sums owed were cleared, it was virtually impossible for the farmer to turn elsewhere for credit; furthermore, typically all the books and records were kept by the storekeeper. If a farmer's debt became great enough, the merchant might ultimately demand a mortgage on the farmer's land before extending more loans; foreclosures could then be only a matter of time. The once independent yeoman perhaps soon found himself reduced to the status of a tenant tilling another man's farm.[4]

Such a happenstance was by no means uncommon. An unexpected crop failure, sickness in the family, or other misfortunes could deplete the small savings of even the most frugal and hardworking Cincinnatus; once enmeshed in the web of the crop-lien system, it could be almost impossible to extricate oneself. The gravity of the situation is highlighted by the tenancy statistics for Arkansas. In 1880, out of a total of 94,433 farmers, 29,188 or 30.9 percent were classified as tenants; by 1900, of 178,694 farmers, 81,140 or 45.4 percent were in the tenant class.[5] By the latter year, moreover, although 34,962 tenants, or 43 percent, were black, a good majority, 46,178 or 57 percent were white.[6] With the bottom falling out of the cotton market, significant numbers of whites were being placed in economic circumstances that were at least starting to resemble those of the most debased class of blacks.

Country store owners were only partly at fault for the developing state of affairs. Although there were ample opportunities for the hard-eyed and unscrupulous,[7] rural merchants themselves operated at considerable risk. Since they often possessed limited assets and were frequently strapped for ready money, a bad season could bring disaster and bankruptcy; in addition, the more humane and feeling often took financial risks for friends and relatives not justifiable by the strictest business judgment. Equally important, rural proprietors had to buy their wares with advances obtained from bankers and businessmen in Memphis, Little Rock, and other large towns. A share of the rewards went to the wholesalers in the Southern cities, who took a handsome middleman's cut for themselves, and ultimately to the manufacturers and creditors outside the South.[8]

In the broadest sense much of the distress of the Southern region grew out of the ruin and devastation wrought by the Civil War. In addition to the trail of physical destruction left by the fighting, the war, as economic historian Robert Higgs has shown, dealt a tremendous blow to the South's asset structure. All of the capital invested in Confederate securities and currency had become so much worthless paper, and the emancipation of the slaves had created a massive "portfolio disequilibrium."[9] Although some scholars, such as Roger Ransom and Richard Sutch, have stressed that other factors have been responsible for the persistence of poverty in the South,[10] their perspective is in fact not inherently inconsistent or necessarily mutually incompatible with that of Higgs and his followers: it is quite possible, for example, for one to believe that such factors as sharecropping and the crop-lien system have contributed to the South's economic retardation while also acknowledging the devastating impact which the South's defeat had. Since there was nothing like a "Marshall Plan" for the prostrate Confederacy, money for resuscitation had to come from the private sector, often at severe financial and social cost.

It is true that the economic picture also contained its roseate hues. Although some of the profits exacted from Dixie's white and black farmers were squandered by Yankee barons on lavish Newport "cottages," much was rechanneled back into the economy in the form of capital investments for business expansion. Such funds helped to underwrite the industrialization of America and also the urbanization of the South. Yet, as has been true in so many areas of the world, part of the burden inherent in the transition to an advanced modern economy was being shouldered by an exploited agricultural class.

In light of the above conditions, it is hardly surprising that rumblings of agrarian discontent began to be heard within Arkansas soon after the collapse of political Reconstruction. The Granger movement surfaced briefly during the 1870s, at one time attracting as many as 20,471 members.[11] Toward the end of the decade the Greenback party appeared, advocating inflation of the money supply with greenback dollars in order to relieve debtors. In 1880, just six years after the end of Carpetbagger rule, the Greenbackers challenged Democratic hegemony by running W. P. "Buck" Parks for governor; an indefatigable campaigner and man of fixed determination, Parks drew large crowds and created a considerable stir—and considerable alarm—among the Democrats. Despite a strong bid for farmer support, however, and the absence of a Republican contender, he garnered less than 37 percent of the votes.[12] The Greenbackers tried again two years later, running for governor Rufus K. Garland, the maverick brother of Arkansas Redeemer leader Augustus H. Garland. But once more the party registered a poor showing.[13] Fresh memories of the turmoil of Reconstruction, a general desire for tranquility, and fears for white supremacy all militated against the Greenbackers' chances of success.

Although the Greenbackers had made little headway, their insurgency augured a more potent rebellion to come. On February 15, 1882, depression and low cotton prices caused seven farmers to meet at McBee's schoolhouse in Prairie County and found the Agricultural Wheel.[14] None present that Saturday night could have dreamt that within six years their numbers would have jumped to over seventy-five thousand within Arkansas and half a million throughout the nation as a whole;[15] neither could anyone have predicted that their order would mount the most serious challenge to Arkansas Democratic rule since the success of Redemption. These original seven Wheelers at first had little program, merely a feeling that they were victims of injustice and that their only hope lay in organization. Within a matter of months, their initial Wheel had expanded to include three additional Wheels. As new spokes constantly were added about the original hub, the Wheel began to roll.[16]

During their initial two years, the Wheelers were absorbed with problems of education, consolidation, and growth. Information was disseminated to members on fertilizers, improved equipment, farm management, and the latest techniques of scientific agriculture. To break the grinding dependence on cotton, farmers were urged to diversify their crops; above all, they were encouraged to avoid taking out crop mortgages, dubbed "Anaconda" mortgages, after the sinister Latin American snake that entwines and crushes its prey. The entire agricultural commodities system was denounced in the strongest terms. The preamble of the order's first constitution stated that "Farmers should save their own meat and bread, raise more corn, wheat and oats and the grasses and less cotton, so as to increase the demand far beyond the actual supply, securing better prices, and holding the stock of provisions from the greedy paws of merciless speculators."[17] In the same vein the Wheel, hoping to avoid the snares of the merchandisers, became interested in cooperative buying and kept a purchasing agent at St. Louis.[18]

Thus, in its earliest days the Wheel concentrated on matters of self-help and group solidarity; the society in no way thought of itself as being directly political. However, as the farmers studied and groped with their plight, there was a gradually dawning awareness that many of their problems suggested governmental solutions. The Wheel was particularly impatient about securing legislation which would outlaw the crop mortgage,[19] and it also desired antitrust statutes and the creation of a state railroad commission.[20] Democratic candidates, in the view of many members, seemingly promised everything and then after the elections delivered nothing. Angry discontent began boiling over first on the local level; although in some counties Wheelers stayed within the dominant party, in others they began to nominate and run their own slates of candidates for office.[21] Starting in 1886, the order also entered the state political fray when Charles E. Cunningham, a prominent Wheel leader, ran for governor as an Independent. Cunningham polled 19,169 votes, compared to 54,070 cast for Republican Lafayette Gregg and 90,650 for the Democratic winner, Simon P. Hughes.[22] The returns were less disappointing than they appeared at first glance, for Hughes' majority over the combined Wheel and Republican vote was only 17,411. This was the lowest majority polled by any Democratic candidate since the close of Reconstruction, a fact noted with some concern by Democratic newspapers.[23] If the opposition forces could somehow unite, the Democracy would have a lion's share of trouble on its hands.

In 1888, this was exactly what happened. Farmers who favored independent action massed under the standard of the Union Labor party, a new third party recently sprung from a meeting of agricultural protest groups at Cincinnati, Ohio.[24] Leadership of the new party in Arkansas was virtually synonymous with that of the Wheel; when Union Labor held its convention in Little Rock during the last week of April 1888, Isaac McCracken of Ozone, president of the national Agricultural Wheel, presided as chairman, and other prominent Wheelers were active in the proceedings.[25] Elements of the Knights of Labor also participated.[26] As its candidate for governor, the convention selected Charles M. Norwood, a country doctor, one-legged Confederate veteran, and former state senator from Prescott. Norwood, in the upcoming election, would joust with Democratic gubernatorial nominee James P. Eagle, a Lonoke planter and popular Baptist evangelist.[27]

Soon after the Union Labor convention adjourned, the State Wheel of Arkansas assembled in Little Rock to hold its own conclave. Despite the great overlap in membership, the Wheelers refrained from formally backing the Union Labor candidates; by its constitution the Wheel was ostensibly nonpartisan, and most of the order's leaders wanted to avoid an open rift with the uncompromising Democrats in their ranks. The Wheel convention, nevertheless, did adopt a resolution thanking the Union Labor party for accepting a list of its demands, an action conspicuous in the case of the Democrats by its absence.[28] One Union Labor spokesman insisted that this amounted to an endorsement and left this taunt with an *Arkansas Gazette* reporter: "You may be sure we will down you Democrats this year by twenty or thirty thousand majority."[29]

The Democrats themselves would have sneered at the threat but for an unforeseen action by the state's Republicans. The first inkling of the Republican strategy came when a *Gazette* correspondent at Benton asked Judge M. W. Benjamin what his party aimed to do about a ticket. "We are going to elect Norwood," the judge responded.[30] A few days later a Chicago *Tribune* reporter cornered federal judge John A. Williams, a Jefferson County Republican then in Chicago attending the Republican National Convention. Williams, noted the journalist, "talked interestingly about the possibility of a combination that would end the Democratic dynasty in rock-ribbed Arkansas. They expect to do so through that queerly-named organization known as the Wheel, which Williams said had 75,000 members."[31]

By now alerted to the possible danger, the *Arkansas Gazette* warned grass-roots Wheelers not to be led astray by the machinations of Powell Clayton, in league with "political farmers who farm with their mouth."[32] When their worst fears came to pass and the Republican state committee, on July 18, endorsed Norwood's candidacy, the announcement was met with a thunder of denunciation from the Democratic press. "The mask has been torn off," exclaimed the *Gazette*, "and the authors of the crimes of the Reconstruction era stand forth in bold relief."[33]

Both rival camps sounded the battle cry and frantically began mobilizing their forces. Eagle's followers, trying to bring out their full strength, made a strenuous effort to organize at least ten Democratic clubs in every county in the state.[34] The executive committee of the national Union Labor party convened in Chicago on August 1 and decided to "give special attention to Arkansas until the September election." A. J. Streeter of Illinois, the Union Labor presidential nominee, cancelled all appointments and came to Arkansas to stump for the ticket.[35] Following the custom of the day, Norwood and Eagle canvassed the state together, crossing swords in a series of sharp debates. When the dust finally settled on election day, Monday, September 3, the official returns gave Eagle 99,229 votes to Norwood's 84,223, a difference of just over 15,000.[36]

While it had not reached its goal, Union Labor's impressive showing in the 1888 contest inspired the party to a renewed assault. In 1890, the same coalition of Wheelers, Knights of Labor, and Republicans again gave Colonel Eagle a run for his money, this time backing the gubernatorial candidacy of the Reverend N. B. Fizer, a Methodist minister. In this second contest Fizer bested Norwood's previous total by a few hundred votes, although Union Labor's percentage of the total ballots fell somewhat, owing to a larger turnout at the polls.[37] That the Democracy had managed to keep its place in the saddle was of minimal comfort to its supporters, however; it still faced its most formidable opposition in years.

Indeed, in the exigencies of the hour, some Democrats had already turned in panic to desperate measures. The old methods of fraud and intimidation, once used with such deadly effect against the Carpetbaggers and their allies, were again dusted off and placed into ready service. In the gubernatorial election of 1888 there appear to have been massive irregularities. In Conway County, for example, Republican leader Powell Clayton claimed that a local Democratic club had been armed by the governor and converted into a state militia company; the militia unit was said to have ostentatiously paraded daily until the election, although Clayton wryly noted that their "military zeal" had "since died out."[38] On the day of the election itself, the militia allegedly seized control of several polling places, ousting the regularly appointed Republican judges of election. Democrats, denying action by the militia, insisted that the judges had simply not appeared at the appointed time and that the voters present had chosen new officials in their place. Whatever the facts, Conway County, previously Republican, went Democratic by seventy-six votes.[39] Norwood supporters in Union County stated that roving bands of mounted Democrats, armed with Winchester rifles, had patrolled for weeks before the balloting, causing large numbers to flee the county out of fear for their lives. Union Laborites and Republicans, traveling to the polls, were assaulted and fired at, and at least one man was gunned down and killed.[40] In the Delta county of Crittenden, where elected black officers had been forcibly expelled less than two months earlier, Norwood received 1,597 votes to 1,323 for Eagle, a majority of only 274; in prior elections the Republicans had ordinarily won with majorities of as much as four to one over their opponents in Crittenden County, and the United States Census of 1890 showed that its population contained only 787 adult white males.[41] In several other counties ballot boxes were burned or destroyed, and ballot-box stuffing was said to be widespread and pandemic.[42] The November 1888 congressional elections witnessed similar irregularities, although the presence of federal supervisors may have somewhat dampened the ardor of the dishonest. In the First District, comprised of eastern Arkansas Delta counties, state Wheel president Lewis P. Featherston of Forrest City, running as an Independent, challenged Democrat W. H. Cate, a lawyer, banker, and circuit court judge. The returns credited Featherston with 14,238 votes to 15,576 for his opponent.[43] In the Second District, in central Arkansas, Wheelers backed Republican John M. Clayton, a Pine Bluff attorney and younger brother of Powell Clayton, against Clifton R. Breckinridge, the Democratic incumbent. Breckinridge was certified the winner by a vote of 17,857 to 17,011.[44] Democratic opposition was much less strong in the Third District, where John A. Ansley, Independent, was easily defeated by Representative Tom McRae, 20,046 to 13,553 votes, and in the Fourth, where national Wheel president McCracken, also campaigning as an Independent, lost to Democrat J. H. Rogers, 14,933 to 20,448 votes. In the Fifth District, Democrat S. W. Peel routed his opponent by a heavy margin.[45]

Featherston, Cate's opponent in the First District, maintained he had been unfairly counted out and appealed to the United States House of Representatives. A special committee came to Arkansas and held hearings; upon receipt of its report, the Republican-controlled House on March 5, 1890, removed Cate and installed Featherston in his place.[46] Clayton, in the Second District, likewise filed a contest and began tracking down evidence on his own. Following the trail of fraud, Clayton visited the town of

142

Plumerville in Conway County, where a ballot box had been heisted from a Republican precinct. On the evening of January 29, 1889, the Plumerville boarding house where he was lodging became the scene of one of the bloodiest political murders in the annals of Arkansas. While Clayton was sitting near an open window, writing by the light of a coal-oil lamp, a shotgun blast rang out in the night; the Republican candidate slumped to the floor, instantly dead.[47] From virtually every pulpit and newspaper in the state came a horrified outcry of indignation. Though the governor and the Democratic state committee offered rewards for information about the murder, as did the victim's brother, Powell Clayton, the assassin or assassins were never apprehended. The U.S. House of Representatives, holding that the deceased had been rightfully elected to Congress, declared his seat vacant, removing Breckinridge.[48] There was, incidentally, no evidence implicating the latter in the crime.[49]

Although they deplored the Clayton killing, most Democrats contended that Breckinridge and Cate had been wrongfully excluded from Congress, the U.S. House investigation being dismissed as a partisan, trumped-up affair.[50] The Democratic leadership, however, seemed noticeably reluctant to undertake an independent finding of its own regarding the various election allegations. In the 1888 gubernatorial race, for example, Union Labor aspirant Norwood asserted that the Democrats had stolen the election and offered to present overwhelming proof documenting the charge. Governor Eagle, to his credit, urged a full investigation of Norwood's case, promising to step down should it be substantiated.[51] The Arkansas legislature proved somewhat less scrupulous. It consented to undertake hearings only if Norwood would post bond defraying their entire cost, the bond to be forfeited if his claims went unsustained. Since this entailed a sum estimated at between twenty and sixty thousand dollars, Norwood was forced to ask reluctantly for a withdrawal of his contest, although he did not retract his charges of fraud. When the legislature passed a bill accepting his withdrawal petition, it was vetoed by Governor Eagle, but, though the House subsequently voted to fund hearings, the Senate remained intransigent. So the matter was left to expire; no investigation was ever held.

Only in one instance did the legislature conduct a formal inquiry into alleged misconduct by Democratic officials. In the state and local races in Pulaski County, burglars had entered the courthouse in Little Rock on the night following the election, breaking open a safe and making away with several ballot boxes from what unofficial tally sheets showed to be heavily Union Labor–Republican districts.[52] The sensational incident made the front pages throughout the state and was universally denounced. John Gould Fletcher, president of the German National Bank and one of the capital city's former mayors, capsuled the general sentiment. "My verdict in matters of the kind," he stated, "is that no condemnation can be too severe. It is robbery in any sense and our people should be educated up to view it in that light. Among business men it cannot be regarded in any other light than the same as robbing a house or breaking into a bank."[53]

The Union Labor–Republican claimants went before the county election board, but that body ruled that the unofficial tally sheets could not be used in computing the voting returns. The decision, complained the *Arkansas Democrat*, "was one of those cases where the law and justice part company."[54] The *Arkansas Gazette* urged the Democratic candidates in question voluntarily to resign,[55] and their refusal to do so evoked much criticism. Encouraged by the public response, Union Labor–Republican nominees for state representative carried their appeal to the General Assembly. Spurred on by the uproar caused by the recent Clayton assassination, the lawmakers were induced to act; on February 18, 1889, Pulaski's Democratic representatives unwillingly surrendered their seats in the House,[56] their places being taken by contestants Henry R. Morehart, E. J. Owens, A. F. Rice, and Green W. Thompson.[57]

◆     ◆     ◆

Perhaps the most important consequence of the 1888 and 1890 election contests was the effect it had on Democratic attitudes toward the Negro. In the beginning, the ominous Union Labor–Republican challenge caused the Democrats to make unprecedented overtures for black support. Party officials, anxious to corral every possible vote, were encouraged in their effort by recollections of black political behavior during the earlier Greenback insurgency; in 1880, the Republicans had failed to nominate a state ticket, and many Negroes had simply stayed home on election day; reportedly, a considerable number had even voted for Democratic candidates.[58]

Democratic hopes of obtaining black ballots were further kindled by a sudden racial flare-up within the Arkansas Republican party. At the Republican state convention in 1888, a group of young blacks had unexpectedly attempted to wrest control of the party machinery from Powell Clayton and his faction of "Regulars"; although the blacks' candidate for temporary convention chairman, J. A. Simmons of Drew County, had been defeated, the incident left ruffled feelings on both sides.[59] Further trouble developed later in the year, when a group of white Republicans in Little Rock organized a "Harrison and Morton Club" which closed its doors to black membership.[60] On July 18, the club founders listened to an address delivered by Judge John "Poker Jack" McClure, a former state supreme court justice during the Reconstruction period. In a long speech, McClure gave an expanded reprise of comments he had made earlier during the state convention affray.[61] He argued that Negroes were retarding the party's growth among whites; that as long as they voted, Republicans could never expect a fair count in the South; and concluded by suggesting that they be tossed overboard.[62]

McClure's speeches produced a veritable furor among blacks. Delighted Democrats predictably worked the racial imbroglio for all it was worth. The *Arkansas Gazette* reprinted McClure's remarks in their entirety and sent a reporter to ascertain the reaction of well-known local black leaders, who responded with indignation and dismay.[63] J. Talbot Bailey, professor of literature and belles-lettres at Philander Smith College and editor of the Little Rock *Sun*, a black newspaper, expressed the feelings of many when he charged that the real motivation of the white Republicans was simply a venal hunger for patronage:

> The probable favorable indications for the election of a republican president has awakened the old political bosses from a four years of lethargy, and tantalizing visions of postoffices, marshalships and sinecures are dancing before their gleaming and bewildering eyes. But these glittering prizes, which in auld lang syne dropped naturally and certainly into their clutches, have excited the cupidity of a greedy rival and the children of the kingdom are in danger of being cast out . . .

when the federal pap comes to be dished out Mr. Negro will be on hand with a big spoon, and—"aye, there's the rub." With the progress of events the negro has "caught on" to all the secrets of the party organization. He has passed through democratic administrations, both state and national. The result is that if there were any so ignorant as to fear being put back into slavery they find that such has not been the case, and the intelligent colored men who feared that a democratic administration would break down the free school system no longer entertain any apprehensions upon that point. Now the working capital and influence of these bosses were built up wholly upon these conditions, which are so rapidly passing away. Even in the matter of intelligence, wealth, and character the colored men can find in their own ranks men vastly superior to the average light-weights who became his champions in reconstruction days.[64]

The capital city's blacks proceeded to organize their own Harrison and Morton Club at a mass gathering held at Jackson's Park in North Little Rock. As its first official action, the Negro group passed a resolution vowing not to support any man running for office who belonged to the white Harrison and Morton Club.[65]

Such action did not go without effect. It seems quite possible that McClure and his followers had only intended to alarm the blacks and frighten them into moderating their demands. In any event, the white leaders swiftly proceeded to shift their sails. The white Harrison and Morton Club changed its name to the "Lincoln Club" and assured Negroes that it only purported to be a strictly social organization: there was no intention of drawing the color line in party appointments. Just in case there were any black skeptics, such prominent Negro leaders as Mifflin W. Gibbs were conspicuously invited to address its meetings.[66]

Some tensions persisted; when the Pulaski County Republican convention convened in August, a faction of blacks, led by white saloonkeeper Angelo Marre, walked out in protest over plans for forming a county fusion ticket with the local Union Labor party.[67] Although Republican chieftains went ahead with the fusion arrangements, no member of the Lincoln Club was nominated for office. All of the white candidates, in fact, both Republican and Union Labor, were younger men or newcomers to politics not identified with the old Reconstruction leadership. As a final gesture to the blacks, two Negroes were placed on the fusion ticket:

Elias Rector, a member of the Little Rock school board, was nominated for circuit clerk, while Green W. Thompson, a city councilman from Little Rock's Third Ward, was picked for one of the four state representative spots.

On the whole, blacks seemed satisfied with these arrangements. When the Marre faction attempted to field an independent slate, the effort ignominiously collapsed; practically all the blacks nominated withdrew their names.[68] The plain truth was the position of Negroes, white Republicans, and third-party agrarians was none too secure in Arkansas, and each group needed the help and support of the others for advancement and political success. By election day, a large majority of black Republicans had re-enlisted in the old ranks.

While the whole affair appears in retrospect to have been of little consequence, it nonetheless encouraged Democrats in believing that they had an unparalleled opportunity to gain black support. In marked counterpoint to the exclusionist policy of the Lincoln Club, Little Rock's Old Hickory Club began enthusiastically embracing new Negro members.[69] When a state conclave of Democratic clubs was held, two blacks, Thomas Morgan of Woodruff County and Benjamin F. Adair, a Little Rock attorney, addressed the delegates (among whom were several Negroes) and were tendered a vote of thanks.[70] Also, separate "colored Eagle" clubs were established in Little Rock, Pine Bluff, and elsewhere;[71] at a rally held at the steps of Little Rock's Capital Hotel, Mrs. Eagle, the Democratic standard-bearer's wife, presented the local colored Eagle club a special embroidered silk banner.[72] During July and August Democratic newspapers made repeated editorial appeals for black votes.[73]

Precisely while this was happening, Democrats were warning white voters that a Union Labor–Republican victory would mean a return to Reconstruction conditions. Trying to reconcile the seeming contradiction, aged Civil War governor Henry M. Rector told an audience at Little Rock he "knew the negro. It was not him he feared, but the . . . adventurers and the carpet-baggers, these men who had involved both county and state in debt. It was these the people feared and not negro domination."[74]

Expanding upon this theme, the editor of the Pine Bluff *Press-Eagle* wrote:

Republics are proverbially ungrateful; so are republicans. It was with the negro vote that such men as Judge McClure were enabled to get possession of the southern states during the era of reconstruction and inaugurate systems of wholesale plunder that foisted debts upon the southern people which they are paying to this day. The white people of the south are intolerant of negro domination, it is true; but republicans of the McClure and Clayton stripe taught them to be so. They have learned from bitter experience in the past, that negro domination is but another name for carpetbag radical domination and its attendant train of evils; and until the negroes manifest wisdom and independence enough to cut loose from their old political bosses, the white people of the south will ever remain "solid" in their resistance of negro domination in politics. This the negroes now seem inclined to do.[75]

However, the newspaper tried to make it clear that although it welcomed Negro votes, it did not endorse the "social equality" of the races.[76] In a somewhat similar vein, the *Arkansas Gazette* qualified its appeal to blacks with reassurances to whites: Negroes were being offered no special favors. The black man, the paper stated, "now knows that he can obtain nothing from the government not open to all other citizens; that the republican leaders can do nothing for him; that he is not under any obligations to them; that, like his neighbors, he must take care of himself, and that to him as to others it is a matter of 'root, hog, or die.'"[77] In brief, blacks could expect little more from the Democracy than laissez faire and equality before the law.

Since the Negroes chief disagreement with the white Republicans had been over division of the patronage—i.e., the contention that they had not been receiving enough from the government—such overtures were bound to fall on deaf ears. Although Democrats were welcoming Negroes into their clubs, rallies, and parades, the ambiguities and limitations in their approach probably explain why so many blacks ultimately supported the Union Labor–Republican nominees.

Many Democrats expressed frank disappointment in the only marginal success they had achieved in winning black support; nevertheless, at least some were willing to try once more. In 1890, as they had occasionally in the past, Democrats in Little Rock and Pulaski County placed a black man on their ticket: Negro Benjamin F. Adair was selected as one of their four candidates for state representative.[78] The action must have been encouraging to Negroes and perhaps appeared a hopeful sign of the Democracy's direction. It is possible that Adair's name on the ballot may have drawn off enough black votes to ensure the victory of the local Democratic nominees in that year—although, it should be noted, allegations of fraud were again lodged by the Union Laborites and Republicans. In January 1891, Adair, along with the rest of the Democratic candidates from Pulaski County, was admitted to the House of Representatives; he was the only black Democrat serving in the new session of the General Assembly.

The example of the Pulaski County Democrats was not followed by the state party at large. Attempting to allay rural defections, county organizations sent "a great many" farmer delegates to the Arkansas Democratic convention in 1890.[79] Probably expressing more wish than firm conviction, the *Arkansas Gazette* stated, "To see so many farmers in Little Rock making a State ticket is a good omen and goes to show in advance how the farmer vote will be cast at the September election."[80] Rural influences were reflected in portions of the state platform denouncing the McKinley tariff and calling for free coinage of silver, antitrust legislation, government regulation of railroad rates, an end to railroad land grants, and the reservation of public lands for actual settlers; other planks advocated an end to alien ownership of land and curtailment of state leasing practices which placed "honest workmen in competition with paupers and convicts." Reform of state election laws was also endorsed.[81]

One other action may also have demonstrated the agrarian temper of the meeting. Although other measures had been passed quietly and without undue commotion, a resolution demanding segregated coaches for white and black passengers on railway lines brought the delegates to their feet. "Amid the wildest cheering and the greatest enthusiasm" and "with a whoop and a hurrah," the convention sent the separate-coach resolution through to adoption.[82]

# VIII

# A Journey
# Backward: The
# Separate-Coach Law
# of 1891

> We are opposed to the measure
> because it seeks . . . to gratify
> and keep alive a prejudice among
> our citizens, fast becoming
> extinct.
> —John Gray Lucas, Arkansas
>   House of Representatives,
>   1891

Soon after the legislature of 1891 convened in Little Rock, the members of the House of Representatives voted to remove a portrait of George Washington hanging behind the Speaker's rostrum and to replace it with one of Jefferson Davis.[1] The gesture was to prove to be suitably emblematic, for especially in the matter of racial policy, the lawmakers of the Twenty-eighth Session would be impelled by a spirit of genuine reaction. The 1891 Assembly would adopt a whole series of measures designed to reverse the racial progress of the preceding three decades.

The first of these measures was a statute requiring segregation of black and white passengers on the railroads. The action of the Democratic state convention in 1890 had virtually assured enactment of a separate-coach law, and a number of assemblymen rushed to attach their names to the impending legislation.[2] After briefly deliberating, party leaders decided to endorse a proposal introduced by Senator J. N. Tillman of Washington County.[3] There had been some fear that opposition to the separate-coach proposal might arise from the mountain country of the Northwest, where there was only a minuscule number of blacks,[4] and sponsorship by Tillman, a well-known senator of that region,[5] was in all likelihood intended to forestall any such development.

The Tillman bill was certainly thorough enough to achieve its purposes. Its principal sections required the railroads to maintain "equal but separate and sufficient" passenger coaches and waiting rooms for members of the white and black races. Small companies operating roads less than twenty-five miles long could conform to the law by dividing coaches with a partition, and street railways were exempted from its provisions altogether. All persons "in whom there is a visible and distinct admixture of African blood" were to be adjudged Negroes. Other features not directly concerned with race ordered the railroads to provide drinking water at stations and on passenger trains and subjected individuals using profane language to a five- to twenty-five-dollar fine. Failure to carry out the law would cost the companies from one hundred to five hundred dollars, with each train run in violation and each day's noncompliance constituting a separate offense. In addition, the law charged all railroad officers with the duty of enforcement, on pain of a twenty-five- to fifty-dollar penalty. Passengers refusing to follow these officers' directions could be assessed from ten to two hundred dollars.[6]

These provisions were admittedly Draconian, but advocates claimed the uncleanliness and rowdiness of the black travelers made them necessary. The editor of the Fort Smith *Times* was especially explicit on this point:

> The people of Arkansas have borne with this negro nuisance on railroads a long time, hoping that the negroes would learn how to be decent, and while a great many of them do behave themselves, others are intolerable. In this portion of the State [western Arkansas] the people have no conception of the degree of offensiveness borne by respectable people at the hands of drunken, insolent blacks in the black district of the State. A Saturday night train out from Little Rock to Pine Bluff is hardly safe, to say nothing of the fact that not one in eighty uses Pear's soap or any other kind.[7]

151

Fear of "social equality" was perhaps equally emphasized by the bill's friends, and the proposal was frankly advanced as a means of sharpening race distinctions. Opponents maintained that such an attitude was not in harmony with America's traditional democratic ideals. This attack was met by laying great stress upon the equal-accommodations section of the act. Time and again it was stated that facilities would be "equal and sufficient" and that only Negroes ashamed of their own race could possibly object to separate coaches. The author of the measure, Senator Tillman, inquired:

> [The Negroes] say that if this bill is passed it will discriminate against them. I call attention to the language of the bill, which says that railway companies must furnish equal but separate and sufficient accommodations for both races. And if they violate any provisions of the act they are subjected to heavy penalties. What more can they ask of the friends of the bill?[8]

Tillman also asserted that his proposal was really no different in principle from the existing segregation found in the examples of separate churches, hotels, and boarding houses.[9]

Finally, proponents of the new act stated that similar legislation had proved satisfactory in other Southern states and had been upheld by the courts.[10] Legal scholar Charles A. Lofgren has insisted that federal court decisions did not trigger the first wave of separate-coach legislation which appeared in the South during the early 1890s;[11] however, evidence from Arkansas suggests that decisions of the federal judiciary were a significant, if not exclusive, factor in engendering the state's separate-coach law. Tillman commented on the floor of the Senate that his bill was "modeled after the Mississippi [separate-coach] statute," which, he noted, had "been tested in the courts and pronounced constitutional."[12] The statement no doubt alluded to the 1890 case of *Louisville, New Orleans, and Texas Railway v. Mississippi*, in which the United States Supreme Court held that the Mississippi separate-coach law did not impose an undue burden on interstate commerce.[13] In Arkansas, it was widely assumed—incorrectly—that the decision had given complete judicial sanction to the separate but equal doctrine (although this would not actually come until the Court's famous *Plessy v. Ferguson* ruling of 1896).[14] The *Arkansas Gazette* reported, "The highest courts in the land have decided that given equal accommodations, such separation of the races as is contemplated by the bill is not 'caste or class legislation'"; rather, it was "strictly lawful and proper in every respect." Later, the newspaper stated, "The Supreme Court of the United States has already decided that accommodations being equal, equality does not require that whites and blacks should occupy coaches in common."[15]

It should be noted that although those supporting the separate-coach law generally followed the same arguments, they varied greatly in their temper and tone. Some were moderate and restrained and probably sincerely believed that separation would be a good means of reducing racial friction.[16] Others were out-and-out Negrophobes who made little attempt to disguise their hatred for the blacks.[17] One newspaper in this latter group warned that failure to pass the act would result in "a summary depopulation of some of the more impudent and venturesome negro districts."[18]

In Little Rock, however, such threats were ignored. Here the urban black community had achieved a measure of freedom and economic security and proved to be both active and articulate, furnishing the principal opposition to the "Jim Crow" cars.

For example, a mass meeting was held at the Negro First Baptist Church on January 19, with over six hundred persons in attendance.[19] A special committee of recognized race leaders, consisting of John E. Bush, co-founder of the Mosaic Templars of America; George N. Perkins, an attorney and former city councilman; W. H. Scott, a landowner and also a former city councilman; the Reverend Y. B. Sims, pastor of the black First Congregationalist Church; and Dr. J. H. Smith, the Little Rock dentist, presented a number of forceful resolutions, all of which were unanimously adopted.[20] The resolutions denounced the separate-coach proposal as caste legislation, warned that attempts to determine an individual's race could lead to embarrassing mistakes, and predicted that segregation would invite rudeness and incivility from conductors and "a certain well-known class of white persons."[21] As an alternative, it was stated that "'An act to promote the comfort of passengers on railway trains' can be better obtained, with honor to the State and justice to all concerned, by compelling the railway companies to provide first-class and second-class accommodations, with charges accordingly, by which means the respectable travelling public would be relieved of contact with objectionable persons of whatever race or class."[22]

A second protest meeting, held on January 27 and chaired by George N. Perkins, met in the House of Representatives' chamber of the State House on Markham Street,[23] which was sometimes used as a public meeting hall. An estimated four hundred blacks plus "a small sprinkling of whites" heard a black quartet open the proceedings with a moving rendition of "Fear Thou Not."[24] The crowd then heard four Negro leaders express keen disapprobation of the Tillman bill: Professor Joseph A. Booker, president of Arkansas Baptist College; Dr. J. H. Smith, the well-known dentist; and two ministers, the Reverend Asberry Whitman and the Reverend H. T. Johnson.[25]

Professor Booker began by alluding to his Arkansas birth and his allegiance to his native state but expressed dismay at recent white comments that the most objectionable Negroes were those, like himself, who had acquired education and property. While disavowing any desire for "social equality," he could not bring himself to believe that well-meaning white people desired to turn back "the wheels of progress" for the "progressive negro." He conceded that objections to Negro cleanliness sometimes had a basis in fact but vowed that blacks "proposed to buy soap even if they couldn't get bread"[26] if the separate-coach bill were defeated.

Booker attacked the proposed law on the grounds that it assumed all blacks were alike, that it would shut off blacks from white people and their example, and that it would not be effective in producing equal accommodations for blacks on the railroads but only would result in "race humiliation." He asked, therefore, that the legislature require the railroads to offer first- and second-class service which would be open to whites and blacks alike on the basis of ability to pay. He also asked that the law empower conductors "to put off a passenger who boards the train on the outside of a barrel of whiskey." Closing his speech, Booker warned that passage of the separate-coach bill would cause Negro labor to emigrate to other areas, a threat he obviously hoped would not be lost on eastern Arkansas planters. He cautioned "that such legislation as the Tillman bill contemplates would drive his race in Arkansas to Oklahoma or Africa, where they are being invited."[27]

154

Dr. Smith, covering much of the same ground as that by Booker, emphasized the differences among his people and the basic unfairness of the separate-coach measure, which would debase the better class of blacks. "Ignorance is contagious," he declared. "To force the better negroes into contact with the more degraded would be to force the race backward."[28] Like Booker, Dr. Smith questioned whether the Tillman bill would compel the railroad to provide equal facilities for blacks; it would be too costly, he argued. He closed by appealing for first- and second-class service to people of all races.[29]

The Reverend Mr. Whitman joined Booker and Smith in pleading for first- and second-class service, fearing, obviously, that a separate-coach law would relegate all blacks to second-class service, or worse, on a segregated basis. He shrewdly appealed to white paternalism and sectional hostility in speculating "that the railroads would not give the negroes equal accommodations, because they are managed and officered by foreigners who have no interest in common with the negro in Arkansas."[30]

The Reverend Mr. Johnson's speech was not summarized, but the *Arkansas Gazette* reporter present at the meeting wrote that "it was beyond question an able one" and "characterized throughout by conservatism and eloquence."[31] The meeting at the State House adjourned with the crowd singing "Come, Where the Lilies Bloom."[32]

In addition to these appeals to the citizenry at large, black leaders turned as a court of last resort to the lawmakers themselves, on whom they showered petitions and memorials.[33] Their efforts were vigorously supported by almost all of the black members of the legislature, who fought the separate-coach law with every ounce of their strength and ability; even a number of their bitterest white adversaries attested to the uncommon quality of some of their addresses.[34] In the Senate, the burden of opposition fell on the only black member, George W. Bell of Desha County.

Initial debate before a packed audience in the galleries occurred on January 29, in a dramatic exchange between Senator Tillman and Senator Bell.[35] Rising in answer to the former's appeal for passage of his bill, Bell denied the alleged need for separate coaches, stating, "The negroes have been riding upon and within the same coaches, in common with all other races, in this

State for more than eighteen years" and without serious trouble.[36] True, a few isolated instances of conflict could be found, but these were no more indicative of general conditions than were occasional fights between two or more white men. Such abuses as did exist could best be remedied by legislation requiring railroads to offer first- and second-class service on trains. This type of statute would be superior to the separate-coach measure, for it would afford protection to decent and orderly persons of all races.

Perhaps exaggerating to win white support, Bell declared he had been proud of Arkansas's attitude toward her black population; while traveling in the North he had "boasted of the equal show that the Negroes have in this state in the procuring of an education and the accumulation of wealth. How just and equitable her laws, and how liberal and well-disposed her rulers."[37] Now it appeared this fine record was to be destroyed.

Mentioning Negro accomplishments in the nation's past, Bell also noted that, if the legislature required separate coaches, "The dirtiest peasants from Europe, the Nihilists, and cut-throats of every government can come here . . . [and] receive better protection before the law, and in their civil rights, than we who have helped to make this country what it is."[38]

Senator Bell concluded his speech with an appeal for good will between Negroes and whites and pictured the advent of a new dawn in Southern history:

> But sir, I thank God that the day is fast approaching when reason, and a proper regard for the rights and privileges of all our countrymen, North, East, West, and South, will be recognized, and that the races here in our fair and beautiful Southland, may feel and know that we have a common cause, a common humanity, and a common interest." And if we would triumph over wrong and place the emblems of peace upon triumphant justice, without distinction of race, color, or previous condition, we must unite and cultivate that spirit of true friendliness which would make us one people in a truly solid South.[39]

Bell's moving oratory may have upset the stereotypes of many whites attending the Senate debates, but their surprise was probably nothing compared to the shock of those who listened to the uncompromising militancy of the chief black spokesman in the

House of Representatives, John Gray Lucas of Jefferson County. After receiving his law degree from Boston University in 1887, the young black man had returned to Arkansas and had won appointment as United States Commissioner for the Eastern District of the state.[40] In 1891, he was serving his maiden, and last, term in the Assembly. Lucas spoke before his fellow legislators on February 17, and his address was published in the *Arkansas Gazette* a few days later under the apt heading "Separate Coaches: All That Can Be Said Against the Bill Just Passed."[41]

In his speech the Jefferson County lawmaker, citing Herodotus and Diodorus, recounted the earliest achievements of his race, alluding to the cities of Napata and Meroë in ancient Nubia and Kush and noting the mulatto character of much of ancient Egypt. He contrasted these early glories with the later debasement and persecution of his people in America, from the horrors of the Middle Passage to the recent attempts to subvert the Constitution of the United States and amendments thereto as they pertained to the rights of Negroes. Fortunately, Arkansas heretofore had been exempt from these latest developments. Harkening back to his days as a student in the East, Lucas recalled his interview with the Boston *Daily Globe* in which he had proudly declared that his state "was an inviting field to young men" where "a liberal public sentiment prevailed and no hindrances were met with anywhere."[42] But apparently some were determined to abandon past policies and instead transport Arkansas "across the Mississippi River, where yoked to the crimson soil of Mississippi, she shall be as incapable of advancement as is a fixed star to alter its course."[43]

Taking up the coach bill itself, Lucas felt that the whole social philosophy of its sponsors was contrary to the most advanced Western thought and the spirit of the age. In addition, segregation went against the grain of the fundamental American principle of personal liberty. "It prohibits and prevents free men [from the right] to choose their own company," he observed, and argued that in essence its enforcement would create "an unlawful imprisonment."[44]

Lucas then went on to give the classic Negro delineation between civil equality and social equality. Social equality was simply a matter of private relations between two or more persons. No intelligent Negro would expect social recognition or acceptance merely because he was a passenger on the railroads. Civil equality, however, was an entirely different matter. It was the right of every citizen to expect equal protection of the law from agencies licensed by the state to carry out public business, such as railroads and hotels. Lucas believed that the railroad was simply a peculiar form of public highway and held that "It would be just as reasonable and proper for the state to place a dividing line through its public roads for the two races, or to require cities to divide their streets, or even to require all white people to live in one particular portion of our cities and the colored people in the other portion, or if you please, in different towns,"[45] as it would be to require separate coaches on the railroads.

Lucas obviously thought he had produced an effect of fine irony by picturing such absurdities. Not apparent to him was another irony appreciated only by the modern reader. While the extreme of separate towns would never become widespread, the years immediately following his address would see the growth and hardening of residential segregation throughout the cities and towns of the South and the nation.[46]

Lucas next considered the objection to Negro cleanliness which was used as a rationale for the separate-coach proposal. In what may have been his most insightful observation, he denied that this was really an important factor; instead, he alleged that the real purpose of the bill was permanently to fix his race in an inferior caste status. Noting a strange discrepancy among advocates on the point of Negro hygiene, Lucas caustically asked:

> Is it true, as charged, that we use less of soap and God's pure water than other people, that it is sought to isolate us from other fellow citizens? It has been heralded to the world by those who would justify the Democratic party of Arkansas in their platform of 1890 demanding "separate coaches," that the negro is not so clean and pleasant to the eye as he should be; but that some few other negroes are less objectionable because refined, intelligent, and genteel. Why, some of our Democratic papers have said that the more money, intelligence, and gentility, the more objectionable the negro. Which is the truth? Do our white friends demand this law that they may not be compelled to travel in the same car with the former class? Or is it the constant growth of a more refined, intelligent, and I might say a more perfumed class, that grow more and more obnoxious as they more nearly approximate to our white friends habits and plane of life?[47]

Indeed, complaints about Negroes on the railroads were ridiculous when one considered the close association of blacks and whites in other aspects of life. Senator Tillman had cited existing cases of separation to support his bill; Representative Lucas now noted the frequent examples of mixed contact as an argument against it:

Who are employed as your servants throughout the South in preference and to the exclusion of every other class? Who is he that attends to the very delicate duties that bring persons in closer relations than any other; that sits by the side of yon delicate and refined white lady, laughing, chatting, covered by the same lapcloth? Who is the scraper of your chin with his face and breath close as the "lover sighing like ballad"? Why, I have heard many say that none but a Negro should shave them. How about those cooks who handle all that goes over your delicate palates and the baker who is said to knead the dough with feet as with hands? How about those nurses that must sleep with the children, go traveling with you, occupy the room with you and the bed with your loved ones? Do you stand all this (and I have not half portrayed it), and yet you can't bear to ride upon the same car, though in a separate seat from your colored fellow citizen? It seems and must appear to every reasonable man to present a peculiar consistency; but "Consistency, thou art a jewel." [48]

The prime motive behind the separate-coach initiative was not mere aversion to physical contact with blacks [49] but instead resentment against Negro social mobility and, ultimately, irrational sexual taboos and phobias about miscegenation and intermarriage. With almost acid contempt, Lucas mockingly assured his white auditors that they need have no fears on this latter score. Alluding to past moral lapses by whites, he observed, "Out of a bounty and plenty of culture and refinement we are satisfied and glad to wed amongst our own; for have we not samples of all complexions and features and texture of hair, if you please, that all the races afford, from the fair-haired daughter of the Caucasus to the raven-haired maid of voluptuous Spain? He or she among us must indeed be an epicure that from our goodly quantity and from among our differing qualities may not find satisfaction." Rather, "It is the dissatisfaction of some of our neighbors with their own, it would seem, that for their own restraint (which does not restrain) they must have laws to prevent this race antipathy of which they love to prate." [50]

Lucas proceeded to try and balance white fears of "social equality" and miscegenation with another fear: that of economic ruin. Passage of the coach bill would lead to a mass exodus of black laborers, he warned, with disastrous consequences to the economy of the state. Repeating lines from Goldsmith's "The Deserted Village," he warned employers that they would rue the day when "your fields have become deserted, your cabins left tenantless, and where the cotton and the corn were wont to grow in plenty and abundance, you find the jimson and the cuckleburr growing in rank profusion over the once fertile fields and the cabin doors."[51]

Lucas ended his address on a conciliatory note. Quoting both from Longfellow's "Hymn to the Night" and The Book of Ruth, he appealed for amity and good will between the races. However, he also issued a forthright challenge to the moral and ethical sensibilities of the white community. "I am not a white man," he declared, "but I here and now proclaim any man my inferior that ostracizes me because of my complexion or who measures my abilities by so shallow a criterion."[52]

It is noteworthy that the protest effort of Lucas and the other black leaders was fairly and fully reported in the capital-city press. Although they disagreed with his stance concerning the separate-coach bill, the Little Rock *Arkansas Gazette* and *Arkansas Democrat* characterized Lucas as "a fluent debater," "unquestionably the ablest and most brilliant representative of his race in the state, and it might be truthfully said (for his age) in the South," "a born leader of his people" for whom in 1891 there was "certainly a bright future in store . . ."[53] The *Gazette* devoted three and one-half columns to its verbatim report of Lucas's speech, more space than was given to any other address delivered during the legislative session. The newspaper also gave front-page coverage to both of the Little Rock protest meetings, relating the proceedings in detail and almost sympathetically.

Nothing, however, could alter the existing political realities; the final legislative tally showed that the separate-coach bill enjoyed insurmountable support. In the Senate it carried easily by a vote of twenty-six to two, with only the black Republican, George W. Bell, and a white Union Laborite, F. P. Hill, voting in the negative.[54] The Senate even adopted an amendment, over the objections of the bill's author and the sponsoring committee, which prohibited Negro nurses from riding in the same railway car with their white charges and employers.[55] The amendment carried handily, eighteen to eight, and revealed significant geographical differences in racial perspective. Of the eight senators who voted against the exclusionary amendment, two represented the districts encompassing Little Rock and Pine Bluff, and their stance may have reflected the greater racial moderation of urban centers. Also, however, the vote revealed significant variations among rural areas. With the exception of Senator Tillman, all the remaining persons who voted against excluding Negro nurses from white coaches represented lowland plantation districts or borderland districts containing major lowland divisions (see table 10). This phenomenon seems readily explainable. Planter families, surrounded by blacks from earliest childhood, often did not find physical contact with blacks objectionable as long as customary social rank and deference were observed. Yeoman whites from mountain regions may have had stronger feelings of color aversion toward blacks; more obvious is the fact that, by insisting on a rigid drawing of the color line, they emphasized the solidarity of the white race at the expense of internal white class distinctions. The desire to forge a herrenvolk democracy of Southern whites was entirely consistent with the egalitarian, Jacksonian heritage of the Ozarks.[56]

By the time the separate-coach bill came before the House of

TABLE 10
*ANALYSIS OF VOTES CAST AGAINST THE NEGRO-NURSE
EXCLUSION AMENDMENT TO THE TILLMAN SEPARATE-COACH
BILL, ARKANSAS SENATE, 1891*

| | |
|---|---|
| Senators Representing Lowland/Urban Districts | 1 |
| Senators Representing Lowland/Rural Districts | 2 |
| Senators Representing Borderland/Urban Districts | 1 |
| Senators Representing Borderland/Rural Districts | 3 |
| Senators Representing Highland Districts | 1 |
| *Total Votes Cast against the Amendment* | 8 |

SOURCE: *Arkansas Senate Journal* (1891), 84; *Arkansas Gazette*, January 28, 1891.

Representatives for final consideration, it was apparent that enactment was certain. The House did, nevertheless, reject a proposed amendment which would have extended coverage to streetcar lines, probably because of the influence of urban business interests. Debate upon the amendment elicited a last sardonic comment from Representative Lucas, reported as follows:

> An amendment, including street cars was proposed, which brought Mr. Lucas to his feet, who made a speech in support of it. He said he knew the [coach] bill would pass, and hoped it would be so amended as to give satisfaction to all classes of citizens. He did not want to associate with white people any more than they desired to associate with him. He would like to see separate coaches placed on all railroads, separate cars or partitions on all street railway lines, and he would also be in favor of having streets and sidewalks divided by some line so that the colored people could go on one side and the white people on the other. He would like to see an end put to all intercourse between white and colored people by day, and especially by night.[57]

The final House tally showed that the separate-coach bill had passed overwhelmingly, seventy-two to twelve. Only two white House members voted against passage, William A. Carlton of Newton County and J. F. Henley of Searcy County, both mountain Republicans. By contrast, of the eleven black House members, only black Democrat Benjamin F. Adair voted for passage.[58]

Adoption of the separate-coach law was a genuine watershed development in the ongoing story of Arkansas's race relations. Paradoxically, though the device of separate coaches was itself new, the intent and purpose of the coach law was to preserve the old: to renew the ancient distinctions of caste, distinctions which were already beginning to decay in the cities and towns. As Representative Lucas had himself put it during the House debates: "We are opposed to the measure because it seeks to pander, not to the convenience of the people, but to gratify and keep alive a prejudice among our citizens, fast becoming extinct."[59]

The urban black middle class understood at once the true import and significance of the coach law and acted much in the fashion of W. E. B. Dubois' "talented tenth," galvanizing the black community into action and spearheading and articulating its demands. The race leaders moved with courage and resolution and deserve to be remembered for their stand. Yet, in the immediate, pragmatic sense their effort accomplished little. It may even have been counterproductive. During the protests some country editors were incensed by the meetings of the "'colored ladies and gentlemen' of Little Rock,"[60] and one editor predicted that their actions would only serve to hasten the passage of the separate-coach bill.[61]

Thus, despite well-organized black resistance, Arkansas determined to board the Jim Crow car and begin a journey into the past. For Arkansas Negroes, the mournful cries of the train whistles in 1891 were both reminders of times gone before and omens of things to come.

# IX

# A Question of Honor: The Election Law of 1891

> Nobody ever achieved honor
> by doing what is wrong.
> —Thomas Jefferson

At the same time that the state's lawmakers were adopting the separate-coach act, they were also placing their imprimatur on a new election statute. Perhaps no other single piece of legislation has had so profound an influence on the character of Arkansas politics as the 1891 election law, yet been the object of so much confusion and misunderstanding. Hailed by its supporters as a typical progressive reform designed to introduce the Australian voting system, the law was long so accepted by most interested historians.[1] In truth, it did contain many praiseworthy features, including provisions for standard, uniform ballots; restrictions on last-minute transfers in the location of polling places; and removal of voting supervision from the hands of local county judges. One section even seemingly outlawed racial discrimination by specifying that blacks and whites should be admitted alternately to the polls at all precincts where more than one hundred votes had been cast in the last election.[2]

Later studies, however, have suggested that the act served in concrete practice as an instrument for massive political disfranchisement and that certain of its key provisions vitiated the principle of universal manhood suffrage.[3] Such investigations plainly have raised new questions about the laws parentage and origins.

164

Initially, demands for a reform of the election statutes were a direct outgrowth of the widespread election irregularities of 1888. Through fraudulent means the Democracy may have survived a crucial political contest, but only at the high cost of tarnishing its vaunted reputation for honesty and integrity and alienating numbers of its own rank and file. More embarrassing still, exposure of major defalcations by a recent state treasurer, William E. Woodruff, Jr., soon followed the election revelations.[4] Ever since the close of Reconstruction, the Arkansas Democrats had crusaded as restorers of honest government; now their chief raison d'être seemed threatened. Undoubtedly, many party leaders were genuinely perturbed by the unsavory doings on the local level. Aside from the moral issues involved, reform presented itself as a cold matter of political survival. In 1890, as previously noted, the Democratic state convention joined the call for improvement of Arkansas's election laws, a call which was echoed by Governor Eagle in his address to the legislature in 1891.[5]

There can be no question but that some revision of the election statutes was needed. Under the old laws, the appointment of voting officers was placed solely in the hands of the county judges and county courts, with virtually no restrictions on who could serve. Sometimes, even men who were themselves candidates for office received positions as precinct judges and clerks.[6] In addition, the county sheriffs were responsible for supervising the polling places and could, when standing for re-election, appoint dozens of deputies to intimidate their opposition.[7] Even if they disapproved, higher party and state officials had no really effective way of bringing such activities to a halt under existing laws.

Almost as soon as the 1891 legislature began its deliberations, two election reform bills were introduced to remedy prevailing conditions. Unfortunately, a full text of these proposals was not recorded in the Assembly journals, though an imperfect synopsis did appear later in the *Arkansas Gazette*. The first measure, House Bill No. 41, was the work of Representative A. H. Sevier of Lafayette County.[8] According to the newspaper descriptions, it provided, among other things, for the use of voting booths and official, uniform ballots printed at state expense. Voting was to be strictly secret, with "no persons other than the electors engaged in receiving, preparing or depositing their ballots [to] . . . be permitted within the booths."[9] Six election judges were to be appointed at every polling place, three each from the first and second largest parties in a given county. Presumably, either the county judge or designated party representatives would appoint the election officials.

Representative E. E. White of Nevada County introduced the second measure, House Bill No. 48.[10] Reportedly similar to the Sevier bill in many respects, it did "not propose any change in the existing laws relating to the appointment of elective officers"[11] but did allow each party to choose its own independent poll watchers. Both the White and Sevier bills were referred to the House Committee on Elections for study and possible revision.[12]

Exactly what transpired in the committee's sessions probably never will be fully known. After conducting two weeks of hearings, the members decided to shelve the original Sevier and White proposals and instead to introduce a third, substitute measure. Entitled House Bill No. 162,[13] it was destined, with a few minor changes in wording, to become the new state election law.[14]

The bill contained two momentous changes which would radically alter the future politics of Arkansas. One section established an elaborate centralization of the election machinery. The governor, auditor, and secretary of state were to be constituted as a State Board of Election Commissioners,[15] and they in turn would have authority to appoint three election commissioners for each of Arkansas's counties.[16] These county officers would select three judges for every voting precinct, and the precinct judges could appoint two clerks to assist them at the polls. Precinct judges were to be of opposite parties "if competent persons of different politics" could be found.[17]

Equally significant were the sections pertaining to voting by illiterates. While illiteracy in the North was by this time insignificant, it remained an acute problem in the poverty-stricken, postbellum South. In Arkansas, among males age twenty or older, 26,160 or 13.4 percent of whites and 40,295 or 55.8 percent of blacks could neither read nor write.[18]

The old law allowed illiterates to ask friends or fellow party members to help prepare their ballots; now, only the precinct judges could mark their tickets. Under the bill's provisions an illiterate was required to apply to two of the precinct judges, who then would order all other electors to vacate the polling place. Afterward, the judges were instructed to prepare the illiterate's ballot as he desired.[19] Further to ensure secrecy, all voters were restrained from leaving the polls with a ballot in their possession, on pain of a twenty-five- to one hundred-dollar fine and a one- to six-month imprisonment.[20]

Soon after leaving committee, the election bill was brought before the Democratic legislative caucus. Here, after a bitter and acrimonious struggle, its supporters managed to win their party's official cachet of approval. It seems that the vote must have been very close; several observers later noted that had it not been for the decision of the caucus, the bill never could have carried,[21] strongly implying that the large numbers of original Democratic opponents plus the sixteen House Republicans and Union Laborites constituted an actual majority against passage.[22]

Complaints continued to be heard, despite the caucus's action. For instance, when the election bill came before the House on its third reading, hostile Representatives made a serious attempt to postpone its consideration. Though the motion to postpone was successfully tabled by a forty-six to thirty-two vote, it is obvious that many Democrats still shied away from giving the bill their endorsement[23] (see table 11).

The introduction of several amendments at the time of the third reading also testifies to the many doubts aroused by the election proposals, while illuminating the nature of some of the more fundamental objections. Republican and Union Labor members were principally concerned with securing an adequate minority voice in the election machinery. Representative John Dunaway, Union Laborite from Faulkner County, introduced an amendment which would have subjected county commissioners to a hundred-dollar fine if they failed to name competent persons of different parties as precinct judges and clerks. An amendment by Representative S. W. Dawson, black Republican of Jefferson County, went even further, conferring on the chairmen of the different parties' county central committees the right to name members of the county election boards. These and other like proposals all were defeated, apparently by voice vote.[24] Fairly or not, Democrats insisted that their opponents could not be trusted with appointive powers. They would, it was claimed, use their posts to bring forth irresponsible and spurious accusations, i.e., to produce

167

## TABLE 11

*ANALYSIS OF VOTES CAST AGAINST A MOTION TO TABLE A MOTION TO POSTPONE CONSIDERATION OF THE ELECTION BILL, ARKANSAS HOUSE OF REPRESENTATIVES, 1891*

| | Against Tabling | Race: Black | Race: White | Party: Dem. | Party: Rep. | Party: ULP |
|---|---|---|---|---|---|---|
| Representatives from Lowland/Urban Districts | 3 | 3 | 0 | 0 | 3 | 0 |
| Representatives from Lowland/Rural Districts | 9 | 4 | 5 | 4 | 3 | 2 |
| Representatives from Borderland/Urban Districts | 2 | 1 | 1 | 2 | 0 | 0 |
| Representatives from Borderland/Rural Districts | 7 | 0 | .7 | 5 | 0 | 2 |
| Representatives from Highland/Urban Districts | 0 | 0 | 0 | 0 | 0 | 0 |
| Representatives from Highland/Rural Districts | 11 | 0 | 11 | 9 | 2 | 0 |

Total House Votes Cast against the Motion to Table the Motion to Postpone Consideration of the 1891 Election Bill: 32.

SOURCE: *Arkansas House of Representatives Journal* (1891), 419–20.

more "Southern outrage" fodder for the Northern Republican grist mills.

On February 25, the election bill came before the House for final consideration. The course of the ensuing debate shows that its purposes could be portrayed in two sharply contrasting ways. In the eyes of Republicans and Union Laborites, it was no reform measure at all; rather, the bill presented itself as a patently obvious fraud, a crude scheme designed to give the Democrats total control over the polling places and untrammeled freedom to count out their adversaries.

Typical of this response was the belligerent address of Searcy County representative J. F. Henley. A vituperative, free-swinging young mountain Republican, Henley castigated the bill as "one of the most damnable and infamous that was ever introduced in a

Legislature." The measure provided that the governor of Arkansas and his board should appoint "discreet persons" to conduct the elections. Who, he asked, would influence the governor to decide who were discreet persons? Would it not be those same courthouse politicians who had committed frauds in the first place? The bill had "the impress of hell upon it"; it permitted "murderers and thieves to steal the ballot boxes." No keen intelligence was needed to discern what the Democrats were about: they were conniving to "turn a jack from the bottom of the pack." [25]

Henley's fierce bellicosity must have startled the Democrats, yet despite this bristling personal attack several joined him in opposition to the election bill. Generally, they were spokesmen for western Arkansas and reflected the resentment of local elites in their region against projected controls from above. Also, they questioned whether the authentic purpose of the bill was to clean up elections, as claimed, or merely to oust Negro Republicans from control of the voting machinery in black districts. Clearly, many western Arkansans opposed surrendering local autonomy and independence and scarcely were moved by any special solicitude for the peculiar electoral problems of the Delta.

Most illustrative of this group's attitude was the speech of Representative Lee Neal of Crawford County. [26] Neal stated that he "admired the pluck of the gentleman from Searcy" but "could not go much on his judgment." Henley "was still a young man" and undoubtedly would grow wiser as he grew older. His problem was that he knew nothing about the history of his own party. For Neal, the election bill was too much a Republican measure to warrant support. Its centralizing features were in fact reminiscent of the hated registration laws used by the Carpetbaggers during Reconstruction; more contemporaneously, the proposal was disquietingly similar to the Lodge "Force" bill,[27] which the Democracy had roundly excoriated during the last canvass. Were the Arkansas Democrats going to abandon the very principles on which they had just won office?

The sponsors of course replied that their measure embodied the spirit and best interests of the Democracy. Its purpose was to prevent, not perpetrate, fraud. Continuing election irregularities had seriously undermined the party's standing at the polls, and the rank and file had demanded reform at the last state convention. The bill under consideration, they insisted, was designed to achieve just that. Furthermore, it had won the approval of the Democratic caucus; anyone who favored honest government would vote for its enactment.[28] Obviously, the crux of the debate centered around the issue of true intent and motive. As the nineteenth century would have phrased it, what was involved at heart was a question of honor.

When the roll was called most Democrats fell into line, the bill easily carrying by a count of sixty-four to twenty-five. Only eleven Democratic members chose to defy their party and vote against passage[29] (see table 12).

Even so, party chieftains seem to have been unusually concerned over the potentially divisive effects of the election proposal. With what seems undue haste, the bill was brought before the Senate on February 27, only two days after the House had

TABLE 12

*ANALYSIS OF VOTES CAST AGAINST THE ELECTION BILL,*
*ARKANSAS HOUSE OF REPRESENTATIVES, 1891*

| | Against Passage | Race: | | Party: | | |
| --- | --- | --- | --- | --- | --- | --- |
| | | Black | White | Dem. | Rep. | ULP |
| Representatives from Lowland/Urban Districts | 3 | 3 | 0 | 0 | 3 | 0 |
| Representatives from Lowland/Rural Districts | 10 | 6 | 4 | 3 | 6 | 1 |
| Representatives from Borderland/Urban Districts | 0 | 0 | 0 | 0 | 0 | 0 |
| Representatives from Borderland/Rural Districts | 8 | 0 | 8 | 6 | 0 | 2 |
| Representatives from Highland/Urban Districts | 0 | 0 | 0 | 0 | 0 | 0 |
| Representatives from Highland/Rural Districts | 4 | 0 | 4 | 2 | 2 | 0 |

Total House Votes Cast against the 1891 Election Bill: 25.

SOURCE: *Arkansas House of Representatives Journal* (1891), 442–43.

completed its action. In addition, it was arranged to have most proponents boycott the senatorial debates, returning only in time for the final balloting. Antagonists therefore were obliged to speak before a nearly empty chamber, with their addresses having, as one reporter observed, "no more effect than the orations of Demosthenes when he spoke against the waves."[30] Discouraged, they nevertheless spent several hours proferring various criticisms of the contemplated law.

George W. Bell, the black senator from Desha, delivered the opening challenge. Reiterating the familiar comparison with the Lodge "Force" bill, he warned against the inherent danger of giving a small cabal of men vast powers and authority:

> Mr. President—This bill comes to us so heavily sugar-coated until it appears at first sight harmless. But, however, upon closer scrutiny we find, sir, many things against which and upon which I shall stamp my solemn protest. The first section . . . provides that the Governor, Secretary and Auditor of State shall constitute a 'State Board of Election Commissioners.' Now, let us see whether this section differs materially in principle from the 'Force bill,' which provided that the Federal Judge should appoint Chief Supervisors of Elections, who in turn would appoint the Judges from the various political parties. It was against this centralization of power that Senators Gray of Delaware, Barbour of Virginia and Voorhees of Indiana hurled such thunderbolts, that the American Congress hesitated, and finally dropped the measure. Will the Democrats of Arkansas, who lauded so justly these great apostles of their faith, now turn their backs upon their teachings? When you thus place the election machinery into the hands of the governor, secretary and auditor of State what will prevent them from appointing their satellites as County Commissioners in every county in the State, who in turn, influenced by their political bosses . . . will do their bidding?
>
> It is true that the present State officers are, from all that I know, upright and honest men. But, sir, you may not always have an Eagle to soar high above fraud, deceit and partisanism. We may behold in a day not far distant, some despot who will desire to perpetuate himself in office; then what is in this bill to prevent him from so doing?[31]

Such questions proved embarrassing to the Democrats, for the bill's centralizing features appeared in fact to go against their traditional espousal of limited government and local independence.

One reply was to argue that under present legislation all power was concentrated in a single individual, the county judge, whereas the new proposal dispersed authority among several boards and officials.[32] Their basic position, however, was expressed in a response delivered by Senator S. A. Miller to Bell's censures. Miller contended that

> there is enough honesty and intelligence in the Democratic party, and the party of the people to come after her to give us free and fair elections. If the better element of the Democratic party will assert itself, we will have no more trouble in Arkansas over elections, and to that extent the bill is in the nature of an experiment: for myself, I am not afraid of the results. If the State should fall into the hands of the enemies of the people and dishonest men of the Democratic party were put at the head of affairs, of course the law would be a failure and the people would suffer; so would they abuse any law. I do not support the bill as a party measure alone, but as a reform measure, and in the hands of its friends, or any honest party, we can reasonably expect favorable results.[33]

Put succinctly, Miller was saying that the Democratic party could always be relied upon to place men of integrity in charge of the affairs of state, ensuring thereby a just execution of the law. Such logic no doubt seemed incontrovertible to many of his Democratic colleagues.

During the course of the Senate debates, reference also was made to voting by blacks. The electoral practices followed in certain Delta counties had for years rankled the sensibilities of many whites. In the so-called "machine" counties, a number of recognized black leaders customarily selected their party's candidates for office, printed and distributed ballots, and then carted the faithful to the polls on election day. In exchange for their support, Negro tenants and croppers could expect to encounter a few friendly black faces when visiting the courthouses or might be extended a helping hand when in difficulty with the law. The system was strikingly analogous to that found among the urban immigrant groups, but respectable Southern progressives had no more love for this style of politics than their middle-class Yankee counterparts in the North. It gave black community spokesmen real power, which perhaps best explains why whites found it so loathsome.

Nevertheless, it probably is true, as the whites constantly charged, that individual black voters who refused to follow their leaders might be subjected to extreme social ostracism or even occasional physical violence.[34] A number of senators voiced the hope that the secret ballot would end "spotting" and arm-twisting by Negro politicians, thus producing a "free ballot" as well as a fair count.

Few Democratic lawmakers, though, were so foolish as to envision any sort of mass conversion by the newly liberated black voters. Later in the session a congressional redistricting bill was introduced, and there was great argument over apportioning the state. Two different approaches were considered: either to create one Negro Republican and five "safe" Democratic districts or else to attempt salvaging six Democratic seats. Though the latter course was ultimately chosen, the heated discussions on this issue strongly indicate that wholesale black disfranchisement was not universally foreseen. If some of the election proposal's supporters did conceive of their measure as principally a disfranchisement devise, then clearly even they did not anticipate just how effective it would be in this regard.[35]

At the conclusion of the Senate debates, the election bill carried overwhelmingly, twenty-five to six. Only three Democrats united with the Republican and Union Labor members to vote against passage.[36] Soon after the senators had given their approval, Governor Eagle signed the measure into law (see table 13).

The new statute was first put to the test on election day, September 1892—with results far more disastrous than anything the Republicans and agrarians had dreamt of in their worst imaginings. From all over the state came reports that the law had driven tremendous numbers of poor blacks and whites away from the ballot box. For instance, the *Arkansas Gazette* correspondent in Hempstead County wired that "Many negroes from pride failed to vote at all, and others scratched their ticket so badly the Judges had great trouble in deciding for whom they intended to vote."[37] The message from Desha County, where the Democrats won their first victory since the end of the Isaac Murphy regime, stated, "The new election law demoralizes the negro, hence the result. Several negroes were arrested in different parts of the county for violating the election law."[38] For the same reason, Democrats scored upset

173

TABLE 13

*ANALYSIS OF VOTES CAST AGAINST THE ELECTION BILL, ARKANSAS SENATE, 1891*

| | Against Passage | Race: | | Party: | | |
|---|---|---|---|---|---|---|
| | | Black | White | Dem. | Rep. | ULP |
| Senators Representing Lowland/Urban Districts | 0 | 0 | 0 | 0 | 0 | 0 |
| Senators Representing Lowland/Rural Districts | 3 | 1 | 2 | 1 | 1 | 1 |
| Senators Representing Borderland/Urban Districts | 1 | 0 | 1 | 1 | 0 | 0 |
| Senators Representing Borderland/Rural Districts | 2 | 0 | 2 | 1 | 0 | 1 |
| Senators Representing Highland/Urban Districts | 0 | 0 | 0 | 0 | 0 | 0 |
| Senators Representing Highland/Rural Districts | 0 | 0 | 0 | 0 | 0 | 0 |

Total Senate Votes Cast against the 1891 Election Bill: 6.

SOURCE: *Arkansas Senate Journal* (1891), 334.

triumphs in three other Delta counties, LaFayette, Monroe, and St. Francis.[39]

Two years later, in 1894, the story was repeated. In Phillips County "The negroes did not vote, largely because of difficulty in handling the official ticket";[40] in consequence, all Republicans were turned out of office for the first time in memory. Likewise, a straight-out Democratic slate carried Jefferson County.[41] Surveying the returns of the fall elections, the editor of the *Arkansas Gazette* noted, "For the first time since the negroes have been allowed to vote there will be no representative of their race in either branch of the Legislature."[42]

Overall, sixty-five thousand fewer persons voted in 1894 than in 1890, an almost one-third drop in elector participation.[43] Republicans and third-party men naturally suffered most from this decline, particularly so in the state's six most predominately black counties.[44] In these areas the combined opposition lost almost eight times as many votes as the Democrats,[45] enabling the latter to regain complete ascendence. More than any other single measure, the 1891 election law established one-party rule and white supremacy as the central motif of Arkansas politics for well over a half century to come.

In some instances the Democrats almost certainly utilized fraud in winning their successes, although the new State Board of Election Commissioners under Governor Eagle does seem to have made an at least minimal effort to administer the elections honestly. Since it was required by law to do so, the board named a Republican or third-party representative to each of the county election commissions; representatives ordinarily were chosen from lists of nominees submitted by the party central committees. However, even when the nominee recommended by the minority party was selected, he easily could be outvoted by the two other county commissioners on all matters, including the appointment of precinct judges. Usually no fewer than two Democrats were placed on the commissions, even in those counties where "minority" groups had polled a majority of the votes. In sixty of the state's seventy-five counties the non-Democratic commissioner was allowed to appoint one of the precinct judges at each polling place, but in fifteen counties this privilege was denied.[46] Not surprisingly, most of these latter were located in East Arkansas and had heavy black populations; they contained the great bulk of the state's traditional Republican strength.

How could such exclusion be rationalized? Democratic apologists claimed that if local Republican bosses helped choose the precinct judges and clerks, then illiterate Negroes still would suffer from the same sort of bulldozing and intimidation they had met in the past. One of the chief purposes of the new election law, to protect the secrecy of the ballot, would be undone. Probably with an eye toward the political power of the Delta, the State Board managed to convince itself that this argument was legitimate.

Experience soon showed, however, that giving East Arkansas Democrats an exclusive monopoly of the election machinery simply was to tempt too much human nature. Aside from the anguished cries of the Republicans, the practice of open corruption is readily shown by an 1892 Democratic campaign song, "Australian Ballot." Sung to the tune of "The Bonnie Blue Flag," the

175

former national anthem of the late Confederacy, the song blatantly praised Negro disfranchisement:

The Australian ballot works like a charm,
It makes them think and scratch,
And when a negro gets a ballot,
He has certainly got his match.

*Chorus*
Hurrah! Hurrah! for Arkansas Hurrah!
And when we elect Old Grover,[47]
We will make them kick and paw.

They go into the booth alone,
Their ticket to prepare,
And as soon as five minutes are out,
They have got to git from there.—Chorus.

They then next to the Judge applies,
With a little tale of woe,
And of course his ticket is well prepared,
Which someone is bound to know.—Chorus.[48]

On the other hand, the actual commission of fraud often simply was unnecessary. Though illiterates legally could ask judges to aid in marking their tickets, few cared to expose their ignorance in such an embarrassingly public way, especially when they never could be sure in their own minds that their ballots were cast honestly. Most reacted by boycotting the polls. The following observations of a reporter at Pine Bluff are enlightening:

In this city it was interesting to note the operation of the new election law. In the first ward and Vangine Township polls crowds of negroes gathered outside the ropes and discussed the situation, and many left for their homes without attempting to vote. There were no ticket peddlers, strikers or heelers visible, and when those who could not read were told to go to the polls and vote the majority of them declined, some being distrustful of the judges and others not caring to expose their inability to make out their tickets unassisted.[49]

Democrats were quick to acknowledge this phenomenon but pretended their opposition had only themselves to blame. The editor of the *Arkansas Gazette* declared:

176

Black leaders at Helena, Arkansas, circa 1880.
Photo courtesy of the University of Central Arkansas Archives
and the Arkansas History Commission

Arkansas black Union troops stationed at Des Arc in 1866: a black color guard. Photo courtesy of the Arkansas History Commission

Arkansas white Union troops stationed at Fayetteville in 1863: The First Light Artillery Battery.
Photo courtesy of the Washington County Historical Society

Powell Clayton.
Photo courtesy of
the University of Central
Arkansas Archives

William H. Grey.
Photo courtesy of
the University of Central
Arkansas Archives

Joseph C. Corbin.
Photo courtesy of
the University of Central
Arkansas Archives

Joseph Brooks.
Photo courtesy of
the Arkansas History
Commission

Elisha Baxter.
Photo courtesy of
the Arkansas History
Commission

Augustus H. Garland.
Photo courtesy of
the Arkansas History
Commission

Scott Bond.
Photo courtesy of
the University of Central
Arkansas Archives

Scott Bond and family at their plantation home, "The Cedars,"
St. Francis County, Arkansas.
Photo courtesy of the University of Central Arkansas Archives

Pickens Black, Jr., next to his private plane.
Photo courtesy of the Arkansas History Commission

"Weighing-up time" on an Arkansas plantation.
Photo courtesy of the Arkansas History Commission

Blacks picking cotton on an Arkansas plantation.
Photo courtesy of the Arkansas History Commission

Blacks picking cotton on an Arkansas plantation.
Photo courtesy of the Arkansas History Commission

Philander Smith College, Eleventh and S. Izard streets, Little Rock, Arkansas. Engraving courtesy of the Arkansas History Commission

Capital Hill School, Eleventh and Wolfe streets, Little Rock, Arkansas, circa 1870.
Location of Little Rock's first black high-school department.
Engraving courtesy of the University of Central Arkansas Archives

"A beacon light in Arkansas."
ARKANSAS BAPTIST COLLEGE, LITTLE ROCK, ARK.

Arkansas Baptist College, 1600 High Street, Little Rock, Arkansas.
Engraving courtesy of the University of Central Arkansas Archives

Shorter College, 602 Locust Street, North Little Rock, Arkansas.
Photo courtesy of the Arkansas History Commission

Shorter College graduating class, 1910.
Photo courtesy of the Arkansas History Commission

Southland College and Normal Institute, Phillips County, Arkansas.
Engraving courtesy of the University of Central Arkansas Archives

Headquarters Building of the Mosaic Templars of America, Ninth and
Broadway streets, Little Rock, Arkansas.
Photo courtesy of the University of Central Arkansas Archives

Black leader Joseph C. Corbin in Masonic regalia. Corbin was Third State Grand Master of the Prince Hall Freemasons of Arkansas from 1878 to 1881.
Photo courtesy of the University of Central Arkansas Archives

Isaac T. Gillam, Sr.
Photo courtesy of the University of Central Arkansas Archives

The Black Diamond Drug Store, 429 Ohio Street, Helena, Arkansas.
An example of a black-owned business enterprise.
Photo courtesy of James W. Leslie

Havis Hall, saloon and meeting hall owned by Ferdinand Havis, Main and Lake (Third) streets, Pine Bluff, Arkansas.
Photo courtesy of James W. Leslie

Ferdinand Havis.
Engraving courtesy of
the University of Central
Arkansas Archives

Mifflin Wistar Gibbs.
Engraving courtesy of
the University of Central
Arkansas Archives

John E. Bush.
Photo courtesy of
the University of Central
Arkansas Archives

Wiley Jones.
Photo courtesy of
the University of Central
Arkansas Archives

Wiley Jones' street railway cars, barn, and stables, at Jones Park,
Harding Avenue and Main Street, Pine Bluff, Arkansas.
Photo courtesy of James W. Leslie

Grandstand of the race track at Jones Park, owned by Wiley Jones.
Harding Avenue and Main Street, Pine Bluff, Arkansas.
Photo courtesy of James W. Leslie

Henry R. Morehart, Union Labor party state representative and Pulaski County election contestant, 1889. The author's maternal great-grandfather.

John N. Tillman. Photo courtesy of Special Collections, University of Arkansas Libraries

George Waltham Bell.
Photo courtesy of the
Arkansas History
Commission

John Gray Lucas.
Engraving courtesy of
Special Collections,
University of Arkansas
Libraries

A Little Rock streetcar from around the turn of the century.
Photo courtesy of Tommy De Vore

Sign from a Little Rock streetcar, early twentieth century.
Photo courtesy of the Little Rock *Arkansas Gazette*

Jeff Davis.
Photo courtesy of
the University of Central
Arkansas Archives

The Australian system is by the majority regarded with favor, and the election yesterday is pronounced the most quiet and fairest ever held. There was nothing that any fair-minded man could find fault with, and we think that after our people fully understand its workings, and its perfect safeguards against fraud and ballot-box stuffing, it will meet with general favor. One thing was particularly noticeable, the total absence of cut and dried tickets on the streets. The hue and cry made by the opposing element against the system kept many from the polls, but not to the material injury of the Democracy. We are satisfied with the result, and if those of the opposing element saw fit to stay away from the polls and not vote—in other words, cut off their nose to spite their face—it was their loss, not ours.[50]

Within a short period, however, candor and a sense of reality required admission that the election law worked as a disfranchisement device. In 1894, the Pine Bluff *Commercial* bluntly proclaimed, "The ignorant and uneducated whites and blacks cannot vote the ticket, which ought to be, and is a blessing to the state, for ignorance should never rule a great commonwealth like Arkansas."[51] The *Arkansas Gazette,* for its part, came full circle. At the time of adoption, it emphatically had denied allegations that the new election law would act as an educational test for the suffrage;[52] by 1896, the paper conceded that this was exactly what had happened. Commenting on a Republican attempt to establish "night schools" where illiterate Negroes could be taught to handle the new ticket, the newspaper observed, "The average negro voter is decidedly inclined to vote, but lacks the necessary qualification of preparing a valid or legible ballot. . . . It has been estimated that perhaps three-fourths of them are incapable of preparing a ballot as required under the Australian system." Hence, "the proposed Republican instruction booths will have ample material to work on."[53]

◆　　◆　　◆

Only once did the legislature seriously consider modifying the new election system. The election of 1896, in which both Democrats and Populists had backed the presidential candidacy of William Jennings Bryan, aroused hopes of wooing third-party agrarians back into the Democratic fold.[54] In order to demonstrate that the Democracy had undergone a genuine change of heart, outgoing governor James P. Clarke, in his farewell message of 1897, appealed for additional revisions in the voting machinery. Though contending that recent elections had been eminently fair, Clarke admitted that more effective minority-party representation was needed.[55] The new incoming governor, Dan W. Jones, further remonstrated upon this point in his inaugural address:

> The election law is a vast improvement upon the system existing before its passage; but it was an entirely new departure, in the main, and its imperfections could only be detected by experience. There can be no doubt that, even with the most perfect laws, frauds in political elections will to some extent be committed. There is entirely too much human nature in man to absolutely prevent this. But the law itself should not be at fault. It should be so construed that all fair-minded men, of every shade of politics, would yield to its fairness. Every qualified elector is entitled to cast his vote according to his own will and to have it counted as cast, and he should not have to rely upon the opposite and dominant political party to know that this is done.[56]

To give all factions a proper voice, Jones recommended that the largest minority party appoint the third member of the state election commission, that it name the third member of the county election boards, and that it select one judge and one clerk in every voting precinct. Furthermore, he urged that illiterates' ballots be prepared by two judges of opposite parties. Jones also denounced the system of numbering ballots established by the state constitution and suggested that the legislature outlaw the practice of candidates buying poll taxes for voters.[57]

Soon afterward, two bills were introduced in the General Assembly to implement Governor Jones's plan for giving the largest minority party a position on state election boards. The first voted upon was that of Ulysses S. Bratton, a Republican from Searcy County; the House debates indicate that the race question was a major cause for its defeat. The following exchange, for example, took place between Lawrence County Populist Benjamin A. Morris and Faulkner County Democrat P. H. Prince:

> Mr. Morris (Pop.) denounced the present bill as a fraud upon its face.
> Mr. Prince—"I see this bill proposes to place the first minority

candidate for governor on the state board of election [commissioners]. Suppose you should run a negro or a thief for governor"—

Mr. Morris—"It would make no difference."

Mr. Prince—"That's just what I thought."

Mr. Prince favored square elections, hence favored the present election law; it brings white people to Arkansas. He was not in favor of placing "black heels on white necks." [58]

Such arguments defeated Bratton's bill by the overwhelming vote of nineteen to seventy. [59]

A week later the House considered similar legislation introduced by Nevada County Populist J. O. A. Bush. Extracts from the discussions on Bush's measure suggest that once again the race issue was paramount. In response to aspersions about the Populists' allegedly close relationship with blacks, Bush retorted that it was the large Democratic landowners who were employing and retaining Negroes in the state. He maintained that not one valid argument had been advanced against his proposal, only partisan demagoguery. [60] Bush's bill won more support than had Bratton's; surprisingly, even eight white Democratic senators from lowland plantation districts voted for its enactment. The most plausible explanation for this was the wholehearted support for election reform given by Governor Jones. Nevertheless, the measure still was rejected, thirty-six to forty-nine [61] (see table 14).

With the failure of the above initiatives, the labyrinthine history of the 1891 election law had run its course. When any measure has the sweeping consequences which the election law had, it is natural to assume that it was planned to have such consequences. In his study of Southern disfranchisement practices, *The Shaping of Southern Politics,* historian J. Morgan Kousser observed that the law's chief sponsor in the House, Representative A. H. Sevier, had stated it was "conceived in the interests of the Democratic party." Kousser also noted that its adoption was contemporaneous with the passage of disfranchisement bills in other Southern states, that it came at a time when a flood of disfranchisement legislation was inundating the South. Hence, he concluded that Arkansas's 1891 election law almost certainly must have originated as a disfranchisement device. [62]

Kousser's argument is a cogent one and may well be correct. Nevertheless, available evidence suggests a second possibility. In

TABLE 14

ANALYSIS OF VOTES CAST IN FAVOR OF THE BUSH ELECTION
BILL, ARKANSAS HOUSE OF REPRESENTATIVES, 1897

| | For Passage | Race: | | Party: | | |
| | | Black | White | Dem. | Rep. | Pop. |
|---|---|---|---|---|---|---|
| Representatives from Lowland/Urban Districts | 0 | 0 | 0 | 0 | 0 | 0 |
| Representatives from Lowland/Rural Districts | 10 | 0 | 10 | 8 | 0 | 2 |
| Representatives from Borderland/Urban Districts | 2 | 0 | 2 | 2 | 0 | 0 |
| Representatives from Borderland/Rural Districts | 12 | 0 | 12 | 6 | 0 | 6 |
| Representatives from Highland/Urban Districts | 1 | 0 | 1 | 1 | 0 | 0 |
| Representatives from Highland/Rural Districts | 11 | 0 | 11 | 7 | 2 | 2 |

Total House Votes Cast in Favor of the 1897 Bush Election Bill: 36.

SOURCE: *House of Representatives Journal* (1897), 62.

the beginning the law may have proceeded out of a search for order, a perhaps sincere attempt to end corruption in elections. While some lawmakers may have been consciously duplicitous, others who backed the measure may have genuinely believed they were voting to end dishonest electoral practices. Many of the bill's initial supporters, at least, earnestly presented themselves as crusaders for reform.

Despite this, once in operation the new law not only failed to prevent irregularities but in some cases actually engendered them; moreover, the election statute led to unprecedented political disfranchisement. This latter result, if not at first foreseen, certainly was cheerfully accepted. Of course, from a conservative perspective, there was nothing inherently unconscionable about support for disfranchisement itself; numerous persons throughout the Western world had opposed the idea of universal suffrage, out of heartfelt conviction, for most of the nineteenth century. What was undeniably culpable, however, was the use of fraud to achieve suffrage restriction. By countenancing a system that experience demonstrated permitted such chicaning methods, Arkansas Democrats violated their own and their society's best standards of conduct—indeed, their own professed reason for originally passing the election law. While a minority of the party, including Governor Jones, had the essential honesty to recognize this, the majority declined to make the required but painful changes—changes which necessarily would involve great sacrifice. In its own way, after all, the law had simply been too successful. The political opposition had been destroyed, Democratic ascendancy was safe, and white rule was assured. Nothing was lost, save honor.

# X

# Further
# Disfranchisement

Here the Democrats shuffle, cut
and deal the cards, then look in
both hands and say 'Walk up, Mr.
Republican, and vote,' and the
Republican has mighty little
chance for that jack pot.
—Powell Clayton

The fact that there is some question as to whether the 1891 election law originated as an intentional disfranchisement device should not be taken to mean that there was no contemporary interest in proposals for suffrage restriction. On the contrary, the near disasters of 1888 and 1890 had left many Democrats badly shaken, and a good number were already contemplating drastic measures to buoy their party's apparently sinking fortunes. For several months following the 1888 contest, the state's press witnessed a lively discussion over possible ways of reducing the number of voters, particularly black voters.[1] Viewed in retrospect, this development does not appear surprising. Most whites, after all, had opposed the initial enfranchisement of the Negro during Reconstruction; in time the idea had been grudgingly accepted, but even moderate men continued to think of black participation in politics as, at best, an experiment. As long as blacks posed no serious threat to continued Democratic control, the experiment seemed perhaps to be working; when they began to demonstrate an independent spirit and even threatened to ally with agrarian radicals, things plainly had gone awry. With unconcealed trepidation, the state's conservative leadership saw their society as tottering on the verge of chaos and disorder, ready to plunge into a dark night of jacobin excess. In such changed circumstances one could logically argue that placing new limitations on the Negro's ballot was only wise and prudent policy. Such a perspective was obviously shaped by partisan and class interest, though not for that reason any less genuinely held.

The simplest and most direct proposal for disfranchisement was also the most popular: repeal of the Fourteenth and Fifteenth Amendments to the United States Constitution. The best-known exponent of the idea in Arkansas was Dr. J. A. Meek, a venerable state representative from Craighead County. Meek advanced repeal during the campaign of 1888 and subsequently set forth his views in a letter to his hometown newspaper, the Jonesboro *Times*. He lamented that "During the Reconstruction period vicious and corrupt practices were introduced in the elections of this state" and that "since the government has passed into the hands of the democracy . . . in some [areas] they manifest a disposition to follow the vile and unlawful practices of their political opponents." These corrupt methods, he warned, "must be suppressed and effectually. To allow [them] to continue would be to ruin us as a party and would overthrow all civil authority in the state and inaugurate anarchy and ruin in its place."[2]

The question, of course, was how to suppress corruption. Meek advocated improved state election laws but candidly acknowledged his doubts that these would prove enough. As Negroes continued to vote, frauds and disorder would continue to occur. Therefore, he avowed, "I am in favor of the repeal of the fourteenth and fifteenth amendments to the Constitution . . . Don't be startled, I am not crazy. It must come to that. The government made a great blunder when it adopted those amendments, and it must retrace its steps. We have our choice—disfranchisement of the colored race or a bloody revolution."[3] It was, he insisted, "no longer a sectional issue, but good men of all sections and all parties recognize the great truth that the Caucasian race must govern America."[4]

Meek's proposal struck a responsive cord and evoked extensive comment; on the surface, his concept held great attraction for the Arkansas Democratic establishment. Direct abolition of Negro suffrage would emasculate the rising political opposition without arousing the white majority. Indeed, by assuaging status anxieties and appealing to deeply held prejudices, repeal of the amendments would forge even stronger traditional Democratic bonds with the average white voter.

Despite this, as a practical matter the chances of revising the Constitution looked slim. In a perceptive series of editorials, the *Arkansas Gazette* pointed out that Meek's suggestions were not so far-fetched as they might at first seem. Popular attitudes in the nation had undergone a decided change of late, and the paper believed that many persons north of the Mason-Dixon line were now willing to admit that enfranchisement of blacks had been a mistake.[5] Even some of the Democracy's Southern opponents appeared to be having second thoughts about the black voter; Judge McClure's "lily-white" address at the recent Republican state convention was cited as a case in point.[6]

Realistically, however, the *Gazette* believed that rescinding of the Fourteenth and Fifteenth Amendments was hardly imminent. Consent of three-fourths of the states would be necessary and could never be obtained; in several closely contested Northern states, the ballots of Negro minorities were simply too vital to the future health and well-being of the Republican party. Thus, because of Northern Republican opposition, any attempt at repeal would be stillborn.[7]

There remained several other possibilities for implementing suffrage restriction. An educational test which would at least bar illiterates from the polls won support from some.[8] To its backers, the idea had one especially pleasing advantage: several states in the North, including Massachusetts, already had a literacy requirement on the books. In an editorial probably written in part for Northern eyes, the *Arkansas Gazette* maintained:

> The intelligent and responsible elements will govern wherever they exist. It is the history of the human race; and it were no more unreasonable to invite the culture of Massachusetts to consent that ignorance should dictate its government, or the mill owners of Rhode Island [to] place the legislative disposition of their property in the hands of pauper labor they employ, than to ask this fair land of ours to submit to the domination of vicious ignorance.[9]

Quite evidently, shielding of their property interests was a prime consideration for many of those calling for educational restrictions; frequently, in fact, demands for a literacy test were coupled with appeals for a poll tax or other property requirements for voting.[10]

Actually, though not tied to the exercise of the suffrage, a poll tax was already in existence: the constitution of 1874 assessed a per capita tax of one dollar on every male inhabitant of Arkansas over the age of twenty-one, with the receipts to be placed in the state's public-school fund.[11] Collection of the tax proved difficult, nevertheless, and payment was at best sporadic, a state of affairs which produced bitter disgruntlement among the wealthy.[12] Since taxes on real property constituted the only reliable source of government revenue, the landless in their eyes got off scot-free (although in reality this latter class helped shoulder the tax burden indirectly through rent payments and receipt of subsistence wages, a fact usually overlooked).[13] Making payment of the per capita levy a prerequisite for the ballot would exact taxes from the poor or drive them from the polls, either a consequence much to be desired.

The most forthright plea for a poll-tax requirement for voting, and the one which assuredly commanded greatest attention, was published by the Reverend Wallace Carnahan in the *Anglo-Saxon Churchman*, the official magazine of the Episcopal Diocese of Arkansas. As rector of Little Rock's Christ Church, Carnahan shepherded a flock with golden fleece; his parish, sometimes referred to as "the Mother Church of the Diocese," was the oldest in the state and boasted a membership of unrivaled affluence and influence.

Like many fellow clergymen, Carnahan was alarmed by the moral rot being induced by the state election system; acceptance of the notion that under certain circumstances one could permissibly steal votes and increasing incidences of fraud were "making scoundrels and ruffians of the sons of gentlemen."[14] Regrettable as it was, however, Carnahan believed the situation would continue while universal black suffrage prevailed. And since specifically racial tests were proscribed by the federal Constitution, some alternative would have to be devised:

> Every intelligent, unprejudiced man in America knows perfectly well that the only thoroughly safe standard is pure Caucasian blood; but as we have assumed the impracticability of returning to that standard, the question is what makeshift shall we substitute for it? We are

persuaded that nothing less, and nothing else, than an educational qualification, a large poll tax and the ownership of unencumbered real estate—to the value say of $1000—will insure us a safe body of voters composed of both white and black citizens.

The negro who can read and write, is able and willing to pay a $10 poll tax, and is able to accumulate and hold $1000 worth of land, is an exceptionally strong negro, and as a rule can be trusted to resist the wiles of the demagogue and vote wisely.[15]

Of course the white person who met these standards could be trusted to "vote wisely" also. All the rhetoric about "Caucasian blood" aside, Carnahan was proposing that, for measuring voter competency, the bourgeois yardstick of social class be substituted for the traditional norm of caste: rich blacks would enjoy favored privileges denied ordinary whites. Carnahan owned that under his plan a great many white as well as black electors would be disfranchised, but felt the former could be prevailed upon to make the "sacrifice" once "the natural leaders of the people" ceased eschewing politics.[16]

It was one thing for an Episcopal priest to advance such views to his wealthy parishioners; for the practical politician, it was less clear that the common whites would order themselves reverently before their betters. Once Carnahan's proposals gained wide currency, they were quickly repudiated. Much to the embarrassment of the Arkansas congressional delegation, a copy of Carnahan's article fell into the hands of Northern Republican advocates of federal election supervision; during the final debates on the Lodge "Force" bill in early 1891, George F. Hoar of Massachusetts read excerpts from the article on the floor of the Senate to prove the existence of widespread corruption in Southern elections. Arkansas senators James H. Berry and James K. Jones immediately disavowed Carnahan's comments, Berry claiming that the facts stated by Carnahan "are not true, and the remedy he proposes . . . absurd."[17]

Back home few rushed to the rector's defense; the idea that poor whites would willingly forsake their ballots in order to deny poor blacks theirs seemed a dubious proposition at best. Even before the Carnahan affair some of those who had briefly flirted with property and educational restrictions had begun to backtrack. The *Arkansas Gazette* reprinted an editorial from the neighboring

Memphis (Tennessee) *Appeal* which stated, among other things, that "The United States could not be a democratic republic if it did not rest . . . upon a basis of consent . . . If only the rich and intelligent voted ours would be an oligarchic government, and there would be no hope for the common people." Regarding the black voter, the Memphis paper asserted, "The Negroes have the right to vote, and are protected in the exercise of that right; they are growing in intelligence, are beginning to think for themselves, and in time will divide, as the white voters do, and cast their votes on opposing sides of every public question. The southern states do not complain of or demur to negro suffrage." The real danger came, not from the Negro, but from "the trusts, monopolies and combines, whose object is the restriction of production and the consequent enslavement of the working masses." [18]

The *Gazette* itself observed that "revolutions cannot go backwards" [19] and that any attempt at suffrage restriction could provoke violent political and social repercussions; the whole effort, moreover, would be futile since its success would require the consent of those to be disfranchised. [20] Reverting to the more traditional stance of urban moderates, the paper cautioned that only time, patience, and good will could ameliorate existing difficulties. [21]

The Arkansas legislature at first displayed a similar unwillingness to embark upon the dangerous waters of suffrage limitation. When the original centralized elections bill was launched in the General Assembly of 1889, it provided, as noted previously, for creation of a State Board of Election Commissioners. In addition, however, this first bill would have established new requirements for voting: to establish proof of residency, the elector would have been ordered to produce a receipt showing he had paid his one-dollar poll tax, or, in lieu of this, sworn testimony from two householders of his election district attesting to his actual place of abode. [22] Though not technically a property requirement for the suffrage, the proposal was clearly a step in that direction. By and large the response was lukewarm; critics maintained the idea probably violated provisions of the state constitution guaranteeing the ballot to all male citizens over the age of twenty-one; [23] along with the rest of the election package, it was rejected by the lawmakers. [24]

When meeting two years later, though, in 1891, the legislature evinced a stiffening mood. The proposal for establishing centralized elections under control of a State Board was reintroduced and passed; simultaneously, the requirement making possession of a poll-tax receipt a prerequisite for the ballot (with the alternative of testimony from two householders now dropped) was brought forth as a proposed constitutional amendment.[25] Democratic leaders tried to push through the amendment as quickly as possible with a minimum of discussion; its author, Senator B. W. M. Warren of the Eighteenth District (Bradley and Union counties), first called the poll tax to a vote late in the session, only cryptically saying that the measure "should have the endorsement of every white man in the State, as well as every intelligent colored man who has the interest of the State at heart."[26] The amendment carried unanimously, twenty-seven to zero, with the black Republican senator, George W. Bell, and white Union Laborite J. P. H. Russ supporting its passage; the other Union Labor senator, F. P. Hill, was among five persons absent and not voting.[27]

A little over a week later the amendment came before the House and faced somewhat greater opposition, though still carrying readily. Sam J. Crabtree, Union Labor representative from White County, tried to lay the amendment on the table, but his motion was rejected, twenty-three to fifty-eight[28] (see table 15). Those unsuccessfully supporting tabling included thirteen white Democrats, the House's two white Republicans, five of the nine black Republicans, two of the four white Union Laborites, and the sole black Union Laborite.[29]

The House also voted down a revision to the amendment suggested by black Republican J. N. Donohoo. Donohoo wanted to allow persons who had lost their receipts to be able to swear an affidavit that they had paid their poll taxes, but his proposal was defeated by voice vote.[30]

By contrast, the representatives accepted two other changes in the amendment; one withheld the ballot from convicted felons,[31] while the other required election officers to stamp or initial poll-tax receipts.[32] This latter requirement hopefully would stop "repeating" or multiple voting by unscrupulous electors. The practice was claimed by whites to be commonplace among blacks;[33] since Negroes all supposedly "looked alike," they allegedly could even vote several times at the same precinct without detection.

With these modifications the poll-tax amendment was approved

## TABLE 15
### ANALYSIS OF VOTES CAST IN FAVOR OF A MOTION TO LAY ON THE TABLE THE PROPOSED POLL-TAX AMENDMENT, ARKANSAS HOUSE OF REPRESENTATIVES, 1891

| | For Tabling | Race: Black | Race: White | Party: Dem. | Party: Rep. | Party: ULP |
|---|---|---|---|---|---|---|
| Representatives from Lowland/Urban Districts | 1 | 1 | 0 | 0 | 1 | 0 |
| Representatives from Lowland/Rural Districts | 7 | 4 | 3 | 2 | 4 | 1 |
| Representatives from Borderland/Urban Districts | 0 | 0 | 0 | 0 | 0 | 0 |
| Representatives from Borderland/Rural Districts | 6 | 0 | 6 | 5 | 0 | 1 |
| Representatives from Highland/Urban Districts | 0 | 0 | 0 | 0 | 0 | 0 |
| Representatives from Highland/Rural Districts | 9 | 0 | 9 | 7 | 2 | 0 |

Total House Votes Cast in Favor of Tabling the Proposed 1891 Poll-Tax Amendment: 23

SOURCE: *House of Representatives Journal* (1891), 894–95.

by the House, fifty-nine to fifteen[34] (see table 16), and sent back to the Senate for final action; the senators gave their assent twenty-six to one; on this final tally Union Laborite J. P. H. Russ switched and cast his vote against the proposal, while his party colleague F. P. Hill and the black senator George W. Bell abstained.[35]

Clearing the legislative hurdle did not ensure the amendment's adoption, for it still had to win acceptance from the voters in the upcoming September 1892 state election. Although most Democratic candidates and editors endorsed the poll-tax prerequisite,[36] both the Republicans and Populists continually excoriated it as an undemocratic measure which would work unnecessary hardships on the poor and lead to increased buying of votes.[37] Debate over the amendment soon became a central issue in the 1892 campaign.

The arguments used by the Democrats in rallying support for

189

TABLE 16

ANALYSIS OF VOTES CAST AGAINST THE PROPOSED POLL-TAX
AMENDMENT, ARKANSAS HOUSE OF REPRESENTATIVES, 1891

| | Against Passage | Race: | | Party: | | |
|---|---|---|---|---|---|---|
| | | Black | White | Dem. | Rep. | ULP |
| Representatives from Lowland/Urban Districts | 0 | 0 | 0 | 0 | 0 | 0 |
| Representatives from Lowland/Rural Districts | 6 | 4 | 2 | 2 | 4 | 0 |
| Representatives from Borderland/Urban Districts | 0 | 0 | 0 | 0 | 0 | 0 |
| Representatives from Borderland/Rural Districts | 5 | 0 | 5 | 4 | 0 | 1 |
| Representatives from Highland/Urban Districts | 0 | 0 | 0 | 0 | 0 | 0 |
| Representatives from Highland/Rural Districts | 4 | 0 | 4 | 3 | 1 | 0 |

Total House Votes Cast against the Proposed 1891 Poll-Tax Amendment: 15

SOURCE: *Arkansas House of Representatives Journal* (1891), 916–17.

the poll tax go a long way toward explaining its eventual ratification and also perhaps the relative weakness of the earlier opposition to it in the General Assembly (including the lack of opposition from urban senators and representatives).[38] Occasionally,
proponents openly touted the amendment as a means of achieving
suffrage restriction. The Arkadelphia *Southern Standard*, for example, exclaimed, "Vote for Amendment No. 2. It requires a poll
tax receipt to entitle a man to vote, and compels thousands of
worthless negroes to show a 'poll tax receipt' or be denied the
sweet privilege of voting."[39]

Usually just the opposite point was stressed, however. Democrats underscored the fact that the poll-tax fee was only one dollar
and that anyone could easily pay the assessment;[40] in fact, this was
only partially true. In comparison to, say, Reverend Carnahan's
proposals the tax was low, but at a time when a dollar a day was
still the frequent wage for unskilled laborers, the levy could be,

190

for some, considerable. Most persons could pay the tax if they were committed enough, but it was precisely the inarticulate poorer classes who were most apathetic and fatalistic about their lot: only acute economic distress had aroused them to political action in the first place.

Along with the assumed paltriness of the poll-tax levy, proponents reiterated that the poll-tax amendment would stop multiple voting.[41] Just how frequently "repeating" occurred it is impossible to say, but, like the 1891 election law, the poll tax was originally promoted as an instrument for securing political reform.[42]

Most importantly, advocates advanced the poll tax as a means of raising additional revenues for the public school system.[43] This was claimed to be the chief motivation for submission of the amendment and was the justification most often given for its adoption. The public schools were indeed starved for revenues, and unquestionably thousands cast their ballots for the poll tax out of a civic-minded concern for public education.

The whole matter of support for schooling also helps explain a curious fact about the poll tax. A survey of the election returns in the state's six most heavily black counties has shown that the 1892 Republican gubernatorial candidate, William G. Whipple, received almost twice as many votes as were cast against the poll-tax amendment.[44] Assuming that most of Whipple's support in these counties came from blacks, then it is apparent that many Negroes voted for the poll tax.

In view of the incessant Republican attacks against the measure, this is hard to fathom. Possibly many blacks as well as whites were motivated by a desire to clean up elections and stop "repeating" incidences. Another likely factor was the not too veiled threat from whites to slash funding for Negro education if the tax were defeated.[45] Since the black middle classes and leadership groups generally saw the public schools as a sine qua non for their race's advancement, such hints were probably not taken lightly.

Still, one last fact should be borne in mind. The state election of 1892, in which the poll-tax amendment was decided upon, was the first major election conducted under the new 1891 voting law. As has been demonstrated, this election law itself excluded large numbers of illiterates—the classes most likely to be opposed to a poll-tax prerequisite—from the polls; thousands of unlettered blacks and whites never had a chance to vote upon the poll tax at all. Moreover, some of those illiterates who did attempt to vote may have had their ballots miscounted by the election judges; fraud is of course the simplest explanation for seeming black support of the poll tax.

Even with the assistance of the new voting law, it was questionable whether the poll-tax amendment in fact carried. The final statewide tally showed 75,847 votes for adoption to 56,589 against.[46] Nevertheless, of the 156,186 persons who cast ballots in the election, only 132,436 cast ballots on the amendment.[47] The 75,847 total for adoption, therefore, was some 2,200 less than an absolute majority of all persons participating in the general voting. Since Article XIX, section 22 of the state constitution specified that an amendment had to be approved by a majority of those voting in the election,[48] there was serious doubt concerning ratification; a number of leading Democratic newspapers, as well as most of the state's Populists and Republicans, insisted that the poll-tax prerequisite had failed.[49]

When the legislature met in joint session in January 1893 to survey the election returns, several lawmakers arose to protest certification of the amendment's passage by the Speaker of the House. The presiding officer of the joint session, E. B. Kinsworthy, president of the Senate, quickly gaveled the dissidents down, commenting, "The law declares that the Speaker of the House shall canvass the returns of the election and declare the result. That is the end of the matter so far as the law is concerned. I declare you out of order (applause)."[50] An act to enforce the amendment was speeded through the legislature,[51] and the poll-tax requirements took effect after April 14, 1893.

In 1895, the General Assembly passed a second poll-tax enforcement measure specifying the times during which payment of the poll tax had to be made. The prospective elector had to pay his tax between the first Monday in January and the Saturday before the first Monday in July to be qualified to vote in any election held before July of the next succeeding year.[52] The purpose may have been innocent enough, to establish an annual registration list of voters and facilitate bookkeeping by county officers. Yet, the law assumed that a voter would possess enough commitment and sense of involvement to pay his tax and register months before the actual election day, a procedure which had to be repeated every year. Regardless of the intent, the effect of the poll-tax requirements was to amplify the strength of the ruling party and to silence further the voice of the underclasses in state politics.

During the time between paying of the poll tax and the election, it was easy to misplace or lose the poll-tax receipt; this was particularly true of itinerant sharecroppers and field hands, who frequently moved from cabin to cabin and who often were not used to keeping permanent records or papers. Fortunately, the 1895 act did allow individuals who had paid their taxes but lost their receipts to vote anyway; their names were recorded and later checked against the tax lists.[53] Anyone whom the election judges suspected of not having paid the poll tax could be made to take a formal oath that he had done so.[54] Of course, persons who perjured themselves could be prosecuted. Again, the purpose may have been well intentioned—to stop "repeating"—but inevitably some honest but timid voters were frightened from the polls.

Another revision in the poll-tax statutes, also made in 1895, specified that the taxpayer's race be designated on the receipt;[55] this enabled authorities to determine the maximum possible black vote in any given election.

Although the poll-tax amendment initially went into force in 1893, complaints continued to be heard for years about its questionable adoption. In January 1905, federal district judge Jacob Trieber delivered a ruling in a Little Rock case contesting the requirement of a poll tax for voting in a congressional election. A Republican appointee and a political associate of Powell Clayton, Trieber's broad interpretations of the equal-protection clause of the Fourteenth Amendment to the federal Constitution sometimes exceeded what was allowed by higher tribunals. In the case in question, the plaintiff had met all necessary residency and age requirements but had been prevented from voting because he had not paid his poll tax. Contending that Arkansas's poll-tax prerequisites had never been properly ratified, he sued for damages. Trieber accepted his plea and awarded a judgment of twenty-five hundred dollars.[56]

The following year, in *Rice v. Palmer*,[57] the Arkansas Supreme Court at last redefined the necessary requirements for adopting state constitutional amendments. The decision concerned Amendment No. 3, which gave the governor authority to fill any vacancies in state and local offices until the next general election. Submitted to the electors in 1894, this proposal, like the poll-tax amendment, had received a plurality but not an absolute majority of all votes cast in the election. In its ruling, the Supreme Court struck down Amendment No. 3, declaring that ratification required approval of a complete majority.

The *Rice v. Palmer* decision did not immediately overturn the original poll-tax amendment, but it was clear that any suit brought against it would be successful. Hoping to deflect impending judicial assaults, the legislature submitted a second poll-tax amendment, Amendment No. 9, to the voters in 1908. As events would have it, this second poll-tax measure won approval by means as doubtful as the first. Although the new proposal was permitted on the ballot, the old prerequisites, since they had not yet been overturned by the courts, were construed still to be in full force and effect.[58] Strangely, an elector had to possess a poll-tax receipt before he could participate in the election and vote on the poll-tax amendment. Under these circumstances, the amendment received the necessary majority.[59]

◆     ◆     ◆

Even after the poll tax and the new state election laws successfully disfranchised a majority of Negroes, a remaining group of middle-class, literate blacks could still retain some political voice by voting in Democratic primaries. Here, they could conceivably hold a balance of power during close election contests and might extract concessions from competing candidates. It was to prevent such situations from developing that Arkansas Democrats instituted a third and final means of disfranchisement, the "white primary."

Democratic primary elections began appearing in some counties as early as the 1870s, as a substitute for the older convention system of choosing nominees. Under the new primaries, selection of nominees for county offices was transferred from delegate conventions to the party rank and file, i.e., instead of sending delegates to the county convention to represent them, party members now voted directly for local and county candidates running for the various positions on the ballot.[60]

The Populist insurgency, with its charges of elitist domination, did much to hasten the collapse of nomination by conventions; fearing massive farmer defections, Democratic organizations in one county after another began authorizing the use of primary

194

contests. Recognizing the importance of the new practice, the legislature in 1895 adopted a law legalizing the holding of primaries. Under this act, it was possible but not mandatory for county central committees to utilize the primary system. If a county committee chose to hold a primary, though, the law required that it be conducted in accordance with the general election statutes, except that election officials naturally all could be of the same political faith. Requirements for voting were to be the same as at regular general elections (including payment of the poll tax), with specific penalties laid down for the various violations.[61]

The primary movement reached its culmination in May 1898 when the Democratic state central committee directed that every county committee in Arkansas inaugurate primary contests. Statewide primaries to nominate the candidates for governor and other state offices were also instituted. The state committee's action was nothing short of revolutionary; it did much to democratize the party structure and paved the way for the later ascent of "new model" agrarian leaders, such as the flamboyant Jeff Davis, within the Democratic household.

As was so often true of reform initiatives for this era, however, the primary elections were an example of democracy restricted to whites. Some Democratic organizations, attempting to emphasize the claim that they represented the party of the white race and trying to reforge white voter solidarity, began welcoming former white Populists into their ranks; simultaneously, they began excluding all blacks, regardless of past loyalties, from participation in their party primaries.[62] Not every Democrat approved of these new experiments; the Little Rock *Arkansas Gazette*, expressing a conservative fear of agrarian extremism, and also perhaps the greater racial moderation of urban localities, argued that the test for admission to primary elections should be past party fealty, not race.[63] Following the newspaper's advice, the Little Rock city central committee, in 1901, rejected a "white primary" proposal by a vote of eighteen to five.[64] Yet, whites-only restrictions continued to spread, especially in rural areas, and finally in January 1906 the Arkansas Democratic committee ordered their use throughout the state.[65]

The "white primary" was the last major instrument of disfranchisement to be employed in Arkansas elections. In 1911, the legislature submitted a proposed constitutional amendment which would have established new educational tests for the suffrage; the amendment also contained a "grandfather clause" exempting white illiterates from its provisions. However, the Arkansas Democratic convention, despite appeals of delegates from some Delta counties, declined to endorse it. Negro spokesmen, led by Little Rock attorney Scipio A. Jones, organized a State Suffrage League which urged blacks to pay their poll tax and vote against adoption. In the November 1912 general election, the proposed amendment lost heavily, 51,334 to 74,950.[66]

Probably the chief reason the amendment lost is that many persons regarded the new measure as simply unnecessary. And little wonder: using ecological regression analysis, J. Morgan Kousser has demonstrated that the earlier 1891 election law contracted voting in Arkansas by about 17 percent (21 percent among blacks and 7 percent among whites). Subsequently, the poll tax curtailed voter participation by an additional 10 percent (15 percent among blacks, 9 to 12 percent among whites). Together, these two laws, as Kousser has observed, "shrank opposition strength enough to ensure permanent Democratic hegemony."[67]

The defeat of the proposed 1912 amendment guaranteed that some blacks would always continue to vote in Arkansas even after effective disfranchisement had been achieved. Such black participation was tolerated because it was essentially meaningless. From the Democrats' standpoint it even served a useful purpose, for it helped to camouflage the true character of the Arkansas election system, the reality of which was dominance by the white middle- and upper-classes. Nomination in the state and congressional Democratic primaries, from which blacks were excluded, was at least after 1900 virtually tantamount to victory: Republican opposition in the general state elections was token and *pro forma*. And in the era of the "solid South," Democratic presidential candidates could usually expect to carry Arkansas handily. Only when they cast their ballots upon initiated acts and proposed constitutional amendments did the remaining black voters exercise a modicum of real political power.

♦    ♦    ♦

Blacks who lived through the period of the 1890s and early twentieth century did not always fully comprehend the complex forces and motivations responsible for their disfranchisement. In his book *The Philosophy of Negro Suffrage*, published in 1895, Arkansas Negro Democrat Jerome R. Riley blamed the recent turn of events on his race's allegedly unshakable allegiance to the Republican party. Riley recalled an 1875 contest for state representative in Jefferson County, where the Republican candidate was one Ned Hill, a Negro. Hill could neither read nor write, but his "fighting weight was two hundred pounds, drunk or sober"; his ticket was overwhelmingly elected. Riley believed that at that time "he, or even Judas Iscariot, if branded with the party stamp, could just as easily have defeated Gov. Garland or Major Breckenridge, or any one else in the front rank of statesmanship."[68]

Riley was reiterating an argument commonplace among whites, an argument already well on its way to becoming a hallowed regional myth. It held that the mass enfranchisement of the ex-slaves during Reconstruction had been a momentous error, the opening act in what was seen as a tragedy of misrule. Forcible removal of blacks from politics, when it came in the nineties, could be justified as merely a belated effort to right the mistakes of the past.[69]

Like many historical legends, this one had a certain basis in fact. Even most of those authorities who feel that long-term democratic gains warranted the action would still concede that suddenly placing the ballot in the hands of largely illiterate, inexperienced freedmen caused serious problems; most would concede that at least some of the corruption and extravagance of Reconstruction governments stemmed from this policy. Yet, to state this alone is to give only half the truth. Blacks knew perfectly well that they were often regarded by whites as inherently unfit for self-government; even during Reconstruction blacks tended to thrust their best men forward, especially for the higher and more important offices. Such black spokesmen as Joseph Carter Corbin, State Superintendent of Public Instruction; Mifflin W. Gibbs, Municipal Judge of Little Rock; and others were able to command considerable respect from both races.

With the overthrow of the Carpetbaggers the political position of blacks became more tenuous yet, and if anything the race moved with even more prudence and circumspection. The conduct of Ferdinand Havis, black leader of the Jefferson County Republican organization during the 1880s and 1890s, was fairly representative. Mifflin W. Gibbs recalled that Havis "As a member of the Arkansas legislature in 1873 and Clerk of Jefferson County for many years . . . by honesty as an official and courtesy of manner made an unimpeachable record, and was only dethroned 'by fraud and force and iron will.'" During his primacy in the county, where three-fourths of the voters were black, "he was ever conservative and regardful of the views and business interests of the numerically weak but financially strong minority of Democrats, and by supporting a compromise ticket that gave most prominence to the minority sought to preserve harmony." [70]

That Gibbs' assessment is essentially correct is suggested by an incident which occurred in 1897, when Havis tried to secure the office of United States Postmaster at Pine Bluff. To refute charges that his appointment would be objectionable to the white community, he secured recommendations from over fifty white Democrats of Jefferson County; included in the list were state senator W. P. Grace, Citizen's Bank president W. H. Langford, former county judge J. W. Bocage, two ex-mayors of Pine Bluff, and dozens of prominent merchants and businessmen. [71]

It would be wrong to assume that a man like Havis was rare and exceptional. In a careful study of the twelve black legislators who served in the General Assembly of 1891, historian Willard Gatewood found that in wealth, degree of education, and previous experience, the black lawmakers differed little from their white counterparts. [72] At least one of the black representatives, John Gray Lucas, an honor graduate of the Boston University School of Law, was a man of genuinely superior talents and abilities.

Ironically, in spite of the recognition they sometimes achieved, Negroes like Havis and Lucas could awaken intense hostility. Havis, for instance, found the support he received for postmaster from Pine Bluff whites was insufficient to overcome the opposition of the Arkansas congressional delegation, responsible to a larger constituency. [73] Although the Congress approved Mifflin W. Gibbs' nomination to become United States Consul to Tamatave, Madagascar, it rejected Havis's own bid for preferment. One white editor chortled that Havis "should have applied for the consulship at Timbuctoo, instead of the Pine Bluff post office." [74]

Men such as Havis and Lucas may actually have prompted their race's enforced rustication from politics. If the ignorant black politician was despised, the capable one could be bitterly resented, particularly by impoverished rural whites whose own status and self-esteem were already threatened by economic depression. Viewed from this perspective, disfranchisement took place in the 1890s perhaps not so much because black leaders lacked competence; rather, it occurred because, increasingly, they possessed it.

# XI

# Blacks and the Agrarian Revolt

This is a white man's country, and white men are going to rule it, and when the third party opened its arms to the negro at its State convention, it invited its certain death at the polls . . .
—Arkadelphia *Siftings*, (n.d.), in *Arkansas Gazette*, June 30, 1892.

For the Democrats, the disfranchisement measures enacted during the 1890s not only had the advantage of destroying black political participation; they also simultaneously ruined whatever chance of success an independent agrarian movement may have had. In 1892, the rebellious Arkansas farmers who had previously gathered under the Union Labor banner easily moved into the new Populist crusade then sweeping through the rural South and West. At first glance, in no state did the outlook for Populism seem brighter. In the rest of Dixie, agricultural organizations had initially tried to achieve their goals within the framework of the Democratic party.[1] In Arkansas, a more radical leadership had already created a vigorous third-party effort, one which had very nearly seized control of the government.

Actually, however, the state's Populists were beginning life under circumstances which were far from sanguine. The Republicans, reversing their strategy of 1888 and 1890, declined to endorse the Populist candidates for state office; instead, they put forth a separate ticket, hoping that their normal opposition vote might split between the Democrats and Populists and ensure a Republican upset.[2] Even more disheartening, in 1892 the new election law first was placed in operation. When the balloting was over in September, the returns disclosed that Populist gubernatorial candidate J. P. Carnahan and Republican nominee William G. Whipple had both trailed badly behind the Democratic victor, William M. Fishback.[3]

Two years later, in 1894, the Populists had to contend with the additional hurdle of the poll tax and fared even more poorly in the state election races.[4] Finally, in 1896 the joint selection of William Jennings Bryan as a presidential standard-bearer by the Democratic and Populist national conventions undercut the Arkansas agrarians' remaining strength. Owing to a fusion understanding, three Populists along with five Democrats were chosen as Arkansas members of the Electoral College,[5] but in every other respect the contest was a disaster. In the governor's race, Populist candidate A. W. Files received only 13,990 votes out of a total of approximately 150,000 cast.[6] After 1896 the Populist party underwent rapid disintegration and soon disappeared as an effective political force.[7]

These developments in Arkansas only paralleled what was happening in other Southern states, where the Democrats employed both legal techniques of disfranchisement and extralegal methods of fraud and terror in containing the Populist insurgency.

Some historians have viewed the downfall of Populism as constituting as much a tragedy for the black farmer as his white counterpart.[8] Foremost among those sharing this perspective is C. Vann Woodward. Drawing heavily from his biography of Tom Watson,[9] the flamboyant Populist leader in Georgia, Woodward has argued that the third-party movement offered the Negro "an equalitarianism of want and poverty, the kinship of a common grievance and a common oppressor."[10] Watson, for example, speaking before mixed audiences in his home state, stressed that "the colored tenant . . . is in the same boat with the white tenant, the colored laborer with the white laborer" and declared, "the accident of color can make no difference in the interests of farmers, croppers, and laborers."[11] Heroically defying native racial orthodoxies, he told blacks "if you stand up for your rights and for your manhood, if you stand shoulder to shoulder with us in this fight," the People's party will "wipe out the color line and put every man on his citizenship irrespective of color."[12]

These were not mere empty promises, says Woodward. In Georgia and elsewhere, Negroes were brought "into the inmost councils of the party."[13] Populists placed black men on their executive committees, campaign committees, and their tickets for public office. They decried lynchings and, whenever they had the power, protected the Negroes' ballots and saw that they were assigned to jury duty. Blacks themselves recognized the revolutionary quality of the Populists' racial program and "responded with more enthusiasm and hope than to any other political movement since their disillusionment with radical Republicanism."[14] All in all, Woodward concludes, "It is . . . probable that during the brief Populist upheaval of the nineties Negroes and native whites achieved a greater comity of mind and harmony of political purpose than ever before or since in the South."[15]

A somewhat more qualified assessment of Populism's stance toward blacks is given by Lawrence Goodwyn in his comprehensive study of the agrarian revolt, *Democratic Promise: The Populist Moment in America*.[16] Goodwyn recognizes that the power of the received culture of white supremacy created internal strains and tensions within the Populist organizations; in particular, in spite of their raised levels of racial consciousness, white radicals sometimes manifested a reluctance to accept the most militant black spokesmen as full political equals in the agrarian cause. Moreover, he notes that while "The educational triumph of the . . . movement lay in its success in persuading hundreds of thousands of poor Southern white farmers to forsake the party of white supremacy for a party of economic self-interest," still "Populism's failure ultimately was traceable to its inability to persuade still more thousands to the same conversion."[17] Even so, Goodwyn, like Woodward, stresses the courage of the Populists and the remarkable degree to which they were willing to break with the received racial traditions of their society and time. Goodwyn believes this was especially true in Arkansas. "Arkansas Populists," he writes, "both politically and personally, demonstrated the clearest record of racial liberalism of any of the Southern third parties."[18]

Another group of scholars has advanced a completely contrary argument concerning Populist-black relationships; in essence, they have turned Woodward and Goodwyn's characterization of Populism's racial policies upside down, asserting that the Populists refused to grant blacks any meaningful role or voice in their party. Moreover, on anti-lynching proposals, jury duty for blacks, and related questions the Populists are seen frequently espousing positions antithetical to the best interests of Negroes. Basically, it is alleged, their approaches to the minority race were founded on opportunism and political expediency.[19]

How does evidence from the present study bear upon this controversy? Put most simply, a careful investigation does not seem to lend unqualified support to either perspective. There is no good reason to believe that the Arkansas agrarians were ever consciously duplicitous in their approach to the Negro. But neither was their overall stand consistently bold or daring. If any posture was typical, it was one marked by hesitancy and uncertainty.

This note of ambiguity was present from the very beginning of the farmers' movement in Arkansas; nowhere, in fact, is it more evident than in the policies of one of the earliest farmers' organizations, the Agricultural Wheel. At the time of its inception in 1882, the Wheel had adopted a constitution restricting membership exclusively to white males.[20] Such a limitation had not prevented the new order's rapid growth, but it obviously debarred many potential recruits and divided the unity of the agrarian cause. Particularly in the eastern section of the state, it soon became apparent that successful action required a measure of interracial cooperation.

For their part, blacks appeared eager to participate in the cause once the restrictions were lifted. Already, they had begun to organize a separate protest association called "The Sons of the Agricultural Star" with headquarters in Monroe County.[21] Under these circumstances, the Wheelers undertook reconsideration of their original stand. At the 1886 Wheel convention, held at Litchfield, the delegates—after what the official historian of the order described as "much animated discussion"—dropped the word "white" from the eligibility clause in the constitution and provided for the grouping of black farmers into separate locals.[22] The next year, delegates from these new Negro Wheels were admitted to full representation in the state assembly.[23]

Once they had gained entry into the Agricultural Wheel, Ne-

203

groes assumed a subordinate, though nevertheless important, role. Their precise status is suggested by the organization's composition of leadership in 1888, immediately prior to the Wheel's merger with the Southern Farmers' Alliance. The four state officers, chaplain, trustees, and executive committee of the order were all white, but three of the eight state lecturers were black.[24] There were, additionally, eleven "colored deputies" who acted as Wheel organizers among the black population.[25] Of the 1,947 Wheel locals in Arkansas, 200 were black.[26]

However, the Wheel's relatively open stance was not followed by a number of other important farmer groups. Outstanding among these was the above-mentioned Southern Farmers' Alliance.[27] Led by a skillful organizer and innovative monetary theorist, Charles W. Macune, the Texas-based Alliance began spreading into neighboring states about the same time that the Wheel was spilling over the borders of Arkansas. Since both societies were pursuing virtually identical aims, union seemed logical and desirable. After considerable preparatory discussion, the Wheel and Alliance held simultaneous national conventions at Meridian, Mississippi, in December 1888 in order to bring about consolidation.[28] A joint committee worked throughout the sessions, hammering out a new constitution for the merged orders. Among the delegates at the Meridian gathering were seven Wheel representatives from Arkansas, including one Negro, F. S. Simons from Marion in Crittenden County.[29]

The major stumbling block to cooperation proved to be race. Over the objection of the Arkansans on the constitution committee, who filed a dissenting minority report, a whites-only membership requirement was written into the charter of the new "Farmers' and Laborers' Union of America."[30] The Meridian meeting adjourned with the understanding that when three-fourths of the state assemblies of each order ratified the draft constitution, unification would be complete.

Subsequently, the State Wheel of Arkansas convened at Hot Springs in July 1889 to vote upon consolidation. Forced to choose between defending the Negroes' interests or forging a united front among white farmers, the Wheelers opted for the latter. Although the convention adopted a resolution condemning a recent race riot at Forrest City,[31] it swiftly proceeded to ratify the Meridian constitution and adopted new rules expelling all Negroes from the state organization.[32] Any black man following the proceedings must, to say the least, have been puzzled.

One upshot of the Wheel's action was to encourage the spectacular growth of the Colored Farmers' Alliance. An entirely independent association first born in Houston County, Texas, in 1886, the Colored Alliance claimed a national membership of 1,200,000 by 1890, including 20,000 members in Arkansas.[33] In theory, the Colored Alliance was to pull in tandem with its white partner, the Southern Farmers' Alliance;[34] in practice, relationships were strained and joint action difficult. Both groups, it is true, suffered from hard times in Southern agriculture; both shared numerous common grievances. Still, between them there were also palpable conflicts of economic interest. Many white agrarians were small farmers who might themselves on occasion employ hired help; the majority of blacks were landless sharecroppers or field hands. When a few Negroes tried organizing a cotton pickers' strike in the Arkansas Delta in 1891, they met with bloody repression.[35] The white Farmers' Alliance not only failed to rally to the strikers support; it actively disassociated itself from them.[36] Throughout the rural South, hostility and reprisal against the Colored Alliance became so intense that within a year it entirely passed from the scene, despite the fact that just a few months previously it may have been the largest black farmers' society in American history.[37]

◆　　　◆　　　◆

When the "political farmers" of the Wheel and Alliance moved from self-help and protest into the arena of direct third-party action, they carried their uncrystalized attitudes toward the Negro with them. The question of the agrarian independents' relationship with blacks initially presented itself at the first Union Labor state convention, held at Little Rock in May 1888. Midway during the convention's deliberations, Henry R. Morehart, a white Union Laborite from Pulaski County, announced that a delegation of black Knights of Labor had arrived and asked if they could be admitted.[38] The Negroes, with no apparent objection, were allowed to come forward, present their credentials, and take seats among the other delegates. One of their number, Captain P. M. E.

Thompson, a black officer on the Little Rock municipal police force, played an important role in the remaining sessions and was awarded the honor of serving as an Arkansas delegate to the forthcoming national Union Labor convention.[39]

Much more important to the new party, as far as its support from Negroes was concerned, was the action of the Arkansas Republicans. On July 18, the Republican central committee electrified the voters by announcing endorsement of the Union Labor candidates for state office.[40] For the first time in many years, the Democrats had a real fight on their hands.

The Republican endorsement was a great boon to the Union Labor party, and, at the same time, its greatest liability. Throughout the campaign, Democrats pounded away on the theme that the Union Labor ticket was only a "Republican mask."[41] Since the Democrats themselves were making overtures to black voters, their aversions to the race issue were somewhat muted. Nevertheless, over and over again they reiterated the refrain that the agrarian candidates were mere Republican stooges: their victory, it was claimed, would inevitably mean a return of the old Carpetbagger element to power.[42] By implication, the Reconstruction story would be retold, with Negroes once more holding an important place in the councils of government.

Under a constant barrage of attacks of this nature, the agrarian-black alliance showed signs of strain. When the *Arkansas Gazette* reported that the Reverend Isom P. Langley, an important ULP leader, had spoken to a "colored picnic" at Ozan in Hempstead County, Langley shot back an emphatic denial: "I wish to state I never addressed a colored picnic in Hempstead County in my life. But on the day named I spoke to about 1200 people, mostly Wheelers, and there were not seventy-five colored people on the grounds. It was a white picnic that I addressed, and not a colored picnic."[43] A little later in the canvass the Little Rock *Sun*, a black paper with Democratic leanings, informed its readers that Union Labor gubernatorial candidate Charles N. Norwood had told friends he did not want black support.[44] Norwood, however, seems to have immediately scouted the rumor, for a few days afterward another Democratic newspaper stated, "Dr. Norwood said in his speech at Paragould that he had [once] voted for a negro against a good white man."[45]

Blacks themselves sometimes appear to have been restive with the Republican–Union Labor arrangements. As noted earlier, some blacks in Pulaski County had opposed fusion with the local Union Labor organization.[46] Occasionally, here and there a few other Negro Republicans balked at cooperation.[47] Nevertheless, despite scattered grousing and disaffection, the official Republican endorsement generally seems to have carried the day. It is estimated that Norwood obtained 46 percent of the ballots cast by Negroes and his Democratic opponent 23 percent, with 30 percent of adult black males not voting, figures comparable to those. for previous 1880s contests between Republican and Democratic candidates; most of the traditionally Republican counties with large black populations cast majorities for the Union Labor party in both the state and congressional elections.[48] Typical was the situation in Phillips County where, following the September count, the *Arkansas Gazette* correspondent on the scene wired, "The Union Labor ticket was endorsed by the republicans and the negroes voted for it solid."[49] Essentially, this same basic pattern repeated itself two years later, in 1890, when the Republicans again backed the Union Labor state ticket.[50]

In view of the unstinted support they gave to the Union Laborites, Arkansas blacks must have had mixed feelings about the party's overall performance. The white agrarians believed, as a matter of honest conviction, that the various economic nostrums they were prescribing would cure the farmers' ills, including those of black farmers. There was nothing insincere or merely expediential about their quest for Negro votes. Even so, their single-minded preoccupation with economic questions had its negative aspects. The agrarians tended to dismiss racial or sectional considerations as irrelevant and superfluous, as "scarecrows" used to distract the people's minds from the really substantive issues facing the nation.[51] Insofar as possible, they tried focusing attention and discussion upon the economic planks in their platform: currency inflation, state regulation of railroads and corporations, abolition of the crop-mortgage system, support for the graduated income tax and the subtreasury plan, and so on. On specifically racial topics, however, especially the matter of legally enforced segregation, the party simply had no stand; anything remotely approaching a consensus failed to exist. In fact, the very lack of such a consensus was one more reason why the agrarians preferred not to mention the dangerous subject at all.

Nothing better highlights intraparty divisiveness over race than the record established by Union Labor assemblymen in the state legislature. During the session of 1889, Union Labor representatives joined the Republicans in voting against the unsuccessful election bill of that year; white agrarians proved no more enthusiastic about creating a centralized election machinery under Democratic control than blacks. However, on another, less publicized question, the alliance between the two groups totally broke down.

The issue itself was important only in a symbolic sense. Although black and white lawmakers sat together on the floor of the House of Representatives, the House galleries, where persons of both sexes intermingled, were traditionally segregated: two-thirds of the galleries was allotted to whites and one-third to blacks. While not unusual, this arrangement nonetheless was at times inconvenient. Black women, in particular, took special pride in seeing the leading men of their race introducing bills, raising points of order, and acting alongside other lawmakers on terms of equality; frequently, the "colored" section of the galleries was filled to overflowing. By comparison, the "white" section had numerous empty spaces except on particularly important occasions.

To remedy this state of affairs, a Negro Republican, J. N. Donohoo of Phillips County, introduced a resolution permitting women visitors to take any available seat when there was no more room in the area reserved for their own race. This seemed so manifestly practicable that Donohoo's motion was quickly adopted, with only four dissenting votes.[52]

However, the matter did not end here. The clerk of the House, out of malice or a genuine misunderstanding of the resolution, refused to provide anyone but black women with passes to the gallery. When J. W. Coffman, a white representative from Johnson County, tried to obtain a pass for a "lady friend" of his, he was told that "none but colored ladies would be provided with tickets." Irked, Coffman proceeded to move for reconsideration of the vote by which the resolution passed. With the whole matter thus being suddenly brought to public attention, most whites scrambled to reverse their stands. Although the black members pointed out that Donohoo's measure had been misconstrued by the clerk, it was repealed easily, seventeen to fifty.[53] Of the ten identifiable white Union Labor or Independent members in the House,[54] four voted for repeal, one against, and five abstained.[55]

Minor as the galleries fracas was, it presaged the response of Union Laborites toward a more important segregation proposal introduced two years later, the Tillman separate-coach act. Just as they had in 1889, a majority of the Union Labor representatives in the session of 1891 allied with the Republicans in opposition to the centralized elections proposal. A majority also fought against the poll-tax amendment. On the matter of segregated railroad cars, however, party unity shattered.

For example, when the separate-coach bill first came up for consideration in the Senate, the only white man voting against passage was Union Laborite F. P. Hill from the Seventh District (Crittenden, St. Francis, Cross, and Woodruff counties).[56] The other Union Labor senator, however, J. P. H. Russ of the Twenty-seventh District (White and Faulkner counties) initially supported the coach measure. Russ's vote particularly was important since at the time he was serving as president of the Arkansas Farmers' Alliance.[57]

Within the House, none of the white Union Labor representatives offered resistance to the separate-coach proposal; three, John Dunaway of Faulkner County, W. A. Evans of Carroll County, and William Manning of St. Francis County, voted for its passage, while a fourth party member, Sam J. Crabtree of White County, abstained.[58] Even Crabtree, moreover, at least favored segregation in principle, for he offered an unsuccessful amendment which would have extended coverage of the law to streetcar lines.[59]

The Union Labor stance on the segregation question of course should be borne in perspective. Anyone espousing integration or concepts of racial equality opened himself to the most vicious kind of political attack; the issue was especially treacherous for white agrarians since they were appealing to the depressed rural classes among whom prejudice was strongest and most passionately held. Usually, moreover, agrarian advocacy of segregation came in response to initiatives of the Democrats. Still, even when all these factors are weighed, it remains obvious that the third-party overture to the Negro had definite limitations. In Arkansas, at least, there is no convincing reason to believe that the agrarians ever seriously proposed to "wipe out the color line and put every man on his citizenship irrespective of color."

◆   ◆   ◆

Beginning with the election of 1892, Arkansas's former Union Laborites joined the new Populist party arising throughout the South and West. The state's Republicans, abandoning their strategy of 1888 and 1890, did not endorse the Populist nominees, but the agrarians nevertheless had high hopes of retaining most of the Negro support they had won previously. Believing themselves exponents of a new realism which transcended outworn issues of section and race, the Populists envisioned a mass awakening of oppressed farmers and laborers of whatever color. Indeed, their own state convention, meeting at Little Rock in June, seemed a tocsin of the new dawn; Populist leaders proudly announced that among the 170 delegates were 82 ex-Confederates, 32 Union veterans, and 11 black men.[60]

The convention itself endorsed the Populists' national principles and condemned both of the old parties as tools of the monopolies and trusts. On local questions, the convention platform urged defeat of the proposed poll-tax amendment, advocated free textbooks in the public schools, and condemned public expenditures for such luxuries as the World's Fair. Rotation in office, substitution of official salaries for the fee system, a just road law, federal supervision of elections, abolition of the convict-lease system, and creation of a state penitentiary farm and juvenile reformatory were all recommended. Looting of the treasury by Democratic officials was rebuked. Of special interest to Negroes was a plank which denounced lynchings and asked that criminals be punished only by courts of law. Also directed at Negroes was a resolution promising that the party would uplift all "downtrodden sons of toil," regardless of race; the resolution, introduced by a black delegate, was unanimously adopted. Armed with this new set of principles, the convention proceeded to nominate J. P. Carnahan, a manufacturer of wood products and former mathematics professor at Cane Hill College, for governor, along with a full ticket for state office.[61]

If the Populists believed they could ignore the issues of the past and introduce a new type of dialogue into Arkansas politics, the Democrats lost little time in disabusing them of the notion. A Democratic newspaper, the Arkadelphia *Siftings*, capsuled the dominant mood of the campaign when it declared, "This is a white man's country, and white men are going to rule it, and when the third party opened its arms to the negro at its State convention, it invited its certain death at the polls next fall."[62] The progress of events would soon verify this grim prediction.

There really was nothing very radical about the Populists' appeals for black support. The Democrats themselves had made ritual gestures toward the black community for decades. Furthermore, the more conservative Democratic leaders had always deplored lynchings and acts of violence outside the law. Yet, the fact was that such moderation had never been popular with a large element among the rural electorate. Playing upon racial themes had obviously told against the Union Laborites in the preceding two elections, and the Democracy, hard pressed by growing farmer discontent, had no intention of surrendering a winning issue.

One means of capitalizing upon race was to insist that the Republicans and Populists were acting in collusion, even though they were running separate slates of candidates. Prior Republican support for the Union Laborites lent some credence to the charge, and, as a matter of fact, it did contain at least a modicum of truth: the Republicans clearly hoped to benefit from the Populists' siphoning off of previously Democratic votes. In the minds of Democratic partisans, however, this took on all the trappings of a lurid conspiracy. The Populist organization was christened with a new name, the "Republican Aid Society," and its candidates were painted as "decoy ducks" in league with former Carpetbagger governor Powell Clayton. The *Arkansas Gazette* admitted that the third-party men had openly denounced the Republicans as well as the Democrats yet insisted that "In secret, behind the door, the decoy duck leaders are hand-in-glove with Clayton, who furnishes the brains for the direction of their campaign, and before whom they in secret bow as master." Both groups were working for a common purpose: "the return of the old Republican party to power."[63]

While making repeated general charges of this nature, Democrats did not neglect more specific attacks. The Populists' forthright condemnation of lynchings became a favorite object of criticism. For instance, the editor of the Arkadelphia *Herald* stridently

211

exclaimed, "The third party platform, conceived and promulgated by the Little Rock Convention, which contained that celebrated nigger plank, offering him protection from the wrath of indignant white communities whose wives and daughters he may choose to outrage, was a great body in some sense. Among the conspicuous members of that committee was I. Glasby, a full negro."[64]

Another journal, the Arkadelphia *Siftings*, saw the Populists' lynching stand as a lesson to wavering Democrats:

> No one could make us believe that the plain, practical farmers of Clark County, who have been raised in the South, and venerate Southern institutions and the memory of their fathers, have suddenly become negro lovers, or defenders of negro rapists and criminals. The plank in the third party platform made to catch negro votes, will not only fail to meet the approbation of those who farm with their hands, who remained at home while those who "farm with their mouth" held the convention, but will open the eyes of many to the danger of leaving the old plain beaten paths of Democracy.[65]

In addition to their stand on lynchings, the Populists were hit hard for endorsing federal supervision of Southern elections. Democrats felt their opponents unusually vulnerable on this question because of the action of an influential Populist leader. During his brief tenure in the House of Representatives in 1890, Union Labor Congressman L. P. Featherston had voted for the Lodge "Force" bill. In 1892, Featherston served as chairman of the platform committee at the Populist state convention and as chairman of the Arkansas delegation to the national convention at Omaha.[66] From this connection Democrats inferred that the third party favored federal military occupation, "Negro rule," and a return to the days of Reconstruction.

It is difficult to overemphasize the stress placed upon the "Force" bill by Democratic orators and editors or to exaggerate the extent to which old fears and distrusts were aroused. For a large number of Democratic leaders, the troubled Reconstruction era was still a live memory, and no doubt many really believed their own vaticinations. The *Arkansas Gazette* underscored their general cast of mind:

> Legislation of the character demanded would virtually revolutionize the Government. In the direct interest of political partisanship it would

concentrate all power in Washington. It would reduce the great mass of the white people of the South to serfs, ruled by a few white men, responsible only to the central power, and by the negroes who are especially meant by the term "oppressed and disfranchised Republicans in the South." . . . It is a demand for legislation to enable the white and black Republican minorities in the South to overcome the white majorities, and turn these states over to the old carpetbaggers and the negro hordes who comprise nearly all the voting strength of the Republican party. It is a demand to put and keep "black heels on white necks."[67]

On another occasion the same paper, referring to the "Force" bill, admonished its readers: "Study its provisions. Every line contains the gleam of a half-concealed bayonet. Every sentence contains a menace to the individual liberty of the citizen."[68]

Speaking before Little Rock's Old Hickory Club, city attorney Morris M. Cohn voiced the same sentiment; passage of the Lodge legislation, he warned, would place political power in the hands of an inferior race and lower the level of "Anglo-Saxon civilization." He argued that the South's policy toward the Negro was based upon the same premises as the nation's Chinese exclusion policy and held that if placed in a similar situation Northerners or Europeans would not tolerate Negroes so well as white Southerners had done. Cohn told his Democratic listeners to ignore those who maintained the "Force" bill had no further chance of passage and was no longer a valid issue. Instead, he vehemently proclaimed, "It is an issue. We will keep it an issue. Like Banquo's ghost—it shall not down."[69]

The "Force" bill specter did indeed haunt the Populist party throughout the duration of the campaign and placed Populist leaders in an agonizingly cruel dilemma. Most of them felt that Democratic frauds were robbing them of the fruits of victory and believed that federal supervision of Southern election practices was vitally needed. Yet, by advocating such federal intervention, they opened themselves to the charge of favoring a return to the hated period of Reconstruction and Republican rule.

Some Populists reacted to this attack by abandoning their support of the Lodge bill and similar proposals. The *Faulkner* (County) *Wheel* urged its readers to remind the electorate that the Populists were as much opposed to force bills as the Democracy and its followers.[70] Also, it seems that at least some Populists regretted their earlier willingness to cooperate with the blacks. A Populist speaker at Cotton Plant reportedly refused to debate against Negro Democrat S. S. Odom.[71] And Pulaski County Populists were said to have opposed the inclusion of any blacks on a Republican-Populist county fusion ticket, although previously eight blacks had served as delegates to the Pulaski County Populist convention.[72]

Such waffling may in part explain Populism's limited success in winning black support. The results in the governor's race gave Democrat William Fishback 90,115 votes, Republican William Whipple 33,644, and Populist J. P. Carnahan 31,117.[73] A survey of the returns discloses that the third party had made no headway whatever in the traditionally Negro Republican areas of the Delta;[74] in counties where Negroes were in the minority, however, and had no hope of winning office in their own right, they appear frequently to have backed Populist candidates in preference to the Democrats.[75] A similar situation prevailed in 1894 and 1896, except that overall third-party strength rapidly declined in each succeeding election;[76] in the latter contest, the Populist candidate reportedly received less than 0.5 percent of the Negro vote.[77] In retrospect, the Arkansas Populists seem to have created the worst of all possible political worlds: their overtures toward Negroes had been just heterodox enough to antagonize and frighten away large numbers of whites, yet they were not so thoroughgoing or consistent as to win a really enthusiastic response from blacks.

# XII

# Drawing the Color Line

Clans and classes grow out of natural affiliations and peculiar racial affinities. The adjustment of such is a matter of taste and fitness of things and does not come within the bounds of legislation. All the combined laws of nations and the best legal jurisprudence cannot compel one individual to associate with another nor can such laws separate kindred spirits whose hearts beat in union and whose sympathies run along lines of common good will among the bustling multitudes.
—The Reverend J. H. Reed, Pastor, Wesley Chapel Methodist Episcopal Church, Little Rock

We have come to a parting of the ways with the Negro.
—Governor Jeff Davis

Following adoption of the Tillman separate-coach law in 1891, a period of twelve years elapsed before Arkansas enacted any further segregation statutes. There are a number of possible explanations for this rather extended interlude. The demise of the Popu-

215

list party during the mid-nineties may have served to delay new initiatives toward racial separation: with the collapse of the agrarian insurgency, there was no longer any immediate political imperative to support segregation legislation.[1] Another reason may lie in a dramatic upsurge in reported lynchings and mob violence.[2] Though it was a direct outgrowth of their own party's earlier exploitation of the race question, the more conservative Democratic leaders were thoroughly frightened by this development;[3] consequently, they probably were reluctant to undertake any new steps which might ignite passions or augment the dangerously high level of existing tensions.

The election of Jeff Davis as governor in 1900, however, prepared the way for additional expansion of the Jim Crow system. Davis campaigned as the champion of the one-gallus farmer against the "high-collared roosters" and "squirrel-headed editors" in Little Rock and roasted the "vested interests" at crossroads debates and rustic barbecues throughout the state.[4] As chief executive, he proposed stricter regulation of railroads and insurance companies, supported a series of dramatic antitrust prosecutions against out-of-state corporations, and called for increased assistance to state charitable institutions and public education.[5] There was, though, more than a little demagoguery in his methods, and the victories he claimed to have won for the people of Arkansas were sometimes more rhetorical than real. Political observers in Davis's own day disagreed concerning his sincerity and character, and later historians and biographers have been no less divided.[6] Since few of his personal papers have survived, the question of his inner motivations may never be fully resolved.

If Davis was in fact a progressive, there can be little doubt that his progressivism was basically for whites only: he showed scant concern for the state's black citizens, and frequently he did not hesitate to use race prejudice for his own benefit, sometimes employing the crudest kinds of racial epithets in his stump speeches and election campaigns. Moreover, at least as important as such verbal abuse was Davis's endorsement, in 1905, of an abortive effort to fund Negro educational programs only with tax revenues collected from blacks, a plan which, if adopted, would almost have destroyed educational opportunities for the state's black schoolchildren. Although bills incorporating the proposal had been before the legislature since the 1890s, Davis was the first chief executive to support the idea.[7]

In retrospect, what Davis's career really symbolizes is a conjoining of the two principal threads of the agrarian revolt in Arkansas, Populist economic unrest and Democratic support for white supremacy. Davis, though admittedly a dubious heir to the agrarian movement in Arkansas and never an authentic Populist (he was frankly distrusted by many of the old radicals),[8] still provided a kind of cathartic relief for his rural followers by excoriating Yankee trusts and by lashing out at local urban, commercial elites. By weaving together at least the rhetorical flourishes of Populism and traditional Democratic racial appeals, he gave the pattern of rural discontent unified political expression. It is hardly surprising that pressures for expansion of the Jim Crow system should have arisen during his administration or that the legislature should have passed a new series of segregation statutes during his tenure in office— although, curiously, Davis seems to have taken no direct part in promoting such legislation.[9]

Just at the moment when race conditions within the state were so badly deteriorating, national and international developments began increasingly to work to the Negroes' disadvantage.[10] At the close of the nineteenth century, the powers of Europe and the empire of Japan scuffled for the last remaining colonial territories in Asia, Africa, and the Pacific. Moreover, after the Spanish-American War the United States itself acquired imperial holdings in the Philippines, Puerto Rico, and other places. By 1900, the editor of the *Arkansas Gazette* could caustically note:

> There are in the Philippines some ten million of the dark races, from the yellow to the black, and their civil and social status is to be determined. Then there are already the colored races of Puerto Rico and Hawaii, and sooner or later those of Cuba to complicate the race and color problems. Under these conditions the president and the Republican party cannot well afford to stir up new and formidable troubles of which the negroes of the Southern states are to be made the object and occasion.[11]

Many American Negroes were aware of the connection between imperialism abroad and destruction of their rights at home. Although a Republican, former United States Consul Mifflin W.

Gibbs gave a scathing critique of American Philippine policy in his autobiography, contending that acquisition of the islands had been prompted by economic greed and a lust for territory. For those who professed to support imperialist ventures out of a humanitarian desire to uplift the darker-skinned peoples of the globe, Gibbs had heavy sarcasm. He wondered why self-proclaimed "world reformers" were so much more distressed over the plight of the alien "Cuban and Filipino colored brothers" than the "colored American brother," wryly concluding, "Really, it would seem that to duty and the bestowal of justice 'tis distance that lends enchantment to the view.'"[12]

Perceptive as they may have been, however, Gibbs' observations could hardly change the nature of American foreign policy or the drift of international events. At the beginning of the new century, the current of world opinion was decidedly inimical to the preservation of opportunities for American Negroes.

As has been seen, conditions within Arkansas itself were even more unfavorable. During the preceding decade the state's blacks had been disfranchised and evicted from public office, and the governor's chair had fallen to a man who had little concern for the welfare of the minority race. Thus, when additional legal measures for extension of the Jim Crow system were introduced in the General Assembly of 1903, their adoption was virtually assured.

The first of these measures required that separate jail cells and furnishings be provided for state and county prisoners of the black and white races. It also forbade the handcuffing or chaining together of prisoners of different races and provided for a fifty- to two hundred-dollar fine for any public official who violated provisions of the act.[13]

Introduced as House Bill No. 66 by Benjamin F. Witt of Faulkner County, the proposal encountered little opposition from the legislators. The House of Representatives approved it without debate by a vote of eighty-three to zero,[14] and the Senate overwhelmingly accepted the bill with only two members in dissent.[15] Senator William P. Fletcher of the Twelfth District (Lonoke and Prairie counties) did not give his reasons for opposition,[16] but Albert W. Rison, of the Tenth District (Pulaski and Perry counties), argued that his home county, Perry, could not afford separate facilities. He believed, furthermore, that the measure would work a hardship on officers required to transport prisoners.[17]

Despite the lawmakers' near unanimity for the Witt bill, it seems to have effected a real change of conditions in several localities. During the Senate discussions, Thomas C. Jobe of the Twentieth District (Hempstead and Nevada counties) exclaimed, "In my own county I saw a big buck negro charged with a crime he could not mention handcuffed to an innocent white man, whom he led into the cell and who was forced to sleep with him."[18] In fact, even after the passage of the Witt bill mixed accommodations still continued to be found in some areas, for the new measure did not apply to municipal prisoners. Pulaski County, for example, divided white from black prisoners prior to 1903, but in the Little Rock city jail there was no such separation. A newspaper reporter described the somewhat topsy-turvy arrangements:

> Should the Witt bill for separate cells for white and black prisoners pass it will not affect Pulaski county, as they have always been separated in the jail in this city. The white prisoners are kept on the first floor of a double-decked cell room, with the negroes above. This excepts United States safekeepers. The white and black women are kept in separate rooms.
>
> The bill applies to state and county prisoners, which leaves out city prisoners confined in the city calaboose. The calaboose here was built many years ago, and consists of two parts, one for men and one for women. The men's department is divided into two parts, both opening into a corridor. It has been the custom to leave both the inner doors open, and the prisoners white and black, separated as they saw fit. If there were more negroes than whites in jail the negroes had the best bunks, and in vice versa the whites took the best. There is no provision for the separation of white and black women.[19]

No state law was ever passed requiring the segregation of city prisoners, although it is plausible to assume that de facto separation gradually increased over the years.

The second Jim Crow statute enacted by the 1903 legislature, the streetcar-segregation act, met with considerably more resistance than the Witt bill; oddly enough, opposition came both from avowed segregationists and from those who opposed the segregation principle. Introduced by Reid Gantt of Garland County, a representative from the spa city of Hot Springs, the streetcar bill was modeled after similar measures already in force in Virginia and Georgia.[20] It provided that conductors should assign white and black passengers to different portions of the streetcar coach;

the demarcation line between the races could be adjusted at will by the streetcar conductor. For example, if three-fourths of the passengers aboard were white, three-fourths of the coach could be allotted for the exclusive use of the white race, or vice versa. Passengers who refused to move to another seat when so ordered by the conductor could be ejected; the especially recalcitrant passenger could be subjected to a twenty-five-dollar fine. Adhering to the "separate but equal" formula, the bill also prohibited discrimination in the quality or convenience of services offered the two races.[21]

The legislative history of the streetcar-segregation act presents an instructive study in microcosm of the subtle but significant differences between town and country racial mentalities. As early as 1891, the Arkansas General Assembly had considered a proposal to extend provisions of the separate-coach law for railroads to streetcar lines. Opponents had moved quickly to secure defeat of this measure and had successfully deflected attempts in later legislative sessions to institute streetcar-segregation requirements.[22]

By 1903, however, it was obvious that some sort of concession to the growing demand for segregation would have to be made. Soon after the General Assembly convened, an eastern Delta representative, Jasper N. Ferguson of Lonoke County, introduced a bill directing streetcar companies to provide separate coaches (or single cars divided by permanent, immobile partitions) for whites and blacks. Ferguson's proposal was referred to the House Committee on Cities and Towns, where it was quietly buried.[23] Instead, the committee, very possibly responding to the streetcar interests, reported out the more moderate bill of Representative Gantt as a substitute. This latter measure, of course, did not require separate coaches but only contemplated segregation within the same car, with the line dividing the races to be moved at the discretion of the conductor. When brought before the full House, the Gantt bill gained easy acceptance. Because of the operation of a number of disfranchisement laws enacted during the preceding decade,[24] there were no black representatives present to offer opposition, and the measure was unanimously adopted without discussion.[25]

In the Senate the bill encountered difficulties. A large group insisted that the bill did not go far enough and supported alternative legislation by Senator Joseph C. Pinnix of the Thirtieth

District (Clark and Pike counties) which would have prescribed separate coaches for each race.[26] Several senators hotly denounced the Gantt proposal, variously characterizing it as a "farce," "a miserable makeshift," and "a mere shadow on its face" which would provoke fights and disturbances. Senator Paul G. Matlock of the Sixteenth District (Lincoln, Cleveland, and Dallas counties) capsuled their viewpoint, describing the Gantt bill as "a mere subterfuge . . . gotten up to defeat the Pinnix bill, and endorsed by the streetcar people themselves." Matlock acknowledged that his own South Arkansas plantation, farming, and timber district contained no streetcar lines. He noted, however, that his constituents rode on streetcars when they visited the cities, and he felt that he "reflected the views of a vast majority of the people in saying they wanted the separate coach."[27]

One of the strongest pleas for the moderate approach was made by Senator George Sengel of the Twenty-eighth District (Sebastian County). Sengel openly admitted that he was a stockholder in the street-railway company of Fort Smith and based his appeal on economic arguments. He urged his colleagues to "adopt laws of this character in mild doses" and asserted:

> The street car systems of our state are not yet profitable property. I have been interested for several years in a system in Fort Smith and have not yet been the happy recipient of dividends. Help us to develop our cities and in doing so we are willing to meet you halfway, but don't strike too hard at one fell blow. Separate seats will please everybody, and enable the car companies to exist. To use separate cars means confiscation of the street car companies, for it means double capital and double employment of help.[28]

By an extremely close margin, a motion deferring action on the Gantt bill until the Pinnix bill could be considered was defeated, thirteen to fourteen.[29] On the concluding tally the Senate finally approved the Gantt bill, twenty-five to four.[30] The former issue was decided on a rising vote, without a roll call being taken or recorded. Newspaper accounts indicate, though, that every senator from the districts encompassing Little Rock, Pine Bluff, Hot Springs, and Fort Smith, Arkansas's four major urban centers, supported the Gantt legislation; those reported as endorsing the Pinnix bill all represented predominantly rural counties.[31]

Interestingly, while this legislative contest was transpiring, the

Isidor Newman and Sons banking house of New Orleans was negotiating purchase of a controlling interest in the Little Rock Traction and Electric Company, which operated the capital city's streetcars.[32] The directors of the Little Rock concern were all influential business and civic leaders. W. E. Hemingway, its president, was a former associate justice of the Arkansas Supreme Court; and George B. Rose, its secretary, was possibly the best-known attorney in the state. Other men of weight connected with the traction company were J. Fairfax Loughborough and D. H. Cantrell, law partners of Hemingway and Rose; H. G. Bunn, the incumbent chief justice of the Supreme Court; J. A. Trawick, the streetcar line's general manager; and W. J. Tharp, the line's cashier.[33] Circumstantial evidence suggests that the traction-company management and directors may have been discreetly endeavoring to secure defeat of the Pinnix bill. In his previously cited address, Senator Sengel had also remarked that "Nearly all our streetcar systems are owned by local capital and they are hoping to interest foreign capital to help them in extending and improving their systems, but [the latter] will not do so if the Pinnix bill is passed."[34] Probably not coincidentally, the agreement transferring ownership of the Little Rock street railways was consummated on the very day that Governor Davis signed the Gantt legislation.[35]

The enactment of the Gantt streetcar law may have pleased Little Rock's businessmen, but even this measure naturally proved unpalatable to many blacks. Recalling the events of 1891, Little Rock's middle-class black leadership launched a spirited protest. On March 11 a mass rally convened at the Negro First Baptist Church in the capital, with the participants demanding that the legislature defeat any new segregation proposals. The principal speakers were Mifflin W. Gibbs, former U.S. Consul to Tamatave, Madagascar; John E. Bush, Receiver of the U.S. Land Office; two physicians, Drs. D. B. Gaines and G. W. Hayman; and two ministers, the Reverend J. H. Reed, pastor of Wesley Chapel Methodist Episcopal Church, and the Reverend W. A. J. Phillips, pastor of Bethel A.M.E. Church.[36] All of these men resemble closely the description of the typical leader of black streetcar boycotts in other Southern cities given in a study by historians August Meier and Elliott Rudwick.[37] They were established spokesmen, well known for their moderation and advocacy of interracial cooperation. Indeed, several were close associates of Booker T. Washington, the apostle of racial accommodation.[38] Their protest did not signal the appearance of a sudden new militancy among blacks. Rather, it represented a desperate attempt by essentially conservative leaders to preserve a relatively open status quo, now seriously threatened.

In addition to protest meetings and resolutions, blacks also tried utilizing the weapon of economic coercion. When the streetcar law took effect on May 27, 1903, black boycotts of the car lines were organized in Little Rock, Pine Bluff, and Hot Springs.[39] The Little Rock blacks even formed a "We Walk League" whose members agreed to submit voluntarily to fines whenever they relented and rode the streetcars.[40] The president of the new league was said to be a porter in a Fifth Street saloon,[41] suggesting that the boycott effort obtained support from blacks of all social classes, even though it had been launched by middle-class leaders. Initially, black traffic on the street railways dropped by over 90 percent in Little Rock, and it appears to have fallen precipitously in Pine Bluff and Hot Springs as well; in all three cities the boycott continued for weeks.[42] The race's ministers actively rallied their congregations' support, and black newspapermen and journalists appealed to their readers.[43] *The Voice of the Twentieth Century*, edited by students at Shorter University in North Little Rock, told its readers:

> Let us be obedient to the law. Let no one get on the cars and attempt to undo what the Legislature of the great state of Arkansas has done. This law was intended to humiliate negroes and every time a negro man, woman, or child goes to the back seat or rides on the cars while this iniquitous law is in force, the negro is humiliated. Never mind about forming resolutions or arguing the merits or demerits of the affair with anyone. Simply stay off the cars. Stay off the cars.[44]

In spite of the drastic fall off in black traffic and a certain obvious concern on their part, the management of the streetcar companies maintained their composure. Alleging that they had no choice but to enforce the law, they philosophically waited for the boycotts to run their course. The white press evinced a similar attitude. The *Arkansas Gazette* retained its equanimity about the whole affair and punned: "The We Walk Club, organized by negroes in protest against the new streetcar law, is of the opinion that these are times which try men's soles."[45]

223

On the first day of segregated streetcars, the *Arkansas Gazette* conducted a survey of public reaction to the new system in Little Rock. Because most blacks were participating in the boycott effort, there were only a few black passengers traveling on the city's streetcars.[46] There were, however, numerous objections lodged against the new segregation arrangements—from white patrons. The streetcar company's general manager, J. A. Trawick, related, "There has been no trouble . . . today [from Negroes] on account of the putting into effect of the separate accommodations law. All the trouble we have had was from whites, who either did not know the law or were constrained to argue the point."[47] Surprisingly, "nearly all . . . white women . . . when they were seated, refused to move without a protest. One told the conductor that she would report him to Mr. Trawick for making her give up her seat to a negro."[48]

Several white men also resisted the enactment. One individual "tried to argue that the law was not constitutional, but was told that had nothing to do with the question, for he must get out of the negroes' seats."[49] Another, described as "a prominent lawyer," declined to leave his seat in the rear of a streetcar unless he could be shown an actual line separating the races. Only the "sight of a bluecoat" made him move.[50]

Perhaps the most notable confrontation, designated by the *Arkansas Gazette* reporter as "The incident of the day," occurred on the Choctaw depot line:

> A white man sat down in the rear of the car, and was asked to move up front. He refused to do so. The conductor explained that the seats were for negroes. Then the man said:
> "Well, I'll stay here then. I would rather sit in the same seat with a negro than with a good many white people."
> Then he waxed warm and broke forth in this wise: "In fact, I would much rather trust my wife and children with a negro than with some white people. The negro is all right, and I am for him."
> As he still refused to move, the conductor handed him his nickel back, with the remark that perhaps it would be better for him to get off and walk, like the negroes were doing. He got off.[51]

Complaints against the streetcar-segregation requirements persisted for several days. For example, "Front-End Patron," the anonymous author of a letter to the editor of the Little Rock *Arkansas Democrat*, made the following tongue-in-cheek proposal:

224

Noticing the difficulties encountered by the street-car management in separating whites and blacks under the new so-called law, recognizing its impracticability . . . I would suggest that Manager Trawick have the front end of each coach painted white, the rear end black, and in the black end put up only advertisements of Red Raven Splits, Gold Dust Twins and a life-size picture of the author of the bill, to whom the manager is directed to issue [a] pass over the road on [the] rear end of [the] car whenever he visits the capital city.[52]

Though such grumblings continued, eventually most whites acquiesced in the new order of things. The fact that infractions of the streetcar law could entail ejection or a fine must have been inducement to do so, as was noted by the press at the time.[53]

It would be easy to magnify the significance of urban white resistance to racial separation on Arkansas streetcars. No doubt many white passengers simply disliked changes in their habits. Some whites may have disapproved of separate accommodations because they did not want to give up their places to blacks. Yet, at least a few whites seem to have protested because they believed the segregation law was unjust, and most appear to have regarded the new seating arrangements as unnecessary and uncalled for. It is difficult to believe that the white patrons did not understand the rationale behind segregated streetcars. Separation of persons by race had existed on the state's railroads for twelve years and had at times been employed at public gatherings since before the Civil War.

Also revealing were the actions of the streetcar managements. The traction owners, like so many urban businessmen, seem to have been more interested in maximizing their profits than with upholding traditional caste distinctions. After apparently resisting legislative pressures for segregation for over a decade, they finally capitulated, but even then succeeded in having segregation inaugurated in its mildest and most inexpensive form.

At the very least, the response of Little Rock whites to segregated streetcars in 1903 indicates that there was no unanimous demand for extension of the Jim Crow principle into every aspect of daily life in the city. While it is undeniably the case that some impulses toward segregation existed within urban areas, what may have proved decisive was the reinforcement they received from without.

# Conclusion

What final conclusions can be drawn in light of the information and evidence presented in the foregoing chapters? To begin with, it might be noted that a major thesis advanced in this study—namely, that segregation legislation applicable to urban areas did not emanate entirely from the city (where, in Arkansas, race relations were promising) but often from rural areas where whites demanded that cities conform to rural views of proper race relations—is compatible with other previously offered explanations and descriptions of southern racial behavior. The thesis, if true, easily harmonizes with C. Vann Woodward's central contention in *The Strange Career of Jim Crow* that, prior to the 1890s, an "era of stiff conformity and fanatical rigidity" had not yet "precluded all variety and experiment in types of interracial association." As Woodward observed, "There were still real choices to be made, and alternatives to the course eventually pursued with such single-minded unanimity and unquestioning conformity were still available." The example of Arkansas's urban centers also lends credence to Woodward's assertion that "on balance . . . the urban contribution to racial segregation in the South would seem to be less impressive than the encouragement that city conditions gave to interracial contact, familiar association, and intimacy."[1]

However, if the arguments presented here generally complement those of Woodward, they are not necessarily inconsonant with some of the ideas of his critics. In *The Crucible of Race* Joel Williamson has suggested that after the Civil War, still rankled by memory of military defeat, southern white men found their ability to care for their families being eroded by their region's growing poverty. Williamson believes that they compensated for their economic powerlessness by stressing their role as protectors of white women, especially against black criminals and rapists, whose numbers were perceived to be increasing. The fury of the resulting backlash against blacks was intensified by the prevailing Victorian code of sexual morality, which left white males feeling either guilty or frustrated. If this interpretation is valid, it certainly helps to explain white rural anger against the more casual and flexible racial mores of the cities and rural insistence on strict observance of the color line within urban areas. Presumably, moreover, rural resentments were heightened by the comparative prosperity and affluence of the cities.[2]

Even the perspectives of historian Howard Rabinowitz are not completely incompatible with the viewpoints that have been expressed herein. In his important regional study *Race Relations in the Urban South, 1865–1890*, in which he investigated racial conditions in five southern cities (Atlanta, Montgomery, Nashville, Raleigh, and Richmond), Rabinowitz emphasized the resistance that blacks encountered in their quest for personal and group advancement. While recognizing that blacks who lived in cities and towns usually fared somewhat better than their fellows in rural districts, Rabinowitz highlighted the barriers confronting black town dwellers and the persistence of prejudice among the urban white majority. Concerning segregation, he contended that frequently the only choice open to urban blacks was to accept new, separate Jim Crow facilities or to continue to be excluded from opportunities and services; viewed from this perspective, the inauguration of segregation could even be seen as an improvement for blacks.[3]

Rabinowitz brought genuinely original insights to his area of inquiry and, as has been shown, some particular cases in Arkansas's urban centers do conform to the pattern he delineated. To acknowledge this, however, is not to concede, as Rabinowitz has argued, that "by 1890, before the resort to widespread de jure segregation, de facto segregation had replaced exclusion as the norm in Southern race relations. In the process the stage of integration had been largely skipped." Nor does evidence substantiate his claim that "for most whites the [individual and class] distinctions among Negroes were unimportant. The only difference that mat-

227

tered was between blacks and whites."[4] Findings from Arkansas simply do not support such sweeping generalizations.

A final few questions remain: Was Arkansas in some way unique; were there special conditions in the state that might conceivably have made it different from other states in the South in regard to race relations? In *The Strange Career of Jim Crow*, C. Vann Woodward hypothesized that blacks residing in the older, settled regions of the South, where the paternalistic traditions of the eastern plantation lingered, may have fared better than those residing in the newer states only then emerging from frontier life.[5] Edwin S. Redkey has echoed this view in his study of black emigration movements in the South during the late nineteenth century.[6] Nevertheless, as both this writer and J. Morgan Kousser have argued in previous articles,[7] possibly the opposite may have been the case: blacks may have received more humane treatment and enjoyed more real opportunity in the less structured societies of the newer regions, where social relationships were less constrained by inherited mores, at least in their rapidly developing cities and towns. The more quick-paced advancement of blacks in such areas also explains why a noticeable backlash against blacks occurred initially in the newer states, which were generally the first to adopt, for example, separate coach laws for the railroads. Thus Arkansas's being a newer state of the western South could conceivably have affected its racial outlooks and practices. Of course, Arkansas was also to some extent a state of the upper South, which could have had a moderating influence.

Still, one suspects that the same process of urbanization that opened new avenues of advancement to blacks in Arkansas was having a similar influence throughout Dixie. Already, studies by John W. Blassingame and Dale A. Somers on New Orleans suggest that this was so.[8] And such advancement had a strange impact on white racial attitudes: paradoxical as it may seem, the very phenomenon that heightened racial tension and intensified prejudice—that of rapid black economic and social mobility—also worked to erode prejudice. Admittedly, few urban whites living during the New South era ever embraced the fully articulated racial egalitarianism of such advocates as George Washington Cable or Lewis Harvie Blair. Yet pioneer liberals like Cable and Blair may have been less exceptional than has usually been assumed.[9]

Significantly, both men were products of the emerging urban, commercial New South culture of their day. Cable, though best remembered for his nostalgic romances of old Creole days, was a native of the cosmopolitan city of New Orleans; and Blair was a wealthy and successful Richmond businessman. While it is perhaps correct to say, as Woodward does, that "acceptance of their doctrines had to await the development of urban liberalism, which did not arrive in any force until the second quarter of the twentieth century,"[10] the seeds for such liberalism had already been planted.

# Notes

## INTRODUCTION

1. C. Vann Woodward, *The Strange Career of Jim Crow* (3rd rev. ed.; New York, 1974).

2. See especially "The Strange Career of a Historical Controversy" in C. Vann Woodward, *American Counterpoint: Slavery and Racism in the North-South Dialogue* (Boston and Toronto, 1964), 234–60; and Joel Williamson, comp., *The Origins of Segregation* (Lexington, Massachusetts, 1968). See also Howard N. Rabinowitz, "More than the Woodward Thesis: Assessing *The Strange Career of Jim Crow*," *Journal of American History* 75 (December 1988): 842–56; C. Vann Woodward, "*Strange Career* Critics: Long May They Persevere," ibid.: 857–68.

3. U.S. Census Office, *Abstract of the Twelfth Census . . . 1900* (Washington, D.C., 1904), 38.

4. John W. Cell, *The Highest Stage of White Supremacy: The Origins of Segregation in South Africa and the American South* (Cambridge, U.K., 1982), 99.

5. Cell, ibid., 132–34.

6. Woodward, "*Strange Career* Critics," 858–59, summarizing the interpretations in Cell, *The Highest Stage of White Supremacy*, 132–34.

7. Ibid.

8. Woodward, "*Strange Career* Critics," 857–58.

## I

1. Woodward, *The Strange Career of Jim Crow*, 5.

2. Orville W. Taylor, *Negro Slavery in Arkansas* (Durham, North Carolina, 1958), 48–49. It should be noted, however, that the entire state

population in 1840 was only 97,574; thus, proportionally, slaves already accounted for 20 percent of the state's residents—up from 11 percent in 1820.

3. Four of these counties were located in the eastern Delta and showed per capita incomes in excess of $2,000; the remaining two were located in the Gulf Coastal Plain and had per capita incomes of between $1,000 and $2,000. Because of more limited amounts of bottom land, the large plantation was less prevalent and the small farm more commonplace in the latter region. Moreover, the river systems connected the area with New Orleans rather than Memphis markets, while the old Southwest Trail established important connections with the newly developing lands in Texas. These distinctions have caused some writers to see three major geographic regions within Arkansas—mountains, Delta, and Gulf Coastal Plain—rather than the customary division of the highlands and lowlands. George H. Thompson, *Arkansas and Reconstruction: The Influence of Geography, Economics, and Personality* (Port Washington, New York, 1976), 9–10; Ralph Wooster, "The Arkansas Secession Convention," *Arkansas Historical Quarterly*, XIII (Summer 1954): 189, 191.

4. Taylor, *Negro Slavery in Arkansas*, 48–49. After the Civil War and Reconstruction periods, immigration of large numbers of blacks into Arkansas would begin anew; by 1900 blacks would account for 366,856 of the state's 1,311,564 inhabitants—approximately 28 percent of the state's total population. See *Abstract of the Twelfth Census, 1900,* 40–41.

5. Jimmy Driftwood, "Down in the Arkansas," in *Music of the Ozarks,* A Sounds of the World Recording from National Geographic Society, c. 1972.

6. Taylor, *Negro Slavery in Arkansas*, 57.

7. Ibid., 50.

8. David Y. Thomas, *Arkansas and Its People, A History, 1541–1930,* I (New York, 1930), 118–27; James M. Woods, *Rebellion and Realignment, Arkansas's Road to Secession* (Fayetteville, Arkansas, 1987), 133–60; Michael B. Dougan, *Confederate Arkansas: The People and Policies of a Frontier State in Wartime* (University, Alabama, 1976), 47–63; *Journal of Both Sessions of the Convention of the State of Arkansas, Which Were Begun and Held in the Capitol, in the City of Little Rock* (Little Rock, 1861), 82, 121–24.

9. For comments on Union sentiment in western Arkansas, see P. B. Cox, Brown's Landing, Arkansas, July 15, 1861, letter to Confederate governor Henry Rector, Little Rock, Arkansas. Mason Brayman Collection, Manuscripts Division, Library of Chicago Historical Society, Chicago, Illinois.

10. David Y. Thomas, *Arkansas in War and Reconstruction, 1861–1874*

(Little Rock, 1926), 382–90; John L. Ferguson and J. H. Atkinson, *Historic Arkansas* (Little Rock, 1966), 142–43.

11. Thomas S. Staples, *Reconstruction in Arkansas, 1862–1874* (New York, 1923), 9–43; Martha A. Ellenburg, "Reconstruction in Arkansas," (Ph.D. diss., University of Missouri, 1967), 1–16.

12. George M. Fredrickson, *The Black Image in the White Mind: The Debate on Afro-American Character and Destiny* (New York, 1971), 43–70.

13. Taylor, *Negro Slavery in Arkansas*, 251–58; Florence R. Beatty-Brown, "Legal Status of Arkansas Negroes before Emancipation," *Arkansas Historical Quarterly*, XXVIII (Spring 1969): 11–12.

14. Staples, *Reconstruction in Arkansas*, 30–33. Later the new Unionist state legislature, meeting in special session, ratified the proposed Thirteenth Amendment to the United States Constitution abolishing slavery. Ibid., 72–73.

15. *Journal of the Convention of Delegates of the People of Arkansas. Assembled at the Capitol, January 4, 1864 . . .* (Little Rock, 1870), 37.

16. *Arkansas Constitution* (1864), ARTICLE 5, SECTION 1. A minority of Unionists, however, did tentatively endorse suffrage for blacks. See Little Rock *Unconditional Union*, July 27, 1865.

17. *Journal of the Convention . . . 1864*, 37.

18. Staples, *Reconstruction in Arkansas*, 71; Ellenburg, "Reconstruction in Arkansas," 25–26.

19. Little Rock *Arkansas Gazette*, September 6, 1865; Washington (Arkansas) *Telegraph*, October 4, 1865.

20. *Rison et al. v. Farr*. 24 Ark. 161.

21. Paige E. Mulhollan, "The Arkansas General Assembly of 1866 and Its Effect on Reconstruction," *Arkansas Historical Quarterly*, XX (Winter 1961): 333.

22. Des Arc *Citizen*, August 14, 1866, quoted in ibid., 339.

23. *Journal of the House of Representatives. Arkansas. Sixteenth Session. Begun at the Capitol, in the City of Little Rock, on the Fifth Day of November, 1866, and Ending on the Twenty-third Day of March, 1867* (Little Rock, 1870), 199–200. Hereinafter cited, for all years and sessions, as *Arkansas House of Representatives Journal*.

24. *Acts of the General Assembly of the State of Arkansas, Passed at the Session Held at the Capitol, in the City of Little Rock, Arkansas . . .* [1866–67] (Little Rock, 1867), 98–100; state statutes hereinafter cited, for all years, as *Acts of Arkansas*.

25. Ibid., 99.

26. *Arkansas House of Representatives Journal* (1866–67), 791.

27. Taylor, *Negro Slavery in Arkansas*, 187–88.

28. *Acts of Arkansas* (1866–67), 550; *Arkansas House of Representatives Journal* (1866–67), 285–89; *Journal of the Senate of Arkansas. Sixteenth Session. Begun at the Capitol, in the City of Little Rock, on the Fifth Day of November, 1866, and Ending on the Twenty-third Day of March, 1867* (Little Rock, 1870), 262. Hereinafter cited, for all years and sessions, as *Arkansas Senate Journal*.

29. Mulhollan, "The Arkansas General Assembly of 1866 and Its Effect on Reconstruction," 334.

30. Dan A. Rudd and Theodore Bond, *From Slavery to Wealth; The Life of Scott Bond* (Madison, Arkansas, 1917), 25.

31. See Leon F. Litwack, *North of Slavery; the Negro in the Free States, 1790–1860* (Chicago, 1961), *passim*.

32. Ibid., 91, 94.

33. A former state's rights Jacksonian Democrat and Southern Unionist, Johnson had been chosen as Lincoln's running mate in 1864 simply to balance the Republican national ticket. Unexpectedly, he became President following Lincoln's assassination in April 1865. Johnson rigidly insisted that since secession had been invalid, the Southern states had never left the Union; Congress, therefore, had no power to establish preconditions for their readmission to the Union or abridge the reserved powers of the Southern states. His veto of the Civil Rights Act of 1866, the Freedmen's Bureau Act, and other relatively moderate measures angered and stiffened the attitudes of many Northerners. Johnson had no real constituency in the North or among the Republican party, but he may have misled the South concerning Northern peace requirements and expectations. See Eric L. McKitrick, *Andrew Johnson and Reconstruction* (Chicago, 1960), *passim;* for Johnson's impact on Arkansas, see Mulhollan, "The Arkansas General Assembly of 1866 and Its Effect on Reconstruction," 342–43.

34. Staples, *Reconstruction in Arkansas*, 124–25.

35. Ibid., 125–26.

36. Ibid., 127–53.

## II

1. Ellenburg, "Reconstruction in Arkansas," 57.

2. Fort Smith *Herald*, July 13, 1867.

3. *Arkansas Gazette*, June 18, 1867.

4. Pine Bluff *Dispatch*, May 4, 1867.

5. Ellenburg, "Reconstruction in Arkansas," 59; Thompson, *Arkansas and Reconstruction*, 83–87.

6. Thompson, *Arkansas and Reconstruction*, 63–64.

7. For an example of noncooperationist attitudes, see John R. Eakin, Washington, Arkansas, August 27, 1867, letter to David Walker, Fayetteville, Arkansas. David Walker Letters, University of Arkansas Library, Fayetteville, Arkansas.

8. Thompson, *Arkansas and Reconstruction*, 63–64.

9. Ibid., 102; *Debates and Proceedings of the Convention which Assembled at Little Rock, January 7th, 1868, under the Provisions of the Act of Congress of March 2d, 1867, and the Acts of March 23d and July 19th, 1867, Supplementary Thereto, to form a Constitution for the State of Arkansas* (Little Rock, 1868), 27–31.

10. *Debates and Proceedings of the Convention . . . 1868*, 770.

11. Staples, *Reconstruction in Arkansas*, 176–77.

12. Ibid., 169–71. *Arkansas Gazette*, November 17, 1867; Pine Bluff *Dispatch*, November 23, 1867; Fort Smith *Herald*, November 18, 1867.

13. Richard L. Hume, "The Arkansas Constitutional Convention of 1868: A Case Study in the Politics of Reconstruction," *Journal of Southern History*, XXXIX (May 1973): 199–200; for biographical sketches of leading Carpetbaggers, see Ellenburg, "Reconstruction in Arkansas," 33–46.

14. Hume, "The Arkansas Constitutional Convention of 1868," 200.

15. Ibid., 199.

16. Ibid., 186. A lawyer and native of Iowa, Bowen in later years would serve as territorial governor of Idaho and United States Senator from Colorado. See Ellenburg, "Reconstruction in Arkansas," 38–39.

17. Hume, "The Arkansas Constitutional Convention of 1868," 195.

18. Ibid., 201–02. The eight Negro delegates were James W. Mason of Chicot County, Richard Samuels of Hempstead County, William Murphy of Jefferson County, Monroe Hawkins of Lafayette County, William H. Grey and James T. White of Phillips County, and Thomas P. Johnson and Henry Rector of Pulaski County. The average value of their property holdings was $3,557.14 and the median value $500.00.

19. Joseph M. St. Hilaire, "The Negro Delegates in the Constitutional Convention of 1868: A Group Profile," *Arkansas Historical Quarterly*, XXXIII (Spring 1974): 43, 60; Llewellyn W. Williamson, *Black Footprints around Arkansas* (Hope, Arkansas, 1979), 61–62. Grey later moved with his parents to Pittsburgh, Pennsylvania, and thence to Cin-

cinnati, Ohio. Following their death from cholera, he traveled to St. Louis, Missouri, where he worked on steamboats of the Mississippi and Ohio rivers. By 1863 he was residing in Arkansas. He made his home at Helena, where he entered a partnership in the grocery and baking business and served as a local minister of the A.M.E. Church. He later held several important offices during radical Reconstruction, including service as a Phillips County state representative, and also played an active role in Republican party affairs, being named an Arkansas delegate to the Republican national conventions of 1868 and 1872. Additionally, Grey was elected the first State Grand Master of the Prince Hall Freemasons of Arkansas. Grey's career was struck short by an attack of paralysis in 1873, although later he was able, even in his stricken condition, to serve as Clerk of the County and Probate Court of Phillips County until 1878; after years of illness he died on November 8, 1887.

20. St. Hilaire, "The Negro Delegates in the Constitutional Convention of 1868," 46, 64. White was a Baptist minister who reportedly arrived at Helena during the Civil War while serving with a detachment of black federal troops. He later served as a Phillips County state representative in 1868–1869 and a Phillips County state senator from 1871 to 1873.

21. James W. Mason was the illegitimate mulatto son of a wealthy white bachelor-planter. Mason was sent by his father to France for his education; his sister, Martha, attended school in the North. When their father died intestate, a lawsuit arose over the inheritance, and eventually the United States Supreme Court upheld the children's claims. In the 1868 convention Mason presented an unsuccessful proposal which asserted that illegitimate children should have the right to inherit property from their parents. During radical Reconstruction Mason served as a state senator from Chicot County from 1868 to 1871 and as sheriff of Chicot County from 1872 to 1874. In later years his widow secured a position as clerk in the United States Land Office through the patronage of Senator Augustus H. Garland and other Democratic congressmen from Arkansas. She afterwards left the country and moved to Paris, France, where her daughter became an aspiring young art student. See Mifflin Wistar Gibbs, *Shadow and Light: An Autobiography, with Reminiscences of the Past and Present Century, with an Introduction by Booker T. Washington* (Washington, D.C., 1902), 228–29; *Debates and Proceedings of the Convention . . . 1868*, 539. (St. Hilaire, the chief biographer of the black delegates, provides some useful information on Mason but apparently was unaware of the unusual circumstances surrounding his parentage; see St. Hilaire, "The Negro Delegates in the Constitutional Convention of 1868," 44–45, 62.)

22. St. Hilaire, "The Negro Delegates in the Constitutional Convention of 1868," 66–69.

23. Hume, "The Arkansas Constitutional Convention of 1868," 199–200.

24. See *Proceedings of the Convention of Colored Citizens of the State of Arkansas, Held in Little Rock, Thursday, Friday and Saturday, Nov. 30, Dec. 1 and 2* [1865], (Helena, Arkansas, 1866), 3, 7–10.

25. *Debates and Proceedings of the Convention . . . 1868*, 91.

26. Ibid., 93.

27. Ibid., 97.

28. Ibid., 682.

29. Hume, "The Arkansas Constitutional Convention of 1868," 186–87.

30. Ibid.

31. Ibid., 191, 195–97.

32. Ibid., 363.

33. Hume, "The Arkansas Constitutional Convention of 1868," 189.

34. *Debates and Proceedings of the Convention . . . 1868*, 376–78.

35. Ibid., 379.

36. Ibid., 375–76.

37. Hume, "The Arkansas Constitutional Convention of 1868," 190–91. The 1868 General Assembly never followed the convention's suggestion that it enact an anti-miscegenation law. However, in an 1895 case, the Arkansas Supreme Court ruled that an original anti-miscegenation statute adopted in 1838 still remained in force; in the justices' view, it had never been rescinded by the constitutions of 1864, 1868, and 1874 or by the Fourteenth Amendment to the United States Constitution. See *Ark. Rev. Stat.* (1838), Chap. 94, Sec. 4; *Dodson v. State.* 61 Ark. 57.

38. *Arkansas Constitution* (1868), ART. 6; Staples, *Reconstruction in Arkansas*, 243–44. The legislature of 1868 bestowed further sweeping powers upon the governor, including the right to name all county and township officers. See Staples, ibid., 277–78.

39. *Arkansas Constitution* (1868), ARTS. 5 and 14. Thompson, *Arkansas and Reconstruction*, 64–71.

40. *Arkansas Constitution* (1868), ART. 8. Despite the experience of the state elections of 1866, a minority of white Scalawags and even one Negro delegate, James W. Mason, charitably spoke against disqualifying any citizen from voting or holding office. See *Debates and Proceedings of the Convention . . . 1868*, 671–72.

41. *Arkansas Constitution* (1868), ART. 8.

42. *Arkansas Constitution* (1868), ART. 9; *Debates and Proceedings of the Convention* . . . *1868*, 645, 659–60, 666, 673–75; Staples, *Reconstruction in Arkansas*, 244–45.

43. *Arkansas Constitution* (1868), ART. 1, SEC. 1; ART. 5, SECS. 37, 38.

44. *Arkansas Constitution* (1868), Schedule.

45. Staples, *Reconstruction in Arkansas*, 251–53.

46. In 1860 the Northwest had 46 percent, the eastern Delta 28 percent, and the Southwest 26 percent of the representation in the state legislature; this essentially reflected the distribution of the white population within Arkansas. Under the new apportionment based upon the convention registration figures, the Northwest, with approximately 40 percent of the adult male population, received 30.6 percent of the legislative representation; the eastern Delta, with 34 percent of the population, 38 percent; and the Southwest, with 26 percent of the population, 31.2 percent. See Thompson, *Arkansas and Reconstruction*, 64, 68.

47. See letter from George C. Watkins, Little Rock, Arkansas, March 6, 1868, to David Walker, Fayetteville, Arkansas. David Walker Letters, University of Arkansas.

48. Staples, *Reconstruction in Arkansas*, 249–51.

49. *Campaign Gazette*, March 10, 1868.

50. Ellenburg, "Reconstruction in Arkansas," 87–88; Staples, *Reconstruction in Arkansas*, 255; for an inside view of Klan operations by a contemporary, see Samuel H. Chester, *Pioneer Days in Arkansas* (Richmond, Virginia, 1927), 62–64.

51. Staples, *Reconstruction in Arkansas*, 260–64; letter from George C. Watkins, Little Rock, Arkansas, March 29, 1868, to David Walker, Fayetteville, Arkansas. David Walker Letters, University of Arkansas.

52. Thompson, *Arkansas and Reconstruction*, 71–75.

53. Staples, *Reconstruction in Arkansas*, 262–64.

54. Ibid., 265–67.

55. Ibid., 274–75.

## III

1. See letter of F. W. Compton, Little Rock, Arkansas, June 25, 1868, to David Walker, Fayetteville, Arkansas. David Walker Letters, University of Arkansas.

2. Thompson, *Arkansas and Reconstruction*, 72–73; Eugene G. Feistman, "Radical Disfranchisement in Arkansas, 1867–1868," *Arkansas Historical Quarterly*, XII (Summer 1953): 158–59.

3. C. Armitage Harper, ed., *Historical Report of the Secretary of State* (Arkansas), (Little Rock, 1968), 249–50; Thomas Rothrock, "Joseph Carter Corbin and Negro Education in the University of Arkansas," *Arkansas Historical Quarterly*, XXX (Winter 1971): 278–81.

4. Joe Tolbert Segraves, "Arkansas Politics, 1874–1918" (Ph.D. diss., University of Kentucky, 1973), 118; Powell Clayton, *The Aftermath of the Civil War in Arkansas* (New York, 1915), 307–10; for descriptions of Negro members in the Reconstruction legislature of 1873, see *Arkansas, Gazette*, February 1, 1873.

5. John William Graves, "The Arkansas Negro and Segregation, 1890–1903" (M.A. thesis, University of Arkansas, 1967), 70–90; Segraves, "Arkansas Politics, 1874–1918," 118–21. Some blacks were particularly restive with the secondary role they played in state party politics. As early as 1869 Tabbs Gross, the founder of Arkansas's first black-owned and operated newspaper, the Little Rock *Arkansas Freeman*, attacked tokenism and demanded a larger role for blacks in Republican-party affairs. Pressure from his newspaper did cause Little Rock Republicans to nominate and elect five blacks to the city council (out of a total of eight) and also to other local offices in 1869. However, the blacks' minority status among the general population as well as fears of the Arkansas Democrats and their intentions limited the room for maneuver of leaders like Gross. Most blacks appear to have felt that the continued exercise of meaningful black political rights in Arkansas required the support of the Republican party and its influential white spokesmen, bolstered in turn by the federal government. Diane Neal, "Seduction, Accommodation, or Realism? Tabbs Gross and the *Arkansas Freeman*," *Arkansas Historical Quarterly*, XLVIII (Spring 1989): 57–64; Little Rock *Arkansas Freeman*, October 5, 1869; Little Rock *Daily Republican*, August 19, 1870; for a general survey of the Arkansas Republican party and the role blacks played in it, see Marvin Frank Russell, "The Republican Party in Arkansas, 1874–1913" (Ph.D. diss., University of Arkansas, 1985), 4–7, 85–87, 103–4, 111–13, 166, 178–80, 190–91, 208–9, 215–20. See also Carl H. Moneyhon, "Black Politics in Arkansas during the Gilded Age, 1876–1900," *Arkansas Historical Quarterly*, XLIV (Autumn 1985): 232–35.

6. Adolphine Fletcher Terry, *Charlotte Stephens: Little Rock's First Black Teacher* (Little Rock, 1973), 51–57, 64–69. There had been only a few black congregations in antebellum Arkansas. Most blacks worshipped in white churches where they were supervised and controlled by their

masters and either confined to the galleries or back pews or met in separate services. The origins of this custom are obscure and may first have had more to do with consciousness of class than of race; possibly it derived from the English practice, where white servants were often seated in galleries apart from the rest of the congregation.

Occasionally churches dispensed with these segregated arrangements altogether. In these instances blacks attended the worship services alongside their owners, took part in joint baptismal ceremonies, and were even called to preach before mixed congregations. Regardless of the practices followed, most blacks abandoned the white churches soon after freedom. See ibid., 14–15, 33–35; Taylor, *Negro Slavery in Arkansas*, 168–87. See also Larry M. James, "Biracial Fellowship in Antebellum Baptist Churches," and Randy J. Sparks, "Religion in Amite County, Mississippi," in John B. Boles, ed., *Masters and Slaves in the House of the Lord* (Lexington, Kentucky, 1988), 37–57, 58–80.

7. *Debates and Proceedings of the Convention . . . 1868*, 649–50, 660; Little Rock *Arkansas Gazette*, July 21, 1868; Clayton, *The Aftermath of the Civil War in Arkansas*, 225–27; Ellenburg, "Reconstruction in Arkansas," 137–40; *Annual Report of the Public Schools of the School District of Little Rock, Arkansas . . . 1877* (Little Rock, 1877), 11; James T. Haley, comp., *Afro-American Encyclopedia . . .* (Nashville, Tennessee, 1896), 562–63. There is evidence that the request for black teachers may have been in response to the prejudiced attitudes of some white teachers. Such a policy would also give needed employment to the emerging class of black urban professionals. Moreover, since blacks were excluded from teaching in white schools, the policy could be justified in terms of equity. See Selma Ann Plowman Hobby, "The Little Rock Public Schools during Reconstruction," Ed.D. diss., University of Arkansas, 1967), 93.

8. Reprinted in *Arkansas Gazette*, July 11, 1868.

9. Ellenburg, "Reconstruction in Arkansas," 192. An outstanding case in point concerned Charlotte Andrews (later Mrs. John Stephens), a black teacher in the Little Rock public schools. In August 1870 Miss Andrews left the Arkansas capital to attend Oberlin College in Ohio. Accompanying her on her journey was the Little Rock school board secretary and Joseph Carter Corbin, soon to be state Superintendent of Public Instruction. Boarding a train at the Little Rock railway station in eager anticipation of her trip, Miss Andrews happiness was dampened when she entered the passenger coach. Two of the trio, the white woman and Corbin, a light-skinned mulatto who could easily pass for a white person, were allowed to ride in the main section of the coach; however, the young black teacher was forced to sit apart in a small anteroom. Terry, *Charlotte Stephens: Little Rock's First Black Teacher*, 78–79; Clara B.

Kennan, "The First Negro Teacher in Little Rock," *Arkansas Historical Quarterly*, IX (Autumn 1950): 199–201.

10. *Acts of Arkansas* (1873), 15–19; ibid., (1907), 728.

11. Charles Nordhoff, *The Cotton States in the Spring and Summer of 1875* (New York, 1876), 35–36; see court documents in the above-mentioned case reprinted in the *Pulaski County Historical Review*, V (September 1957): 47–50.

12. Nordhoff, *The Cotton States in . . . 1875*, 36.

13. Boston *Daily Globe*, December 6, 1886; *Arkansas Gazette*, January 29, 1891; Charles Dudley Warner, "Studies of the Great West: Memphis and Little Rock," *Harper's New Monthly Magazine*, LXXVI (September 1888): 55; Little Rock *Arkansas Democrat*, May 29, 1903 (hereinafter cited, for all dates, as *Arkansas Democrat*).

14. Cheryl Griffith Nichols, "Pulaski Heights: Early Suburban Development in Little Rock, Arkansas," *Arkansas Historical Quarterly*, XLI (Summer 1982): 139–40.

15. *Little Rock City Directory, 1900–01* (Little Rock, 1901), 97–214.

16. *Arkansas Gazette*, August 10, October 8, 1897; James W. Bell, "The Early Parks of Little Rock: Part I," *Pulaski County Historical Review*, XXX (Spring 1982): 20–21.

17. *Arkansas Gazette*, July 10, 1892; Bell, "Early Parks of Little Rock," 20.

18. In his autobiography black Arkansan Mifflin Wistar Gibbs describes his attendance at the Folies-Bergère in Paris, France, in 1898. Gibbs mentioned, "The appearance of the occupants of the front row of seats very forcibly reminded me of a smaller locality at the Capital Theater in the City of Roses [Little Rock], on similar occasions, where many of my old friends loved to congregate." Although the race of the friends is not clearly identified, the sentence strongly suggests that blacks were not confined to the theater balcony but were using the main parquet section as well. Of course, this would not preclude possible segregation within the parquet section. When Frederick Douglass spoke at the Capital Theater in Little Rock in 1889, it appears that blacks sat on one side of the theater and whites on the other. Still, in a 1967 interview with this writer, Miss Dorothy Gillam, a school teacher and older black resident, stated that she remembered no theater segregation or exclusion of blacks in Little Rock during her youth prior to World War I. Miss Gillam recounted painfully how theater segregation and exclusion began to be inaugurated during the 1920s and 1930s. Finally, only one downtown theater, the Roxy on Main Street, continued to admit blacks, and it restricted black patrons to the balcony. Gibbs, *Shadow and Light*, 227; *Arkansas Ga-*

zette, February 6, 1889, October 17, 1896; interview by the author with Miss Dorothy Gillam, Little Rock, Arkansas, July 29, 1967. (Miss Gillam was the daughter of the late Isaac T. Gillam, Jr., principal of Little Rock's M. W. Gibbs' High School, and granddaughter of the late Isaac T. Gillam, Sr., former black Little Rock city councilman during the 1870s and Pulaski County state representative in 1879. Little Rock *Arkansas Democrat*, January 23, 1986, 10A.

19. Tim Hackler, "When on a Dry Day You Could Walk to Town, Little Rock—1891: An Era of Change and Growth," in *Arkansas Democrat*, March 5, 1972, 14A. Hereinafter cited as "Little Rock—1891."

20. *Arkansas Gazette*, January 30, 1891.

21. Margaret Smith Ross, "Nathan Warren, a Free Negro of the Old South," *Arkansas Historical Quarterly*, XV (Spring 1956): 59.

22. *Arkansas Gazette*, March 21, 1888; Joe Neal, "Fraternal Cemetery: Reflections on a Southern Negro Graveyard," *Pulaski County Historical Review*, XXV (March 1977): 1–13. On the emergence of separate cemeteries elsewhere, see Rudd and Bond, *From Slavery to Wealth*, 307–11.

23. Jerry Dean, "History of Arkansas Can Be Read in Stones Dotting Martin Cemetery," *Arkansas Gazette*, October 11, 1987, 5A; D. Michael Finnigan, "Martin Cemetery: Mabelvale History in Marble and Granite," Little Rock *Arkansas Democrat* (March 8, 1979): 7F.

24. Orval Truman Driggs, Jr., "The Issues of the Powell Clayton Regime, 1868–1871," *Arkansas Historical Quarterly*, VIII (Spring 1949): 40.

25. Ibid.

26. By 1867–1868, 51 such schools had been established, serving approximately 3,500 students. Ferguson and Atkinson, *Historic Arkansas*, 154; see also Larry Wesley Pearce, "The American Missionary Association and the Freedmen in Arkansas, 1863–1878," *Arkansas Historical Quarterly*, XXX (Summer 1971): 123–44; ibid., XXX (Autumn 1971): 242–59; ibid., XXXI (Autumn 1972): 246–61.

27. *Acts of Arkansas* (1873), 423.

28. William Preston Vaughn, *Schools for All: The Blacks and Public Education in the South* (Lexington, Kentucky, 1974), 59.

29. Driggs, "The Issues of the Powell Clayton Regime," 45–46.

30. The main campus of the new Arkansas Industrial University (later renamed the University of Arkansas), located at Fayetteville in the far northwest corner of the state, was inaccessible to most blacks. One Negro did enroll there in 1872, but he was instructed separately and not allowed to attend classes with white students. In light of these condi-

tions, blacks preferred having their own institution. John H. Reynolds and David Y. Thomas, *History of the University of Arkansas* (Fayetteville, Arkansas, 1910), 96–97; Rothrock, "Joseph Carter Corbin and Negro Education in the University of Arkansas," 281.

31. *Fifth Biennial Report of the Trustees and Superintendent of the Arkansas Institute for the Education of the Blind, for the Two Years Commencing November 1, 1868, and Ending October 21, 1870* (Little Rock, 1871), 11, 84–90.

32. *Acts of Arkansas* (1868), 115–21.

33. *Arkansas Gazette,* February 5, March 26, 1889; *Fourteenth Biennial Report of the Board of Trustees and Superintendent of the Arkansas School for the Blind, for the Two Years Commencing October 1, 1886, and Ending September 30, 1886* (Little Rock, 1888), 45–46; *Tenth Biennial Report of the Board of Directors and Officers of the Arkansas Deaf Mute Institute to the Governor of the State of Arkansas, for the Years 1887 and 1888* (Little Rock, 1888), 15; Mattie Cal Maxted, "Training of Deaf Children in Arkansas," *Arkansas Historical Quarterly,* V (Fall 1946): 199–200; Garland Erastus Bayliss, "Public Affairs in Arkansas 1874–1896" (Ph.D. diss., University of Texas, 1972), 227, 230.

34. State reports show that by 1888, five years after the opening of the asylum, 90 of the 408 patients confined were black. *Sixth Annual Report of the Board of Trustees and Superintendent of the State Lunatic Asylum at Little Rock, Ark., for the Year Ending December 1, 1888* (Little Rock, 1889), 33.

35. Warner, "Studies of the Great West: Memphis and Little Rock," 556. Although assigned to separate wards, black and white patients appear to have mingled freely when using the recreational areas on the asylum grounds [James Cooke Warde], *Jimmy Warde's Experiences as a Lunatic* (Little Rock, 1902), 189, 257.

36. See letter of J. H. Barton, private secretary of Governor Powell Clayton, Little Rock, Arkansas, to J. W. Browning, New York, New York, January 10, 1870. Letterbook of Governor Powell Clayton, Arkansas History Commission, Little Rock, Arkansas.

37. Jane Zimmerman, "The Convict Lease System in Arkansas and the Fight for Abolition," *Arkansas Historical Quarterly,* VIII (Autumn 1949): 172.

38. Garland E. Bayliss, "The Arkansas State Penitentiary under Democratic Control, 1874–1896," *Arkansas Historical Quarterly,* XXXIV (Autumn 1975): 208–13. Segregation of convicts by race was not begun until required by state law in 1903. *Acts of Arkansas* (1903), 160–62.

39. Driggs, "The Issues of the Powell Clayton Regime," 35.

40. Thompson, *Arkansas and Reconstruction*, 77.

41. Staples, *Reconstruction in Arkansas*, 359–60.

42. Average annual tax collections for the six years of radical Reconstruction government, 1868–1874, were over seven times greater than under the Murphy regime, 1864–1866; total property assessments increased almost three-fold over the Murphy period. Ibid., 356–59.

43. Ibid., 360–63.

44. Thompson, *Arkansas and Reconstruction*, 234. Large issues of county and municipal script fell even more disastrously, in some instances to as low as ten cents on the dollar.

45. Staples, *Reconstruction in Arkansas*, 324–25.

46. Thompson, *Arkansas and Reconstruction*, 231–35.

47. Ibid., 232–33.

48. Ibid., 231–32, 234–35; Ellenburg, "Reconstruction in Arkansas," 105–6.

49. Thompson, *Arkansas and Reconstruction*, 237–39.

50. Staples, *Reconstruction in Arkansas*, 255.

51. Clayton gives a detailed listing of dozens of murders and other outrages in his memoirs. Clayton, *The Aftermath of the Civil War in Arkansas*, 56–105.

52. Michael P. Kelly, "Partisan or Protector: Powell Clayton and the 1868 Presidential Election," *Ozark Historical Review*, III (Spring 1974): 44–58.

53. Otis A. Singletary, "Militia Disturbances in Arkansas during Reconstruction," *Arkansas Historical Quarterly*, XV (Summer 1956): 140–50; Staples, *Reconstruction in Arkansas*, 294–308; Ferguson and Atkinson, *Historic Arkansas*, 156–57. For descriptions of continuing intimidation of Negroes see letter of J. H. Barton, private secretary of Governor Powell Clayton, Little Rock, Arkansas, to I. S. Ford, Springfield, Arkansas, January 17, 1870; letter of J. H. Barton, Little Rock, Arkansas, to R. M. Peshall, Mouth of White River, Arkansas, March 31, 1870. Powell Clayton Letterbook, Arkansas History Commission; letter of Keyes Danforth, private secretary of Governor O. A. Hadley, Little Rock, Arkansas, to J. H. Mason, Reu Lowand, Arkansas, December 7, 1872. O. A. Hadley Letterbook, Arkansas History Commission.

54. Staples, *Reconstruction in Arkansas*, 375–77.

55. Ibid., 374.

56. Van Buren *Press*, August 7, 1868; see also letter of Augustus H. Garland, Little Rock, Arkansas, July 30, 1868, to David Walker, Fayetteville, Arkansas. David Walker Letters, University of Arkansas.

57. *Arkansas Gazette,* August 1, 1868.

58. Ibid., August 4, 1868.

59. Letter of William E. Woodruff, Jr., Little Rock, Arkansas, September 11, 1868, to David Walker, Fayetteville, Arkansas. David Walker Letters, University of Arkansas. Woodruff was the son of the *Gazette's* founder.

60. Letter of William E. Woodruff, Jr., Little Rock, Arkansas, October 16, 1868, to David Walker, Fayetteville, Arkansas. A. Howard Stebbins, Jr., Collection, Arkansas History Commission, Little Rock, Arkansas.

61. For an excellent discussion of these internal disagreements within the Conservative camp, see Thompson, *Arkansas and Reconstruction,* 77–96.

62. Letter of David Walker, Fayetteville, Arkansas. September 24, 1868, to William E. Woodruff, Jr., Little Rock, Arkansas. David Walker Letters, University of Arkansas. In an identical vein, see the letter of former antebellum Whig spokesman and ex-Confederate brigadier Albert Pike in the Memphis *Appeal,* September 10, 1868.

63. Letter of David Walker, Fayetteville, Arkansas, August 6, 1869, to John R. Eakin, Washington, Arkansas. David Walker Letters, University of Arkansas.

64. The praise came from Conservative member John M. Bradley of Bradley County. *Debates and Proceedings of the Convention . . . 1868,* 655.

65. *Arkansas Gazette,* February 18, 1869.

66. Staples, *Reconstruction in Arkansas,* 389–95. The party leader in question was John G. Price, editor of the Little Rock *Daily Republican.*

67. Ibid.

68. Thompson, *Arkansas and Reconstruction,* 98–99. See also letters of B. F. Rice, Little Rock, Arkansas, September 7, 14, October 7, 1872, to former Confederate governor Harris Flanagin, Arkadelphia, Arkansas; letter of C. B. Moore, Little Rock, Arkansas, October 4, 1872, to Harris Flanagin, Arkadelphia, Arkansas. Harris Flanagin Papers, Arkansas History Commission, Little Rock, Arkansas.

69. Thompson, *Arkansas and Reconstruction,* 98.

70. Jerome R. Riley, *The Philosophy of Negro Suffrage* (Hartford, Connecticut, 1895), 60–61; *Arkansas Gazette,* May 22, 1872.

71. Letter of Augustus H. Garland, Little Rock, Arkansas, June 6, 1872, to Harris Flanagin, Arkadelphia, Arkansas. Harris Flanagin Papers, Arkansas History Commission; Thompson, *Arkansas and Reconstruction,* 98–99.

72. Staples, *Reconstruction in Arkansas*, 386; *Arkansas Gazette*, March 19, 1871; Little Rock *Daily Republican*, March 15, 1871.

73. Baxter had been born in North Carolina, but he had lived in Arkansas ever since 1852. A resident of the town of Batesville, he had been variously engaged as a lawyer, merchant, and editor in antebellum days and had served as a state representative from Independence County in 1854 and 1858. During the Civil War he served as an officer in the Fourth Arkansas Infantry (Union) and was at one time held as a Confederate prisoner. Thompson, *Arkansas and Reconstruction*, 108; Thomas, *Arkansas in War and Reconstruction*, 202, 242; James H. Atkinson, "The Arkansas Gubernatorial Campaign and Election of 1872," *Arkansas Historical Quarterly*, I (December 1942): 31.

74. Staples, *Reconstruction in Arkansas*, 62.

75. Ibid., 393–95; Clayton, *Aftermath of the Civil War in Arkansas*, 346–47.

76. Eugene Cypert, "Constitutional Convention of 1868," *Publications of the Arkansas Historical Association*, IV (1917): 55.

77. State law gave the governor exclusive authority to appoint a three-man registration board for each county. Appointments were for two years, but the governor could make removals at pleasure and fill all vacancies. Registrars were empowered to pass on the qualifications of all voters and appoint three judges of election for every voting precinct. In practice, registration officers were chosen strictly on the basis of party loyalty, with the names of nominees forwarded to the governor by the regular Republican county and township committees. *Acts of Arkansas* (1868), 52; letter of Governor Powell Clayton, Little Rock, Arkansas, March 11, 1870, to James A. Davis, Fort Smith, Arkansas. Letterbook of Governor Powell Clayton, Arkansas History Commission; letter of Edward Saxton, private secretary of Governor O. A. Hadley, Little Rock, Arkansas, July 21, 1872, to William C. Petty, Searcy, Arkansas; letter of Edward Saxton, Little Rock, Arkansas, August 13, 1872, to W. J. McClud, Hamburg, Arkansas. Letterbook of Governor O. A. Hadley, Arkansas History Commission, Little Rock, Arkansas.

78. The official returns gave Baxter 43.9 percent of the vote in Northwest Arkansas, 48.7 percent in Southwest Arkansas, and 62 percent in the eastern Delta. Brooks own totals showed him winning 40,549 to 38,353, with 60 percent of the Northwest ballots, 56 percent of those of the Southwest, and 41 percent of those of the Delta. Both sets of returns suggest that a majority of Delta blacks, probably suspicious of Democratic support for Brooks, stayed loyal to the regular Republican ticket. Thompson, *Arkansas and Reconstruction*, 100–105.

79. Ibid., 104–5.

80. Thompson, *Arkansas and Reconstruction*, 104–16; letter of E. H. English, Little Rock, Arkansas, January 28, 1873, to Governor Elisha Baxter, Little Rock. L. C. Gulley Collection of State Papers, Arkansas History Commission, Little Rock, Arkansas; letter of U. M. Rose, Little Rock, Arkansas, March 31, 1873, to Harris Flanagin, Arkadelphia, Arkansas. Harris Flanagin Papers, Arkansas History Commission.

81. Thompson, *Arkansas and Reconstruction*, 108–11.

82. Staples, *Reconstruction in Arkansas*, 401. The amendment was ratified by a majority of 21,504 out of a total of 28,894 votes cast.

83. *Arkansas Gazette*, March 20, 1874.

84. Thompson, *Arkansas and Reconstruction*, 147–48. Among other points, Baxter noted that the 1868 constitution specified that no act could take effect until 90 days after the close of the legislative session in which it had been passed. Since the session in which the railway-aid act had been passed had not expired until April 10, 1869, the act could not become law before July 10, 1869. However, the act itself had directed that a referendum election be held on November 3, 1868, in which the voters would approve the issuance of railway-aid bonds. Although the voters had in fact approved the bond issue on that date, the act authorizing the referendum had not yet formally become law at the time the referendum was conducted. Baxter therefore contended that the election had been a nullity and that state railroad bonds had been issued without authority of law. In an 1877 case, the Arkansas Supreme Court accepted Baxter's reasoning and voided $5,350,000 worth of railroad bonds. See *State of Arkansas v. Little Rock, Mississippi River and Texas Railway Company*, 31 Ark. 701 (1877).

85. One of the railroads which had received state bonds constructed part of its line through "Linwood," Powell Clayton's plantation in Jefferson County; Clayton, however, donated the land for its right-of-way. In his memoirs he insisted that he at least had never owned state railroad bonds during the Reconstruction period and had never personally profited from their issuance. Clayton, *Aftermath of the Civil War in Arkansas*, 237–50.

86. James H. Atkinson, "The Brooks-Baxter Contest," *Arkansas Historical Quarterly*, IV (Summer 1945): 124–25.

87. Dallas T. Herndon, *Centennial History of Arkansas* (Chicago, 1922), 309, quoting the New York *Herald*, n.d.

88. Atkinson, "The Brooks-Baxter Contest," 129; Earl F. Woodward, "The Brooks and Baxter War in Arkansas, 1872–1874," *Arkansas Historical Quarterly*, XXX (Winter 1971): 326–27.

89. Atkinson, "The Brooks-Baxter Contest," 126.

90. Ferguson and Atkinson, *Historic Arkansas*, 167.

91. Atkinson, "The Brooks-Baxter Contest," 127–28, 131–32, 144. Former Confederate brigadier general Robert C. Newton led the Baxter troops; the Brooks' forces were commanded by former Confederate major general James F. Fagan.

92. Ibid., 133–35.

93. John Gould Fletcher, *Arkansas* (Chapel Hill, North Carolina, 1947), 255–57.

94. Ibid., 251.

95. Ferguson and Atkinson, *Historic Arkansas*, 167; some estimates placed the casualty figures much lower, as low as twenty or thirty. *Arkansas Gazette*, May 17, 24, 1874.

96. John M. Harrell, *The Brooks and Baxter War: A History of the Reconstruction Period in Arkansas* (St. Louis, Missouri, 1893), 208–10, 246–47.

97. Ibid., 230; ART. 6, SEC. 19 of the 1868 constitution stated, "Contested elections shall . . . be determined by both houses of the General Assembly in such manner as is or may hereafter be prescribed by law."

98. Ibid., 209; *Brooks v. Page.* 29 Ark. 199 (1874).

99. Staples, *Reconstruction in Arkansas*, 416–18; Thompson, *Arkansas and Reconstruction*, 155–56.

100. Staples, *Reconstruction in Arkansas*, 417–18.

101. Ibid., 418–19.

102. Ibid., 420.

103. Harrell, *The Brooks and Baxter War*, 256–57; Mrs. U. M. Rose, "Clayton's Aftermath of the Civil War in Arkansas," *Publications of the Arkansas Historical Association*, IV (1917): 63.

104. Harrell, *The Brooks and Baxter War*, 258–59; Benjamin S. Johnson, "The Brooks-Baxter War," *Publications of the Arkansas Historical Association*, II (1908): 125–32.

105. Dallas T. Herndon, *Annals of Arkansas*, I (Hopkinsville, Kentucky, 1947), 197.

106. James M. Pomeroy, ed., *The Constitution of the State of Arkansas . . . 1874 . . . A Documentary History . . .* (Little Rock, 1876), xx; "Manuscript Journal of the Arkansas Constitutional Convention, 1874" (2 vols.), I, 31. The manuscript journal is on microfilm at the University of Arkansas Library, Fayetteville, Arkansas.

107. Staples, *Reconstruction in Arkansas*, 424; for a complete listing of convention delegates, see Fay Hempstead, *A Pictorial History of Arkansas* (St. Louis and New York, 1890), 644.

108. James Harris Fain, "Political Disfranchisement of the Negro in Arkansas" (M.A. thesis, University of Arkansas, 1961), 16–18. The Negro delegates were W. L. Copeland, Crittenden County; J. Pennoyer Jones, Desha County; Silas Berry and William Murphy, Jefferson County; Robert Polk and James T. White, Phillips County; and Jesse Butler and George N. Perkins, Pulaski County. Historian Thomas Staples' observation that there were only four Negro delegates at the convention was in error. Staples, *Reconstruction in Arkansas*, 425.

109. *Arkansas Gazette*, June 13, 1874.

110. Little Rock *Daily Republican*, July 3, 15, 22, 1874. It is possibly significant that the county election commissioners in charge of the convention balloting were named, not by Governor Baxter, noted for his honesty, but by a special three-man board of supervisors appointed by the legislature. *Acts of Arkansas* (1874), 4–5.

111. Pomeroy, *The Constitution of the State of Arkansas . . . 1874*, xx. In addition to Phillips, six other counties, Cross, Fulton, Green, Lee, Saline, and St. Francis, reported no votes in opposition.

112. *Arkansas Constitution* (1874), ART. 6.

113. Ibid., ART. 6, SEC. 3; ART. 7, SECS. 6, 17, 29, 38, 44, 46, 47.

114. Ibid., ART. 3, SEC. 2.

115. Ibid., ART. 16, SEC. 8.

116. Ibid., ART. 16, SEC. 1. This section stipulated, "Neither the State, nor any city, county, town or other municipality in this State shall ever loan its credit for any purpose whatever. Nor shall any county, city, town, or municipality ever issue any interest bearing evidences of indebtedness; except such bonds as may be authorized by law to provide for and secure the payment of the present existing indebtedness. And the State shall never issue any interest bearing Treasury warrants or scrip."

117. Ibid., ART. 16, SECS. 9, 10, 11.

118. *Arkansas Constitution* (1874), ART. 8, SEC. 1.

119. Ibid., ART. 8, SEC. 2. There appear to have been no obvious attempts at gerrymandering under these provisions. See Bayliss, "Public Affairs in Arkansas," 77–78.

120. *Arkansas Constitution* (1874), ART. 14.

121. *Arkansas Gazette*, August 2, 1874.

122. Fain, "Political Disfranchisement of the Negro in Arkansas," 19–20; Joseph W. House, "The Constitutional Convention of 1874—Reminiscences," *Publications of the Arkansas Historical Association*, IV (1917): 210–68.

123. *Arkansas Gazette*, August 2, 1874; for the full text of the law see *Debates and Proceedings of the Convention . . . 1868*, 810–11.

124. *Arkansas Constitution* (1874), ART. 3, SECS. 1, 2; Joseph T. Robinson, "Suffrage in Arkansas," *Publications of the Arkansas Historical Association*, III (1911): 173.

125. *Arkansas Constitution* (1874), ART. 2, SEC. 3.

126. Thompson, *Arkansas and Reconstruction*, 161–63; John H. Moore, *A School History of Arkansas* (Little Rock, 1924), 177. Baxter apparently had anticipated, wrongly, that he could win appointment to the U.S. Senate instead. See Gibbs, *Shadow and Light*, 159.

127. Alfred Holt Carrigan, "Reminiscences of the Secession Convention," *Publications of the Arkansas Historical Association*, I (1906): 307.

128. Thompson, *Arkansas and Reconstruction*, 145–46, 152–54; Walter Scott McNutt, Olin Eli McKnight, and George Allen Hubbell, *A History of Arkansas*, (Little Rock, 1932), 241–42.

129. On Garland's life and career, see Beverly Nettles Watkins, "Augustus Hill Garland, 1832–1899: Arkansas Lawyer to United States Attorney-General" (Ph.D. diss., Auburn University, 1985), and Farrar Newberry, *A Life of Mr. Garland of Arkansas* (n.p., 1908). See also Josiah H. Shinn, *Pioneers and Makers of Arkansas* (Little Rock, 1908), 307–31; John Hugh Reynolds, *Makers of Arkansas History* (New York, 1905), 268–74; Thompson, *Arkansas and Reconstruction*, 135–58. For one of the few negative critiques of Garland, see John Hallum, *Biographical and Pictorial History of Arkansas*, I (Albany, New York, 1887), 410.

130. Staples, *Reconstruction in Arkansas*, 429–31.

131. Pomeroy, *The Constitution of the State of Arkansas . . . 1874*, xxiii; Thompson, *Arkansas and Reconstruction*, 164–65.

132. Staples, *Reconstruction in Arkansas*, 435–38; letter of A. H. Garland, Little Rock, Arkansas, February 11, 1875, to Alexander H. Stephens, Washington, D.C., Alexander H. Stephens Papers, Library of Congress. Quoted in Thompson, *Arkansas and Reconstruction*, 168.

133. Little Rock *Daily Republican*, March 5, 1875; Staples, *Reconstruction in Arkansas*, 438–40.


*IV*


1. Gibbs, *Shadow and Light*, 159.

2. Staples, *Reconstruction in Arkansas*, 431.

3. Newberry, *A Life of Mr. Garland of Arkansas*, 26.

4. Riley, *The Philosophy of Negro Suffrage*, 19–20.

5. Clayton, *Aftermath of the Civil War in Arkansas*, 309–10.

6. Segraves, "Arkansas Politics, 1874–1918," 115–16; *Arkansas Gazette*, May 14, 18, 1892; Pine Bluff *Graphic*, April 29, 1892.

7. Clayton, *Aftermath of the Civil War in Arkansas*, 309–10. Rarely, Democrats would dispense with fusion arrangements and place blacks directly on their own tickets. In 1890, for example, Monroe County Democrats backed four Negroes for local offices. See *Arkansas Democrat*, January 18, August 15, 19, 1890.

8. Letter of Charles Nordhoff in the New York *Herald*, April 13, 1875, quoted in the *Arkansas Gazette*, April 17, 1875.

9. Letter of Jerome R. Riley to Ferd Havis, printed in the *Arkansas Gazette*, January 16, 1875.

10. Riley, *The Philosophy of Negro Suffrage*, 19–20.

11. Herndon, *Annals of Arkansas*, I, 205.

12. Gibbs, *Shadow and Light*, 228–29; *Arkansas Gazette*, September 9, October 12, 1897.

13. Newberry, *A Life of Mr. Garland of Arkansas*, 33–35.

14. *Arkansas Gazette*, December 28, 1883.

15. Gibbs, *Shadow and Light*, 158–60; Riley, *The Philosophy of Negro Suffrage*, 19–20. For similar comments from other black leaders in Arkansas, see *Arkansas Gazette*, March 11, June 4, 1875.

16. Newberry, *A Life of Mr. Garland of Arkansas*, 96.

17. *Arkansas Gazette*, January 12, 25, 1877; Josiah H. Shinn, *The History of Arkansas* (Richmond, Virginia, 1900), 233.

18. *Arkansas Gazette*, June 2, 7, 16, 17, 24, 1881. Churchill later reinstated the commander in question, but in the meantime the white militia unit at Pine Bluff had angrily disbanded its organization. Although use of black militia continued, ordinarily they functioned simply as drill teams and black social clubs and were rarely called to active duty.

19. Ibid., March 31, 1882.

20. Ibid., February 3, 1889.

21. Ibid., February 28, 1889, quoting the New York *World*, (n.d.). For related expressions of opinion, see *Gazette*, September 19, 1888; January 6, 9, February 3, 1889; *Arkansas Democrat*, December 2, 1880.

22. *Arkansas Gazette*, February 28, 1889.

23. Ibid., January 2, 1889; *Arkansas City Journal*, August 15, 1883.

24. Rothrock, "Joseph Carter Corbin and Negro Education in the University of Arkansas," 284.

251

25. Bayliss, "Public Affairs in Arkansas," 148–66; Segraves, "Arkansas Politics, 1874–1918," 62–67.

26. *Acts of Arkansas* (1875), 54–82.

27. Bayliss, "Public Affairs in Arkansas," 163.

28. *Biennial Report of the Superintendent of Public Instruction for the State of Arkansas . . . 1891–92* (Little Rock, 1893), 438–39. However, some whites, even while supporting black schooling, expressed anxiety that it might erode the traditional caste system, especially if white education were neglected. See James B. Craighead, "The Future of the Negro in the South," *Popular Science Monthly*, XXVI (November 1884): 41–42, 45. (Craighead was an Arkansas planter.)

29. Ibid., 438; Stephen B. Weeks, *A History of Arkansas* (Washington, D.C., 1912), 123. The slight disparity in favor of the black students was due to the fact that school funds were apportioned between the races on the basis of total school-age population enumerations. However, because of the absence of a compulsory attendance law, only 52 percent of white and 47 percent of black children of school age were enrolled in classes. More important than the above differentiations was the lack of adequate support for schools of both races. During the next year, 1891, a slight drop in total school revenues and, simultaneously, an over 7 percent increase in total enrollment caused the average per capita expenditure for all school children to decline further, to $4.80.

30. Nordhoff, *The Cotton States in . . . 1875*, 29.

31. Letter of Augustus H. Garland, Little Rock, Arkansas, November 9, 1868, to Alexander H. Stephens, n.p. Alexander H. Stephens Papers, Library of Congress. Quoted in Thompson, *Arkansas and Reconstruction*, 145.

32. Economic growth in the period following the Civil War is discussed in John Ewing Kane, "Business Fluctuations in Arkansas since 1866" (master's thesis, School of Business Administration, University of Arkansas, 1939); Evert Eugene Mapes, "Business Cycles in Arkansas" (master's thesis, School of Business Administration, University of Arkansas, 1939); and Rufus D. Wolff, "The Industrial Development of Arkansas" (M.A. thesis, Vanderbilt University, 1929). Also useful is Mattie Brown's "A History of River Transportation in Arkansas from 1819 to 1880" (M.A. thesis, University of Arkansas, 1933). On twentieth-century development, see James Emmet Pool Griner, "The Growth of Manufactures in Arkansas, 1900–1950" (Ph.D. diss., George Peabody College for Teachers, 1957).

33. Segraves, "Arkansas Politics, 1874–1918," 61.

34. *Acts of Arkansas* (1874–75), 157–58. Dallas T. Herndon, *Outline*

*of Executive and Legislative History of Arkansas* (Fort Smith, Arkansas, 1922), 104.

35. Segraves, "Arkansas Politics, 1874–1918," 58–61; David Y. Thomas, "A History of Taxation in Arkansas," II, *Publications of the Arkansas Historical Association* (1908): 75, 78–80.

36. *Acts of Arkansas* (1879), 16, 24, 31–33, 73–81.

37. Ibid., 70–73; *Arkansas Gazette*, August 21, 1879. For studies of immigration patterns, see J. M. Lucey, "History of Immigration to Arkansas," III, *Publications of the Arkansas Historical Association* (1911): 201–19; Robert B. Walz, "Migration into Arkansas, 1834–1880" (Ph.D. diss., University of Texas, 1958).

38. For examples of adverse Northern reactions to election scandals in Arkansas, from both Republican and Democratic newspapers, see Chicago *Tribune*, Dec. 19, 25, 1888; January 5, 12, 1889; *St. Louis Post-Dispatch*, September 6, 7, 8, 15, 1888; Philadelphia *Press*, (n.d.), in *Arkansas Gazette*, February 6, 1889.

39. Pine Bluff *Graphic*, (n.d.), in *Arkansas Gazette*, September 16, 1888. See also *Gazette*, September 7, 1888; January 25, 1889.

40. Clarksville *Herald*, August 12, 1878; Washington, Arkansas, *South-Western Press*, July 18, 1880; *Appleton's Annual Cyclopaedia and Register of Important Events . . . of the Year 1880* (New York, 1880), 26; Fain, "Political Disfranchisement of the Negro in Arkansas," 25–28.

41. For example, in 1891 blacks admonished that adoption of a proposed "Jim Crow" segregation law for railroad passengers would cause an evacuation of Negro laborers from the state. When the measure passed anyway and was followed by a series of disfranchisement legislation, several hundred Arkansas Negroes moved to black communities in Oklahoma, Mexico, and the Republic of Liberia in Africa. Only a lack of money and support stopped thousands more from joining them. *Arkansas Gazette*, January 28, February 21, 28, March 11, 21, April 5, 1891; March 12, 13, December 3, 10, 14, 18, 1892; March 8, 21, August 3, 1895; *Arkansas Democrat*, February 28, 1891; Pine Bluff *Press-Eagle*, March 3, 1891; Van Buren *Press*, September 5, 1891; Edwin S. Redkey, *Black Exodus: Black Nationalist and Back-to-Africa Movements, 1890–1910* (New Haven, 1969), 107–26.

42. *St. Louis Post-Dispatch*, September 7, 9, 15, 1888.

43. *Arkansas Gazette*, September 7, 8, 21, 1888; February 3, 1889; Dardanelle *Post*, (n.d.), in *Arkansas Gazette*, September 15, 1888.

44. J. Morgan Kousser, *The Shaping of Southern Politics; Suffrage Restriction and the Establishment of the One-Party South, 1880–1910* (New Haven, 1974), 123; Bayliss, "Public Affairs in Arkansas," 82, 96–100.

45. Kousser, *The Shaping of Southern Politics*, 15; Segraves, "Arkansas Politics, 1874–1918," 121–24.

46. *Arkansas Gazette*, March 31, 1882.

47. Kousser, *The Shaping of Southern Politics*, 15, 28.

48. Fredrickson, *The Black Image in the White Mind*, 212. Most of the Redeemer leaders who served as governor between 1874 and 1900 were men of education and means. All but two, William R. Miller and James H. Berry, had attended college. Eight of the nine governors in this period were members of the bar. The sole exception, James P. Eagle, was a prominent Lonoke County planter, merchant, and Baptist minister who left an estate worth from $150,000 to $200,000. Every governor until 1893 had served in the Confederate military or government, as had most state legislators and members of the state's congressional delegation. The Redeemers' social eminence, Confederate war records, and leadership in overturning Reconstruction enabled them to gain wide popular backing; however, their governmental philosophy and programs often reflected their own special class backgrounds and interests. See Daniel Ross Grant, "The Role of the Governor of Arkansas in Administration" (Ph.D. diss., Northwestern University, 1948), 22; Segraves, "Arkansas Politics, 1874–1918," 48–52; Timothy P. Donovan, and Willard B. Gatewood, Jr., *The Governors of Arkansas: Essays in Political Biography* (Fayetteville, Arkansas, 1981), 61–110.

49. *Acts of Arkansas* (1874–75), 84–85.

50. Ibid., 230–32; Little Rock *Daily Republican*, (n.d.), in *Arkansas Gazette*, March 11, 1875.

51. *Acts of Arkansas* (1874–75), 149. Under provisions of the 1874 constitution, no more than 10 percent annual interest could be charged on ordinary commercial loans; also, Article 9 of the constitution exempted from seizure for debt $500 worth of personal property and a homestead of up to 160 acres per each head of family. These strictures purportedly made it difficult for all but the surest risks to negotiate loans, with landless tenants, having no collateral but their crops, being the worst penalized. A dearth of credit facilities exacerbated the situation. The entire state in 1880 could boast only seventeen banks; their combined capital and surplus totaled but $500,000, and their deposits were only $913,000. While the crop mortgage helped give the poorest farmers access to credit, this proved, as will be shown, to be more a curse than a blessing. *Arkansas Constitution* (1874), ART. 9; ART. 19, SEC. 13; Segraves, "Arkansas Politics, 1874–1918," 148–50.

52. *Acts of Arkansas* (1874–75), 129–30.

53. Francis Clark Elkins, "The Agricultural Wheel in Arkansas,

1882–1890" (Doctor of Social Science thesis, Syracuse University, 1953), 26.

54. *Acts of Arkansas* (1885), 225–26.

55. Ibid. (1874–75), 112.

56. Craighead, "The Future of the Negro in the South," 40, 43–44.

57. *Arkansas Gazette*, January 16, 1875; Bayliss, "Public Affairs in Arkansas," 73–75.

58. *Arkansas Gazette*, January 22, 1879.

59. *Arkansas Biennial Report of the State Penitentiary, 1903–04* (Little Rock, 1904), 6.

60. It was not until 1905 that the legislature, responding to appeals by Governor Jeff Davis, finally created a juvenile reform school. Thomas, *Arkansas and Its People*, I, 278.

61. Segraves, "Arkansas Politics, 1874–1918," 68.

62. Bayliss, "The Arkansas State Penitentiary under Democratic Control, 1874–1896," 198.

63. Segraves, "Arkansas Politics, 1874–1918," 70–72; Hirum U. Ford, "A History of the Arkansas Penitentiary to 1900" (M.A. thesis, University of Arkansas, 1936), 81.

64. *Arkansas Democrat*, March 27, 1879; Bayliss, "The Arkansas State Penitentiary under Democratic Control, 1874–1896," 202.

65. Bayliss, "The Arkansas State Penitentiary under Democratic Control, 1874–1896," 202–3.

66. *Acts of Arkansas* (1881), 120–28. Under provisions of this law, a new contract for the letting of prisoners was given to J. P. Townshend and L. A Fitzpatrick of Helena in 1882. With other associates, they formed the Arkansas Industrial Company, which remained the lessee until 1893; the company, in turn, sublet convicts to other parties, chiefly planters and mining concerns. The state was relieved of all expense for the care of prisoners and received $3.75 a month for each convict leased. This produced $24,613.13 during the first year in which the contract took effect, 1883. Fitzpatrick already had control of county prisoners from several Delta counties at the time the state contract was negotiated; Townshend, who resided in Helena but farmed in neighboring Mississippi, was a subcontractor for the Mississippi prison. As one student has observed, in view of the sorry reputations of the Arkansas county-lease and Mississippi prison systems, their prior experience "hardly recommended them, at least to critical posterity." Bayliss, "The Arkansas State Penitentiary under Democratic Control, 1874–1896," 204–5; *Arkansas Gazette*, November 15, 18, 22, 24, 1882. On abuses before

255

1883, under earlier lessees, see especially Segraves, "Arkansas Politics, 1874–1918," 69–72.

67. Bayliss, "The Arkansas State Penitentiary under Democratic Control, 1874–1896," 207–8; *Arkansas Gazette*, March 24, 27, 1888.

68. Bayliss, "The Arkansas State Penitentiary under Democratic Control, 1874–1896," 208.

69. Segraves, "Arkansas Politics, 1874–1918," 74; *Arkansas Gazette*, March 24, 27, April 1, 5, 8, 1888. The Coal Hill disclosures were partly responsible for Hughes' failure, in 1888, to gain renomination for a third term as governor. They also induced the legislature to appoint a full-time inspector of convicts, responsible for making regular visits to state convict camps and bimonthly reports to the state prison board. This innovation produced a 40 percent decline in the mortality rate of state prisoners by 1891. *Acts of Arkansas* (1889), 89–90; Bayliss, "The Arkansas State Penitentiary under Democratic Control, 1874–1896," 208–9.

70. Blake McKelvey, "Penal Slavery and Southern Reconstruction," *Journal of Negro History*, XX (April 1935): 177; Bayliss, "Public Affairs in Arkansas," 213–17.

71. *Acts of Arkansas* (1881), 144–45. Owing to population increases, the number of state convicts continued rising in spite of the change in law; the state convict population jumped from 600 in 1882 to 816 in 1889. Bayliss, "The Arkansas State Penitentiary under Democratic Control, 1874–1896," 200.

72. *Acts of Arkansas* (1881), 148–54. For several grisly examples of mal-use of county convicts, see Bayliss, "Public Affairs in Arkansas," 215–17.

73. *Arkansas Gazette*, March 26, 27, 1889.

74. Ibid., February 15, 1888.

75. Ibid. For similar defenses of the use of fraud to maintain white supremacy, see letter of "Democrat," printed in *Arkansas Gazette*, September 8, 1888; letter of Mr. John M. Rose, printed in *Arkansas Democrat*, September 18, 1888.

76. *Arkansas Gazette*, January 6, 1889.

77. Ibid., February 3, 1889.

78. Ibid., January 6, 1889.

79. Ibid.; *White County Wheel*, (n.d.), in Forrest City *Times*, June 16, 1888. Under state law, the county court appointed local election judges and clerks, ordinarily upon the recommendation of the county judge. A county judge, if determined and unscrupulous enough, could use his influence over the election machinery to defraud the opposition of their votes. *Acts of Arkansas* (1874–75), 92–111. Fear of federal interference

against such above practices caused the General Assembly to delay consolidating the date for holding federal and state elections until 1915. Even after 1915, irregularities were not uncommon. See Segraves, "Arkansas Politics, 1874–1918," 112–13, 367; statement of the Reverend Mr. Benjamin S. Grinage, director of the Arkansas Project of the Student Nonviolent Coordinating Committee, to the U.S. Commission on Civil Rights, reported in *Arkansas Gazette*, February 27, 1966.

80. *Arkansas Gazette*, October 17, 1876; Segraves, "Arkansas Politics, 1874–1918," 111.

81. *Arkansas Gazette*, August 8, 1879; address of former governor Powell Clayton, printed in ibid., September 23, 1888.

82. Ibid., July 14, 16, 18, 1888.

83. Ibid., July 17, 18, 1888.

84. Ibid., July 31, August 1, 14, September 23, 1888.

85. Ibid., July 14, 1888.


## *V*

1. *Arkansas Gazette*, July 18, 1888.

2. Staples, *Reconstruction in Arkansas*, 183.

3. Ibid., 183–84; Carmichael, "The Plantation System in Arkansas," 311; John Eaton, *Grant, Lincoln, and the Freedmen; Reminiscences of the Civil War with Special Reference to the Work for the Contrabands and Freedmen of the Mississippi Valley* (New York, 1907), 54.

4. Eaton, *Grant, Lincoln, and the Freedmen*, 58–61. The Reverend Joseph Warren, ed., *Extracts from Reports of Superintendents of Freedmen* (Vicksburg, Mississippi, 1864), 61–63.

5. Eaton, *Grant, Lincoln, and the Freedmen*, 110–11.

6. Ibid., 125–26; Carmichael, "The Plantation System in Arkansas," 322–23.

7. War of the Rebellion, *Official Records of the Union and Confederate Armies*, Series III, v. 4 (Washington, D.C., 1902), 166–70; *Report of the General Superintendent of Freedmen, Department of the Tennessee and State of Arkansas, December 31, 1864* (Washington, D.C., 1865), 15–16.

8. *Appleton's Annual Cyclopaedia, 1863*, 428; Staples, *Reconstruction in Arkansas*, 184.

9. *Report of the General Superintendent of Freedmen*, 11–16; Carmichael, "The Plantation System in Arkansas," 320–21.

10. Carmichael, "The Plantation System in Arkansas," 320. Practices varied widely; some planters, for instance, gave hands both food

257

and clothing gratis while others charged for both. *Report of the General Superintendent of Freedmen*, 28–29.

11. *Report of the General Superintendent of Freedmen*, 36, 64.

12. Carmichael, "The Plantation System in Arkansas," 321–22.

13. Staples, *Reconstruction in Arkansas*, 187.

14. *Report of the General Superintendent of Freedmen*, 29–34.

15. Ibid., 37, 39–40.

16. Ibid., 37, 49–50; Carmichael, "The Plantation System in Arkansas," 324.

17. *Report of the General Superintendent of Freedmen*, 50–51.

18. Washington (Arkansas) *Telegraph*, August 9, 30, 1865; Staples, *Reconstruction in Arkansas*, 200.

19. Carmichael, "The Plantation System in Arkansas," 476–77.

20. Ibid., 526; Des Arc *Citizen*, July 14, 1866.

21. *Debates and Proceedings of the Constitutional Convention of . . . 1868*, 250; Staples, *Reconstruction in Arkansas*, 233.

22. *Arkansas Gazette*, August 24, 1870; W. W. Mansfield, *A Digest of the Statutes of Arkansas* . . . (Little Rock, 1884), 161.

23. Carmichael, "The Plantation System in Arkansas," 386–87.

24. In their studies for Alabama and Georgia, Jonathan Weiner and Lewis Nicholas Wynne have argued that the planter class as a whole survived Reconstruction in those states with its economic, social, and political primacy largely intact. Regrettably, as yet no study of the planter-persistence rate for Arkansas has been conducted. See Jonathan M. Weiner, *Social Origins of the New South, Alabama, 1860–1885* (Baton Rouge, 1978), 3–34; and Lewis Nicholas Wynne, *The Continuity of Cotton, Planter Politics in Georgia, 1865–1892* (Macon, Georgia, 1986), 1–117.

25. Little Rock *Weekly Republican*, January 9, 1872; *Arkansas Gazette*, January 13, 1872. For sale procedures see *Acts of Arkansas* (1868), 45–51, 58–60.

26. Mound City *Post*, (n.d.), in *Arkansas Gazette*, December 11, 1873.

27. Mansfield, *A Digest of the Statutes of Arkansas*, 652.

28. Nordhoff, *The Cotton States in . . . 1875*, 37.

29. *Twelfth Census, 1900*, V, *Agriculture*, Pt. 1: *Farms, Live Stock, and Animal Products*, 6, 52; as noted previously, beginning in 1879 lands confiscated by the state for back taxes were available to homesteaders. Homesteads of up to 160 acres could be secured upon payment of a $5.50 fee. *Acts of Arkansas* (1879), 70–73.

30. *Twelfth Census, 1900*, V, *Agriculture*, Pt. 1: *Farms, Live Stock, and Animal Products*, 53.

31. Ibid., 174–75.

32. *Acts of Arkansas* (1895), 179–80.

33. *Twelfth Census, 1900*, V, *Agriculture*, Pt. 1; *Farms, Live Stock, and Animal Products*, 53.

34. Mike Masterson, "Hard Work, Savings Built Empire," in *Arkansas Gazette*, July 25, 1971, 6E.

35. Rudd and Bond, *From Slavery to Wealth, passim.*

36. Ibid., 145–50.

37. Masterson, "Hard Work, Savings Built Empire," 6E.

38. Staples, *Reconstruction in Arkansas*, 53–54; for individual examples see George P. Rawick, ed., *The American Slave: A Composite Autobiography*, VIII, *Arkansas Narratives*, (Westport, Connecticut, 1972), 8, 17, 20, 137, 227.

39. Diary of Mrs. Alfred Holt Carrigan, January 1, 1866, quoted in Carmichael, "The Plantation System in Arkansas," 432.

40. Carmichael, "The Plantation System in Arkansas," 430.

41. Extracts from the diary of James M. Hanks, January 21, 1868, through January 12, 1871, quoted in Carmichael, "The Plantation System in Arkansas," 442–51.

42. Extract from a letter written by the wife of a Southern soldier returning to Phillips County at the close of the war, (n.d.), quoted in Carmichael, "The Plantation System in Arkansas," 429.

43. Diary of Mrs. Alfred Holt Carrigan, December 25, 1865, quoted in Carmichael, "The Plantation System in Arkansas," 432.

44. Van Buren *Press*, February 17, 1866.

45. Ibid.

46. Des Arc *Citizen*, May 26, 1866.

47. Carmichael, "The Plantation System in Arkansas," 437.

48. Van Buren *Press*, June 23, 1866.

49. Mapes, "Business Cycles in Arkansas," 37. By the end of the decade, however, cotton production was rapidly reviving; by the 1870s it usually exceeded the highest prewar levels.

50. Ibid.

51. Carmichael, "The Plantation System in Arkansas," 431.

52. Roger L. Ransom and Richard Sutch, *One Kind of Freedom: The Economic Consequences of Emancipation* (Cambridge, England, 1977), 44–47; Robert Higgs, *Competition and Coercion; Blacks in the American Economy, 1865–1914* (Cambridge, England, 1977), 40.

53. Carmichael, "The Plantation System in Arkansas," 453, 509–21.

Carmichael believed that the cumulative effect of these woes was to cause the breakup of the large plantation in Arkansas. However, she made one fatal error in her otherwise excellent study. Relying on U.S. census data which showed an increase in the number of small farms in selected Delta counties, she concluded that the large plantation had largely broken up during the postwar decades. Carmichael apparently was unaware that census authorities classified each parcel of land on a plantation worked by an individual sharecropper as a separate "farm." The increase in the number of such "farms" and a decline in white population in several counties suggests another possibility: that while some old families were indeed wiped out, others, along with newcomers, may have survived and acquired more land and wealth than ever before—the process in fact documented by Jonathan Weiner for Alabama.

54. Ibid., 484–91.

55. New Orleans *Times*, (n.d.), in Arkadelphia *Southern Standard*, November 11, 1869.

56. Carmichael, "The Plantation System in Arkansas," 490.

57. Ibid., 489.

58. Ibid., 491–501. In his study for Alabama, Jonathan Weiner argued that planters drove out independent furnishing merchants from plantation counties since the new merchant class threatened to weaken planter domination over black laborers. Also, a prosperous and growing merchant class would threaten planter social and political preeminence and power. The plantation store thus prevailed over the country store. See Weiner, *Social Origins of the New South*, 77–136. Although the subject cries for attention, no modern investigation of the postbellum planter class in Arkansas has yet been conducted.

59. Carmichael, "The Plantation System in Arkansas," 491–501.

60. Joseph D. Reid, "Sharecropping as an Understandable Market Response: The Post-Bellum South," *Journal of Economic History*, XXXIII (March 1973): 106–30.

61. Herbert G. Gutman, *The Black Family in Slavery and Freedom, 1750–1925* (New York, 1976), 442–50.

62. Stephen J. DeCanio, *Agriculture in the Postbellum South: The Economics of Production and Supply* (Cambridge, Massachusetts, 1974), 1–15.

63. Ransom and Sutch, *One Kind of Freedom*, 94–105, 171–99.

64. DeCanio, *Agriculture in the Postbellum South*, 13–15.

65. Carmichael, "The Plantation System in Arkansas," 504–7.

66. Ibid., 505–6; Gavin Wright, *Old South, New South: Revolutions in the Southern Economy since the Civil War* (New York, 1986), 99–107.

67. Rawick, ed., *The American Slave*, VIII, *Arkansas Narratives*, 178.

68. See Joel Williamson, *The Crucible of Race: Black-White Relations in the American South since Emancipation*, (New York, 1984), 24–35.

69. Rudd and Bond, *From Slavery to Wealth*, 266.

70. Ibid., 238–42.

71. Ibid., 324. On racial discrimination elsewhere in Arkansas, in the lumbering and sawmill industries, see Kenneth L. Smith, *Sawmill: The Story of Cutting the Last Great Virgin Forest East of the Rockies* (Fayetteville, Arkansas, 1986), 37, 47, 56, 58, 68, 96, 126–27.

72. Masterson, "Hard Work, Savings Built Empire," 6E. It is possible, of course, that these acts of arson could have been inspired as much by class as by racial antagonism, and it is even possible that the arsonists could have been black themselves. Arson was often utilized as a means of class protest in the postbellum South. See Albert C. Smith, " 'Southern Violence' Reconsidered: Arson as Protest in Black-Belt Georgia, 1865–1910," *Journal of Southern History*, LI (November 1985): 527–64.

73. Edward King, "The Great South," *Scribner's Monthly*, VIII (October 1874): 653.

74. Jay R. Mandle, *The Roots of Black Poverty: The Southern Plantation Economy after the Civil War* (Durham, North Carolina, 1978), 10–15, 28–38; for an excellent summary of Mandle's perspectives, see Harold D. Woodman, "Sequel to Slavery: The New History Views the Postbellum South," *Journal of Southern History* XLIII (November 1977): 544–45, 548–50. For indepth examination of postbellum peonage arrangements, see Roger L. Ransom and Richard Sutch, "Debt Peonage in the Cotton South after the Civil War," *Journal of Economic History*, XXXII (September 1972): 641–69. On the continuation of peonage well into the twentieth century, see Pete Daniel, *The Shadow of Slavery: Peonage in the South, 1901–1969* (New York, 1973), *passim*.

75. Margaret Ross, "The New Madrid Earthquake," *Arkansas Historical Quarterly*, XXVII (Summer 1968): 83–104; Virgil Holder, "Historical Geography of the Lower White River," ibid., 132–45.

76. See Elmo Howell, "Mark Twain's Arkansas," ibid., XXIX (Autumn 1970): 195–208; Foy Lisenby, "A Survey of Arkansas's Image Problem," ibid., XXX (Spring 1971): 60–71; Evan Burr Bukey "Frederick Gerstaecker and Arkansas," ibid., XXXI (Spring 1972): 3–14.

77. Taylor, *Negro Slavery in Arkansas*, 49–53; Carmichael, "The Plantation System in Arkansas," 70–116. In the initial territorial period, Arkansas pioneers had generally avoided the eastern Delta, preferring the westward upland districts instead. While the land in the latter area was often poorer, the climate was decidedly healthier.

78. See Lee A. Dew, "The J.L.C. and E.R.R. and the Opening of the 'Sunk Lands' of Northeast Arkansas," *Arkansas Historical Quarterly*, XXVII (Spring 1968): 22–39; Lee A. Dew and Louis Koeppe, "Narrow Gage Railroads in Arkansas," ibid., XXXI (Autumn 1972): 276–93.

79. *Tenth Census, 1880*, I, Pt. 2, *Population*, 381.

80. Ibid. The state's white population rose from 324,143 to 591,531 between 1860 and 1880, while the black population increased from 111,259 to 210,666.

81. Ibid. The counties were Arkansas, Chicot, Crittenden, Desha, Hempstead, Jefferson, Mississippi, and Phillips.

82. *Arkansas Gazette*, May 5, 1866.

83. For limited use of Italian peasant and Chinese labor on Arkansas plantations, see Robert L. Brandfon, "The End of Immigration to the Cotton Fields," *Mississippi Valley Historical Review*, L (March 1964): 595–97, 605–6, 610; Lucey, "History of Immigration to Arkansas," 216–18.

84. Carmichael, "The Plantation System in Arkansas," 464.

85. *Arkansas Gazette*, December 11, 1898.

86. George B. Tindall, *South Carolina Negroes, 1877–1900* (Columbia, South Carolina, 1952), 170–77, 184; Frenise A. Logan, *The Negro in North Carolina, 1876–1894* (Chapel Hill, North Carolina, 1964), 127; *Arkansas Democrat*, March 27, 1889; *Arkansas Gazette*, January 6, 1888; March 26, 1889; December 11, 1898.

87. William Pickens, *Bursting Bonds* (Boston, Massachusetts, 1923), 22–23.

88. Ibid., 23–24.

89. Ibid., 24–25.

90. Ibid., 25–26.

91. Ibid., 27.

92. Ibid., 28.

93. Ibid., 30–31. Such animal tales were derived from the oral folk traditions of West African societies. See John W. Blassingame, *The Slave Community, Plantation Life in the Antebellum South* (New York, 1972), 26–27.

94. Pickens, *Bursting Bonds*, 26.

95. Ibid., 26–27.

96. Ibid., 27.

97. Ibid., 28–29.

98. Ibid., 29–30.

# VI

1. Woodward, *Origins of the New South,* 140.

2. Ibid., 629–54. However, there is one entry for "City-manager plan."

3. Paul M. Gaston, *The New South Creed* (New York, 1970).

4. Woodward, *Origins of the New South,* 140.

5. *Abstract of the Twelfth Census, 1900,* 38.

6. Wright, *Old South, New South: Revolutions in the Southern Economy since the Civil War,* 39–43.

7. Ibid., 40, 101; *Eighth Census, 1860,* I, *Population,* 18–19.

8. Ira Don Richards, *Story of a Rivertown, Little Rock in the Nineteenth Century* (n.p., 1969), 103–5.

9. Ibid., 109.

10. *Twelfth Census, 1900,* VIII, *Manufactures,* Pt. 2., *States and Territories,* 25. For statewide totals and developments see Griner, "The Growth of Manufactures in Arkansas," 39.

11. *Little Rock City Directory, 1900–01* (Little Rock, 1900), 589–643.

12. Hackler, "Little Rock—1891," 14A.

13. Quoted in Ibid.

14. Richards, *Story of a Rivertown,* 99. The honor was to be bestowed on Markham and Main streets before their paving.

15. *Arkansas Democrat,* (n.d.), in Hackler "Little Rock—1891," 14A.

16. Hackler, "Little Rock—1891," 14A; *Biographical and Historical Memoirs of Pulaski, Jefferson, Lonoke, Faulkner, Grant, Saline, Perry, Garland, and Hot Spring Counties, Arkansas* (Chicago, 1889), 518. Hereinafter cited as *Biographical and Historical Memoirs of Central Arkansas.*

17. *Eighth Census, 1860,* I, *Population,* 19; Richards, *Story of a Rivertown,* 81.

18. Edward King, "The Great South," 661.

19. *Tenth Census, 1880,* XIX, *Social Statistics of Cities,* Pt. 2, *The Southern and Western States,* 211.

20. Lucey, "The History of Immigration to Arkansas," 217.

21. Ibid., 205, 214–15; Jonathan James Wolfe, "Background of German Immigration [part III]," *Arkansas Historical Quarterly,* XXV (Winter 1966): 356–57.

22. Wolfe, "Background of German Immigration," 377.

23. Richards, *Story of a Rivertown,* 93.

24. *Biographical and Historical Memoirs of Central Arkansas*, 415; *Little Rock City Directory, 1900–01*, 73.

25. Lucey, "The History of Immigration to Arkansas," 216–19; Jan Sarna, ed., "Marche, Arkansas: A Personal Reminiscence of Life and Customs," *Arkansas Historical Quarterly*, XXXVI (Spring 1977): 31–49.

26. *Arkansas Gazette*, July 15, 1888.

27. Shinn, *Pioneers and Makers of Arkansas*, 213–19.

28. The Right Reverend William Montgomery Brown, *The Crucial Race Question, or, Where and How Shall the Color Line Be Drawn* (Little Rock, 1907), xxvii; E. C. Hubbard, Thirteenth Illinois Volunteers, Batesville, Arkansas, May 9, 1862, letter to A. S. Hubbard, Chicago, Illinois. Hubbard Papers, Manuscripts Division, Library of Chicago Historical Society. The author demonstrates strong hostility toward blacks and German troops in the Union army.

29. King, "The Great South," 653.

30. Richards, *Story of a Rivertown*, 84. By the close of Reconstruction, however, a majority of Germans appear to have joined the Democrats in efforts to oust the radical Republicans. Charges of local misgovernment, strong appeals from native whites, and the Grant administration's approval of U.S. arms sales to France during the Franco-Prussian War were responsible for the shift in loyalties. Wolfe, "Background of German Immigration [part I]," 163–64.

31. Interview with Miss Dorothy Gillam, daughter of Isaac Gillam, Jr., Little Rock, Arkansas, July 29, 1967.

32. Ferguson and Atkinson, *Historic Arkansas*, 64–65.

33. Richards, *Story of a Rivertown*, 43–48, 127–28; Walter L. Brown, "Albert Pike, 1809–91," (Ph.D. diss., University of Texas, 1955), 230; Gene Wells Boyett, "The Whigs of Arkansas, 1836–56," (Ph.D. diss., Louisiana State University, 1972), i, 97–98.

34. Richards, *Story of a Rivertown*, 87–89; even radical governor Powell Clayton had made attempts to woo the old Whig vote. See Powell Clayton, Little Rock, Arkansas, May 22, 1870, letter to William Brian, Jacksonport, Arkansas. Letterbook of Governor Powell Clayton, Arkansas History Commission, Little Rock.

35. Richards, *Story of a Rivertown*, 88.

36. Ibid., 89.

37. Ibid., 88.

38. Ibid., 102.

39. Ibid., 87.

40. *Biographical and Historical Memoirs of Central Arkansas,* 518; *Arkansas Gazette,* July 6, 7, 1892.

41. See for example the protests of William G. Whipple and other white Republicans against election frauds in 1888. *Arkansas Gazette,* September 7, 1888.

42. Hackler, "Little Rock—1891," 14A; *Arkansas Gazette,* February 24, April 6, 1892; March 21, 1902; minute books of the Little Rock city council, 1871–1893, Office of the City Clerk, Little Rock, Arkansas.

43. For example, Redeemer mayor John Gould Fletcher kept four to six blacks on the city police force during his administration from 1875 to 1881 and filled other minor posts with Negroes. *Arkansas Gazette,* August 30, 1882; *Little Rock City Directory, 1881–82* (Little Rock, 1881), 17–18. Blacks continued to serve on the city police force throughout the century. See *Little Rock City Directory, 1900–01,* 63.

44. *Annual Report of the Public Schools of . . . Little Rock, 1896* (Little Rock, 1896), 295–96.

45. Ibid., 2.

46. Selma Ann Plowman Hobby, "The Little Rock Public Schools during Reconstruction, 1865–74," (Ed.D. diss., University of Arkansas, 1967), 19, 35.

47. Pickens, *Bursting Bonds,* 72–74.

48. Hobby, "The Little Rock Public Schools during Reconstruction," 46–47, 56–58; Weeks, *History of Public School Education in Arkansas,* 116.

49. *Annual Report of the Public Schools of . . . Little Rock, 1896,* 70.

50. *Annual Report of the Public Schools of . . . Little Rock, 1880* (Little Rock, 1880), 44–45.

51. *Annual Report of the Public Schools of . . . Little Rock, 1896,* 70.

52. Ibid.

53. Ibid., 137, 140.

54. Thomas, "A History of Taxation in Arkansas," 72; *Annual Report of the Public Schools . . . of Little Rock, 1890* (Little Rock, 1890), 15–16.

55. *Biennial Report of the Superintendent of Public Instruction for the State of Arkansas . . . 1891–92* (Little Rock, 1893), 63, 68–69.

56. Ibid., 97. By comparison, the national average expenditure per enrolled pupil in 1900 was $21.14. Woodward, *Origins of the New South,* 398.

57. Hobby, "The Little Rock Schools during Reconstruction," 85, 92–93.

58. *Annual Report of the Public Schools . . . of Little Rock, 1880,* 38.

59. De Lois Gibson, "A Historical Study of Philander Smith College, 1877 to 1969," (Ed.D. diss., University of Arkansas, 1972), 17–79; Ellis Greenlee Mosley, "The History of Higher Education for Negroes in Arkansas," (M.A. thesis, University of Texas, 1944), 40–46; W. N. Hartshorn, ed., *An Era of Progress and Promise, 1863–1910: The Religious, Moral, and Educational Development of the American Negro since His Emancipation* (Boston, 1910), 197, hereinafter cited as *An Era of Progress; Arkansas Gazette,* February 8, May 24, 1903.

60. *Arkansas Gazette,* December 28, 1898; see also *Gazette,* May 21, 1897; Mosley, "The History of Higher Education for Negroes in Arkansas," 48–50; Williamson, *Black Footprints around Arkansas,* 91; Booker was the brother-in-law of the Reverend E. C. Morris, president of the National Baptist Convention. Interviews with Mr. James Booker, son of Joseph A. Booker, Little Rock, Arkansas, August 19, 1967, and with O. A. Rogers, Jr., president of Arkansas Baptist College, Little Rock, Arkansas, July 24, 1967.

61. *Arkansas Gazette,* May 23, 1897; Mosley, "The History of Higher Education for Negroes in Arkansas," 46–48; Hartshorn, *An Era of Progress,* 283–368; Williams, *Black Footprints around Arkansas,* 92–93.

62. *Annual Report of the Public Schools of . . . Little Rock, 1877* (Little Rock, 1877), 11. See also J. T. Haley, *Afro-American Encyclopedia* (Nashville, 1895), 562–63, and Hobby, "The Little Rock Public Schools during Reconstruction," 93.

63. Terry, *Charlotte Stephens: Little Rock's First Black Teacher,* 104–5.

64. Ibid., 128.

65. Ibid., 104.

66. See *Annual Report of the Public Schools . . . of Little Rock, 1880,* 6–7; Ibid., *1896,* 68–69.

67. Terry, *Charlotte Stephens: Little Rock's First Black Teacher,* 102.

68. Ibid.

69. William Grant Still, "My Arkansas Boyhood," *Arkansas Historical Quarterly,* XXVI (Autumn 1967): 285–92.

70. Pickens, *Bursting Bonds,* 121–38; for local reports on Pickens' receipt of the Ten Eyck Prize, see *Arkansas Gazette,* April 3, 7, 12, May 24, 1903; also see *The Freeman* (Indianapolis, Indiana), April 18, May 23, 1903. In later years Pickens, as an NAACP official, assisted defendants in the famous Scottsboro trials. See Dan T. Carter, *Scottsboro: A Tragedy of the American South* (Baton Rouge, 1969), 60, 73, 85–87, 90–91, 95.

71. Terry, *Charlotte Stephens: Little Rock's First Black Teacher,* 88.

72. Ibid.; *Arkansas Gazette*, January 3, August 15, 1888; July 2, 22, 1896; August 26, 1898; January 2, 1902; *The Freeman* (Indianapolis, Indiana), January 17, 1891; June 13, 1903.

73. Terry, *Charlotte Stephens: Little Rock's First Black Teacher*, 90.

74. Ibid.

75. *Little Rock City Directory, 1900–01*, 71–81; *Arkansas Gazette*, July 9, 1892; March 17, 1894; March 7, 1900; Terry, ibid., 77.

76. A. E. Bush and P. L. Dorman, *History of the Mosaic Templars of America—Its Founders and Officials* (Little Rock, 1924), 82–83; 174–75.

77. Richards, *Story of a Rivertown*, 93–94.

78. Conversations of the author with the late Mrs. Jack Steele. The roguish scion of a distinguished Jefferson County planter family, Mrs. Steele's husband was reportedly the "vice lord" of Little Rock throughout much of the early twentieth century.

79. Richards, *Story of a Rivertown*, 94.

80. *Arkansas Gazette*, June 24, 1903.

81. Ibid., February 2, 1888.

82. Quoted in Hackler, "Little Rock: 1891," 14A.

83. Pickens, *Bursting Bonds*, 35.

84. Ibid., 42–43.

85. Ibid., 58–59.

86. For example, see Rawick, ed., *The American Slave*, VIII, *Arkansas Narratives*, 26.

87. D. B. Gaines, *Racial Possibilities as Indicated by the Negroes of Arkansas* (Little Rock, 1898), 173–84. For a good sketch of a successful urban artisan, see Rawick, *The American Slave*, VIII, *Arkansas Narratives*, 132–34. On the development of a postbellum black middle class in other Southern cities, see John W. Blassingame, *Black New Orleans, 1860–1880* (Chicago and London, 1973), 69–77, 139–71; Lawrence Oland Christensen, "Black St. Louis: A Study in Race Relations, 1865–1916," (Ph.D. diss., University of Missouri, 1972), 160–80; John Dittmer, *Black Georgia in the Progressive Era, 1900–1920* (Urbana, Illinois, 1977), 23–49; Leroy Graham, *Baltimore: The Nineteenth Century Black Capital* (Lanham, Maryland, 1982), 252–308; Robert E. Perdue, *The Negro in Savannah, 1865–1900* (New York, 1973), 105–21; Michael Leroy Porter, "Black Atlanta: An Interdisciplinary Study of Blacks on the East Side of Atlanta, 1890–1930," (Ph.D. diss., Emory University, 1974), 42–68; Bernard Edward Powers, Jr., "Black Charleston: A Social History, 1822–1885," (Ph.D. diss., Northwestern University, 1982), 137–77; Faye Welborne Robbins, "A World within a World: Black Nash-

ville, 1880–1915," (Ph.D. diss., University of Arkansas, 1980), 239–52; Jerry John Thornberry, "The Development of Black Atlanta, 1865–1885," (Ph.D. diss., University of Maryland, 1977), 191–225; George C. Wright, *Life behind a Veil: Blacks in Louisville, Kentucky, 1865–1930* (Baton Rouge, 1985), 93–101.

88. *Biographical and Historical Memoirs of Central Arkansas*, 806.

89. Ibid., 806–7.

90. Ibid., 802–3.

91. Tom Dillard, "To the Back of the Elephant: Racial Conflict in the Arkansas Republican Party," *Arkansas Historical Quarterly*, XXXIII (Spring 1974): 13; Williamson, *Black Footprints around Arkansas*, 13–14; interview with Miss Dorothy Gillam, granddaughter of Isaac Gillam, Sr., Little Rock, Arkansas, July 29, 1967.

92. *Biographical and Historical Memoirs of Central Arkansas*, 806; *Annual Report of the Public Schools of . . . Little Rock, 1896*, 296.

93. *Biographical and Historical Memoirs of Central Arkansas*, 808.

94. *Arkansas Gazette*, May 10, 1902.

95. Ibid., January 16, 1889; January 26, 1902; Haley, *Afro-American Encyclopedia*, 289; Gaines, *Racial Possibilities as Indicated by the Negroes of Arkansas*, 78.

96. *Biographical and Historical Memoirs of Central Arkansas*, 807–8; Gaines, *Racial Possibilities as Indicated by the Negroes of Arkansas*, 95.

97. Gaines, *Racial Possibilities as Indicated by the Negroes of Arkansas*, 87.

98. Tom Dillard, "Scipio A. Jones," *Arkansas Historical Quarterly*, XXXI (Autumn 1972): 201–19.

99. I. Garland Penn, *The Afro-American Press and Its Editors* (Springfield, Massachusetts, 1891), 240–45; *Biographical and Historical Memoirs of Central Arkansas*, 795–96.

100. *Biographical and Historical Memoirs of Central Arkansas*, 796–97; Gibbs, *Shadow and Light, passim*.

101. Ibid.

102. Ibid. For an excellent summary of Gibbs' Arkansas career, see Tom W. Dillard, "'Golden Prospects and Fraternal Amenities': Mifflin W. Gibbs's Arkansas Years," *Arkansas Historical Quarterly*, XXXV (Winter 1976): 307–33.

103. Bush and Dorman, *History of the Mosaic Templars of America—Its Founders and Officials*, 19–102; C. Calvin Smith, "John E. Bush of Arkansas, 1890–1910," *Ozark Historical Review*, II (Spring 1973): 48–59.

104. Bush and Dorman, *History of the Mosaic Templars of America—Its Founders and Officials*, 83–84.

105. See, for instance, black support for Clayton at the Republican State League convention in 1895. *Arkansas Gazette*, June 6, 8, 1895. On Clayton's backing for Negroes, see H. L. Remmel, Little Rock, Arkansas, October 18, 1899, letter to Powell Clayton, Mexico City, Mexico, Harmon Remmel MSS, University of Arkansas Library; Powell Clayton, Mexico City, Mexico, October 23, 1899, letter to H. L. Remmel, Little Rock, Harmon Remmel MSS, University of Arkansas Library.

106. Smith, "John E. Bush of Arkansas, 1890–1910," 52; interview with Mrs. C. E. Bush, granddaughter of John E. Bush, Little Rock, July 23, 1967.

107. Ibid.

108. *Fort Smith and Van Buren Directory, 1900*, (Fort Smith, 1899), 342–65; *Racial Possibilities as Indicated by the Negroes of Arkansas*, 138–44.

109. William J. Schafer and Johannes Riedel, *The Art of Ragtime, Form and Meaning of an Original Black American Art* (Baton Rouge, 1973), 47, 51–54, 205–225.

110. St. Hilaire, "The Negro Delegates in the Arkansas Constitutional Convention of 1868: A Group Profile," 43, 60–61; *Arkansas Gazette*, November 11, 1888; The Reverend Lewis G. Jordan, *Negro Baptist History, U.S.A., 1750–1930* (Nashville, 1930), 394.

111. *The Freeman* (Indianapolis, Indiana), January 31, 1891.

112. Jordan, *Negro Baptist History, U.S.A., 1750–1930*, 96, 394; Hartshorn, *An Era of Progress*, 481.

113. Hartshorn, *An Era of Progress*, 261–62; Mosley, "The Higher Education of Negroes in Arkansas," 51; Thomas C. Kennedy, "Southland College: The Society of Friends and Black Education in Arkansas," *Arkansas Historical Quarterly*, XLII (Autumn 1983): 207–38.

114. *Biographical and Historical Memoirs of Central Arkansas*, 124–47.

115. Rothrock, "Joseph Carter Corbin and Negro Education in the University of Arkansas," 277–314; Mosley, "The History of Higher Education for Negroes in Arkansas," 16–33.

116. Hartshorn, *An Era of Progress*, 261–62; Mosley, "The History of Higher Education for Negroes in Arkansas," 16–33.

117. J. M. Lucey, "The Catholic Church in Arkansas," *Publications of the Arkansas Historical Association*, II (1908), 448–49; the school was at first operated by the white Sisters of Charity, but in 1900 a black order of New Orleans, the Sisters of the Holy Family, assumed control of operations. *Arkansas Democrat*, January 24, 1890; *Arkansas Gazette*, August 27,

October 12, 1899; September 4, 5, 1901. See also James W. Leslie, "The Colored Industrial Institute Was City's First School for Blacks," in Pine Bluff *Commercial*, March 26, 1972, 15; and Leslie, "St. Peter's School Was Established before Church," in Pine Bluff *Commercial*, May 21, 1972, 13.

118. *Biographical and Historical Memoirs of Central Arkansas*, 803–4.

119. Ibid., 797–98; *Arkansas Gazette*, March 21, 1900.

120. *Biographical and Historical Memoirs of Central Arkansas*, 798; Williamson, *Black Footprints around Arkansas*, 12; James W. Leslie, "Ferd Havis: Jefferson County's Black Republican Leader," *Arkansas Historical Quarterly*, XXXVII (Autumn 1978): 240–51. Havis usually sided with Powell Clayton in the various factional disputes within the Arkansas Republican party; in 1897, as a reward for his loyalty, Clayton and the Republican state committee recommended him for the postmastership at Pine Bluff. Because of the strong opposition of Arkansas senator James H. Berry, the United States Senate refused to confirm Havis's appointment. Even so, Havis reportedly remained influential enough to compel the eventual white appointee, white Republican Louis Altheimer, to pay him seventy-five dollars out of the postmaster's monthly salary; in exchange, the black leader consented to Altheimer's filling the post.
In 1910 Havis finally broke with Powell Clayton when the latter, probably responding to pressures from the Taft administration, tried to impose "lily-white" policies on the Jefferson County Republican organization. Havis successfully beat back the attempt, and Negroes retained twenty-eight of thirty-one positions on the Republican county committee. *Arkansas Democrat*, February 23, 1898; *Arkansas Gazette*, February 22, 1900; June 30, 1910; Pine Bluff *Press-Eagle*, January 25, 1910.

121. Haley, *Afro-American Encyclopedia*, 234, 289; *Biographical and Historical Memoirs of Central Arkansas*, 798–802; James W. Leslie, "Wiley Jones: A Slave Who Left His Mark on Pine Bluff's Business World," in Pine Bluff *Commercial*, April 5, 1970, 13; Leslie, "Street Cars: Earliest Public Transportation Was Drawn by Mules," in Pine Bluff *Commercial*, February 8, 1976, 11; Leslie, "Jones Park: Races, Baseball Drew Crowds to Harding and Main," Pine Bluff *Commercial*, August 15, 1976, 13; Leslie, *Land of Cypress and Pine: More Southeast Arkansas History* (Little Rock, 1976), 127–37; Leslie, *Pine Bluff and Jefferson County; A Pictorial History* (Norfolk, Virginia, 1981), 63, 73, 84, 85, 91, 100; Willard B. Gatewood, Jr., "Arkansas Negroes in the 1890s," *Arkansas Historical Quarterly*, XXXIII (Winter 1974): 306.

122. *The Freeman* (Indianapolis, Indiana), January 31, 1891; Kousser,

"A Black Protest in the 'Era of Accommodation': Documents," 152–55; letter to the author from Edwin G. Sanford, Reference Librarian, Boston Public Library, Boston, Massachusetts, April 14, 1972; letter to the author from Richard Dugas, Transcript Supervisor, Boston University, Boston, Massachusetts, March 28, 1972.

123. Boston *Daily Globe*, December 6, 1886.

124. Goldfield traces the beginnings of this change during the antebellum period, while Gaston describes postbellum developments, stressing especially how the dream of an industrialized, urbanized "New South" was used to sustain Southern morale after the region's defeat in the Civil War. See Goldfield's "Pursuing the American Dream: Cities in the Old South" in Blaine A. Brownell and David R. Goldfield, eds., *The City in Southern History: The Growth of Urban Civilization in the South* (Port Washington, New York, 1977), 52–91, and Gaston, *The New South Creed, passim*.

125. *Arkansas Gazette*, January 1, 1899.

126. Ibid.

127. Gibbs, *Shadow and Light*, 199.

128. *Arkansas Gazette*, January 5, 26, 1888.

129. *Biographical and Historical Memoirs of Central Arkansas*, 797.

130. *Arkansas Gazette*, February 1, 2, 1888.

131. Bush and Dorman, *History of the Mosaic Templars of America—Its Founders and Leaders*, 15–16.

132. Leslie, *Land of Cyprus and Pine*, 127–37.

133. *Arkansas Gazette*, March 23, 1897.

134. Bush and Dorman, *History of the Mosaic Templars of America—Its Founders and Leaders*, 33.

135. Ibid., 33–34. On Booker T. Washington's continuing support of Bush, see letter of John E. Bush, Little Rock, Arkansas, January 27, 1906, to Emmett J. Scott, Tuskegee, Alabama; letter of John E. Bush, Little Rock, Arkansas, April 2, 1906, to Booker T. Washington, Tuskegee, Alabama. Booker T. Washington Papers, Library of Congress, Washington, D.C.

136. Woodward, *Origins of the New South*, 464.

137. Fay Hempstead, *Historical Review of Arkansas*, I (Chicago, 1911), 298, quoting the New York *Graphic*, April 26, 1880.

138. *Arkansas Gazette*, April 17, 1880; Gibbs, *Shadow and Light*, 356–58.

139. *Arkansas Gazette*, February 6, 1889.

140. For an excellent examination of this phenomenon in Latin America, see Carl N. Degler, *Neither Black nor White; Slavery and Race Relations in Brazil and the United States* (New York, 1971).

141. *Arkansas Gazette*, February 6, 1889.

142. Indianapolis *World*, February 23, 1889, quoted in Willard B. Gatewood, Jr., "Frederick Douglass in Arkansas," *Arkansas Historical Quarterly*, XLI (Winter 1982): 313–14. The comment concerning an "unpropitious time" to visit Arkansas probably referred to the recent election troubles in the state and the political assassination of John M. Clayton, a Republican congressional candidate, in 1888. Douglass had remarked on Clayton's murder earlier in his interview.

143. Ibid., 314–15.

144. *Arkansas Gazette*, February 6, 1889; Douglass also visited Pine Bluff. See Pine Bluff *Press-Eagle*, February 12, 1889.

145. Pierre L. van den Berghe, *Race and Racism: A Comparative Perspective* (New York, 1967), 25–37.

146. Ibid., 30.

147. C. Vann Woodward, "The Strange Career of a Historical Controversy," in *American Counterpoint: Slavery and Racism in the North-South Dialogue* (Boston, 1964), 244. The quotation by Woodward is summarizing van den Berghe's thesis.

148. *Arkansas Gazette*, May 14, 1892.

149. Ibid.

150. A brief experiment in integration of the local barbers' union appears to have failed. A separate Negro barbers' union and a Negro musicians' union, however, participated in the Little Rock Trades Council along with other union locals. Some of these latter may have been successfully integrated, but other local unions excluded blacks. See *Arkansas Gazette*, December 13, 1899; September 27, 1900; July 14, 1901; February 27, September 3, December 21, 1902; John E. Bush, "Afro-American People of Little Rock," *Colored American Magazine*, VIII (January 1905): 41.

151. David E. Finch, "Little Rock's Red Bishop Brown and His Separate Black Church," *Pulaski County Historical Review*, XX (September 1972): 28.

152. Dr. Charles E. Nash, *The Status of the Negro, from a Negro's Standpoint in His Own Dialect—A Country Negro Visits the City and Takes In the Surroundings—His Conversation after His Return* (Little Rock, 1900), 9–10.

153. Ibid., 14.

## VII

1. Lawrence C. Goodwyn, *Democratic Promise, The Populist Moment in America* (New York, 1976), 11–24, 574.

2. Goodwyn, ibid., 113–20; Woodward, *Origins of the New South*, 185; for an excellent survey of agrarian thinking on the "money question" and proposed solutions to this problem, see Bruce Palmer, *"Man Over Money": The Southern Populist Critique of American Capitalism* (Chapel Hill, 1980), 81–110.

3. Goodwyn, 113–20; Woodward, *Origins of the New South*, 185.

4. Woodward, *Origins of the New South*, 180–85; Ransom and Sutch, *One Kind of Freedom*, 149–68.

5. Earl Blake, "From Tenancy in Arkansas," (M.A. thesis, University of Arkansas, 1939), 16.

6. Ibid.

7. W. W. Tedford, one of the founders of the Agricultural Wheel, recalled an Arkansas merchant who began trading with a small stock of provisions and twenty-five years later, through shrewd use of the crop lien, had acquired title to 18,000 acres of land, plus large numbers of mules, horses, cattle, and several stores. W. Scott Morgan, *History of the Wheel and Alliance and the Impending Revolution* (Fort Scott, Kansas, 1889), 56.

8. Woodward, *Origins of the New South*, 184–85; Michael Schwartz, *Radical Protest and Social Structure: The Southern Farmers' Alliance and Cotton Tenancy, 1880–1890* (New York, 1976), 41–45.

9. Robert Higgs, *The Transformation of the American Economy, 1865–1914: An Essay in Interpretation* (New York, 1971), 112–14.

10. Ransom and Sutch, *One Kind of Freedom*, 40–55. For an excellent overview of recent scholarship on this question, see Woodman, "Sequel to Slavery," 523–54.

11. Theodore Saloutos, "The Agricultural Wheel in Arkansas," *Arkansas Historical Quarterly*, II (June 1943): 129.

12. *Arkansas Secretary of State Biennial Report, 1879–1880* (Little Rock, 1880), 34–35. Parks received 31,424 votes to 84,185 cast for Thomas J. Churchill, his Democratic opponent.

13. *Arkansas Secretary of State Biennial Report, 1881–1882* (Little Rock, 1882), 74–75. The vote was Democrat J. H. Berry, 87,675; Republican W. D. Slack, 49,352; and Greenbacker R. K. Garland, 10,142.

14. F. Clark Elkins, "Arkansas Farmers Organize for Action: 1882–1884," *Arkansas Historical Quarterly*, XIII (Autumn 1954): 232–33.

15. Clifton Paisley, "The Political Wheelers and Arkansas' Election of 1888," *Arkansas Historical Quarterly*, XXV (Spring 1966): 3–4.

16. Elkins, "Arkansas Farmers Organize for Action," 237.

17. Morgan, *History of the Wheel and Alliance*, 63, quoted in Paisley, "The Political Wheelers and Arkansas' Election of 1888," 12.

18. Morgan, *History of the Wheel and Alliance*, 71–74.

19. Ibid., 70–71.

20. Ibid., 65, 70, 73.

21. Paisley, "The Political Wheelers and Arkansas' Election of 1888," 12.

22. *Arkansas Secretary of State Biennial Report, 1887–1888* (Little Rock, 1888), 47.

23. *Arkansas Gazette*, April 28, 1888.

24. Goodwyn, *Democratic Promise*, 100–102.

25. *Arkansas Gazette*, May 1, 1888; Paisley, "The Political Wheelers and Arkansas' Election of 1888," 4.

26. *Arkansas Gazette*, May 1, 1888.

27. Paisley, "The Political Wheelers and Arkansas' Election of 1888," 4–5.

28. Ibid., 7–8. A resolution urging endorsement of Wheel demands had been introduced at the Democratic state convention but had been withdrawn amidst derision and laughter.

29. *Arkansas Gazette*, July 29, 1889, quoted in ibid., 8.

30. *Arkansas Gazette*, June 9, 1888, quoted in ibid., 6.

31. Chicago *Tribune*, n.d., quoted in ibid., 6.

32. *Arkansas Gazette*, June 21, 1888.

33. Ibid., quoted in Paisley, "The Political Wheelers and Arkansas' Election of 1888," 7.

34. Thomas, *Arkansas and Its People*, I, 212.

35. *Arkansas Gazette*, August 3, 1888.

36. *Arkansas Secretary of State Biennial Report, 1887–1888*, 49.

37. *Arkansas Secretary of State Biennial Report, 1889–1890* (Little Rock, 1891), 55. The vote was Eagle, 106,267; Fizer, 85,181.

38. *Arkansas Gazette*, September 23, 1888.

39. Bayliss, "Public Affairs in Arkansas," 304–5.

40. *Arkansas Gazette*, September 22, 23, 1888.

41. Bayliss, "Public Affairs in Arkansas," 305.

42. *Arkansas Gazette*, September 22, 23, 1888.

43. *Arkansas Secretary of State Biennial Report, 1887–1888*, 267.

44. Ibid.

45. Ibid., 268–69.

46. *Congressional Record*, 51st Cong., 1st sess. (March 1–5, 1890), 1843–1955. See also *United States House of Representatives Digest of Contested Election Cases in the Fifty-first Congress Compiled under Resolution of the House, by Chester H. Rowell, Clerk to the Committee on Elections* (Washington, D.C., 1891), 77–146. Hereinafter cited as *Digest of Contested Election Cases.*

47. Thomas, *Arkansas and Its People,* I, 219.

48. *Digest of Contested Election Cases,* 679–81; *Congressional Record,* 51st Cong., 1st sess. (September 2–5, 1890), 9559–751. Both Breckinridge and Cate ran for Congress again in 1890 and were certified as narrowly victorious by state authorities. Although the opposition once more charged fraud, the U.S. House of Representatives had by now passed under Democratic control and both men were allowed to retain their seats. The official state returns in the First District gave W. H. Cate, 15,437 votes, L. P. Featherston, 14,834; in the Second District the totals were C. R. Breckinridge, 20,017, Isom P. Langley, 19,941. See *Arkansas Secretary of State Biennial Report, 1889–1890,* 64–65.

49. Thomas, *Arkansas and Its People,* I, 219.

50. Ibid., 225; *Arkansas Gazette,* March 6, 1890; *Appleton's Annual Cyclopaedia, 1890,* 24.

51. Thomas, *Arkansas and Its People,* I, 218.

52. Woodward, *Origins of the New South,* 56; *Appleton's Annual Cyclopaedia, 1889,* 35, 36; *Arkansas Gazette,* September 6, 7, 23, 1888.

53. *Arkansas Gazette,* September 9, 1888.

54. *Arkansas Democrat,* (n.d.), in *Arkansas Gazette,* September 15, 1888.

55. *Arkansas Gazette,* September 28, 1888.

56. *Arkansas Gazette,* February 19, 1889. The ejected Democrats were C. W. Coffman, William Nickell, John R. Walters, and George Granberry.

57. Ibid.; *Biographical and Historical Memoirs of Central Arkansas,* 380. Of "Pennsylvania Dutch" origins, the oldest known progenitor of the Morehart family in America was John Morehart, a Revolutionary War veteran who served in the Continental Line. In 1805, he moved from Pennsylvania to Fairfield County in central Ohio, his family making the trek by covered wagon via the old "Forbes Military Road" and Zane's Trace. John's great-grandson, Henry R. Morehart, was born in Fairfield County on October 30, 1841. During the Civil War he enlisted in Company C, 114 Ohio Volunteers, and did part of his fighting in Arkansas. In

1881, Henry Morehart returned to Arkansas, journeying part of the way by steamboat, and homesteaded land in the Mabelvale community, then ten miles southwest of Little Rock. Little Rock's *Morehart Park* is named in honor of Henry Morehart's eldest son, Amos Morehart, a former president and director of the Mabelvale Rural School District, and the latter's wife, Emma Harrison Morehart. Henry Morehart was this writer's maternal great-grandfather, and Amos and Emma Harrison Morehart his maternal grandparents.

58. Thomas, *Arkansas and Its People,* I, 172–73, 177–78. Although the Greenbackers had carried several southwestern counties and scored scattered victories elsewhere, they had made particularly no headway at all in the predominately black counties of the eastern Delta. See *Arkansas Secretary of State Biennial Report, 1879–1880,* 34–35.

59. *Arkansas Gazette,* April 11, 1888.

60. Ibid., July 7, 1888. Named for Benjamin Harrison and Levi P. Morton, Republican presidential and vice-presidential candidates in 1888.

61. Ibid., July 22, 1888.

62. Ibid.

63. Ibid., July 8, 1888.

64. Little Rock *Sun,* (n.d.), in *Arkansas Gazette,* July 15, 1888.

65. *Arkansas Gazette,* July 12, 1888.

66. Ibid., July 11, 19, December 14, 1888.

67. Ibid., August 17, 1888.

68. Ibid., August 23–31, 1888.

69. Little Rock *Sun,* (n.d.), in *Arkansas Gazette,* July 15, 1888.

70. *Arkansas Gazette,* August 18, 1888.

71. Ibid., August 3, 17, 1888; Jonesboro *Sun,* (n.d.), in ibid., August 14, 1888.

72. Ibid., August 18, 1888.

73. Ibid., July 15, 27, 28, August 18–29, September 21, 1888; *Arkansas Democrat,* August 27, 1888.

74. *Arkansas Gazette,* July 27, 1888.

75. Pine Bluff *Press-Eagle,* July 24, 1888.

76. Ibid., July 10, 1888.

77. *Arkansas Gazette,* August 24, 1888.

78. *Arkansas Democrat,* August 8, 1890; Willard B. Gatewood, Jr., ed., "Negro Legislators in Arkansas, 1891: A Document," *Arkansas Historical Quarterly,* XXXI (Autumn 1972): 222–23.

79. *Arkansas Gazette*, June 18, 1890.

80. Ibid.

81. Ibid.

82. Ibid., June 18, 19, 1890.

## VIII

1. Arkadelphia *Southern Standard*, April 17, 1891.

2. *Arkansas Senate Journal* (1891), 15; *Arkansas House of Representatives Journal* (1891), 80, 85; *Arkansas Gazette*, January 14, 20, 1891.

3. *Arkansas Senate Journal* (1891), 15; *Arkansas Gazette*, January 14, 20, 1891.

4. Pine Bluff *Commercial*, December 30, 1890.

5. Tillman later served as president of the University of Arkansas from 1905 to 1912.

6. *Acts of Arkansas* (1891), 15–17. For earlier studies of the law's enactment, see John William Graves, "The Arkansas Separate Coach Law of 1891," in the *Journal of the West*, VII (October 1968): 531–41; and in the *Arkansas Historical Quarterly*, XXXII (Summer 1973): 148–65.

7. Fort Smith *Times*, (n.d.), in *Arkansas Gazette*, January 26, 1891.

8. Speech delivered by Senator John N. Tillman of Washington County in the Arkansas Senate, January 29, 1891, printed in the *Arkansas Gazette*, January 30, 1891. Hereinafter cited as "Tillman speech"; *Arkansas Senate Journal* (1891), 106.

9. Ibid.

10. Fayetteville *Arkansas Sentinel*, March 10, 1891; Pine Bluff *Press-Eagle*, January 20, February 3, 1891.

11. Charles A. Lofgren, *The Plessy Case: A Legal-Historical Interpretation* (New York, 1987), 203.

12. Tillman speech.

13. Lofgren, *The Plessy Case*, 33–35.

14. Ibid., 174–95.

15. *Arkansas Gazette*, January 21, August 11, 1891.

16. Fayetteville *Democrat*, January 30, 1891; *Arkansas Gazette*, January 20, 1891.

17. Morrilton *Pilot*, January 9, 1891; Nashville *News*, March 7, 1891; Yellville *Mountain Echo*, February 27, 1891.

18. Pine Bluff *Commercial*, December 29, 1890.

19. *Arkansas Gazette,* January 20, 1891.

20. Ibid.

21. Ibid.

22. Ibid.

23. Ibid., January 28, 1891.

24. Ibid.

25. Ibid.

26. Ibid.

27. Ibid.

28. Ibid.

29. Ibid.

30. Ibid.

31. Ibid.

32. Ibid.

33. *Arkansas House of Representatives Journal* (1891), 150; *Arkansas Gazette,* January 14, 1891.

34. Pine Bluff *Press-Eagle,* February 3, 1891.

35. Although born in Tennessee in 1855, Bell had been reared in Arkansas. Left fatherless at the end of the war, Bell somehow managed to earn enough money to support his family, attend private schools, and put himself through Lincoln University in Pennsylvania, where in 1883 he was graduated first in a class of twenty. Active in the Republican party and the Knights of Labor, Bell was a school teacher who later in life became a practicing physician. He also must have been fairly wealthy, for he purportedly paid the tuition costs of some 140 college students. A Quaker, nonsmoker, and teetotaler, Bell gained the respect of his white colleagues mainly because of his courteous manner and quiet demeanor. Even so, he was a firm and often eloquent defender of his race's interests. Kousser, "A Black Protest in the 'Era of Accommodation'," 156; Gaines, *Racial Possibilities as Indicated by the Negroes of Arkansas,* 133–34.

36. Speech delivered by Senator George Waltham Bell of Desha County in the Arkansas Senate, January 29, 1891, printed in the *Arkansas Gazette,* January 30, 1891; and in *The Freeman* (Indianapolis, Indiana), February 21, 1891; *Arkansas Senate Journal* (1891), 106. Bell's reference to "eighteen years" suggests that the state's 1873 civil-rights act may have been effective in ending incipient railway segregation.

37. Ibid.

38. Ibid.

39. Ibid.

40. Ibid. In 1893, however, Lucas would leave Arkansas, probably because of the worsening racial situation, and would settle in Chicago. He soon established there a lucrative legal practice with both white and black clients; occupying a spacious suite of law offices on Dearborn Avenue, by the early twentieth century he was being referred to as a "black millionaire." Active in local politics, he was elected to several county offices on the Republican ticket. Later, during the Great Depression, Lucas switched parties (like so many of his race) and became a Democrat; he was named Assistant United States Attorney for Cook County during the administration of Franklin D. Roosevelt. Gatewood, "Negro Legislators in Arkansas, 1891: A Document," 220–25; Kousser, "A Black Protest in the 'Era of Accommodation'," 155–56; Thomas Yenser, ed., *Who's Who in Colored America, 1938–40* (New York, 1940), 341; *The Broad-Ax* (Chicago, Illinois), November 29, December 27, 1902; March 30, October 20, 1906; *Arkansas Democrat*, April 1, 1891; *Arkansas Gazette*, January 31, 1891.

41. Speech of Representative John Gray Lucas of Jefferson County, delivered in the Arkansas House of Representatives, February 17, 1891, printed in the *Arkansas Gazette*, February 21, 1891, and in *The Freeman* (Indianapolis, Indiana), April 4, 1891. Hereinafter cited as Lucas speech; *Arkansas House of Representatives Journal* (1891), 344–45.

42. Boston *Daily Globe*, December 6, 1886.

43. Lucas speech.

44. Ibid.

45. Ibid.

46. Ibid.

47. Ibid. Lucas's comments strikingly anticipate the typology of race relations developed by Pierre van den Berghe, who argues that when paternalistic racial patterns give way to competitive ones, the dominant race responds with hatred and violence; moreover, to the extent that social distance diminishes, physical segregation is introduced as a second line of defense for preservation of the dominant group's superior position. Van den Berghe, *Race and Racism*, 25–37.

48. Lucas speech.

49. Ibid.

50. *Arkansas Gazette*, February 21, 1891.

51. Ibid.

52. Ibid.

53. *Arkansas Gazette*, January 31, 1891, and *Arkansas Democrat*, April 1, 1891, quoted in Kousser, "A Black Protest in the 'Era of Accommodation'," 155.

54. *Arkansas Senate Journal* (1891), 106. Hill's Seventh District consisted of several Delta counties (Crittenden, Cross, St. Francis, and Woodruff). He undoubtedly had been elected with a good deal of black support.

55. *Arkansas Senate Journal* (1891), 84; *Arkansas Gazette*, January 28, 1891. Those voting against the exclusionary amendment were S. H. Davidson of the Second District (Lawrence, Randolph, and Sharp counties); J. N. Tillman of the Fifth District (Washington County): J. E. Williams of the Tenth District (Perry and Pulaski counties); J. W. Campbell of the Eleventh District (Jefferson County); C. W. Bricknell of the Thirteenth District (Arkansas and Monroe counties); James P. Clarke of the Fourteenth District (Lee and Phillips counties); W. P. McElroy of the Twenty-first District (Howard, Little River, Polk, and Sevier counties); and E. B. Kinsworthy of the Thirtieth District (Clarke and Pike counties).

56. Ten years later, in 1901, Representative E. B. Waddell of Jefferson County, in the Delta, reintroduced a Negro nurse-exemption proviso, but the House of Representatives rejected it by a vote of forty-two to thirty. At least one lawmaker opposed it "because it would be legislation in favor of the wealthy, who are alone able to employ nurses." Though slightly less pronounced, the 1901 vote revealed geographical divisions similar to the 1891 vote. Only six of the thirty supporters of the Negro-nurse proviso represented Ozark or Ouachita mountains counties. The remaining twenty-four supporters all represented counties with major urban centers, lowland counties, or borderland counties with major lowland divisions. *Arkansas House of Representatives Journal* (1901), 335; *Arkansas Gazette*, March 19, 1901.

57. *Arkansas Gazette*, February 14, 1891.

58. *Arkansas House of Representatives Journal* (1891), 344–45. In addition to George W. Bell in the Senate, the following blacks served in the House: Henry A. Johnson of Chicot County; G. W. Watson of Crittenden County; R. C. Weddington of Desha County; S. W. Dawson, John Gray Lucas, and Sam L. Woolfork of Jefferson County; H. N. Williams of Lincoln County; George W. Lowe of Monroe County; John H. Carr and J. N. Donohoo of Phillips County; and B. F. Adair of Pulaski County. All were Republicans except Adair, a Democrat, and Lowe, president of the state Colored Wheel, who was elected on the Union Labor ticket. Of the twelve black legislators, only Democrat Adair backed the separate-coach law; all the rest cast their votes against enactment. For biographical sketches, see *The Freeman* (Indianapolis, Indiana), April 4, 1891; Gatewood, "Negro Legislators in Arkansas, 1891," *passim*.

59. *Arkansas Gazette,* February 21, 1891.

60. Camden *Beacon, Fort Smith Call,* and Helena *World,* (n.ds.), quoted in *Arkansas Gazette,* January 24, 1891.

61. Nashville *News,* January 24, 1891.


## IX

1. For examples, see Thomas, *Arkansas and Its People,* I, 231–32; James Harris Fain, "Political Disfranchisement of the Negro in Arkansas," (M.A. thesis, University of Arkansas, 1961), 39–40.

2. *Acts of Arkansas* (1891), VII, 36.

3. John William Graves, "Negro Disfranchisement in Arkansas," *Arkansas Historical Quarterly,* XXVI (Autumn 1967): 199–225; Graves, "A Question of Honor: Election Reform and Black Disfranchisement in Arkansas," University of Virginia, *Essays in History,* XV (1969–71), 9–26.

4. Thomas, *Arkansas and Its People,* I, 233–34. Woodruff was the son of the *Arkansas Gazette* founder of the same name.

5. *Arkansas Gazette,* January 14, 1891.

6. Ibid., March 1, 1891. This practice violated ART. 3, SEC. 10 of the state constitution but nevertheless occurred.

7. Ibid.

8. *Arkansas House of Representatives Journal* (1891), 86; *Arkansas Gazette,* January 20, 1891; Arkadelphia *Southern Standard,* January 30, 1891.

9. *Arkansas Gazette,* January 20, 1891.

10. *Arkansas House of Representatives Journal* (1891), 87; *Arkansas Gazette,* January 21, 1891.

11. *Arkansas Gazette,* January 21, 1891.

12. White and Sevier were both on the election committee, White being the committee chairman. Other members were P. D. Brewer of Sebastian County, Sam J. Crabtree of White County, H. A. Johnson of Chicot County, A. S. Morgan of Union County, and C. A. Otey of Lee County. All were white Democrats except Johnson, a black Republican, and Crabtree, a white Union Laborite.

13. *Arkansas House of Representatives Journal* (1891), 87; *Arkansas Gazette,* January 31, 1891; Arkadelphia *Southern Standard,* March 6, 1891. All committee members endorsed the substitute except Representative Johnson, who submitted a minority report contending that present laws were adequate if honestly administered. Crabtree, despite his initial approval, later voted against the bill's passage.

14. House Bill No. 162 was later redrafted to eliminate awkward phraseology and reintroduced as House Bill No. 240. The two measures seem to have been identical, however, in all important respects. Sevier's sponsorship was important. His father, of the same name, had been one of Arkansas's first two U.S. Senators, and he was a descendant of the Conway-Sevier-Johnson family, the antebellum "dynasty" that had supplied Arkansas with numerous governors, U.S. Senators, congressmen, and judges. No doubt endorsement from a member of such an old and distinguished Democratic family enhanced the bill's chances of success.

15. *Acts of Arkansas* (1891), I, 33.

16. Ibid.

17. Ibid., II, 35.

18. *Eleventh Census, 1890*, I, *Population*, Pt. 2, lii–lv.

19. *Acts of Arkansas* (1891), XXXVI, 47; ibid. (1891), 130–32. Under previous statutes each party could supply voters with its own ballots. These usually were differentiated from the other parties in size and color and automatically destroyed any possibility of secrecy. The new ballot was standard and uniform but contained one awkward feature: instead of placing the customary "x" mark beside candidates' names, the elector had to scratch out completely the names of all persons except those for whom he intended to vote. This especially was difficult for the semiliterate and increased the possibility of technical errors which could invalidate his ballot. Also, party emblems were not included on the ballot, so illiterates had no way of preparing ballots on their own behalf. Despite the claims of its sponsors, the bill thus did not fully establish the Australian voting system.

20. *Acts of Arkansas* (1891), XXXVI, 47.

21. *Arkansas Gazette*, February 28, 1891.

22. A Democratic party caucus had been organized for the first time at the opening of the 1891 legislature. During the previous session, the Assembly of 1889, a coalition of Republicans, Union Laborites, and western Arkansas Democrats, under Speaker B. B. Hudgins of Boone County, narrowly defeated an election bill similar to the proposal now under consideration. Democratic leaders may well have had this event in mind when they decided to establish the caucus. Perhaps it also should be noted that this writer's great-grandfather, Pulaski County representative Henry Morehart, helped lead the successful drive to kill the election bill in 1889. *Arkansas Gazette*, February 6, March 1, 7, 20, 23, 26, 27, 1889; January 11, February 26, 1891; childhood conversations of the author with the late Dr. Henry Calvin Lewis, page boy to Mr. Morehart in 1889.

23. In addition, seventeen persons were recorded as absent and not voting. *Arkansas House of Representatives Journal* (1891), 240–42.

24. Ibid.

25. Ibid., 442–43; *Arkansas Gazette*, February 26, 1891.

26. Ibid. The aversion to murderers probably referred to the assassins of John M. Clayton.

27. Ibid. The "Force bill" referred to the bill of Representative Henry Cabot Lodge of Massachusetts which would have placed federal supervisors at Southern polls during congressional and presidential elections. Though defeated in Congress in 1890, the Democrats had used it as an issue in the subsequent campaign—with great effect. To many white Southerners the "Force bill" evoked painful memories of Reconstruction.

28. Ibid.

29. Ibid. Of the eleven black House members, all voted against enactment except Pulaski Democrat B. F. Adair and one Republican, G. W. Watson of Crittenden County. The House's two white Republicans, Representatives Henley and Carlton, voted against enactment, as did two white Union Labor representatives, Sam J. Crabtree of White County and John Dunaway of Faulkner County. White Union Laborites W. A. Evans of Carroll County and William Manning of St. Francis County voted for the bill.

30. *Arkansas Gazette*, February 28, 1891.

31. *Arkansas Senate Journal* (1891), 334; *Arkansas Gazette*, February 28, 1891.

32. See particularly the *Arkansas Gazette* editorial of March 1, 1891; also the letter of the Honorable E. E. White, printed in the *Gazette*, May 7, 1892.

33. *Arkansas Senate Journal* (1891), 334; *Arkansas Gazette*, February 28, 1891. Miller, representing Crawford and Franklin counties, was one of the few Democratic proponents who remained on the floor during the debates.

34. *Arkansas Gazette*, September 19, October 5, November 27, 1888; December 25, 1888.

35. According to the Arkadelphia *Southern Standard*, soon after the passage of the separate-coach and election laws a secret caucus was held between leading Democratic solons and prominent Negroes. In order to forestall a threatened exodus of Negro laborers and soothe the troubled racial waters, the Democrats promised to carve out a new black congressional district from counties bordering the Mississippi River. This

report is highly creditable since the *Standard* was owned by Senator E. B. Kinsworthy, a member of the Committee on Apportionment. The plan eventually was dropped because of fierce resistance from representatives of the Delta. Had these representatives fully anticipated the extent of the disfranchisement which would result from the election law, then they logically would have favored the proposed new district since the small handful of whites in the area would have had a congressional seat all to themselves. Since blacks were unable to retain political control in even a single county in the Delta after the law's enactment, it seems unlikely they could ever have captured the proposed new district. Arkadelphia *Southern Standard*, February 27, 1891; *Arkansas Gazette*, March 5, 6, 7, 14, 24, 1891.

36. *Arkansas State Journal* (1891), 334. In addition to the black Republican George W. Bell, there were two white Union Labor senators, F. P. Hill of Woodruff County and J. P. H. Russ of White County. All other members of the Senate were white Democrats.

37. *Arkansas Gazette*, September 7, 1892.

38. Ibid.

39. Ibid.

40. *Arkansas Gazette*, September 4, 1894.

41. Pine Bluff *Commercial*, September 7, 1894.

42. *Arkansas Gazette*, September 12, 1894. Following the session of 1893, and lasting for the next eighty years, no black person would serve in the legislative branch of Arkansas's state government. In 1973, three black representatives, Richard Mays, Dr. William H. Townsend, and Henry Wilkins, and one black senator, Jerry D. Jewell, were seated in the Assembly.

43. *Arkansas Secretary of State Biennial Report, 1889–1890*, 53–55; *Arkansas Secretary of State Biennial Report, 1893–1894* (Little Rock, 1895), 44–46. In 1894, Arkansas's new poll tax went into effect and accounted for some of the drop in voter participation. However, in the majority of Delta counties, blacks were eliminated from office in 1892, before the poll tax had become operative. Contemporary observers generally voiced the belief that the election law was a more important factor in bringing about disfranchisement.

44. Chicot, Crittenden, Desha, Jefferson, Lee, and Phillips, the counties with approximately 75 percent or more black populations.

45. *Arkansas Secretary of State Biennial Report, 1890*, 53–55; *Arkansas Secretary of State Biennial Report, 1893–1894*, 44–46.

46. *Arkansas Gazette*, August 30, 1894; August 7, 8, September 6, 11, 1896.

47. The reference is to Democratic presidential candidate Grover Cleveland.

48. *Arkansas Gazette*, September 9, 1892. For additional evidence of corruption by judges, see the editorial of the Walnut Ridge *Telephone*, (n.d.), published in the *Arkansas Gazette*, May 28, 1896, and the speech of Democratic gubernatorial candidate Dan W. Jones in the *Gazette*, June 21, 1896.

49. Pine Bluff *Press-Eagle*, September 6, 1892.

50. *Arkansas Gazette*, September 9, 1892.

51. Pine Bluff *Commercial*, September 4, 1894.

52. *Arkansas Gazette*, March 7, 1891.

53. Ibid., July 17, 1896.

54. Arkansas U.S. Senator James K. Jones, as Democratic National Chairman, helped promote cooperative efforts between the state's Populists and Democrats. See Robert F. Durden, *The Climax of Populism: The Election of 1896* (Lexington, Kentucky, 1965), 73–74.

55. *Arkansas Gazette*, January 15, 1897. Clarke himself, as Phillips County state senator, was a prime sponsor of the original centralized election bill in 1889. In that year he had spoken against minority representation on state election boards, arguing that the blurring of party lines made it too cumbersome (see ibid., March 20, 1889). Also, Clarke may have been the real brainchild of the 1891 law; at the time of its enactment Senator Kinsworthy's paper, the Arkadelphia *Southern Standard*, reported that "The leading features of the bill are the conceptions of the Hon. J. P. Clarke, President of the Senate, and embodies, in the main, the features of the bill introduced in the Senate two years ago" (Arkadelphia *Southern Standard*, March 6, 1891). That Clark was now willing, on the basis of trial and error, to consent to minority representation on election boards can be construed as additional evidence that the 1891 law was not, in the beginning, conceived of as an instrument to promote ballot stealing and fraud. Of course, it is equally possible that Clarke merely changed his position because of changed political conditions. Clarke subsequently served as one of Arkansas's U.S. Senators from 1903 to 1916.

56. *Arkansas Gazette*, January 19, 1897.

57. Ibid.

58. *Arkansas House of Representatives Journal* (1897), 51; *Arkansas Gazette*, May 21, 1897.

59. Ibid.

60. *Arkansas House of Representatives Journal* (1897), 63–64; *Arkansas Gazette*, May 27, 1897.

61. Ibid.

62. Kousser, *Shaping of Southern Politics*, 123–30.

## X

1. *Arkansas Gazette,* December 1, 1888; Pine Bluff *Press-Eagle,* (n.d.), in *Arkansas Gazette,* January 4, 1889.

2. Jonesboro *Times,* (n.d.), in *Arkansas Gazette,* December 29, 1888.

3. Ibid.

4. Ibid.

5. *Arkansas Gazette,* November 17, 1888; January 2, 1891.

6. *Arkansas Gazette,* November 17, 1888.

7. Ibid., January 2, 1891.

8. Ibid., November 17, 18, December 9, 22, 1888; Texarkana *Democrat,* (n.d.), in *Arkansas Gazette,* December 2, 1888.

9. *Arkansas Gazette,* November 18, 1888.

10. Pine Bluff *Press-Eagle,* (n.d.), in *Arkansas Gazette,* January 4, 1889; Fordyce *Enterprise,* (n.d.), in *Arkansas Gazette,* January 9, 1889.

11. *Arkansas Constitution* (1874), ART. 14, SEC. 3.

12. Morrilton *Pilot,* July 1, 1892; *Arkansas Gazette,* August 18, 1892.

13. Fordyce *Enterprise,* (n.d.), in *Arkansas Gazette,* January 9, 1889; Pine Bluff *Press-Eagle,* (n.d.), in *Arkansas Gazette,* January 4, 1889.

14. The Reverend Wallace Carnahan, "Safety without Rascality," *Anglo-Saxon Churchman,* VII (January 1891), published in the *Congressional Record,* 51st Cong., 2nd sess., (January 16, 1891), 1399.

15. Ibid.

16. Ibid.

17. *Congressional Record,* 51st Cong., 2nd sess. (January 16, 1891), 1402.

18. Memphis *Appeal,* (n.d.), in *Arkansas Gazette,* January 3, 1889.

19. *Arkansas Gazette,* December 29, 1888.

20. Ibid., January 4, 1889.

21. Ibid., December 12, 29, 1889.

22. *Arkansas Gazette,* March 9, 1889.

23. See especially the speech of Representative, J. C. Floyd of Marion County, published in the *Arkansas Gazette,* March 26, 1889.

24. *Arkansas Gazette,* March 27, 1889.

25. *Acts of Arkansas* (1891), 314.

26. *Arkansas Gazette,* March 20, 1891.

27. *Arkansas Senate Journal* (1891), 512.

28. *Arkansas House of Representatives Journal* (1891), 894–95.

29. Ibid. Blacks voting to table the poll tax were Henry A. Johnson of Chicot County, G. W. Watson of Crittenden County, S. W. Dawson of Jefferson County, John H. Carr and J. N. Donohoo of Phillips County, all Republicans, and George W. Lowe of Monroe County, a Union Laborite. However, four other Negroes, Republicans R. C. Weddington of Desha County, John Gray Lucas of Jefferson County, H. N. Williams of Lincoln County, and Democrat B. F. Adair of Pulaski County were among fourteen persons absent and not voting. Only one black man, Republican Sam L. Woolfork of Jefferson County, actually voted against tabling the poll-tax amendment.

30. Ibid.

31. Ibid.

32. Ibid.

33. *Arkansas Gazette,* March 27, September 19, December 5, 1888; Pine Bluff *Press-Eagle,* (n.d.), in *Arkansas Gazette,* January 4, 1889.

34. *Arkansas House of Representatives Journal* (1891), 916–17; *Arkansas Gazette,* April 2, 1891.

35. *Arkansas Senate Journal* (1891), 701; *Arkansas Gazette,* April 4, 1891.

36. Fain, "Political Disfranchisement of the Negro in Arkansas," 41–43.

37. Thomas, *Arkansas and Its People,* I, 237–39; *Arkansas Political Farmer* and Fort Smith *Republican,* (n.ds.), in *Arkansas Gazette,* May 14, July 14, 1892; *Arkansas Gazette,* June 22, July 17, 21, 1892.

38. Fain, "Political Disfranchisement of the Negro in Arkansas," 41–43.

39. Arkadelphia *Southern Standard,* July 8, 1892.

40. Hot Springs *Graphic,* (n.d.), in *Arkansas Gazette,* July 22, 1892; *Arkansas Gazette,* April 10, July 14, 1892.

41. Ibid.

42. Ibid. Needless to say, a permanent registration system could have been created to halt "repeating" without adding a poll-tax requirement.

43. Ibid.

44. Fain, "Political Disfranchisement of the Negro in Arkansas," 45–46.

45. *Arkansas Gazette*, July 14, 1892.

46. *Arkansas Secretary of State Biennial Report 1891–1892* (Little Rock, 1893), 57–59.

47. Ibid.

48. *Arkansas Constitution* (1874), ART. 19, SEC. 22.

49. For example, see the Fort Smith *Elevator*, October 14, 1892.

50. *Arkansas Gazette*, January 13, 1893; Sidney R. Crawford, "The Poll Tax" (M.A. thesis, University of Arkansas, 1944), 38. The law in question was more ambiguous than Kinsworthy's ruling indicated. It read: ". . . the returns shall be opened and counted in the presence of the General Assembly in joint convention assembled. If it shall appear that a majority of the electors voting at such election adopt such amendment, then the Speaker shall declare such proposed amendment duly adopted by the people of Arkansas." *Acts of Arkansas* (1883), II, 71.

51. *Acts of Arkansas* (1893), 245–46.

52. *Acts of Arkansas* (1895), V, 55–56.

53. Ibid., VI, 56–57.

54. The original poll-tax enforcement act of 1893 allowed individuals who had lost their receipts to swear an affidavit that they had paid the poll tax and still vote. This was identical to the provision which Negro representative J. N. Donohoo had unsuccessfully tried, in 1891, to include in the actual amendment itself. The 1895 act further liberalized the procedure by dropping the requirement of a formal oath, except when ordered at the discretion of the election judges. Under this more flexible provision, however, a biased judge could require oaths from members of the opposite race or party, yet dispense with them in the case of members of his own group. *Acts of Arkansas* (1893), VII, 246; ibid. (1895), VI, 56–57.

55. *Acts of Arkansas* (1895), 179–80.

56. *Knight v. Shelton*, 134 Fed. 423.

57. *Rice v. Palmer*, 78 Ark. 432.

58. Fain, "Political Disfranchisement of the Negro in Arkansas," 47–48.

59. *Arkansas Secretary of State Biennial Report, 1907–08* (Little Rock, 1909), 378. The vote was 88,386 for adoption, 46,835 against. Since 167,789 voters participated in the general balloting, the requisite absolute majority was obtained.

60. John Gardner Lile, *The Government of Arkansas* (Arkadelphia, 1916), 119–21; Thomas, *Arkansas and Its People*, I, 91–92; Fain, "Political Disfranchisement of the Negro in Arkansas," 56–57.

61. *Acts of Arkansas* (1895), 240–41.

62. For instance, in 1902 the Clark County Democratic committee invited ex-Populists back into the fold and simultaneously expelled Negroes. The Arkadelphia *Southern Standard* commented that the policy of "absolutely excluding the negro" and "throwing the doors wide open for the populists brethren, is all for the future good of the party." Arkadelphia *Southern Standard*, February 6, April 3, 1902.

63. *Arkansas Gazette*, October 22, 1899.

64. Ibid., February 10, 1901.

65. Ibid., February 1, 1906. Despite the state committee's directive, here and there a few blacks were occasionally permitted to continue voting in Democratic primaries. Boyce A. Drummond, "Arkansas Politics: A Study of a One-Party System," (Ph.D. diss., University of Chicago, 1957), 75–76.

66. *Arkansas Secretary of State Biennial Report, 1909–1912* (Little Rock, 1913), 411.

67. Kousser, *Shaping of Southern Politics*, 128–30.

68. Riley, *The Philosophy of Negro Suffrage*, 58–59.

69. For an expression of this view, see the address of the Honorable Clifton R. Breckinridge, "Is Lynching Advisable?" in *Race Problems of the South; Report of the First Annual Conference . . . of the Southern Society for the Promotion of the Study of Race Conditions and Problems in the South* (Montgomery, Alabama, 1900), 170–77. Breckinridge served as an Arkansas congressman during the 1880s and 1890s and later as U.S. Minister to Russia from 1894 to 1897.

70. Gibbs, *Shadow and Light*, 215–16.

71. Pine Bluff *Press-Eagle*, November 9, 1897. It should be noted, however, that the *Press-Eagle* itself, and a number of the Pine Bluff whites, opposed Havis's confirmation. Ibid., November 2, 1897.

72. Gatewood, "Negro Legislators in Arkansas, 1891," 225.

73. *Congressional Record*, 55th Cong., 2nd sess. (March 30, 1898), 3378.

74. Pine Bluff *Press-Eagle*, October 12, 1897.


## XI

1. Woodward, *Origins of the New South*, 235–43.

2. Thomas, *Arkansas and Its People*, I, 240.

3. *Arkansas Secretary of State Biennial Report, 1891–1892* (Little Rock, 1893), 56.

4. *Arkansas Secretary of State Biennial Report, 1893–1894*, (Little Rock, 1895), 46.

5. Durden, *The Climax of Populism*, 73–74.

6. *Arkansas Secretary of State Biennial Report, 1895–1896* (Little Rock, 1896), 59.

7. In 1898, Populist gubernatorial candidate W. S. Morgan polled no more than 8,332 votes against 75,362 for Democrat Dan W. Jones and 27,524 for Republican W. S. Auten. At the same time Polk County in western Arkansas, the last stronghold of Populism, fell to the Democrats, and all Populists were removed from the legislature. In 1900, 3,641 Populist die-hards voted for A. W. Files in the governor's race, but by 1902 the party was reduced to endorsing the Prohibitionist nominee, George H. Kimbell, rather than running its own candidate. Reportedly, the Populists' last major victory in Arkansas occurred in 1904, when one of their members was elected to the legislature. *Arkansas Secretary of State Biennial Report, 1897–1898* (Little Rock, 1898), 193; *Arkansas Secretary of State Biennial Report, 1899–1900* (Little Rock, 1900), 415; *Arkansas Gazette*, September 7, 13, 1898; August 14, 1902; Thomas, *Arkansas and Its People*, I, 277.

8. C. Vann Woodward, "The Populist Heritage and the Intellectual," in *The Burden of Southern History* (Baton Rouge, 1960), 141–66, and his *The Strange Career of Jim Crow*, 60–65; Jack Abramowitz, "The Negro in the Agrarian Revolt," *Agricultural History*, XXIV (1950), 89–95, and "The Negro in the Populist Movement," *Journal of Negro History*, XXXVIII (July 1953): 257–89. More guarded is William H. Chafe, "The Negro and Populism: A Kansas Case Study," *Journal of Southern History*, XXXIV (August 1968): 402–19.

9. C. Vann Woodward, *Tom Watson: Agrarian Rebel* (New York, 1938).

10. Woodward, *The Strange Career of Jim Crow*, 61.

11. Quoted in ibid., 63.

12. Ibid.

13. Ibid., 64.

14. Ibid.

15. Ibid.

16. Goodwyn, *Democratic Promise*, 276–306.

17. Ibid., 299.

18. Ibid., 298.

19. Robert M. Saunders, "The Ideology of Southern Populists, 1892–

1895" (Ph.D. diss., University of Virginia, 1967); "The Southern Populists and the Negro in 1892," History Club, University of Virginia *Essays in History* XII (1967), 7–25, and "Southern Populism and the Negro, 1893–1905," *Journal of Negro History*, LIV (July 1969): 240–57. For support of Saunders' viewpoint, see Herbert Shapiro, "The Populists and the Negro: A Reconsideration," in August Meier and Elliott Rudwick (eds.), *The Making of Black America*, 2 vols. (New York, 1969), II, 27–36, and Francis M. Wilhoit, "An Interpretation of Populism's Impact on the Georgia Negro," *Journal of Negro History*, LII (April 1967), 116–27; Gerald H. Gaither, *Blacks and the Populist Revolt: Ballots and Bigotry in the "New South"* (University, Ala., 1977), *passim*. For an excellent, in-depth examination of this subject, see Gregg Cantrell and D. Scott Barton, "Texas Politics and the Failure of Biracial Politics," *Journal of Southern History*, LV (November 1989): 659–92.

20. Morgan, *History of the Wheel and Alliance*, 64.

21. F. Clark Elkins, "The Agricultural Wheel: County Politics and Consolidation, 1884–1885," *Arkansas Historical Quarterly*, XXIX (Summer 1970): 174.

22. Morgan, *History of the Wheel and Alliance*, 73; Elkins, "The Agricultural Wheel in Arkansas," 149–50.

23. Elkins, "The Agricultural Wheel in Arkansas," 175–76.

24. Little Rock *Wheel-Enterprise and Stockman*, February 23, 1889. The three Negro lecturers were F. S. Simons of Marion, E. A. Head of Hollywood, and G. C. King of Ashley.

25. Ibid.

26. Bayliss, "Public Affairs in Arkansas," 291.

27. Theodore Saloutos, *Farmer Movements in the South, 1865–1933* (Berkeley, 1960), 69–87.

28. Henry C. Taylor, *The Farmers' Movement, 1620–1920* (New York, 1953), 209; Solon Justus Buck, *The Agrarian Crusade: A Chronicle of the Farmer in Politics* (New Haven, 1920), 117–22.

29. Elkins, "The Agricultural Wheel in Arkansas," 208.

30. Ibid., 239–40. Shortly thereafter, under a complicated reorganization plan, the agrarian orders were incorporated into the "National Farmers' Alliance and Industrial Union"; for purposes of simplification, the term "Southern Farmers' Alliance" will be used to describe the merged orders hereinafter.

31. Ibid., 245–49.

32. Ibid.

33. While the Colored Alliance enjoyed mass support, its membership claims were likely considerably exaggerated. See Robert C. McMath,

*Populist Vanguard: A History of the Southern Farmers' Alliance* (Chapel Hill, 1975), 45.

34. Goodwyn, *Democratic Promise,* 278–94.

35. William F. Holmes, "The Arkansas Cotton Pickers Strike of 1891 and the Demise of the Colored Farmers' Alliance," *Arkansas Historical Quarterly,* XXXII (Summer 1973): 107–19.

36. Ibid., 118–19.

37. Ibid., 108.

38. *Arkansas Gazette,* May 1, 1888. On the Negro knights, see William W. Rogers, "Negro Knights of Labor in Arkansas: A Case Study of the Miscellaneous Strike," *Labor History,* X (Summer 1969): 498–505.

39. *Arkansas Gazette,* May 1, 1888.

40. Ibid., July 19, 1888.

41. Ibid., June 27, July 14, 1888.

42. Ibid.

43. Ibid., July 14, 15, 1888.

44. Newport *News,* (n.d.), quoting the Little Rock *Sun* in *Arkansas Gazette,* August 26, 1888.

45. Paragould *Press,* (n.d.), in *Arkansas Gazette,* August 29, 1888.

46. *Arkansas Gazette,* August 17, 23, 1888.

47. Ibid., November 2, 7, 1888.

48. *Arkansas Secretary of State Biennial Report, 1887–1888,* 267–69; ibid., *1889–1890,* 47–49. Kousser, *Shaping of Southern Politics,* 15, 28.

49. *Arkansas Gazette,* September 5, 1888.

50. *Arkansas Secretary of State Biennial Report, 1889–1890,* 53–55, 64–66. In the governor's race, the combined totals in the six most heavily black counties (Chicot, Crittenden, Desha, Jefferson, Lee, and Phillips) were Democrat James P. Eagle 8,296, Union Laborite N. B. Fizer 15,155.

51. Van Buren *Graphic,* (n.d.), in *Arkansas Gazette,* August 3, 1888.

52. *Arkansas Gazette,* February 22, 1889.

53. Ibid., February 23, 1889.

54. Ibid. Those listing their party affiliation as Union Laborite, Wheeler, or Independent were Sam J. Crabtree of White County, J. W. Dollison of Clay County, J. P. Dunn of Pike County, R. S. Hill of Van Buren County, W. P. Huddleston of Independence County, A. B. Jones of Hempstead County, O. S. Jones of Nevada County, and William Manning of St. Francis County. Representatives Henry Morehart and A. F. Rice were elected on the Union Labor–Republican fusion ticket in Pulaski County but were members of the Union Labor party. *Arkansas Secretary of State Biennial Report, 1887–1888,* 285–86.

55. *Arkansas Gazette*, February 23, 1889.

56. *Arkansas Senate Journal* (1891), 106.

57. Ibid. After clearing the Senate the coach bill was passed by the House with several amendments being added. The measure was then sent back to the Senate for final adoption. On this second, *pro forma* Senate vote, Russ did reverse his position and join Hill in opposing enactment. *Arkansas Gazette*, February 20, 1891.

58. *Arkansas House of Representatives Journal* (1891), 344–45.

59. *Arkansas Gazette*, February 14, 1891.

60. Thomas, *Arkansas and Its People*, I, 240.

61. *Appleton's Annual Cyclopaedia, 1892*, 19–20.

62. Arkadelphia *Siftings*, (n.d.), in the *Arkansas Gazette*, June 30, 1892.

63. *Arkansas Gazette*, April 9, 1892.

64. Arkadelphia *Herald*, (n.d.), in the *Arkansas Gazette*, July 10, 1892.

65. Arkadelphia *Siftings*, (n.d.), in the *Arkansas Gazette*, July 16, 1892.

66. *Arkansas Gazette*, June 29, 1892.

67. *Arkansas Gazette*, April 10, 1892. For numerous other examples see Richard Baker Dixon, "Press Opinion toward the Populist Party in Arkansas, 1890–1896" (M.A. thesis, University of Arkansas, 1953), *passim*.

68. *Arkansas Gazette*, August 14, 1892.

69. *Arkansas Gazette*, October 5, 1892.

70. Faulkner *Wheel*, (n.d.), in the *Arkansas Gazette*, August 5, 1892.

71. Woodruff County *Vidette*, (n.d.), in the *Arkansas Gazette*, August 19, 1892.

72. *Arkansas Gazette*, July 27, August 4, 1892.

73. *Arkansas Secretary of State Biennial Report, 1891–1892*, 56.

74. Ibid. In the governor's race, the totals in the six most heavily Negro counties (Chicot, Crittenden, Desha, Jefferson, Lee, and Phillips) were Democrat William Fishback, 6543; Republican William Whipple, 3844; and Populist J. P. Carnahan, 246. The greatly reduced vote from 1890 and the Democratic majority may be attributed to the operation of the new election law. Few of those blacks who still voted, however, preferred the Populist ticket.

75. Negro support, for example, was said to have contributed to Populist victories in Faulkner and Nevada counties. *Arkansas Gazette*, September 7, 1892.

76. In the 1894 gubernatorial election, the vote was Democrat James P. Clarke, 74,809; Republican Harmon L. Remmel, 26,085; and Populist D. E. Barker, 24,541; in 1896, the returns were Democrat Dan W.

Jones, 91,114; Republican Harmon L. Remmel, 35,836; and Populist A. W. Files, 13,990. See *Arkansas Secretary of State Biennial Report, 1893–1894*, 46; *Arkansas Secretary of State Biennial Report, 1895–1896*, 59.

77. Kousser, *Shaping of Southern Politics*, 42.

## XII

1. It is important to note, however, that extension of segregation in the private sector continued throughout these years. During the nineties, Negroes were discreetly excluded from white professional societies and forced to organize their own bar and medical associations. Gibbs, *Shadow and Light*, 199; *Arkansas Gazette*, June 17, July 3, 1898.

2. Between 1882 and 1937, a total of at least 285 persons were lynched or otherwise put to death without trial in Arkansas. Blacks accounted for 226 cases or about 80 percent of the illegal executions. Slightly less than one-third of all deaths occurred during the 1890s alone. Ferguson and Atkinson, *Historic Arkansas*, 274; James Elbert Cutler, *Lynch-Law: An Investigation into the History of Lynching in the United States* (New York, 1905), 183; Arthur F. Raper, *The Tragedy of Lynching* (Chapel Hill, 1933), 28, 483; Walter White, *Rope and Faggot: A Biography of Judge Lynch* (New York, 1929), 254.

3. Both Governors James P. Clarke (1893–1896) and Dan W. Jones (1897–1900) deplored lynchings as a disgrace to the state. *Arkansas Gazette*, July 17, 1895; August 27, 1898.

4. Woodward, *Origins of the New South*, 376–77; Thomas, *Arkansas and Its People*, I, 267–68; Charles Jacobson, *The Life Story of Jeff Davis, The Stormy Petrel of Arkansas Politics* (Little Rock, 1925), *passim*.

5. Rupert B. Vance, "A Karl Marx for Hillbillies, Portrait of a Southern Leader," in *Social Forces* (Chapel Hill), IX (1930–31), 180–90; *Arkansas House of Representatives Journal* (1903), 133; *Arkansas House of Representatives Journal* (1905), 28–48.

6. For the best critical biography of Davis, see Raymond Arsenault, *The Wild Ass of the Ozarks: Jeff Davis and the Social Bases of Southern Politics* (Philadelphia, 1984). For two other recent studies see Cal Ledbetter, Jr., "Jeff Davis and the Politics of Combat," *Arkansas Historical Quarterly*, XXXIII (Spring 1974): 16–37; and Richard L. Niswonger, "A Study in Southern Demagoguery: Jeff Davis of Arkansas," *Arkansas Historical Quarterly*, XXXIX (Summer 1980): 114–24.

7. Arsenault, *The Wild Ass of the Ozarks*, 205–7.

8. Ibid., 97–109, 217–18.

9. Ibid., 214–15.

10. Woodward, *The Strange Career of Jim Crow*, 69–74; Rayford W. Logan, *The Negro in American Life and Thought: The Nadir, 1877–1901* (New York, 1954), 271–73; Fredrickson, *The Black Image in the White Mind*, 305–11; I. A. Newby, *Jim Crow's Defense: Anti-Negro Thought in America, 1900–1930* (Baton Rouge, 1965), 15–16; Claude H. Nolen, *The Negro's Image in the South: The Anatomy of White Supremacy* (Lexington, Kentucky, 1968), 91–92.

11. *Arkansas Gazette*, November 21, 1900.

12. Gibbs, *Shadow and Light*, 283.

13. *Acts of Arkansas* (1903), 160–62.

14. *Arkansas House of Representatives Journal* (1903), 237–38; *Arkansas Gazette*, February 22, 1903.

15. *Arkansas Senate Journal* (1903), 162; *Arkansas Gazette*, March 4, 1903. At the last minute Senator Rison changed to vote for adoption in order later to be able to move for reconsideration. He dropped the idea for lack of support. See *Arkansas Senate Journal* (1903), 195.

16. *Arkansas Gazette*, March 4, 1903.

17. Ibid.

18. Ibid.

19. Ibid., March 7, 1903. It should be noted, though, that at least as late as 1889 the county jail apparently had integrated facilities. See ibid., January 13, 1889.

20. Ibid., April 5, 1903.

21. *Acts of Arkansas* (1903), 178–80.

22. *Arkansas House of Representatives Journal* (1891), 286. For instance, Representative A. G. Gray of Independence County had introduced an unsuccessful streetcar-segregation bill in 1901. See *Arkansas Gazette*, March 6, 1901.

23. *Arkansas House of Representatives Journal* (1903), 69, 106, 186.

24. See Graves, "Negro Disfranchisement in Arkansas," 199–225, and "A Question of Honor," 9–26.

25. *Arkansas House of Representatives Journal* (1903), 226; *Arkansas Gazette*, February 20, 1903.

26. *Arkansas Senate Journal* (1903), 314; *Arkansas Gazette*, March 7, 1903.

27. *Arkansas Gazette*, March 7, 1903.

28. Ibid.

29. Ibid.

30. *Arkansas Senate Journal* (1903), 314; *Arkansas Gazette*, March 7, 1903.

31. *Arkansas Gazette*, March 7, 1903.

32. *Arkansas Gazette*, December 12, 1902; January 8, 25, April 4, 18, 1903.

33. Ibid., April 5, 1903. Hemingway was the brother of William L. Hemingway, the Democratic treasurer of Mississippi who was sentenced to five years in the penitentiary for embezzlement of state funds. Jackson, Mississippi, *Clarion-Ledger*, February 27, March 20, July 3, December 4, 1890; Woodward, *Origins of the New South, 1877–1913*, 70; interview with Linn Hemingway Bealke, great-nephew of Justice Hemingway, Fayetteville, Arkansas, March 15, 1964.

34. *Arkansas Gazette*, March 7, 1903.

35. Ibid., April 5, 1903.

36. Ibid., March 12, 1903. For biographical sketches of these men, see Gaines, *Racial Possibilities as Indicated by the Negroes of Arkansas*, 78–80, 92, 94, 149. Also, see W. A. J. Phillips, *The Autobiography of W. A. J. Phillips* (Little Rock, 1916).

37. August Meier and Elliott Rudwick, "The Boycott Movement Against Jim Crow Streetcars in the South, 1900–1906," *Journal of American History*, LV (March 1969): 756–75.

38. Washington was the author of an introduction to Mifflin W. Gibbs' autobiography, and he assisted John E. Bush in the latter's successful effort to be reappointed Receiver of the U.S. Land Office at Little Rock. See Gibbs, *Shadow and Light*, v–viii; letter of John E. Bush, Little Rock, Arkansas, January 27, 1906, to Emmett J. Scott, Tuskegee, Alabama; letter of John E. Bush, Little Rock, Arkansas, April 2, 1906, to Booker T. Washington, Tuskegee, Alabama. Booker T. Washington Papers, Library of Congress, Washington, D.C.

39. *Arkansas Democrat*, June 2, 9, 1903; *Arkansas Gazette*, May 28, June 19, 1903; Pine Bluff [Daily] *Graphic*, May 28, 1903; Pine Bluff *Weekly Graphic*, June 27, 1903; *The Freeman* (Indianapolis, Indiana), June 13, 1903.

40. *Arkansas Gazette*, May 28, 1903.

41. Ibid.

42. *Arkansas Democrat*, June 2, 9, 1903; *Arkansas Gazette*, May 28, June 19, 1903; Pine Bluff *Weekly Graphic*, June 27, 1903; *The Freeman* (Indianapolis, Indiana), June 13, 1903.

43. *Arkansas Democrat*, June 2, 5, 1903; *The Freeman* (Indianapolis, Indiana), June 13, 1903.

44. *The Voice of the Twentieth Century*, (n.d.), in the Fort Smith *News Record*, June 22, 1903.

45. *Arkansas Gazette*, May 29, 1903.

46. Ibid., May 28, 1903. Those few blacks riding the streetcars reportedly were either federal letter carriers or women.

47. Ibid.

48. Ibid.

49. Ibid.

50. Ibid.

51. Ibid.

52. *Arkansas Democrat*, May 29, 1903.

53. *Arkansas Gazette*, May 28, 1903; *Acts of Arkansas* (1903), 178–80.

## CONCLUSION

Portions of this chapter are taken from John William Graves, "Jim Crow in Arkansas: A Reconsideration of Urban Race Relations in the Post-Reconstruction South," *Journal of Southern History* LV (August 1989): 422, 445–48.

1. Woodward, *The Strange Career of Jim Crow*, 16, 44. The statement was made principally in regard to Richard C. Wade's *Slavery in the Cities: The South, 1820–1860* (New York, 1964). Focusing on selected antebellum southern cities, Wade observed that slavery there had crumbled under pressures of urban life. Alarmed masters responded with demands for new legal restrictions on slave activities and segregation ordinances that compelled separation of the races. Although Wade did not advance or pursue the idea, some of his evidence suggests that antebellum urban segregation came about in part because of pressures from rural planters. Ibid., 126–27. On urban white resistance to restrictive measures, especially from town merchants, see ibid., 253–55. For a general discussion of social tensions between planters and the urban bourgeoisie in one antebellum city, Charleston, South Carolina, see William W. Freehling, *Prelude to Civil War: The Nullification Controversy in South Carolina, 1816–1836* (New York, 1965), 13, 23–24, 86, 177–79, 254.

2. Williamson, *The Crucible of Race*, passim.

3. Howard N. Rabinowitz, *Race Relations in the Urban South, 1865–1890* (New York, 1978), 329–39.

4. Ibid., 332, 336.

5. Woodward, *The Strange Career of Jim Crow*, 41.

6. Redkey, *Black Exodus*, 107–26.

7. Graves, "The Arkansas Separate Coach Law of 1891," 531–32; and Kousser, "A Black Protest in the 'Era of Accommodation'," 151–52.

8. Blassingame, *Black New Orleans, 1860–1880*, 173–217; Dale A. Somers, "Black and White in New Orleans: A Study in Urban Race Relations, 1865–1900," *Journal of Southern History* XL (February 1974): 19–42.

9. At least one notable white Arkansan during this era openly expressed views approximating those of Cable and Blair. The Right Reverend J. M. Lucey, a Catholic priest at Pine Bluff and a Confederate veteran, courageously denounced efforts to adopt a separate coach law in 1890–1891 and appealed for fair and equal treatment for blacks. Monsignor Lucey also served as secretary of the Board of Trustees of the Colored Industrial Institute, the Catholic vocational school for blacks founded at Pine Bluff in 1889. In later years he was an unusually outspoken foe of lynching. *Arkansas Democrat*, January 24, 1890; *Arkansas Gazette*, February 2, 1890; August 27, October 12, 1899; September 4, 5, 1901. See also Lucey, "The Catholic Church in Arkansas," 448–49. On liberalism elsewhere in the post-Reconstruction South see Williamson, *Crucible of Race*, 85–107.

10. Woodward, *The Strange Career of Jim Crow*, 47.

# Bibliography

## PRIMARY SOURCES

### Manuscripts

Bliss, Calvin C., MSS. Arkansas History Commission, Little Rock, Arkansas.

Brayman, Mason, Collection, MSS. Library of the Chicago Historical Society, Chicago, Illinois.

Clayton, Powell, Letterbook, MSS. Arkansas History Commission, Little Rock, Arkansas.

Flanagin, Harris, MSS. Arkansas History Commission, Little Rock, Arkansas.

Gulley, Luther C., Collection of State Papers, MSS. Arkansas History Commission, Little Rock, Arkansas.

Hadley, Ozra A., Letterbook, MSS. Arkansas History Commission, Little Rock, Arkansas.

Hubbard, Family, MSS. Library of the Chicago Historical Society, Chicago, Illinois.

Remmel, Harmon, MSS. University of Arkansas Library, Fayetteville, Arkansas.

Stebbins, A. Howard, Jr., Collection, MSS. Arkansas History Commission, Little Rock, Arkansas.

Walker, David, MSS. University of Arkansas Library, Fayetteville, Arkansas.

Washington, Booker T., MSS. Library of Congress, Washington, D.C.

### Newspapers

Arkadelphia *Southern Standard*, Nov. 11, 1869; Jan. 30, Feb. 6, 20, 27, Mar. 6, Apr. 17, 1891; July 8, 1892; Feb. 6, Apr. 3, 1902.

Arkansas City *Journal*, Aug. 15, 1883.
Boston, Mass. *Daily Globe*, Dec. 6, 1886.
Chicago, Ill. *The Broad-Ax*, Nov. 29, Dec. 27, 1902; Mar. 30, Oct. 20, 1906.
Chicago, Ill. *Tribune*, Dec. 19, 25, 1888; Jan. 5, 12, 1889.
Clarksville *Herald*, Aug. 12, 1878.
Des Arc *Citizen*, May 26, July 14, Aug. 14, 1866.
Fayetteville *Arkansas Sentinel*, Mar. 10, 1891.
Fayetteville *Democrat*, July 12, 19, 26, 1873; Apr. 25, May 2, 1874; Jan. 30, 1891.
Forrest City *Times*, June 16, 1888.
Fort Smith *Elevator*, July 18, 1890; Oct. 14, 1892.
Fort Smith *Herald*, July 13, Nov. 18, 1867.
Fort Smith *News Record*, June 22, 1903.
Indianapolis, Ind. *The Freeman*, Jan. 17, 31, Feb. 21, Apr. 4, 1891; Apr. 18, May 23, June 13, 1903.
Jackson, Miss. *Clarion-Ledger*, Feb. 27, Mar. 20, July 3, Dec. 4, 1890.
Little Rock *Arkansas Democrat*, Mar. 27, 1879; Dec. 2, 1880; Aug. 27, Sept. 18, 1888; Mar. 27, 1889; Jan. 18, 24, Aug. 8, 15, 19, 1890; Feb. 28, Apr. 1, Aug. 19, 1891; Feb. 23, 1898; May 29, June 2, 5, 9, 1903.
Little Rock *Arkansas Freeman*, Oct. 5, 1869.
Little Rock *Arkansas Gazette*, Jan. 1, 1865–Dec. 31, 1905.
Little Rock *Daily Republican*, Aug. 19, 1870; Mar. 15, 1871; Apr. 10, 1873; July 3, 15, 22, 1874; Mar. 5, 1875.
Little Rock *Unconditional Union*, July 27, 1865.
Little Rock *Weekly Republican*, Jan. 9, 1872.
Little Rock *Wheel-Enterprise and Stockman*, Feb. 23, 1889.
Memphis, Tenn. *Appeal*, Sept. 10, 1868.
Morrilton *Pilot*, Jan. 9, 1891; July 1, 1892.
Nashville *News*, Jan. 24, Mar. 7, 1891.
Pine Bluff *Commercial*, Dec. 29, 30, 1890; Sept. 4, 7, 1894.
Pine Bluff *Dispatch*, May 4, Nov. 23, 1867.
Pine Bluff [Daily] *Graphic*, Apr. 29, 1892; May 28, 1903.
Pine Bluff *Weekly Graphic*, June 27, 1903.
Pine Bluff *Press-Eagle*, July 24, 1888; Feb. 12, 1889; Jan. 20, Feb. 3, Mar. 3, 1891; Sept. 6, 1892; Oct. 12, Nov. 2, 9, 1897; Jan. 25, 1910.
*St. Louis*, Mo. *Post-Dispatch*, Sept. 6–9, 15, 1888.
Van Buren *Argus*, Oct. 15, 1902.
Van Buren *Press*, Feb. 17, June 23, 1866; Aug. 7, 1868; Sept. 5, 1891.
Washington *South-Western Press*, July 18, 1880.
Washington *Telegraph*, Aug. 9, 30, Oct. 4, 1865.
Yellville *Mountain Echo*, Feb. 27, 1891.

## Official Records: Public Documents

Arkansas. Board of Deaf Mute Institute. *Biennial Report of the Board of Directors and Officers of the Arkansas Deaf Mute Institute*, 1887/88.

Arkansas. Board of Institute for the Education of the Blind. *Biennial Report of the Trustees and Superintendent of the Arkansas Institute for the Education of the Blind*, 1868/70.

Arkansas. Board of School for the Education of the Blind. *Biennial Report of the Trustees and Superintendent of the Arkansas School for the Blind*, 1886/88.

Arkansas. Board of State Lunatic Asylum. *Annual Report of the Board of Trustees and Superintendent of the State Lunatic Asylum*, 1888.

Arkansas. Board of State Penitentiary. *Biennial Report of State Penitentiary*, 1903/04.

Arkansas. Cities of Fort Smith and Van Buren. *City Directory*, 1900.

Arkansas. City of Helena. *City Directory*, 1908.

Arkansas. City of Little Rock. *Annual Report of the Public Schools of Little Rock*, 1877, 1880, 1890, 1896.

Arkansas. City of Little Rock. *City Directory*. 1881/82, 1900/01.

Arkansas. City of Little Rock, "Minute Books of the Little Rock City Council" (1871–1893).

Arkansas. City of Pine Bluff. *City Directory*, 1911.

Arkansas. City of Texarkana. *City Directory*, 1908.

Arkansas. *Constitution* (1836, 1864, 1868, 1874).

Arkansas. Constitutional Convention, 1864. *Journal of the Convention of the People of Arkansas*. Assembled at the Capitol, January 4, 1864. Little Rock: Price and Barton, 1870.

Arkansas. Constitutional Convention, 1868. *Debates and Proceedings of the Convention Which Assembled at Little Rock*, January 7th, 1868. Little Rock: J. G. Price, 1868.

Arkansas. Constitutional Convention, 1874. "Proceedings of the Constitutional Convention of the People of the State of Arkansas, Convened at the Capitol, July 14, 1874." 2 vols. (handwritten manuscript). Film 24, Reel 21, University of Arkansas Library, Fayetteville, Arkansas.

Arkansas. *Digest of the Statutes of Arkansas* (Mansfield), 1884.

Arkansas. General Assembly, *Acts and Resolutions* (1866–67, 1868, 1873, 1874, 1874–75, 1875, 1879, 1881, 1883, 1885, 1889, 1891, 1893, 1895, 1899, 1903, 1907).

Arkansas. General Assembly. House of Representatives. *Journal* (1866–67, 1891, 1897, 1901, 1903, 1905).

Arkansas. General Assembly. Senate. *Journal* (1866–67, 1891, 1903).

Arkansas. Office of the Auditor of State. *Biennial Report of the Auditor of State*, 1897/98, 1907/08.

Arkansas. Office of the Secretary of State. *Biennial Report of the Secretary of State*, 1879/80, 1881/82, 1887/88, 1889/90, 1891/92, 1893/94, 1895/96, 1897/98, 1899/1900, 1905/06, 1907/08, 1909/12.

Arkansas. Office of the Secretary of State. *Historical Report of the Secretary of State*, 1968, 1978, 1986.

Arkansas. Office of the Superintendent of Public Instruction. *Biennial Report of the Superintendent of Public Instruction*, 1891/92.

Arkansas. *Revised Statutes* (Ball and Roane), 1837.

Arkansas. Secession Convention, 1861. *Journal of Both Sessions of the Convention of the State of Arkansas, Which Were Begun and Held in the Capitol, in the City of Little Rock*. Little Rock: Johnson and Yerkes, 1861.

U.S. Bureau of the Census. *Eighth Census of the United States, 1860*. Through *Twelfth Census of the United States, 1900*. Washington, D.C.: Government Printing Office, 1864–1906.

U.S. Bureau of the Census. *Negro Population, 1790–1915*. Washington, D.C.: Government Printing Office, 1918.

U.S. Bureau of Education. *History of Public School Education in Arkansas*, by Stephen B. Weeks, U.S. Bureau of Education *Bulletin* (Nov. 27, 1912). Washington, D.C.: Government Printing Office, 1912.

U.S. Congress. *Congressional Record*. 51st Cong., 1st sess. (1890).

U.S. Congress. *Congressional Record*. 51st Cong., 2d sess. (1891).

U.S. Congress. *Congressional Record*. 55th Cong., 2d sess. (1898).

U.S. Congress. House of Representatives. 51st Cong., 2d sess. (1891). *Miscellaneous Document*, No. 137, *Digest of Contested Election Cases*, compiled by Chester H. Rowell. Washington, D.C.: Government Printing Office, 1891.

U.S. *Constitution*.

U.S. *Extracts from Reports of Superintendents of Freedmen, Compiled by the Reverend Joseph Warren, from Records in the Office of Colonel John Eaton, Jr., Department of the Tennessee and State of Arkansas. Two Series, June, 1864*. Washington, D.C.: Government Printing Office, 1864.

U.S. *General Report of the Superintendent of Freedmen, Department of the Tennessee and State of Arkansas*. Washington, D.C.: Government Printing Office, 1865.

U.S. *Report of the Superintendent of Freedmen, Department of the Tennessee and State of Arkansas, December 31, 1864*. Washington, D.C.: Government Printing Office, 1865.

U.S. *War of the Rebellion. A Compilation of the Official Records of the Union and Confederate Armies*. Washington, D.C.: Government Printing Office, 1880–1901.

## Official Records: Legal Decisions

*Brooks v. Page.* 29 Ark. 199 (1874).
*Dodson v. State,* 61 Ark. 57 (1895).
*Dunn v. Lott.* 67 Ark. 591. (1899).
*Knight v. Shelton,* 134 Feb. 423 (1905).
*Rice v. Palmer,* 78 Ark. 432 (1906).
*Rison et al. v. Farr.* 24 Ark. 161 (1865).
*State v. Little Rock, Mississippi River, and Texas Railway Company.* 31 Ark. 701 (1877).

## Personal Interviews

Bealke, Linn Hemingway. Fayetteville, Arkansas. Interview, March 15, 1964.
Booker, James. Little Rock, Arkansas. Interview, August 19, 1967.
Bush, Clota. Little Rock, Arkansas. Interview, July 23, 1967.
Gillam, Dorothy. Little Rock, Arkansas. Interview, July 29, 1967.
Lewis, Henry Calvin. Little Rock, Arkansas. The author's remembrances of childhood conversations.
Rogers, O. A., Jr. Little Rock, Arkansas. Interview, July 24, 1967.

## Reminiscences, Memoirs

Carrigan, Alfred Holt. "Reminiscences of the Secession Convention," *Publications of the Arkansas Historical Association* I (1906): 305–13.
Chester, Samuel H. *Pioneer Days in Arkansas.* Richmond, Va.: Presbyterian Committee of Publication, 1927.
Clayton, Powell. *The Aftermath of the Civil War in Arkansas.* New York: Neale Publishing Co., 1915.
Cypert, Jesse N. "Secession Convention," *Publications of the Arkansas Historical Association* I (1906): 314–23.
Dunaway, Louis Sharp, ed. *Jeff Davis, Governor and Senator: His Life and Speeches, with Personal Reminiscences.* Little Rock: Democrat Printing and Lithographing Co., 1913.
Eaton, John. *Grant, Lincoln, and the Freedmen: Reminiscences of the Civil War, with Special Reference to the Work for the Contrabands and Freedmen of the Mississippi Valley.* New York: Longmans, Green and Co., 1907.
Gibbs, Mifflin Wistar. *Shadow and Light: An Autobiography, with Reminiscences of the Past and Present Century, with an Introduction by Booker T. Washington.* Washington, D.C.: Published by the author, 1902.

House, Joseph W. "The Constitutional Convention of 1874—Reminiscences." *Publications of the Arkansas Historical Association* IV (1917): 210–68.

Jacobson, Charles. *The Life Story of Jeff Davis: The Stormy Petrel of Arkansas Politics*. Little Rock: Parke-Harper Publishing Co., 1925.

Miller, Reverend A. H. *How I Succeeded in My Business*, 1911.

Morris, E. C. *Sermons, Addresses, and Reminiscences*. National Baptist Publishing Board, 1901.

Phillips, W. A. J. *The Autobiography of W. A. J. Phillips*. Little Rock: Published by the author, 1916.

Pickens, William. *Bursting Bonds*. Boston: Jordan and More Press, 1923. Enlarged edition of *The Heir of Slaves*, 1911.

Pope, William F. *Early Days in Arkansas, Being for the Most Part the Personal Recollections of an Old Settler*. Little Rock: Frederick Allsopp, 1895.

Rawick, George P., ed. *The American Slave: A Composite Autobiography*. Vols. 8–11. *Arkansas Narratives*. Westport, Conn.: Greenwood Publishing Co., 1972.

Rose, Margaret T. "Clayton's Aftermath of the Civil War in Arkansas," *Publications of the Arkansas Historical Association* IV (1917): 57–65.

Rudd, Daniel A., and Theophilus Bond. *From Slavery to Wealth: The Life of Scott Bond; The Rewards of Honesty, Industry, Economy, and Perseverance: with Preface by Hon. J. C. Napier*. Madison, Ark.: Journal Printing Co., 1917.

Sarna, Jan, ed. "Marche, Arkansas: A Personal Reminiscence of Life and Customs," *Arkansas Historical Quarterly* XXXVI (Spring 1977): 31–49.

Still, William Grant. "My Arkansas Boyhood," *Arkansas Historical Quarterly* XXVI (Autumn 1967): 285–92.

Warde, James Cooke. *Jimmy Warde's Experiences as a Lunatic*. Little Rock: Tunnah and Pittard, 1902.

Williams, Harry Lee. *Forty Years Behind the Scenes in Arkansas Politics*. Little Rock: Parkin Printing and Stationery Co., 1949.


**Travel Accounts**

*A History of the North-Western Editorial Excursion to Arkansas*. Little Rock: T. B. Mills and Co., 1876.

King, Edward. "The Great South: Down the Mississippi—the Labor Question—Arkansas," *Scribner's Monthly* VIII (October 1874): 641–69.

Nordhoff, Charles. *The Cotton States in the Spring and Summer of 1875*. New York: D. Appleton and Co., 1876.

Warner, Charles Dudley. "Studies of the Great West: Memphis and Little Rock," *Harper's New Monthly Magazine* LXXVI (September 1888): 551–60.


## Miscellaneous Sources

*Appleton's Annual Cyclopaedia and Register of Important Events.* 42 vols. New York: D. Appleton and Co., 1862–1903.

*Biographical and Historical Memoirs of Pulaski, Jefferson, Lonoke, Faulkner, Grant, Saline, Perry, Garland, and Hot Spring Counties, Arkansas.* Chicago: Goodspeed Publishing Co., 1889.

Bishop, Albert W. *Loyalty on the Frontier, or, Sketches of Union Men of the South-West, with Incidences and Adventures in Rebellion on the Border.* St. Louis: R. P. Studley and Co., 1863.

Blair, Lewis Harvie. *The Prosperity of the South Dependent upon the Elevation of the Negro.* Richmond, Va.: Everett Waddey, 1889.

Breckinridge, Clifton R. "Is Lynching Advisable?" in *Race Problems of the South: Report of the First Annual Conference . . . of the Southern Society for the Promotion of the Study of Race Conditions and Problems in the South at Montgomery, Alabama.* Richmond, Va.: 1900.

Brown, William Montgomery. *The Crucial Race Question, or, Where and How Shall the Color Line Be Drawn.* Little Rock: Arkansas Churchman's Publishing Co., 1907.

Bush, A. E., and P. E. Dorman. *History of the Mosaic Templars of America—Its Founders and Officials.* Little Rock: Central Printing Co., 1924.

Bush, John E. "Afro-American People of Little Rock," *Colored American Magazine* VIII (January 1905): 39–42.

Cable, George W. *The Silent South.* New York: Charles Scribner's Sons, 1885.

Carnahan, Wallace. "Safety Without Rascality," *Anglo–Saxon Churchman* XII (January 1891), reprinted in the *Congressional Record*, 51st Cong., 2d sess. (January 16, 1891): 1399.

Craighead, James B. "The Future of the Negro in the South," *Popular Science Monthly* XXVI (November 1884): 39–46.

Gaines, D. B. *Racial Possibilities as Indicated by the Negroes of Arkansas.* Little Rock: Philander Smith College Printing Department, 1898.

Haley, James T. *Afro-American Encyclopedia.* Nashville, Tenn.: Haley and Florida, 1895.

Hartshorn, W. N., ed. *An Era of Progress and Promise, 1863–1910: The Religious, Moral, and Educational Development of the American Negro since His Emancipation.* Boston: Priscilla Publishing Co., 1910.

Jordan, Lewis G. *Negro Baptist History, U.S.A., 1750–1930.* Nashville:

Sunday School Publishing Board, National Baptist Convention, 1930.

Lemke, W. J., ed. *Appendix to the Walker Family Letters*. Fayetteville: Washington County Historical Society, 1956.

Lemke, W. J., ed. *The Life and Letters of Judge David Walker of Fayetteville*. Fayetteville: Washington County Historical Society, 1957.

Morgan, W. Scott. *History of the Wheel and Alliance and the Impending Revolution*. Fort Scott, Kan.: J. H. Rice and Sons, 1889.

———. *The Red Light: A Story of Southern Politics and Election Methods*. Moravian Falls, N.C.: Yellow Jacket Press, 1904.

Nash, Charles E. *The Status of the Negro, from a Negro's Standpoint in His Own Dialect—A Country Negro Visits the City and Takes in the Surroundings—His Conversation after His Return*. Little Rock: Tunnah and Pittard, 1900.

Payne, Daniel Alexander. *History of the African Methodist Episcopal Church*. Nashville: Publishing House of the A.M.E. Sunday School Union, 1891.

Penn, I. Garland. *The Afro-American Press and Its Editors*. Springfield, Mass.; Willey and Co., 1891.

Phillips, Charles Henry. *History of the Colored Methodist Episcopal Church in America, Comprising Its Organization, Subsequent Development, and Present Status*. Jackson, Tenn.: C.M.E. Publishing House, 1898.

Pomeroy, James M., ed. *The Constitution of the State of Arkansas . . . 1874 . . . ; A Documentary History . . . and a Digest*. Little Rock: P. A. Ladue, 1876.

*Proceedings of the Convention of Colored Citizens of the State of Arkansas, Held in Little Rock, Thursday, Friday, and Saturday, Nov. 30, Dec. 1 and 2* (1865). Helena, Ark.: Clarion Office Printing, 1866.

Riley, Jerome R. *The Philosophy of Negro Suffrage*. Hartford: American Publishing Co., 1895.

Simmons, William. *Men of Mark: Eminent, Progressive, and Rising*. Cleveland: G. M. Rewell, 1887.

Woods, E. M. *Blue Book of Little Rock and Argenta, Arkansas*. Little Rock: Central Printing Co., 1907.

Wright, Richard Robert, Jr. *Centennial Encyclopedia of the African Methodist Episcopal Church*. Philadelphia: A.M.E. Church Book Concern, 1916.

Yenser, Thomas, ed. *Who's Who in Colored America, 1938–1940*. New York: Who's Who in Colored America Corporation, 1940.

# SECONDARY SOURCES

## Books

Arsenault, Raymond. *The Wild Ass of the Ozarks: Jeff Davis and the Social Bases of Southern Politics.* Philadelphia: Temple University Press, 1984.

Baskett, Tom, Jr., ed. *Persistence of the Spirit: The Black Experience in Arkansas.* Little Rock: Arkansas Endowment for the Humanities/ Target Printing, 1986.

Berwanger, Eugene H. *The Frontier against Slavery: Western Anti-Negro Prejudice and the Slavery Extension Controversy.* Urbana: University of Illinois Press, 1967.

Blassingame, John W. *The Slave Community: Plantation Life in the Antebellum South.* New York: Oxford University Press, 1972.

———. *Black New Orleans, 1860–1880.* Chicago: University of Chicago Press, 1976.

Boles, John B., ed. *Masters and Slaves in the House of the Lord: Race and Religion in the American South, 1740–1870.* Lexington: University of Kentucky Press, 1988.

Branfon, Robert L. *Cotton Kingdom of the New South: A History of the Yazoo-Mississippi Delta from Reconstruction to the Twentieth Century.* Cambridge: Harvard University Press, 1967.

Brownell, Blaine A., and David R. Goldfield, eds. *The City in Southern History: The Growth of Urban Civilization in the South.* Port Washington, N.Y.: Associated Faculty Press, 1976.

Buck, Solon J. *The Agrarian Crusade: A Chronicle of the Farmer in Politics.* New Haven: Yale University Press, 1920.

Callcott, Margaret Law. *The Negro in Maryland Politics, 1870–1912.* Baltimore: Johns Hopkins Press, 1969.

Carter, Dan T. *Scottsboro: A Tragedy of the American South.* Baton Rouge: Louisiana State University Press, 1969.

Cell, John Whitson. *The Highest Stage of White Supremacy: The Origins of Segregation in South Africa and the American South.* Cambridge, U.K.: Cambridge University Press, 1982.

Commons, John R. *History of Labor in the United States.* 2 vols. New York: MacMillan, 1921.

Cutler, James Elbert. *Lynch-Law: An Investigation into the History of Lynching in the United States.* New York: Longmans, Green and Co., 1905.

Daniel, Pete. *The Shadow of Slavery: Peonage in the South 1901–1969.* New York: Oxford University Press, 1973.

DeCanio, Stephen. *Agriculture in the Postbellum South: The Economics of Production and Supply.* Cambridge, Mass.: MIT Press, 1974.

Degler, Carl N. *Neither Black Nor White: Slavery and Race Relations in Brazil and the United States*. New York: MacMillan, 1971.

Dittmer, John. *Black Atlanta in the Progressive Era, 1900–1920*. Urbana: University of Illinois Press, 1977.

Donovan, Timothy P., and Willard B. Gatewood, Jr., eds. *The Governors of Arkansas: Essays in Political Biography*. Fayetteville: University of Arkansas Press, 1981.

Dougan, Michael B. *Confederate Arkansas: The People and Policies of a Frontier State in Wartime*. University, Alabama: University of Alabama Press, 1976.

Durden, Robert F. *The Climax of Populism: The Election of 1896*. Lexington: University of Kentucky Press, 1965.

Ferguson, John L., and J. H. Atkinson. *Historic Arkansas*. Little Rock: Arkansas History Commission, 1966.

Fischer, Roger A. *The Segregation Struggle in Louisiana, 1862–1877*. Urbana: University of Illinois Press, 1974.

Fletcher, John Gould. *Arkansas*. Chapel Hill: University of North Carolina Press, 1947.

Fredrickson, George M. *The Black Image in the White Mind: The Debate on Afro-American Character and Destiny, 1817–1914*. New York: Harper and Row, 1971.

————. *White Supremacy: A Comparative Study of American and South African History*. New York: Oxford University Press, 1981.

Freehling, William W. *Prelude to Civil War, the Nullification Controversy in South Carolina, 1816–1836*. New York: Harper and Row, 1965.

Gaither, Gerald H. *Blacks and the Populist Revolt: Ballots and Bigotry in the "New South"*. University, Alabama: University of Alabama Press, 1977.

Gaston, Paul M. *The New South Creed: A Study in Southern Mythmaking*. New York: Alfred A. Knopf, 1970.

Goldfield, David R. *Cotton Fields and Skyscrapers: Southern City and Region, 1607–1980*. Baton Rouge: Louisiana State University Press, 1982.

Goodwyn, Lawrence C. *Democratic Promise: The Populist Moment in America*. New York: Oxford University Press, 1976.

Graham, Leroy. *Baltimore: The Nineteenth-Century Black Capital*. Lanham, My.: University Press of America, 1982.

Gutman, Herbert G. *The Black Family in Slavery and Freedom, 1750–1925*. New York: Pantheon Books, 1976.

Hallum, John. *Biographical and Pictorial History of Arkansas*. 2 vols. Albany, N.Y.: Weed, Parsons, and Co., 1887.

Harrell, John M. *The Brooks-Baxter War: A History of the Reconstruction Period in Arkansas*. St. Louis: Slawson Printing Co., 1893.

Hempstead, Fay. *A Pictorial History of Arkansas*. St. Louis and New York: N. D. Thompson Publishing Co., 1890.

————. *The Historical Review of Arkansas: Its Commerce, Industry, and Modern Affairs*. 2 vols. Chicago: Lewis Publishing Co., 1911.

Herndon, Dallas T., ed. *Centennial History of Arkansas*. 3 vols. Chicago: S. J. Clarke Publishing Co., 1922.

————, ed. *The Highlights of Arkansas History*. Little Rock: Arkansas Democrat Co., 1922.

————, ed. *Outline of Executive and Legislative History of Arkansas*. Fort Smith: Calvert-McBride Printing Co., 1922.

————, ed. *Annals of Arkansas*. 4 vols. Hopkinsville, Ky.: Historical Record Association, 1947.

Higgs, Robert. *The Transformation of the American Economy, 1865–1914*. New York: John Wiley and Sons, 1971.

————. *Competition and Coercion: Blacks in the American Economy, 1865–1914*. Cambridge, U.K.: Cambridge University Press, 1977.

Kousser, J. Morgan. *The Shaping of Southern Politics: Suffrage Restriction and the Establishment of the One-Party South, 1880–1910*. New Haven: Yale University Press, 1974.

————. *Dead End: The Development of Nineteenth Century Litigation on Racial Discrimination in Schools*. New York: Oxford University Press, 1986.

Kousser, J. Morgan, and James M. McPherson, eds. *Race and Reconstruction: Essays in Honor of C. Vann Woodward*. New York: Oxford University Press, 1982.

Larsen, Lawrence Harold. *The Rise of the Urban South*. Lexington: University of Kentucky Press, 1985.

Leslie, James W. *Saracen's Country: Some Southeast Arkansas History*. Little Rock: Rose Publishing Co., 1974.

————. *Land of Cypress and Pine: More Southeast Arkansas History*. Little Rock: Rose Publishing Co., 1976.

————. *Pine Bluff and Jefferson County: A Pictorial History*. Norfolk, Va.: The Donning Company/Publishers, 1981.

Lile, John Gardner. *The Government of Arkansas*. Columbus, Ohio: Champlin Press, 1916.

Litwack, Leon. *North of Slavery: The Negro in the Free States, 1790–1860*. Chicago: University of Chicago Press, 1961.

Lofgren, Charles A. *The Plessy Case: A Legal-Historical Interpretation*. New York: Oxford University Press, 1987.

Logan, Frenise A. *The Negro in North Carolina, 1876–1894*. Chapel Hill: University of North Carolina Press, 1964.

Logan, Rayford W. *The Negro in American Life and Thought: The Nadir, 1877–1901*. New York: Dial Press, 1954.

McKitrick, Eric L. *Andrew Johnson and Reconstruction.* Chicago: University of Chicago Press, 1960.

McMath, Robert C. *Populist Vanguard: A History of the Southern Farmers' Alliance.* Chapel Hill: University of North Carolina Press, 1975.

McNutt, Walter Scott, Oli Eli McKnight, and George Allen Hubbard. *A History of Arkansas.* Little Rock: Democrat Printing and Lithographing Co., 1932.

Mandle, Jay R. *The Roots of Black Poverty: The Southern Plantation Economy after the Civil War.* Durham, N.C.: Duke University Press, 1978.

Meier, August, and Elliott Rudwick, eds. *The Making of Black America: Essays in Negro Life and History.* 2 vols. New York: Atheneum, 1971.

Monks, William. *A History of Southern Missouri and Northern Arkansas.* West Plains, Mo.: West Plains Journal Co., 1907.

Moore, John H. *A School History of Arkansas.* Little Rock: Democrat Printing and Lithographing Co., 1924.

Moore, Waddy W., ed. *Arkansas in the Gilded Age, 1874–1900.* Little Rock: Rose Publishing Co., 1976.

Newberry, Farrar. *A Life of Mr. Garland of Arkansas.* N.p.: Published by the author, 1908.

———. *James K. Jones, the Plumed Knight of Arkansas.* Arkadelphia, Ark: Siftings-Herald Printing Co., 1913.

Newby, I. A. *Jim Crow's Defense: Anti-Negro Thought in America, 1900–1930.* Baton Rouge: Louisiana State University Press, 1965.

Nolen, Claude H. *The Negro's Image in the South: The Anatomy of White Supremacy.* Lexington: University of Kentucky Press, 1968.

Palmer, Bruce. *Man over Money: The Southern Populist Critique of American Capitalism.* Chapel Hill: University of North Carolina Press, 1980.

Perdue, Robert E. *The Negro in Savannah, 1865–1900.* New York: Exposition Press, 1973.

Rabinowitz, Howard N. *Race Relations in the Urban South, 1865–1890.* New York: Oxford University Press, 1978.

Ransom, Roger L., and Richard Sutch. *One Kind of Freedom: The Economic Consequences of Emancipation.* Cambridge, U.K.: Cambridge University Press, 1977.

Raper, Arthur. *The Tragedy of Lynching.* Chapel Hill: University of North Carolina Press, 1933.

Redkey, Edwin S. *Black Exodus: Black Nationalist and Back-to-Africa Movements, 1890–1910.* New Haven: Yale University Press, 1969.

Reynolds, John Hugh. *Makers of Arkansas History.* New York: Silver, Burdett and Co., 1905.

Reynolds, John Hugh, and David Y. Thomas. *History of the University of Arkansas.* Fayetteville, Ark.: University of Arkansas, 1910.

310

Richards, Ira Don. *Story of a Rivertown: Little Rock in the Nineteenth Century*. N.p.: Published by the author, 1969.

Saloutos, Theodore. *Farmer Movements in the South, 1865–1933*. Berkeley: University of California Press, 1960.

Schafer, William J., and Johannes Riedel. *The Art of Ragtime: Form and Meaning of an Original Black American Art*. Baton Rouge: Louisiana State University Press, 1973.

Schwartz, Michael. *Radical Protest and Social Structure: The Southern Farmers Alliance and Cotton Tenancy, 1880–1890*. New York: Academic Press, 1976.

Shinn, Josiah H. *The History of Arkansas*. Richmond, Va.: B. J. Johnson Publishing Co., 1900.

———. *Pioneers and Makers of Arkansas*. Little Rock: Genealogical and Historical Publishing Co., 1908.

Smith, Kenneth L. *Sawmill: The Story of Cutting the Last Great Virgin Forest East of the Rockies*. Fayetteville: University of Arkansas Press, 1986.

Staples, Thomas S. *Reconstruction in Arkansas, 1862–1874*. New York: Columbia University Press, 1923.

Taylor, Henry C. *The Farmers' Movement, 1620–1920*. New York: American Book Co., 1953.

Taylor, Orville W. *Negro Slavery in Arkansas*. Durham: Duke University Press, 1958.

Terry, Adolphine Fletcher. *Charlotte Stephens: Little Rock's First Black Teacher*. Little Rock: Academic Press of Arkansas, 1973.

Thomas, David Y. *Arkansas in War and Reconstruction, 1861–1874*. Little Rock: Central Printing Co., 1926.

———, ed. *Arkansas and Its People: A History, 1541–1930*. 4 vols. New York: American Historical Society, 1930.

Thompson, George H. *Arkansas and Reconstruction: The Influence of Geography, Economics and Personality*. Port Washington, N.Y.: Kennikat Press, 1976.

Tindall, George Brown. *South Carolina Negroes, 1877–1900*. Columbia: University of South Carolina Press, 1952.

Van den Berghe, Pierre. *Race and Racism: A Comparative Perspective*. New York: John Wiley and Sons, 1967.

Vaughn, William Preston. *Schools for All: The Blacks and Public Education in the South, 1865–1877*. Lexington: University of Kentucky Press, 1974.

Voegeli, V. Jacque. *Free But Not Equal: The Midwest and the Negro during the Civil War*. Chicago: University of Chicago Press, 1967.

Wade, Richard C. *Slavery in the Cities: The South, 1820–1860*. New York: Oxford University Press, 1964.

Weiner, Jonathan M. *Social Origins of the New South: Alabama, 1860–1885.* Baton Rouge: Louisiana State University Press, 1978.

Wharton, Vernon Lane. *The Negro in Mississippi, 1865–1890.* Chapel Hill: University of North Carolina Press, 1947.

White, Walter. *Rope and Faggot, A Biography of Judge Lynch.* New York: Alfred A. Knopf, 1929.

Williamson, Joel. *After Slavery: The Negro in South Carolina during Reconstruction, 1861–1877.* Chapel Hill: University of North Carolina Press, 1965.

———. *The Crucible of Race: Black-White Relations in the American South since Emancipation.* New York: Oxford University Press, 1984.

Williamson, Llewellyn W. *Black Footprints around Arkansas.* Hope, Ark: Etter Printing Co., 1979.

Woods, James M. *Rebellion and Realignment, Arkansas's Road to Secession.* Fayetteville: University of Arkansas Press, 1987.

Woodward, C. Vann. *Tom Watson: Agrarian Rebel.* New York: MacMillan, 1938.

———. *Origins of the New South, 1877–1913.* Baton Rouge: Louisiana State University Press and the Littlefield Fund for Southern History of the University of Texas, 1951.

———. *The Burden of Southern History.* Baton Rouge: Louisiana State University Press, 1960.

———. *American Counterpoint: Slavery and Racism in the North-South Dialogue.* Boston: Little, Brown and Co., 1964.

———. *The Strange Career of Jim Crow.* 3d rev. ed. New York: Oxford University Press, 1974.

———. *Thinking Back: The Perils of Writing History.* Baton Rouge: Louisiana State University Press, 1986.

Wright, Gavin. *Old South, New South: Revolutions in the Southern Economy since the Civil War.* New York: Basic Books, Inc., 1986.

Wright, George C. *Life behind a Veil: Blacks in Louisville, Kentucky, 1865–1930.* Baton Rouge: Louisiana State University Press, 1985.

Wynes, Charles E. *Race Relations in Virginia, 1870–1902.* Charlottesville: University Press of Virginia, 1961.

Wynne, Lewis Nicholas. *The Continuity of Cotton: Planter Politics in Georgia, 1865–1892.* Macon, Ga.: Mercer University Press, 1986.

**Articles**

Abramowitz, Jack. "The Negro in the Agrarian Revolt," *Agricultural History* XXIV (April 1950): 89–95.

————. "The Negro in the Populist Movement," *Journal of Negro History* XXXVIII (July 1953): 258–89.

Atkinson, James H. "The Arkansas Gubernatorial Campaign and Election of 1872," *Arkansas Historical Quarterly* I (December 1942): 307–21.

————. "The Brooks-Baxter–Contest," *Arkansas Historical Quarterly* IV (Summer 1945): 124–49.

————. "The Adoption of the Constitution of 1874 and the Passing of the Reconstruction Regime," *Arkansas Historical Quarterly* V (Autumn 1946): 288–96.

————, ed., "Clayton and Catterson Rob Columbia County," *Arkansas Historical Quarterly* XXI (Summer 1962): 153–57.

Barjenbruch, Judith. "The Greenback Political Movement: An Arkansas View," *Arkansas Historical Quarterly* XXXVI (Summer 1977): 107–22.

Bayliss, Garland E. "Post-Reconstruction Repudiation: Evil Blot or Financial Necessity?" *Arkansas Historical Quarterly* XXIII (Autumn 1964): 243–59.

————. "The Arkansas State Penitentiary under Democratic Control, 1874–1896," *Arkansas Historical Quarterly* XXXIV (Autumn 1975): 195–213.

Beatty-Brown, Florence R. "Legal Status of Arkansas Negroes before Emancipation," *Arkansas Historical Quarterly* XXVIII (Spring 1969): 6–13.

Bell, James W. "The Early Parks of Little Rock: Part I," *Pulaski County Historical Review* XXX (Spring 1982): 17–21.

————. "The Early Parks of Little Rock: Part II," *Pulaski County Historical Review* XXX (Spring 1982): 44–47.

Bond, Ulysses S. "Highlights in the Life of Scott Bond," *Arkansas Historical Quarterly* XXI (Summer 1962): 146–52.

Branfon, Robert L. "The End of Immigration to the Cotton Fields," *Mississippi Valley Historical Review* L (March 1964): 591–611.

Brough, Charles Hillman. "The Industrial History of Arkansas," *Publications of the Arkansas Historical Association* I (1906): 191–229.

Bukey, Evan Burr. "Frederick Gerstaecker and Arkansas," *Arkansas Historical Quarterly* XXXI (Spring 1972): 3–14.

Buxton, Virginia. "Clayton's Militia in Sevier and Howard Counties," *Arkansas Historical Quarterly*, XX (Winter 1961): 344–50.

Cantrell, Gregg and D. Scott Barton, "Texas Politics and the Failure of Biracial Politics," *Journal of Southern History* LV (November 1989): 659–92.

Carmichael, Maude. "Federal Experiments with Negro Labor on Abandoned Plantations in Arkansas: 1862–1865," *Arkansas Historical Quarterly* VI (June 1942): 101–16.

Chafe, William H. "The Negro and Populism: A Kansas State Study," *Journal of Southern History* XXXIV (August 1968): 402–19.

Cowen, Ruth Caroline. "Reorganization of Federal Arkansas, 1862–1865," *Arkansas Historical Quarterly* XVIII (Summer 1959): 32–57.

Crawford, Sidney. "Arkansas Suffrage Qualifications," *Arkansas Historical Quarterly* II (December 1943): 331–39.

Cypert, Eugene. "Constitutional Convention of 1868," *Publications of the Arkansas Historical Quarterly* IV (1917): 7–56.

Davis, Granville D. "The Granger Movement in Arkansas," *Arkansas Historical Quarterly* IV (December 1943): 340–52.

Dean, Jerry. "History of Arkansas Can Be Read in Stones Dotting Martin Cemetery," Little Rock *Arkansas Gazette* (October 11, 1987): 5A.

————. "Scipio A. Jones, Lawyer and Early Civil Rights Hero," Little Rock *Arkansas Gazette* (February 15, 1989): 1–2 E.

Dethloff, Henry C., and Robert R. Jones. "Race Relations in Louisiana, 1877–1898," *Louisiana History* IX (Fall 1968): 301–23.

Dew, Lee A. "The J.L.C. and E.R.R. and the Opening of the 'Sunk Lands' of Northeast Arkansas," *Arkansas Historical Quarterly* XXVII (Spring 1968): 22–39.

Dew, Lee A., and Louis Koeppe. "Narrow Gage Railroads in Arkansas," *Arkansas Historical Quarterly* XXXI (Autumn 1972): 276–93.

Dillard, Tom W. "Scipio A. Jones," *Arkansas Historical Quarterly* XXXI (Autumn 1972): 201–19.

————. "To the Back of the Elephant: Racial Conflict in the Arkansas Republican Party," *Arkansas Historical Quarterly* XXXIII (Spring 1974): 3–15.

————. "Isaac T. Gillam: Black Pulaski Countian," *Pulaski County Historical Review* XXIV (March 1976): 6–11.

————. "'Golden Prospects and Fraternal Amenities': M. W. Gibbs's Arkansas Years," *Arkansas Historical Quarterly* XXXV (Winter 1976): 307–33.

Dougan, Michael B. "Life in Confederate Arkansas," *Arkansas Historical Quarterly* XXXI (Spring 1972): 15–35.

Driggs, Orval Truman, Jr. "The Issues of the Powell Clayton Regime, 1868–1871," *Arkansas Historical Quarterly* VIII (Spring 1949): 1–75.

Elkins, F. Clark. "Arkansas Farmers Organize for Action: 1882–1884," *Arkansas Historical Quarterly* XIII (Autumn 1954): 231–48.

————. "The Agricultural Wheel: County Politics and Consolidation, 1884–1885," *Arkansas Historical Quarterly* XXIX (Summer 1970): 152–75.

————. "State Politics and the Agricultural Wheel," *Arkansas Historical Quarterly* XXXVIII (Autumn 1979): 248–58.

Ewing, Cortez A. M. "Arkansas Reconstruction Impeachments," *Arkansas Historical Quarterly* XIII (Summer 1954): 137–53.

Feistman, Eugene C. "Radical Disfranchisement in Arkansas, 1867–1868," *Arkansas Historical Quarterly* XII (Summer 1953): 126–68.

Finch, Daniel E. "Little Rock's Red Bishop Brown and His Separate Black Church," *Pulaski County Historical Review* XX (September 1972): 27–34.

Finnigan, D. Michael. "Martin Cemetery: Mabelvale History in Marble and Granite." Little Rock *Arkansas Democrat* (March 8, 1979): 7F.

Fischer, Roger A. "Racial Segregation in Ante-Bellum New Orleans," *American Historical Review* LXXIV (February 1969): 926–37.

Freeman, Felton D. "Immigration to Arkansas," *Arkansas Historical Quarterly* VII (Autumn 1948): 210–20.

Gatewood, Willard B., Jr., ed. "Negro Legislators in Arkansas, 1891: A Document," *Arkansas Historical Quarterly* XXXI (Autumn 1972): 220–33.

———, ed. "Arkansas Negroes in the 1890s: Documents," *Arkansas Historical Quarterly* XXXIII (Winter 1974): 293–325.

———. "Frederick Douglass in Arkansas," *Arkansas Historical Quarterly* XLI (Winter 1982): 303–15.

Goodrich, Carter. "Public Aid to Railroads in the Reconstruction South," *Political Science Quarterly* LXXI (September 1956): 407–42.

Graves, John William. "Negro Disfranchisement in Arkansas," *Arkansas Historical Quarterly* XXXVI (Autumn 1967): 199–225.

———. "The Arkansas Separate Coach Law of 1891," *Journal of the West* VII (October 1968): 531–41.

———. "A Question of Honor: Election Reform and Black Disfranchisement in Arkansas," University of Virginia *Essays in History* XV (1969–1971): 9–26.

———. "The Arkansas Separate Coach Law of 1891 (revised)," *Arkansas Historical Quarterly* XXXII (Summer 1973): 148–65.

———. "Jim Crow in Arkansas: A Reconsideration of Urban Race Relations in the Post-Reconstruction South," *Journal of Southern History* LV (August 1989): 421–48.

Hackler, Tim. "When on a Dry Day You Could Walk to Town, Little Rock—1891: An Era of Change and Growth," Little Rock *Arkansas Democrat* (March 5, 1972): 14A.

Halliburton, William H. "Reconstruction in Arkansas County," *Publications of the Arkansas Historical Association* II (1908): 478–520.

Henningson, Berton E., Jr. "Northwest Arkansas and the Brothers of Freedom: The Roots of a Farmer Movement," *Arkansas Historical Quarterly* XXXIV (Winter 1974): 304–24.

———. "'Root, Hog or Die': The Brothers of Freedom and the 1884 Arkansas Election," *Arkansas Historical Quarterly* XLV (Autumn 1986): 197–216.

Hesseltine, William B., and Larry Gara. "Arkansas Confederate Leaders After the War," *Arkansas Historical Quarterly* IX (Winter 1950): 259–69.

Holder, Virgil. "Historical Geography of the Lower White River," *Arkansas Historical Quarterly* XXVII (Summer 1968): 132–45.

Holmes, William F. "The Arkansas Cotton Pickers Strike of 1891 and the Demise of the Colored Farmers' Alliance," *Arkansas Historical Quarterly* XXXII (Summer 1973): 107–19.

Howell, Elmo. "Mark Twain's Arkansas," *Arkansas Historical Quarterly* XXIX (Autumn 1970): 195–208.

Hume, Richard L. "The Arkansas Constitutional Convention of 1868: A Case Study in the Politics of Reconstruction," *Journal of Southern History* XXXIX (May 1973): 183–206.

Johnson, Benjamin S. "The Brooks-Baxter War," *Publications of the Arkansas Historical Association* II (1908): 125–32.

Kelly, Michael P. "Partisan or Protector: Powell Clayton and the 1868 Presidential Election," *Ozark Historical Review* III (Spring 1974): 44–58.

Kennan, Clara B. "The First Negro Teacher in Little Rock," *Arkansas Historical Quarterly* IX (Autumn 1950): 199–201.

Kennedy, Thomas C. "Southland College: The Society of Friends and Black Education in Arkansas," *Arkansas Historical Quarterly* XLII (Autumn 1983): 207–38.

Kousser, J. Morgan, ed. "A Black Protest in the 'Era of Accommodation': Documents," *Arkansas Historical Quarterly* XXXIV (Summer 1975): 149–78.

Lack, Paul D. "An Urban Slave Community: Little Rock, 1831–1862," *Arkansas Historical Quarterly* XLI (Spring 1982): 258–87.

Ledbetter, Cal, Jr. "Jeff Davis and the Politics of Combat," *Arkansas Historical Quarterly* XXXIII (Spring 1974): 16–37.

———. "The Constitution of 1868: Conqueror's Constitution or Constitutional Continuity?" *Arkansas Historical Quarterly* XLIV (Spring 1985): 16–41.

Leslie, James W. "Wiley Jones: A Slave Who Left His Mark on Pine Bluff's Business World," Pine Bluff *Commercial* (April 5, 1970): 13.

———. "Private School Here Remains Only As a Memory," Pine Bluff *Commercial* (April 18, 1971): 4.

———. "The Colored Industrial Institute Was City's First School for Blacks," Pine Bluff *Commercial* (March 26, 1972): 15.

————. "St. Peters: School Was Established Before Church: Landmark Reduced by Flames," Pine Bluff *Commercial* (May 21, 1972): 13.

————. "Street Cars: Earliest Public Transportation Was Drawn by Mules," Pine Bluff *Commercial* (February 8, 1976): 11.

————. "Jones Park: Races, Baseball Drew Crowds to Harding and Main," Pine Bluff *Commercial* (August 15, 1976): 13.

————. "Ferd Havis: Jefferson County's Black Republican Leader," *Arkansas Historical Quarterly* XXXVII (Autumn 1978): 240–51.

Lisenby, Foy. "A Survey of Arkansas's Image Problem," *Arkansas Historical Quarterly* XXX (Spring 1971): 60–71.

Lucey, J. M. "The Catholic Church in Arkansas," *Publications of the Arkansas Historical Association* II (1908): 425–49.

————. "History of Immigration to Arkansas," *Publications of the Arkansas Historical Association* III (1911): 201–19.

McKelvey, Blake. "Penal Slavery and Southern Reconstruction," *Journal of Negro History* XX (April 1935): 153–79.

McSwain, Bernice Lamb. "Shorter College: Its Early History," *Pulaski County Historical Review* XXX (Winter 1982): 81–84.

Masterson, Mike. "Hard Work, Savings Built Empire," Little Rock *Arkansas Gazette* (July 25, 1971): 6E.

Maxted, Mattie Cal. "Training of Deaf Children in Arkansas," *Arkansas Historical Quarterly* V (Fall 1946): 193–207.

Meier, August, and Elliott Rudwick. "The Boycott Movement against Jim Crow Streetcars in the South, 1900–1906," *Journal of American History* LV (March 1969): 756–75.

Mitchell, John B. "An Analysis of Arkansas' Population by Race and Nativity and Residence," *Arkansas Historical Quarterly* VIII (Summer 1949): 115–32.

Moneyhon, Carl H. "Black Politics in Arkansas during the Gilded Age, 1876–1900," *Arkansas Historical Quarterly* XLIV (Autumn 1985): 222–45.

Moore, Samuel W. "State Supervision of Railroad Transportation in Arkansas," *Publications of the Arkansas Historical Association* III (1911): 265–309.

Mulhollan, Paige E. "The Arkansas General Assembly of 1866 and Its Effect on Reconstruction," *Arkansas Historical Quarterly* XX (Winter 1961): 331–43.

Neal, Diane. "Seduction, Accommodation, or Realism? Tabbs Gross and the *Arkansas Freeman*," *Arkansas Historical Quarterly* XLVIII (Spring 1989): 57–64.

Neal, Joe. "Fraternal Cemetery: Reflections on a Southern Negro Graveyard," *Pulaski County Historical Review* XXV (March 1977): 1–13.

Nichols, Cheryl Griffith. "Pulaski Heights: Early Suburban Development in Little Rock, Arkansas," *Arkansas Historical Quarterly* XLI (Summer 1982): 129–45.

Niswonger, Richard L. "Arkansas and the Election of 1896," *Arkansas Historical Quarterly* XXXIV (Spring 1975): 41–78.

———. "A Study in Southern Demagoguery: Jeff Davis of Arkansas," *Arkansas Historical Quarterly* XXXIX (Summer 1980): 114–24.

Nunn, Walter. "The Constitutional Convention of 1874," *Arkansas Historical Quarterly* XXVII (Autumn 1968): 177–204.

Paisley, Clifton. "The Political Wheelers and Arkansas' Election of 1888," *Arkansas Historical Quarterly* XXV (Spring 1966): 3–21.

Palmer, Paul C. "Miscegenation as an Issue in the Arkansas Constitutional Convention of 1868," *Arkansas Historical Quarterly* XXIV (Summer 1965): 99–119.

Pearce, Larry Wesley. "The American Missionary Association and the Freedmen in Arkansas, 1863–1878," *Arkansas Historical Quarterly* XXX (Summer 1971): 123–44.

———. "The American Missionary Association and the Freedmen's Bureau in Arkansas, 1866–1868," *Arkansas Historical Quarterly* XXX (Autumn 1971): 242–59.

———. "The American Missionary Association and the Freedmen's Bureau in Arkansas, 1868–1878," *Arkansas Historical Quarterly* XXXI (Autumn 1972): 246–61.

Petersen, Svend. "Arkansas in Presidential Elections," *Arkansas Historical Quarterly* VII (Autumn 1948): 194–209.

Ransom, Roger L., and Richard Sutch. "Debt Peonage in the Cotton South after the Civil War," *Journal of Economic History* XXXII (September 1972): 641–69.

Reed, Germaine A. "Race Legislation in Louisiana, 1864–1920," *Louisiana History* VI (Fall 1965): 379–92.

Reid, Joseph D. "Sharecropping as an Understandable Market Response: The Post-Bellum South," *Journal of Economic History* XXXIII (March 1973): 106–30.

Reynolds, John Hugh. "Presidential Reconstruction in Arkansas," *Publications of the Arkansas Historical Association* I (1906): 352–61.

Reynolds, Thomas J. "Pope County Militia War (July 8, 1872, to February 17, 1873)" *Publications of the Arkansas Historical Association* II (1908): 174–98.

Richards, Ira Don. "Little Rock on the Road to Reunion, 1865–1880," *Arkansas Historical Quarterly* XXV (Winter 1966): 312–35.

Robinson, Joseph T. "Suffrage in Arkansas," *Publications of the Arkansas Historical Association* III (1911): 167–74.

Rogers, William W. "Negro Knights of Labor in Arkansas: A Case Study of the Miscellaneous Strike," *Labor History* X (Summer 1969): 498–505.

Ross, Margaret Smith. "Augustus H. Garland—Arkansas's Biggest Man: Leader in Law, in State and National Politics," Little Rock *Arkansas Gazette* (January 22, 1956): 2–3F.

———. "Nathan Warren, A Free Negro of the Old South," *Arkansas Historical Quarterly* XV (Spring 1956): 53–61.

———. "Shift from Slavery to Freedom Brings No Dramatic Change to State's Negroes," Little Rock *Arkansas Gazette* (July 11, 1956): 6E.

———. "Governor Elisha Baxter Was a Unionist—And He Suffered for It in the Civil War," Little Rock *Arkansas Gazette* (December 4, 1966): 6E.

———. "The New Madrid Earthquake," *Arkansas Historical Quarterly* XXVII (Summer 1968): 83–104.

Rothrock, Thomas. "Joseph Carter Corbin and Negro Education in the University of Arkansas" *Arkansas Historical Quarterly* XXX (Winter 1971): 277–314.

Russ, William A., Jr. "The Attempt to Create a Republican Party in Arkansas during Reconstruction," *Arkansas Historical Quarterly* I (September 1942): 206–22.

Russell, Marvin F. "The Rise of a Republican Leader: Harmon L. Remmel," *Arkansas Historical Quarterly* XXXVI (Autumn 1977): 234–57.

St. Hilaire, Joseph M. "The Negro Delegates in the Constitutional Convention of 1868: A Group Profile," *Arkansas Historical Quarterly* XXXIII (Spring 1974): 39–69.

Saloutos, Theodore. "The Agricultural Wheel in Arkansas," *Arkansas Historical Quarterly* II (June 1943): 127–40.

Saunders, Robert M. "The Southern Populists and the Negro in 1892," University of Virginia *Essays in History* XII (1967): 7–25.

———. "Southern Populism and the Negro, 1893–1905," *Journal of Negro History* LIV (July 1969): 240–57.

Scroggs, Jack. "Arkansas in the Secession Crisis," *Arkansas Historical Quarterly* XII (Autumn 1953): 179–224.

Shinn, Josiah H. "Augustus H. Garland Was Born Seventy-Six Years Ago: His Life and Services to Arkansas, the Confederacy and the Nation," Little Rock *Arkansas Gazette* (June 11, 1908): 3, 10.

Singletary, Otis A. "Militia Disturbances in Arkansas during Reconstruction," *Arkansas Historical Quarterly* XV (Summer 1956): 140–50.

Smith, Albert C. "'Southern Violence' Reconsidered: Arson as Protest in Black-Belt Georgia, 1865–1910," *Journal of Southern History* LI (November 1985): 527–64.

Smith, C. Calvin. "John E. Bush of Arkansas, 1890–1910," *Ozark Historical Review* II (Spring 1973): 48–59.

Smith, T. Lynn. "The Redistribution of the Negro Population of the United States, 1910–1960," *Journal of Negro History* LI (July 1966): 155–73.

Somers, Dale A. "Black and White in New Orleans: A Study in Urban Race Relations, 1865–1900," *Journal of Southern History* XL (February 1974): 19–42.

Taylor, Orville W. "Baptists and Slavery in Arkansas: Relationships and Attitudes," *Arkansas Historical Quarterly* XXXVIII (Autumn 1979): 199–226.

Thomas, David Y. "A History of Taxation in Arkansas," II *Publications of the Arkansas Historical Association* (1908): 43–90.

Thompson, George H. "Reconstruction and the Loss of State Credit," *Arkansas Historical Quarterly* XXVIII (Winter 1969): 298–308.

Trieber, Jacob. "Legal Status of Negroes in Arkansas before the Civil War," *Publications of the Arkansas Historical Association* III (1911): 175–83.

Vance, Rupert B. "A Karl Marx for Hill Billies, Portrait of a Southern Leader," *Social Forces* IX (1930–31): 180–90.

Walton, Brian G. "The Second Party System in Arkansas, 1836–1848," *Arkansas Historical Quarterly* XXVIII (Summer 1969): 120–55.

Walz, Robert B. "Arkansas Slaveholdings and Slaveholders in 1850," *Arkansas Historical Quarterly* XII (Spring 1953): 38–74.

———. "Migration into Arkansas, 1820–1880: Incentives and Means of Travel," *Arkansas Historical Quarterly* XVII (Winter 1958): 309–24.

Watkins, Beverly. "Efforts to Encourage Immigration to Arkansas, 1865–1874," *Arkansas Historical Quarterly* XXXVIII (Spring 1979): 32–62.

Wheeler, Elizabeth L. "Isaac Fisher: The Frustrations of a Negro Educator at Branch Normal College, 1902–1911," *Arkansas Historical Quarterly* XLI (Spring 1982): 3–50.

Wilhoit, Francis M. "An Interpretation of Populism's Impact on the Georgia Negro," *Journal of Negro History* LII (April 1967): 116–27.

Wolfe, James Jonathan. "Background of German Immigration," *Arkansas Historical Quarterly* XXV (Summer 1966): 151–82.

———. "Background of German Immigration," *Arkansas Historical Quarterly* XXV (Autumn 1966): 248–78.

———. "Background of German Immigration," *Arkansas Historical Quarterly* XXV (Winter 1966): 354–85.

Wood, Stephan E. "The Development of Arkansas Railroads. Early Interest and Activities," *Arkansas Historical Quarterly* VII (Summer 1948): 103–40.

————. "The Development of Arkansas Railroads: The Great Railroad Boom," *Arkansas Historical Quarterly* VII (Autumn 1948): 155–93.

Woodman, Harold D. "Sequel to Slavery: The New History Views the Postbellum South," *Journal of Southern History* XLIII (November 1977): 523–54.

Woodward, Earl F. "The Brooks and Baxter War in Arkansas," *Arkansas Historical Quarterly* XXX (Winter 1971): 315–36.

Woorster, Ralph. "The Arkansas Secession Convention," *Arkansas Historical Quarterly* XIII (Summer 1954): 172–95.

Worley, Ted R. "The Arkansas Peace Society of 1861: A Study of Mountain Unionism," *Journal of Southern History* XXIV (November 1958): 445–56.

————, ed. "Major Josiah H. Demby's History of Catterson's Militia," *Arkansas Historical Quarterly* XVI (Summer 1957): 203–11.

————, ed. "Documents Relating to the Arkansas Peace Society of 1861," *Arkansas Historical Quarterly* XVII (Spring 1958): 82–111.

Zimmerman, Jane. "The Convict Lease System in Arkansas and the Fight for Abolition," *Arkansas Historical Quarterly* VIII (Autumn 1949): 173–88.

## Unpublished Theses and Dissertations

Bayliss, Garland Erastus., "Public Affairs in Arkansas, 1874–1896." Ph.D. diss., University of Texas, 1972.

Blake, Earl. "Farm Tenancy in Arkansas." M.A. thesis, University of Arkansas, 1939.

Boyett, Gene Wells. "The Whigs of Arkansas, 1836–1856." Ph.D. diss., Louisiana State University, 1972.

Brown, Mattie. "A History of River Transportation in Arkansas from 1819 to 1880." M.A. thesis, University of Arkansas, 1933.

Brown, Walter L. "Albert Pike, 1809–1891." Ph.D. diss., University of Texas, 1955.

Burnside, William H. "Powell Clayton: Politician and Diplomat, 1897–1905." Ph.D. diss., University of Arkansas, 1978.

Carmichael, Maude. "The Plantation System in Arkansas, 1850–1876." Ph.D. diss." Radcliffe College, 1935.

Christensen, Lawrence Oland. "Black St. Louis: A Study in Race Relations, 1865–1916." Ph.D. diss., University of Missouri, 1972.

Crawford, Sidney R. "The Poll Tax." M.A. thesis, University of Arkansas, 1944.

Dillard, Tom W. "The Black Moses of the West: A Biography of Mifflin Wistar Gibbs, 1823–1915." M.A. thesis, University of Arkansas, 1975.

Dixon, Richard Baker. "Press Opinion toward the Populist Party in Arkansas, 1890–1896." M.A. thesis, University of Arkansas, 1953.

Drummond, Boyce A. "Arkansas Politics: A Study of a One-Party System." Ph.D. diss., University of Chicago, 1957.

Elkins, Francis Clark. "The Agricultural Wheel in Arkansas, 1882–1890." Doctor of Social Science thesis, Syracuse University, 1953.

Ellenburg, Martha A. "Reconstruction in Arkansas," Ph.D. diss., University of Missouri, 1967.

Evans, W. C. "The Public Debt of Arkansas: Its History from 1836 to 1885." M.A. thesis, University of Arkansas, 1928.

Fain, James Harris. "Political Disfranchisement of the Negro in Arkansas." M.A. thesis, University of Arkansas, 1961.

Ford, Hirum U. "A History of the Arkansas Penitentiary to 1900." M.A. thesis, University of Arkansas, 1936.

Gibson, DeLois. "A Historical Study of Philander Smith College, 1877 to 1969." Ed.D. diss., University of Arkansas, 1972.

Gordon, Fon. "The Black Experience in Arkansas, 1880–1920." Ph.D. diss., University of Arkansas, 1988.

Grant, Daniel Ross. "The Role of the Governor of Arkansas in Administration." Ph.D. diss., Northwestern University, 1948.

Graves, John William. "The Arkansas Negro and Segregation, 1890–1903." M.A. thesis, University of Arkansas, 1967.

———. "Town and Country, Race Relations and Urban Development in Arkansas, 1865–1905." Ph.D. diss., University of Virginia, 1978.

Griner, James Emmett Pool. "The Growth of Manufactures in Arkansas, 1900–1950." Ph.D. diss., George Peabody College for Teachers, 1957.

Hobby, Selma Ann Plowman. "The Little Rock Public Schools During Reconstruction, 1865–1874." Ed.D. diss., University of Arkansas, 1967.

Howard, James Edgar. "Populism in Arkansas." M.A. thesis, George Peabody College for Teachers, 1931.

Kane, John Ewing. "Business Fluctuations in Arkansas Since 1866." M.A. thesis, University of Arkansas, 1939.

Lewis, Elsie M. "From Nationalism to Disunion: A Study of the Secession Movement in Arkansas, 1850–1861." Ph.D. diss., University of Chicago, 1946.

Mapes, Evert Eugene. "Business Cycles in Arkansas." M.A. thesis, University of Arkansas, 1939.

Mosley, Ellis Greenlee. "The History of Higher Education for Negroes in Arkansas," M.A. thesis, University of Texas, 1944.

Niswonger, Richard Leverne. "Arkansas Democratic Politics, 1896–1920." Ph.D. diss., University of Texas, 1973.

Nunn, Walter. "Revision of the Arkansas Constitution." M.A. thesis, University of Kansas, 1966.

Penrose, William Orestus. "Political Ideas in Arkansas, 1880–1907." M.A. thesis, University of Illinois, 1952.

Porter, Michael Leroy. "Black Atlanta: An Interdisciplinary Study of Blacks on the East Side of Atlanta, 1890–1930." Ph.D. diss., Emory University, 1974.

Powers, Bernard Edward, Jr. "Black Charleston: A Social History, 1822–1885." Ph.D. diss., Northwestern University, 1982.

Robbins, Faye Welborne. "A World Within a World: Black Nashville, 1880–1915." Ph.D. diss., University of Arkansas, 1980.

Russell, Marvin Frank. "The Republican Party in Arkansas, 1874–1913." Ph.D. diss., University of Arkansas, 1985.

Saunders, Robert M. "The Ideology of Southern Populists, 1892–1895." Ph.D. diss., University of Virginia, 1967.

Segraves, Joe Tolbert. "Arkansas Politics, 1874–1918." Ph.D. diss., University of Kentucky, 1973.

Stevenson, George James. "The Political Career of Jeff Davis: An Example of the Southern Protest." M.A. thesis, University of Arkansas, 1949.

Thornberry, Jerry John. "The Development of Black Atlanta, 1865–1885." Ph.D. diss., University of Maryland, 1977.

Walz, Robert Bradshaw. "Migration into Arkansas, 1834–1880." Ph.D. diss., University of Texas, 1958.

Watkins, Beverly Nettles. "Augustus Hill Garland, 1832–1899." Ph.D. diss., Auburn University, 1985.

Wolff, Rufus D. "The Industrial Development of Arkansas." M.A. thesis, Vanderbilt University, 1929.

323

# Index

Landlord's Lien, 61
Langford, W. H., 198
Langley, Rev. Isom P., 206
Langley, Miles L., 21
Larceney Law, 62–63, 64
Lee County, Ark., 53, 54, 77–78
Liberal Republican. *See* Republican
Lincoln, Abraham, 6, 7, 8, 11, 108
"Lily-White" Movement, 121, 127, 184
Lincoln Club. *See* Harrison and Morton Club
Lincoln County, Ark., 54
Litchfield, Ark., 203
Little Missouri River, 5
Little Rock, Ark., 6, 16, 30, 31–33, 41, 45, 60, 100–121, 125–31, 132, 136, 144, 153, 161, 163, 193, 195, 219, 221–22; resistance to streetcar-segregation act, 222–25. *See also* Urbanization
Lodge "Force" Bill, 169, 171, 186, 212–14
Lofgren, Charles A., 152
Loughborough, J. Fairfax, 222
Louisiana, State of, 51, 71
*Louisville, New Orleans, and Texas Railway v. Mississippi*, 152
Loyalty Oath, 7, 8, 12, 15, 23, 39–40, 42, 74
Lucas, John Gray, 124–25, 150, 157–60, 162, 198
Lucey, J. M., 123
Lynching, 10, 123, 132, 202, 203, 210–11, 212, 216

Macune, Charles W., 204
Madison, Ark., 78, 88
*Maifest*, 113
Mandle, Jay R., 89
Manning, William, 209
Marche, Ark., 105
Marre, Angelo, 146–47
Marion, Ark., 68, 70
Martial Law, 37–38, 45
Mason, James W., 17
Massachusetts, State of, 11, 125, 127, 184
Matlock, Paul G., 221
McClure, John, 21, 45, 145–46, 148, 184

McCoy, John, 7
McCracken, Isaac, 139, 142
McKinley, William, 149
McRae, Tom, 142
Meek, J. A., 183–84
Meier, August, 222
Memphis, Tenn., 67, 68, 92, 136
Meridian, Miss., 204
Middlebrooks, A. M., 123, 126
Miller, S. A., 172
Miller, William R., 56, 129
Military Districts. *See* Reconstruction Acts
Militia, 37–38, 45–47, 56, 141
Minstrels. *See* Republicans
Miscegnation, 9–10, 20–22, 131, 159–60
Mississippi River, 5, 16, 71, 81
Mississippi, State of, 67, 152, 157
Monks, William, 37
Monroe County, Ark., 54, 174, 203
Morehart, Henry R., 144, 205
Morgan, Thomas, 147
Morrill Act, Land Grant Funds, 34
Morris, Benjamin A., 178–79
Morris, Rev. E. C., 122, 126
Mosaic Templars of America, 114, 119, 120, 126, 153
Moss, Edgar E., 32
Mountain Districts, 5–8, 24–25, 60, 66, 161. *See also* Farmers
Murphy, Isaac, 7, 8, 9, 12, 22, 33, 40, 43, 49, 50, 173

Nash, Charles E., 133
National Baptist Convention, 122
Neal, Lee, 169
Negroes. *See* Blacks
New Gascony, Ark., 45
New Orleans, La., 229
Newport, Ark., 78
Noncooperationists. *See* Democrats
Nordhoff, Charles, 31, 54, 76
Norwood, Charles M., 139–41, 142, 143, 206–7
North Little Rock, Ark., 80, 111, 115, 146

Oath of Allegiance. *See* Loyalty Oath
Odom, S. S., 214

Old Hickory Club, 147, 213
Ord, Bvt. Maj. Gen. E. O. C.,
    12–13, 15
Ouachita Mountains, 5
Ouachita River, 5
Owens, E. J., 144
Ozan, Ark., 206
Ozark Mountains, 5–6, 7, 38, 66, 161.
    *See also* Mountains, Farmers

Palarm Creek, 45
Paragould, Ark., 207
Parks, W. P. "Buck," 137
Paternalism and Caste, 2, 88, 90,
    131–33, 158, 162, 228
Patillo, Susan, 112
Peel, S. W., 142
Perkins, George N., 153, 154
Perry County, Ark., 218
Pfeifer, Philip, 101, 105
Philander Smith College, 111, 119,
    145
Philippines, 217
Phillips County, Ark., 47, 54, 57, 67,
    77–78, 126, 174, 207
Phillips, Rev. W. A. J., 222
Pickens, William, 92–96, 97, 113,
    115–17
Pine Bluff, Ark., 34, 56, 72, 122–25,
    147, 161, 176, 198, 221, 223; social
    mobility of blacks in, 122–25, 127,
    147
Pinnix, Joseph C., 220–21, 222
Plantation Economy, 5, 35, 59–60,
    61–62, 65, 71–73, 80–86, 87–88,
    89–90, 107, 161; attitude toward
    black social and economic mobil-
    ity, 88–89
*Plessy v. Ferguson*, 152
Plumerville, Ark., 143
Poland, Luke, 50
Poll Tax, 23, 48, 185–94, 201, 209
Populists, 1, 177, 178, 179, 189, 194,
    195, 200–201, 210–14, 215–16,
    217; relations with blacks, 201–3,
    211, 214
Prairie County, Ark., 138
Presbyterian Board of Missions for
    Freedmen, 123
Presidential Reconstruction, 7, 14

Prisons, 35, 62–65, 210, 218–19
Prince, P. H., 178–79
Puerto Rico, 217
Pulaski County, Ark., 26, 45, 50, 105,
    115–16, 118, 119, 120, 121, 126, 128,
    144, 146, 148, 149, 207, 214, 219
Pulaski Heights, 32

Rabinowitz, Howard N., 227–28
Race Relations, Theory, 131–33
Racial Intermarriage. *See*
    Miscegenation
Radical Reconstruction. *See*
    Reconstruction
Ransom, Roger L., 85–86, 136
Read, Opie, 128–29
Reconstruction, 16, 24, 25, 28–52,
    75, 90, 109, 121, 137, 146, 147, 169,
    182, 183, 197, 206
Reconstruction Acts, 11–13, 14, 15,
    18, 23; military districts, 11–13,
    14–15, 26
Reconstructionists, 22, 30
Rector, Elias, 147
Rector, Henry, 22, 101, 147
Rector, James E., 118
Rector, John K., 112, 118, 125
"Redshirt" Movement, 67
Red River, 5, 16
Redeemers, 1, 55–69, 99
Redkey, Edwin S., 228
Reed, Rev. J. H., 215, 222
Republicans, 11, 12, 13, 14, 20–23,
    24–25, 26, 29, 35, 38, 41, 42–43,
    44–45, 46, 50–51, 52, 54, 55, 60,
    67–68, 108, 120–21, 123–24, 127,
    139, 140–43, 144–47, 148, 160,
    162, 167–69, 173–75, 177, 184,
    188–89, 191–92, 193, 196, 197,
    200–201, 206–7, 210, 211, 214;
    Brindletails, 41–42, 43; Minstrels,
    41, 43; Liberal Republicans, 40,
    41; Unionists, 6, 7, 8, 9, 10, 11, 13,
    15, 22, 38, 43, 49; Scalawags,
    16–17, 20, 21, 38
*Rice v. Palmer*, 193–94
Richard Allen Institute, 123
Richmond, Va., 50, 229
Reichardt Family, 105
Reid, Joseph D., 85

330

Van den Berghe, Pierre L., 131–32
Vicksburg, Miss., 71
Violence, 10–11, 25, 37, 45–46, 52, 59, 66–69, 89, 90, 132, 141–44, 216
Virginia, State of, 92, 219

Walker, David, 6, 40, 41, 42
Warren, B. W. M., 188
Warner, Charles Dudley, 97
Washington, Ark., 80, 81
Washington, Booker T., 127, 128, 222–23
Washington County, Ark., 26, 34
Washington, George, 150
Watson, Tom, 201–2
Whigs, 40, 49, 107–8
Whipple, William G., 108, 110, 191, 201, 214
White County, Ark., 37
White, E. E., 166
White, James T., 17, 18, 19, 28, 48, 122
White, King, 46

White Primary, 194–95
White Supremacy, 2, 56, 60, 65, 66, 108, 175, 202, 217
White River, 90
White Sulphur Springs, Ark., 127
Whitman, Rev. Asberry, 154, 155
Williams, John A., 140
Williams, John W., 62
Williams, R. A., 92
Williamson, Joel, 226–27
Wilson, Ira, 21
Wilson, Woodrow, 121
Winchester, Celia, 10–11
Winfrey, Cora, 121
Winfrey, Solomon, 118, 121
Wise, Henry A., 17
Witt, Benjamin, 218–19
Wittsburg, Ark., 10–11
Woodruff, William E., Jr., 39, 40, 42, 165
Woodward, C. Vann, 1–2, 98, 100, 201–3, 226, 228, 229
Worthen, W. B., 101
Wright, Gavin, 100